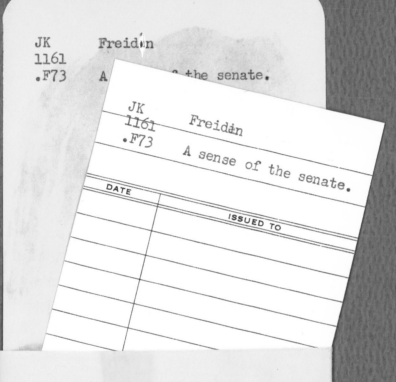

A SENSE OF THE SENATE

A SENSE
OF THE SENATE

SEYMOUR K. FREIDIN

DODD, MEAD & COMPANY

NEW YORK

For Stiva, Josh, and Nick

ISBN: 0-396-06537-6
Library of Congress Catalog Card Number: 72-873
Printed in the United States of America
by The Cornwall Press, Inc., Cornwall, N.Y.

PREFACE

Almost all American institutions are in deep trouble today. Disenchantment is a way of life. Suspicion of established motives and pursuits stalks public working habits and procedures. So it is with the U.S. Senate. This book depicts the battered plight of the Senate, one of our senior and major institutions. It shows its siege mentality. The book is not an historical study nor a political analysis. It is the product of impressions, interviews and in-Senate research during the Nixon Administration.

A divisive war has riddled society and old considerations—or what are euphemistically known as values. Violence, in deed and proposal, has come to be acceptable as part of the new, upside-down life. Corruption when exposed, has caused only deeper discontent. Special investigations and learned panel conclusions have turned off an embittered public. What is wrong and where are we going?

This book depicts a sense of the affliction as it has infected the Senate. The special elected league of 100 is divided against itself, the Presidency, and the public. Thus, it epitomizes a national discontent and uncertainty. The U.S. Senate is stuck in a swamp, bogged down in tradition, hide-bound rules and refusal to reform itself in a way that could re-inspire confidence.

But the Senate does know that change is as essential to its continuity as to other beleaguered citadels of the nation. It is timorous in coming to grips with issues—taxes, health, education, inflation and fear, to cite a few. Less antiquated, built-in prerogatives are watered down or vanish in the process.

v

Occasionally, the Senate seeks to win back key responsibilities it abdicated years before to the Presidency, such as substantive control over foreign affairs. The strategy usually centers on accumulating small points to build up a case. But surgery-providing reforms, not band-aids stemming from debate, are urgent. The Senate hears but does not heed.

In his unyielding campaign to give all Americans a better break out of life, Ralph Nader has turned his talents and troops to speeding reform in the Congress. He has examined myriad aspects of our government, from specialized agencies to faulty automobiles and shoddy goods fobbed off on the consumer. Today Nader sees the only possibility of desperately-needed reform coming from the Congress itself, starting with the Senate rather than the Presidency or other branches of government. Asking for the elected healer to reform himself is a daring thought. But risks are not only imperative but fairly safe because the basic, good sense of American citizens will curb outrageous demands and ambitions.

If the Senate, for example, maintains a go-slow approach towards reform, it can find itself far behind the aspirations of the country. Frustration then can burst and wash like an avenging tidal wave at home and abroad. It will not wash clean but carry off everything in its path in a torrent of rage.

This is the alternative confronting the Senate. It can start quickly to reform itself—the House of Representatives as well— or sooner than later learn that its 100 select members are as anachronistic as the House of Lords as we approach the twenty-first century. The thought of reform may smack of revolution to tradition-tied members so fond of quoting the Founding Fathers. But a little reading of, say, *The Federalist Papers* could reassure them that reform was bound up in the philosophy of this Republic's creators.

In order to obtain material on the crisis of the Senate, I joined the staff of the late Thomas H. Dodd, Democrat of Connecticut. It was an ironic choice in its way. Dodd represented both the best and the worst in the Senate. He had been zealous and meticulous as one of our top prosecutors at the Nuremberg trials, where I first met him, and as a Senator he was among the early crusaders for civil rights.

The gilded roof of Senatorial privilege collapsed on Dodd when he was justly accused of the far too common Senatorial practice of applying campaign funds to personal use. But he probably committed a more strategic mistake by challenging his Senate colleagues to concede they did the same. Dodd had also called Senate ethics overseer John Stennis a bigot.

That finally provoked the Senate to teach him a lesson. Dodd was censured and became a pariah. He ran as an Independent in 1970, lost and died soon thereafter. Only a few years before he was a swiftly rising star, even considered a candidate for Vice-President. Had he gone quietly and deferentially to Stennis, as others have, even the malodorous publicity might have been overlooked.

Despite his censure, Dodd remained a member of imposing Senate committees: Judiciary, Foreign Affairs, and Space and Aeronautical Sciences. For someone doing research in an arcane set-up like the Senate this kind of access was invaluable. It also provided me an eyewitness presence during meetings with other Senators, and an opportunity to check out views of the members about each other and the electorate.

I could not have chosen a more suitable, albeit venomous, classroom to learn firsthand what was going wrong. I had been abroad as a newspaperman most of my adult life, come home to study the tremors in my own country. My stay on the Hill and study of its personalities and methods have convinced me of an urgent need for its reform. This may not be man's last hope, but it is the Senate's.

—SEYMOUR K. FREIDIN

Washington, D.C.
April, 1972

CONTENTS

CONTENTS

I

BOTH MEMBERS OF
THIS CLUB

Bitter cold, unseasonable even for Washington, D.C., congealed the capital. On Thursday, January 21, 1971, the temperature rose a little. It didn't matter much outside. Frost glistened on the naked lawns. There had been lots of scrubbing and cleaning the night before. This was the last-minute cleanup for the Houses of Congress preparing to welcome the ninety-second session.

A few minutes before 6 o'clock that bleak Thursday morning, a four-door 1968 Buick slid slowly into the garage near the old Senate Office Building. In a sharply pressed gray suit and TV-blue shirt, a slight but dapper figure alighted, redolent with a popular brand of after-shaving lotion. As always, he greeted the attendant cheerily. A couple of congressmen had been mugged in the garage a few months before. But except for the two-man police patrols with a giant shepherd dog that checked regularly, everyone pretended service ran smoothly and normally.

So the pretense of nothing ruffled, nothing changed hovered around the edges of the United States Senate. From the garage into the miserable cold stepped the little man. Briskly he strode to the entrance a few yards away. Emerging from the entrance, a uniformed policeman called a surprised good morning.

"How are you?" was the response torn out of his mouth by the wind.

Inside the overheated building the little man strolled purposefully to Room 105, his overcrowded office. The painted sign read:

1

"Mr. Byrd, West Virginia. Welcome." Senator Robert C. Byrd, Democrat of the state named, unlocked the door and entered. He switched on the lights and shucked a dark gray overcoat. Sharp featured, pursed lips and darting brown eyes, Bobby Byrd looked maybe five to ten years younger than his upcoming fifty-third birthday. There was nobody else in the office. His staff, ordinarily on tap between 7:30 and 8:00 A.M., wasn't instructed about the senator's unusually early arrival.

At his massive desk, flanked by the flags of the United States and West Virginia, Bobby Byrd started making telephone calls. A colleague, Senator Herman E. Talmadge, Democrat from Georgia, almost always came to his office by 6:30. Early birds in the Senate are rare. Usually, senators turn up between 9:00 and 10:00 in the morning during working days. Talmadge was a notable exception, as was his Democratic colleague from Georgia, Senator Richard Brevard Russell, the seventy-three-year-old "dean" of the Senate. Russell, a bachelor, worked long and hard at his job. He was alternately feared, respected, and even hated. Moreover, Russell was chairman of the Appropriations Committee. Every senator tugged figuratively at his forelock when he went to see Russell.

Now the old man lay dying in Walter Reed Medical Center. Several months earlier, when he was out of the hospital for a while, he agreed to talk to me. Ailing seriously, he obviously had the premonition of impending death. Emphysema was an official reason circulated. He also had a cancerous condition. A talk with Dick Russell was like being taken on a conducted tour of American history. Like most Southerners in the Capitol, he was immersed with the intricacies of parliamentarianism. Only a few Northerners have recently bothered to absorb all those tedious and tortuous details.

Russell always had been a reflective man. He placed the national interest first. It raised him far above his fellow Southerners. He could be preoccupied with regional concerns such as civil rights. But he was hardly a narrow man even when he exercised all the devices of parliamentary rule to stave off visceral, oft ill-conceived outbursts and legislative probes that could reduce a Southern position to ashes. We talked of the Senate, its format, and its role in national affairs. For just as Sir Winston Churchill regarded himself as a child of the House of Commons, Richard Russell saw himself as a child of the Senate.

When I saw him, he was upset and deeply fatigued. The United States Senate, he observed, was in a state of fragmentation. There were too many colleagues seeking to advance their own personal aggrandizements. No, he said, he wasn't opposed to changes, even what some call reforms. But he was opposed to making a mockery of the Senate and its role to advance personal quests. I deliberately brought up names and personalities. Quite a few Russell couldn't stomach ideologically or personally. To me he never bad-mouthed any. He ignored them and their names. When I mentioned Senator Fulbright, a fellow Southerner, Russell simply said: "He never leaked a word about what he discussed with me in confidence."

Russell may have been the only man in government—high and low—whose confidence Fulbright felt absolutely bound to respect. When it suits him, Fulbright is one of the most porous public officials in the capital. I asked a ranking senator why Fulbright played so unique a game with Senator Russell.

"Simple," came the reply. "He's scared of him. Most others feel the same."

Years before, when Lyndon B. Johnson became Vice-President to the late President John F. Kennedy, Bobby Byrd, who had been devoted to LBJ, turned to Dick Russell as mentor. Johnson always needed senatorial couriers when majority leader. Bobby Byrd, who was a walking adding machine, could not have suited his purpose better. Thus, by 1969, when the Ninety-first Congress lumbered into session, Byrd was ready to have his onerous on-and-off Senate floor chores recognized.

He was elected secretary of the majority party. Senator Mike Mansfield, of Montana, lean, leathery, and often mentally languid, was majority leader. Senator Edward M. (Teddy) Kennedy, of Massachusetts, chose to make the No. 2 spot a challenging one. This is the whip's job. He rounds up the votes before four bells or buzzed signals indicate a live quorum. The details are myriad and frequently dreary. Colleagues impatient with sporadic, listless debate on the floor ask the whip to look after some pet project and let them know. They have to be hunted up in the hideaways the more senior members have in the Capitol—or maybe in the Senate dining room.

Teddy Kennedy, after a full six years in the Senate, decided to make a big thing of getting the whip's assignment. He went after Senator Russell Long, of Louisiana, a Southern entrenched power and son of Huey Long. The third Kennedy in the Senate—after his late brothers, President John F. and Senator Robert F.—Teddy was splashed with glamour and tragedy. A new President, a Republican, was in the White House. The Democrats had a big majority in the Senate, 57 to 43. Teddy challenged Russell Long. He won handily 31 to 26. Long never forgot or forgave. And Teddy, in the ensuing two years, was pretty much an absentee whip. Bobby Byrd did the work. There was no doubt about it in anyone's mind. He had a pocket memorandum book, in which he noted down all requests and favors executed.

The Democrats were down two Senate seats, 55 to 45, after the 1970 mid-term elections. When the Ninety-second Congress was about to be declared in session, Byrd had been active. Kennedy had not. Byrd isn't shy, although he seems the retiring type. Teddy's indifference to a post he made bigger than it was, for headline purposes, also convinced him that he was invulnerable to a fresh challenge. After all, who would really want the drudgery? Bobby Byrd. But you couldn't take him seriously, said the Kennedy entourage.

Bobby Byrd was dismissed in sneering remarks from self-stamped liberals, ultra-reformers, and self-anointed saviors of the Republic. He had been a member of the Ku Klux Klan about thirty years earlier. In 1946 he even wanted the Grand Kleagle of the Klan to restore operations in all states. Questioned, Byrd always had the same answer: a mistake, a bad mistake. When I brought that up to him, Byrd replied bitterly:

"A member of the Kennedy family [Bobby] worked for Joe McCarthy. That's been conveniently forgotten. He had family and background and wealth. A mistake I made about the same age he was when he worked with McCarthy is used against me. Nothing was said then or now about him. Or his brother [Ted]."

Bigger names in the Senate, lumped amorphously as liberals, never thought seriously about Bobby Byrd. He was taken for granted—hard worker, modest suburban dweller. He has a $30,000 house, a quiet wife, and two unpublicized married daughters. By no mean convivial, Byrd does not drink. He'll smoke a couple of fifteen-cent cigars a day. Parties he generally shuns like Sodom and Gomorrah. Byrd is a Baptist lay preacher. Takes it seriously. He was an orphan who assumed his uncle Titus's surname. And he studied nights, even for his law degree at American University, which the late President Kennedy conferred on him.

The contrast between Teddy Kennedy, long on glamour and short on work, and Byrd was great—they were millions of votes apart. Who in New York, or California, for that matter, ever heard of Bobby Byrd? It didn't matter to the little man from West Virginia. He wanted the whip's job. Simultaneously, he wanted to hang a haymaker on Teddy's low-slung jaw. You can't treat a man, especially a senator, too long as an errand boy. Right after the 1970 elections, stormy and replete with synthetic recrimination and outrageous spending on both sides, Bobby Byrd was reelected to his third term with 78 percent of the vote. Teddy won easily but didn't come close to that percentage.

Byrd wasted no time. He returned to Washington and started calling in overdue bills for multifarious favors he'd done senators for two years. Kennedy heard about it quickly. Intrigue of this kind gets around the Senate. He laughed, and took a vacation in sun-baked Jamaica. Nevertheless, he sent out information gatherers. They reported he had a solid majority from among the fifty-five Democrats. There was lots of duplicity. Rhode Island's John Pastore, who voted in the end for Teddy, tried to get support for Byrd. Byrd, notebook in hand, toted up his votes. They came to a minimum of twenty-eight, with a possibility of thirty. His senior senatorial partner from West Virginia, double-chinned Jennings Randolph, from the beginning, nearly two months before, was on the inside of the Byrd tactical operation.

A fortnight before the fifty-five Democratic senators gathered for what was regarded as a *pro forma* vote, one of Byrd's close, old West Virginia friends told me:

"Bobby's got the whip's job. But he's playing it close to the vest. I wonder why? He has the votes and he's the best head counter in the Senate, maybe in the Congress."

His mystification was shared by others. Only at about 10:30, January 21, after the vote was taken by secret ballot without sponsors' names, was the Byrd mystery solved. He had the proxy of the dying Senator Russell. With his blotter technique for detail and minutiae, Bobby Byrd repeatedly ran down the list of names in his memo book. Talmadge, the early riser in the Senate, was contacted twice. He reassured Byrd that he'd follow the fight for life that Dick Russell was losing at Walter Reed. The little man telephoned other senators at their homes who vowed support for him.

"He keeps at it until you can be worn down," remarked one of Byrd's active critics. "That guy's like Captain Queeg. Maybe a combination of Queeg and Uriah Heep is more to the point."

Nevertheless, this particular senator from the North voted for Bobby Byrd. Why? It's simple—past and endless favors. Teddy Kennedy shirked the whip's assignment anyway. A great deal of Teddy's do-nothing feeling suffused the senatorial bloc of Democrats. Kennedy, who knew about the growing pro-Byrd tendencies, shrugged them off. Somehow he also heard about the Russell proxy signed by the dying Senator at the beginning of the week and handed over to Mansfield. Inexplicably, the Kennedy team also knew how Byrd felt about Russell. He would not challenge Kennedy if Russell died before the vote. Why?

"I just don't think it would have been right," said Byrd to me. "There is nothing devious or complicated. I will not expand on it."

Overconfident in that knowledge, Democratic National Chairman Lawrence F. (Larry) O'Brien, veteran political architect for the Kennedys and the Democratic party, waved away any thought that Byrd could go anywhere. Forty-eight hours before, he said, "Forget it," when an old crony raised the question. Even bits of information that Byrd had telephoned fellow senators in the sacrosanct steamroom of the Senate didn't disturb old Larry, who is a real holdover of the "last hurrah" school. But a dogged, humorless little man from West Virginia would soon make him eat his certainty.

O'Brien and the Kennedy crowd weren't the only superconfident people. The media—that weird collective word that signifies something almost occult—concentrated instead on a Republican fight for Senate minority leader. That pitted acute, but aging, Senator Hugh Scott, from Pennsylvania, against small-in-stature and long-on-ambition Howard Baker from Tennessee. Baker, in his mid-forties, was the son-in-law of Everett Dirksen. He had been well coached by Dirksen in the intricacies of Republican machinations. But the old man, then minority leader, had died more than a year before. Scott replaced him, by beating Baker then. This looked like a closer fight. It would be a tussle, proclaimed the media. Teddy Kennedy believed it, while Bobby Byrd kept the phones going until the senators met at ten o'clock to decide by secret vote.

All senators, Democratic and Republican, began appearing at their offices around nine o'clock. Almost none had sideburns, somebody noticed wickedly. There was a trace of longer face hair on Senator George McGovern of South Dakota. That may have been to take attention away from his ever-thinning top. Maybe, observed Henry M. (Scoop) Jackson, of the state of Washington, McGovern had mini-sideburns to identify with the middle-aged. McGovern was already a declared candidate for the presidential nomination. Most of his colleagues were unshaken in the belief that he was really a stalking horse for Teddy Kennedy.

Ever since Teddy Kennedy decided to make a national issue of the whip's job two years before, he had made enemies a roll call long. Once regarded, as his late brothers were not, as a man of the Senate, Kennedy haters nurtured grievances and circulated all the gamy stories they could to do him discredit. A regular Republican crack that always made the rounds: "Teddy can't keep his pants buttoned." Another—more bipartisan—had him closely nuzzling a young Eskimo girl when he was in Alaska inquiring into local injustices. Kennedy had already bent freshman Mike Gravel's nose out of shape. Having beaten old Senator Ernest Gruening of Alaska in an encompassing TV campaign in the primaries, Gravel won election as the Democratic senator.

Out to please veterans and peers alike—Gravel quickly established a reputation in the Senate as an artful dodger—the freshman agreed in 1969 to support Russell Long. It was something of a coup for Long, since Gravel was supposed to be a liberal. Annoyed, Kennedy kept Gravel from appointment to the Commerce Committee. Byrd supported him. When Ted went off in a hail of publicity to Alaska, he ignored collegial facilities offered him by fellow Democrat Gravel. He used those made available by Republican Ted Stevens. Not surprisingly, Kennedy's Eskimo capers made their way, almost on an hourly basis, down to Washington. They were woven into regional strings of tales told with smacking lips and guffaws around the country.

Besides stories of his pre-Chappaquiddick acrobatics, Ted Kennedy's indifference to the minutiae of the whip's job began to irritate his colleagues. It grew into a rash. Even tiny, oracular Pastore was miffed. He made calls to on-the-fence senators advocating Bobby Byrd. That was Pastore's contribution for many past Byrd favors. He then felt free to vote for Ted Kennedy, as he believed a New Englander should.

"Bob Byrd would do the smallest things imaginable for Senators," remarked Hubert Humphrey, who was back again in the Senate and who voted for Kennedy. "Ted Kennedy, let's face it, didn't do a damned thing for anybody."

Little slights, perhaps engendered by casualness or indifference, also rubbed salt into Bob Byrd's hypersensitive skin where Kennedy was concerned. Teddy always insisted on retaining the symbols of the office of which he made national challenge. The substance was Byrd's to handle. Yet days that passed without Kennedy showing on the Senate floor were covered by a standing directive: Teddy had to be summoned to adjourn the chamber. It became a special ritual. He almost never let Byrd call adjournment. There was a time when he tried. Kennedy interrupted Byrd's adjournment motion. He made his own motion as a mark of respect to the late General Charles de Gaulle. In his office, Bob Byrd fumed: "There are times that I can't even make a routine motion. It's been going on for two years. I have to sit there and take it."

Kennedy's blunders on the floor of the Senate occasionally got under the skin of Majority Leader Mike Mansfield. As whip, Kennedy should have mastered the incessant detail, since he had so loudly and solemnly proclaimed his intent to master Senate problems. In the whip's post nearly two years, he decided to bring up the controversial Consumer Protection Act of 1970. Only one other senator was on the floor. Senator Robert P. Griffin, of

Michigan, assistant Republican leader, rushed to protest this breach of ground rules. Wearily Mansfield appeared. Knowledgeable to the core about floor rules and privileges, Mansfield apologized profusely.

"Interested Senators were apparently not consulted," he observed in his low-key manner. "It should not have been done."

The rebuke was clear to every senator. It was at that point that Bob Byrd really made up his mind to see if he could wrest the post away from Kennedy. The seeds had been planted before. Byrd had a base of seventeen Southern senators. Politics and involved jealousies started to play prominent roles. The Senate seemed to have been converted into a hothouse for cultivating candidates for the Democratic nomination for President. It was early, but that didn't curb aspirations. Never before in United States history had so many senators thought themselves candidates to lead the country out of a wilderness of entanglements. A workhorse, and relentless in his own all-work routine, Bob Byrd knew all about—and respected—the exercises of political clout. There were lots of senators who didn't like Kennedy, but feared him. They perked up at suggestions of a Byrd stop-Kennedy-now idea. It would be an unmitigated disaster, declared Byrd, if Ted Kennedy got the presidential nomination in 1972.

Besides Byrd's own dedication to detail and favors, he had broad powers as chairman of an appropriations subcommittee. It dealt with supplemental appropriation bills, which were often employed to slip in money items that were rejected in other bills. Byrd didn't hesitate to use all this subcommittee power of persuasion with his colleagues. He also approached Senators Henry M. (Scoop) Jackson and Warren G. Magnuson, both of the state of Washington. In 1969 Jackson had been an important voice urging the election of Kennedy over Long. Two intervening years made a big difference. Jackson deplored Kennedy's call to withdraw immediately from Vietnam. In addition, Jackson was testing the wind to see if he could compete for the presidential nomination. The decisive factor was the impending fate of the supersonic transport (SST), being built by Boeing in the home state of Jackson and Magnuson.

Kennedy was opposed to the government continuing any more

subsidies to the SST. His attitude enraged Jackson and Magnuson. Ironically, Magnuson often sided with Teddy on many external issues. And both Washington senators had as liberal a record on domestic policies as Kennedy. Theirs was longer as well. Bob Byrd could not by any lively imagination have been considered an intellectual counterpart of Jackson. Long before Byrd was elected to the Senate, Jackson crusaded for civil rights. Byrd was a conservative Southerner on those issues. His KKK past hardly aroused personal popularity with most Northerners. The Bobby Byrd ideology, nevertheless, did not detract from the role in which he saw himself most appropriately cast, that of being a legislative technician.

The inner political machinations of the Senate, added to Byrd's devotion to his role, had an impact on the Jacksons and Magnusons. Byrd, some time before the vote, came to Magnuson. He said tersely that he could help in the SST fight with two votes—his and fellow West Virginian Randolph's. Irritated at the approach, Magnuson said no, thanks. It was a first reaction. Magnuson and Jackson talked about it at length. The pluses for supporting Bobby Byrd outweighed the minuses and personal feelings. What had Ted Kennedy, after all, done for Jackson-Magnuson and in return for their earlier assistance? Suffering from stomach ulcers because of his driving intensity, Byrd shook off pain to canvas members. It didn't take him long to learn that Kennedy never bothered to call freshman Senator Lawton Chiles of Florida. He sewed up the Chiles vote early.

Before the mid-term 1970 elections, Kennedy got wind of the possibility that Byrd might go after him. Having ignored Byrd for the most part, the cloakroom approaches of his deputy and Byrd's suggestions to fence sitters reached Kennedy in good time. He could not or would not take Bob Byrd seriously. Both senators, anticipating easy times with re-elections, dawdled before leaving the Senate for other chores. Kennedy telephoned Byrd late one afternoon. That was another habit Byrd griped about. Kennedy called him, never asked about having a private chat in one office or the other. A newspaper had something of the early and wary Byrd overtures to fellow senators. Was it true? demanded Kennedy over the phone.

"Oh, it's pure speculation," replied Bob Byrd. "Sure, I've given it some thought but it's premature."

Kennedy, eager to take off on a trip, wanted "assurances" from Byrd.

"I can't make any kind of assurances, Ted," answered Byrd. "In these situations you shouldn't even ask. Would anyone ask Mike [Mansfield] for assurances? And would Mike ask for them from anyone?"

"You can tell me whether you'll run or not," Kennedy responded heatedly.

Snapped Byrd: "Well, I won't."

To anyone that kind of standoff would ring alarms. Kennedy apparently paid the matter little additional attention. A couple of months stretched between their telephone colloquy and the vote for whip. Byrd was annoyed but quieted his ulcers and did some plain political thinking. The fears and concerns other Democratic senators held about Kennedy becoming the nominee and maybe even President dissipated greatly after Chappaquiddick. Before, who'd want to lay his career maybe on the line against someone who could be in the White House? Byrd, from complaints and shots at Kennedy from fellow senators in private, had a shrewd idea of the tepid to cold feelings now. On Senate stationery he sent out dozens of little notes. "Byrd-o-grams," they were to members who asked for and received favors in the past. There was no need to explain the notes. A recipient was not puzzled. But he couldn't prove anything, either. To colleagues who seemed interested or promising, Byrd talked his ambitions in covert Byzantine terms. It was the kind of Senate cloakroom intrigue that delighted senators.

A few longer memories recalled how Byrd went after the No. 3 spot—the one he now held—as secretary of the Democratic conference. It was in 1967 and his opponent was Pennsylvania millionaire-liberal Joseph S. Clark. In an organized, carefully repetitive manner, Bob Byrd lined up support. At the time he had already run innumerable errands for colleagues. He hadn't even any designated or elected post on the Senate floor. But Byrd was always around to note the gist of speeches, issues, and to have a look at declarations intended for the *Congressional Record*. His yearning for the place second to that of the whip amused many fellow members. Many, ideologically opposed to him, didn't see any harm in Byrd as No. 3. Clark, later defeated for re-election by a Republican, was beaten by Bob Byrd.

He was the first political victim in the big money-liberal category to fall before the prepared onslaught of Senator Byrd of West Virginia. It was a victory relished by Byrd. The only man besides Byrd who keeps the Clark defeat in mind is young John D. Rockefeller IV, who settled in West Virginia and has been elected to state offices. Rockefeller, presently Secretary of State there, knows that Bob Byrd feels anything but benign toward him and his future hopes to run for governor. Married to a twin daughter of Republican Senator Charles (Chuck) Percy, of Illinois, he conveys a malevolent image to Bob Byrd. Endowed with vast, inherited wealth, he has—in Byrd's eyes—deigned to enter the crucible of leadership. It's out-and-out carpetbagging for someone like John D. IV to trespass in their regions. Byrd considers himself a populist and people like young Rockefeller economic royalists trying to buy their way straight to domination over poor people.

Black leaders in Washington and elsewhere long have regarded Bob Byrd as totally unreconstructed in civil rights. He was implacably against blacks, they charged, going over his KKK background and Confederacy stances in the Senate. Byrd argued back, no; that he was for slower evolution than most but still for reform in co-equality for blacks. His perseverance in having black police officers appointed to important jobs in West Virginia was always pointed to pridefully by Byrd. Strip the façade, contended the Reverend Walter Fauntroy, who was later elected the first non-voting representative to Congress from the District of Columbia. Fauntroy thinks of Bob Byrd as a Janus-faced hypocrite whose record against assisting blacks to human dignity belies any fancy words. He would point to Byrd's adamant opposition to welfare for unemployed blacks and unwed mothers in the District. It's a record that runs eight dreary years as chairman of the Senate Appropriations Subcommittee for the District of Columbia.

Just about every major tenet held high by liberals in the Senate was certainly not shared by Bobby Byrd. None of their distaste rebuffed Byrd if he believed any showed interest. Lots, of course, did. "Hell, Bobby Byrd delivers when he promises," argued a prominent pro-Labor senator. "I'll fight him on the main issues. He understands that. He wants to handle the floor details when nobody else does. Let him do it." Byrd's insistence on reconfirmation also exasperated his friends, though they were good-natured about it. "I'll certainly vote for Bobby Byrd," explained a veteran Southerner. "It's not just good enough. He isn't checking a change of heart for me. It's just the way Bobby is. Check and recheck. There aren't many who do it that way." The Byrd appeals to fellow senators gathered more steam after the mid-term elections and the approaching convening of the Ninety-second session of Congress.

"I just don't want to be cut to pieces," Byrd pleaded with members he called. "Please tell me now if you can't vote for me."

The weekend before the vote, Byrd, Jennings Randolph, and Talmadge got together for strategy sessions. Ted Kennedy felt secure. His outriders who checked came back to say he had a sound majority. They simply swallowed some barefaced lies. Before the actual vote the Kennedy network would double check and come up with the same results. Kennedy and they accepted what was told them. Bobby Byrd, more conscious of the frailties of colleagues, knew better. That's why he kept checking, never letting up. At Byrd's request, Talmadge visited Senator Russell in the hospital. He brought a typed, proposed proxy letter. It read:

Dear Senator Mansfield:

In the event it is not possible for me to be present when the Senate Democrats caucus for the opening of the 92nd Congress, I hereby tender my proxy in favor of Senator Robert C. Byrd of West Virginia if he is a candidate for the position of Assistant Majority Leader.

With best wishes, I am

Sincerely,

The signature was scrawled, "Richard B. Russell." It obviously had been done with great difficulty by the dying Senator. Byrd previously had obtained the proxy of Magnuson. The Russell approval was all important. In Bob Byrd's cautious head-counting, it gave him twenty-eight, or a majority of one. In their skull ses-

sions, Byrd declared he wouldn't use Russell's proxy if by chance
the senior Georgia Senator died. Anti-Byrd senators agreed later
that Bob Byrd really meant it. Nobody could explain why. Thus,
an elaborate deathwatch was maintained on Russell's sickroom at
Walter Reed Hospital. The way it worked was for Talmadge to
keep checking Russell's condition and then to inform Byrd. In
turn, Byrd would signal Randolph—a nod, yes, or a shake of the
head, no. If yes, it meant that Senator Russell still lived. Randolph
could place Bob Byrd's name in nomination. The Democratic
caucus was set for 10:00 A.M.

From the old and new Senate Office buildings, the senators
came casually. The Democrats had, with McGovern, at least eight
senators by this time aspiring to the Democratic presidential
nomination. More astounding than their ambitions was their
early quest—eighteen months and maybe two dozen primaries
before the nominations. Nearly all had been in the bruising chase
for money. The costs of running, even for a senator in a small
state, was upwards of $250,000. Some places as high as $5 to $8
million. Much of the cash had to come over the transom, so to
speak. The easiest way was the formation of D.C. committees.
That's a license to thumb your nose at the so-called Corrupt
Practices Act, fifty years old. Nobody has to report anything. In
his race for the Presidency in 1968, Hubert H. Humphrey reported $350—count it—that he knew about. After all, you've got
to say you knew about the money.

The senators generally used the little Toonerville cars called
the "subway" to get to the Capitol from the old and new buildings, that abut each other. Democrats and Republicans were
scheduled to meet separately and secretly in rococo caucus rooms
in the Capitol. Right after the vote, they could saunter to the
Senate floor. Senators would be sworn in, four at a time, before
the presiding officer—Vice-President Spiro T. (Ted) Agnew.

Most Democrats turned up at their caucus wearing solemn
expressions. Newcomers like Lloyd Bentsen, of Texas, were among
the earliest. He was jollied by Big Jim Eastland, dead cigar in his
fist. In his drawling speech, Eastland asked Bentsen if he didn't
think that a senator's salary should be raised from the present
$42,500 annually to, say, $50,000. More middle-level executives of

horse-shit firms were paid better, guessed Eastland. Bentsen, a multimillionaire, demurred. With the active but covert assistance of LBJ, he had chopped up the incumbent, Ralph Yarborough, in the primaries. Then he had gone on to crush a rising Republican star, George Bush. Cost: no less than $2,500,000 for Bentsen's forces. In their losing effort, the Republicans weren't far behind that figure.

Senator Phil Hart, from Michigan, now fully bearded (on a bet, he said), turned up with McGovern. They were on one of their favorite topics: the military establishment was deceitful and wasteful. Saturnine and well-tailored, Bill Fulbright entered. He listened to senators like smiling Birch Bayh, of Indiana, and huge Harold E. Hughes, of Iowa, worry about our role in Vietnam. Before the vote the known "doves" talked among themselves. They paid little but formal attention to a newcomer like Chiles from Florida, who had walked across his state to attract attention. Instead of big, fund-raising dinners, Chiles had chicken-in-the-basket, al fresco picnics. He clobbered a hand-picked Republican, Bill Cramer, long in the House. Cramer cut up in the Republican primaries Judge G. Harrold Carswell. The Senate rejected Carswell as an associate Supreme Court justice. Chiles spent $400,000. chicken dinners and all. Cramer? Maybe three times as much.

Majority Leader Mansfield turned up toward 10:00 A.M. He shook hands with everybody. By coincidence, Teddy Kennedy came in among the last. He was trailed by Bobby Byrd. Not much time for any formalities. By acclaim, with Byrd in the chair, Mike Mansfield was re-elected majority leader. He had held the post since LBJ went up. Now came the crunch. Byrd slipped away from the chair to consult Talmadge. Jennings Randolph waited for word from Byrd to see if Bobby would challenge Kennedy for the nomination. The media was crowded outside the Republican session. Byrd wanted to know from Talmadge if Dick Russell still lived. At 10:53 A.M., Talmadge nodded, yes. Byrd nodded his head to where Randolph stood.

Robert C. Byrd was placed in nomination for whip by Randolph. A level of red-creased Kennedy chin rose above his white collar. This he didn't expect, warnings and all. Without signatures, the fifty-five senators scribbled down their choices. Freshman Senator, and Teddy's lawschool roommate, John Tunney, of California, was assigned to make the official announcement. Three fellow freshman senators stood by to help with the tally. Tunney, son of the ex-world heavyweight champion of the world, stumbled.

"Keerist, Bobby Byrd's got it!" exclaimed Gale McGee of Wyoming.

He made no secret of the fact early that he would support Byrd—for totally nonideological reasons. An ex-history professor, articulate and photogenic, McGee was the only fluent adversary Bill Fulbright ran up against in the Foreign Relations Committee. His views of Teddy, Ed Muskie (who remained steadfastly silent), and all aspirants but Scoop Jackson dripped with contempt. McGee hides nothing from friend or foe.

"Ed Muskie pretends to be the taciturn type from Maine," McGee once said bitterly. "It's nothing against him but maybe he is so quiet about major issues because he doesn't really understand them."

John Tunney announced the count. It stood: 31 for Byrd; 24 for Kennedy. By any measure, it was a bad licking for a Kennedy. And by whom? A little upstart from West Virginia was the way one of the more charitable pro-Kennedy senators put it. Mumbling a barely audible "congratulations," Teddy shook hands in a perfunctory way with Bobby Byrd. Back of them other senators burned the unsigned ballot papers in a tin wastebasket. There were a few notable questions, though. Kennedy's people swore up and down that he was promised a total of 28 votes minimum out of 55. At least four senators who promised to vote for him made the same pledge to Bobby Byrd. What mattered—to Byrd—was they voted for him.

Teddy Kennedy, flushed to the eyes, walked to the waiting media. The word had gotten out. It was passed jubilantly by Randolph. In a flash of activity, the Republican caucus was deserted by the media. Nobody cared. Scott beat back a tough challenge from Baker, 24 to 20. Still, no excitement in that one.

Before the assembled media, Ted Kennedy said slowly: "I learned a long time ago that unless you know how to lose, you don't deserve to win."

But no Kennedy was raised that way. As soon as he could, Kennedy chewed out his immediately available staff men. They didn't know politics; they had only talked to the obvious friends. Recrimination was the long suit. His brother-in-law, Sargent Shriver, recently returned from being Ambassador to France, had had his own last word at a party that night:

"It's a defeat, but what the hell. You win some and you lose some. It's interesting that all great men have had their defeats. They've all been licked—Churchill, de Gaulle, Nixon, Willy Brandt."

Nobody else in the Kennedy family would ever have compared Teddy with Churchill or General Charles de Gaulle. Of all the tragic Kennedy brothers, Teddy is by far the least able. That's why he worked so hard originally when he went to the Senate. Absorbing a problem doesn't come easily to him. His defeat caused many in the Capitol to cheer. There were remarks about Chappaquiddick. And quite a few remembered how Teddy had once been expelled for cheating on exams at Harvard. As for Shriver? A shrewd little man in Maryland cut him so badly that he didn't dare try for the Democratic governorship in Maryland. Marvin Mandel, elected Governor by the legislature when Agnew ran with Nixon, taught Shriver what a blue zero he is in political life. The Kennedy mantle was becoming threadbare.

But who had reneged on a vote promised Teddy? All United States senators are presumed most honorable men because they belong to the "greatest deliberative body in the world." Nevertheless, a fellow liberal from the Midwest, Harold E. Hughes, did. So did Clinton P. Anderson, of New Mexico, and Stuart Symington, the silvery duke of Missouri. Onetime superhawk and former Secretary of the Air Force, Symington was running lots of interference for Fulbright these days. Senator Russell told me that a tactical mistake he committed was in not giving Symington chairmanship of the subcommittee on preparedness.

"John Stennis talked me out of that one," mused the Senate's Nestor. "So Mr. Symington shopped around for another chairmanship. He got it. Senator Fulbright gave him one on the Foreign Relations Committee. Look what that's done."

Symington headed up a subcommittee on our foreign bases and

commitments. His investigators—"hanging jurors" according to McGee—dented, distorted, and disturbed United States foreign policy associations and commitments around the world. They started with LBJ when he showed the first traces of vulnerability. With virtually a roll of the eye and a lilt to the voice, Symington's private gumshoes happily went after Nixon.

Yet Symington, like thirty others, owed Bobby Byrd lots of little senatorial favors. The strange key to challenging Kennedy remained with the last breaths taken painfully by Senator Russell. He died a few minutes short of four hours after Teddy was defeated. Byrd refused adamantly to explain why he would have withdrawn the Russell proxy and himself if the fatally ill Senator had died before the vote. He stuck to his simplistic thesis.

Some senators lied, though. They promised both Teddy Kennedy and Byrd their votes. Embittered Kennedyites said: "Don't get mad—get even," an old Irish-Mafia injunction. A Kennedy always remained a menace to Presidential aspirations. Even those who posed for a photo as Democratic nominee possibilities said most sanctimoniously that they voted for Kennedy. A few who voted for Byrd—on his list—had the nerve to thrust their best faces forward in a group photograph. It's a sobering but rewarding exercise to run down the list of those voting for Senator Bob Byrd for whip:

Allen, Ala.; Bible, Nev.; Byrd, W. Va.; Byrd, Va.; Anderson, N.M.; Bentsen, Tex.; Burdick, N.D.; Chiles, Fla.; Eastland, Miss.; Ellender, La.; Ervin, N.C.; Gravel, Alaska; Hartke, Indiana; Fulbright, Ark.; Hollings, S.C.; Jackson, Wash.; Magnuson, Wash.; Jordan, N.C.; Long, La.; McClellan, Ark.; McGee, Wyo.; Montoya, N.M.; Randolph, W. Va.; Russell, Ga.; Sparkman, Ala.; Spong, Va.; Stennis, Miss.; Symington, Mo.; Talmadge, Ga.; Williams, N.J.; and Hughes, Iowa.

On that list there are a dozen who would consistently call themselves "liberal." Kennedy had counted on Anderson, Burdick, Ellender, and Symington to vote for him. The omission of Hughes from the Kennedy camp was strictly a personal feud that also involved both senators' wives and Kennedy's near-flagrant tendency to philander. In addition, of course, Hughes had been bitten by the Presidential bug. He was the best speaker in the Senate, a massive figure with a resonant bass voice. Harrison (Pete) Williams got off the Ted Kennedy team in this instance a few days before the vote. He absolutely refused to say why or to comment. Burdick insisted that he voted for Teddy. His name was on a "certain" count held by Byrd's tacticians.

The carelessness of the Kennedy counters and checkers was best exemplified in the belief that Allen Ellender was on their side. He was certain to succeed Dick Russell as chairman of the Appropriations Committee. At eighty, and the oldest in the Senate, Ellender had his eccentricities, but being pro-Kennedy was never one of them. Besides, he was from Louisiana. His junior colleague was Russ Long, beaten two years before by the Kennedy challenge. Ellender bitterly resented that affront to the South and to Louisiana. In the Senate the power of the purse was essentially Ellender's to open or close. Symington's eye, always geared to appropriations and their size, was beamed to Ellender. The vote conclusively showed Kennedy that members of the exclusive club rejected him. They believed he had become vulnerable. In public his nose was tweaked for the country to see. Deception in some key cases was deliberate.

There was almost as much jubilation in the White House as if Nixon had been re-elected. All other calls were held off as communications from the Senate gave news of the vote. Ted Kennedy always had been regarded as the President's principal opponent in 1972.

"Chappaquiddick II," was the immediate aftermath slogan in White House offices.

Ed Muskie, fiercely correct in his associations with Ted Kennedy, had another, more charitable view. He had declined two years before to run for Democratic whip. It was really his refusal that caused Kennedy to take up the challenge. Muskie was not disposed to gloat. A fleeting smile is as close as he can come to gloating. The lank Senator from Maine was also the considered hare in the race for the party's presidential nomination. He was not exactly displeased with Kennedy's defeat.

"I have the feeling," he said, "that I ought to send Teddy the statements I made two years ago about the worthlessness of being whip. He'd understand now."

On the other side of the Capitol, in the House of Representatives, another friend of Ted Kennedy had some piercing words of counsel. Four bells rang. The Ninety-second Congress was in session. The 435 Representatives gathered noisily. Carl Albert was elected Speaker, a triumph to the stamina of a poor boy from the dustbowls of Oklahoma. Ancient John McCormack of Massachusetts had retired. It was a resignation forced by events, principally corruption involving his top assistant, lordly Dr. (Ph.D.) Martin Sweig. New and veteran congressmen spiced their speech with demands for independence. Reform was the brave talk that soon was reduced to a whisper in a wind tunnel. Representative Morris K. Udall, whose brother Stewart had long been Secretary of the Interior under Presidents Kennedy and Johnson, was badly wounded. He bid to become Speaker. Lots of fellow liberals promised him support. Result? Udall was soundly deceived by promises—and badly trounced.

He called Kennedy to say: "As soon as I pick all the liberal buckshot out of my ass, I'll come over and help pull those liberal knives out of your back. It doesn't hurt as much if you just pull them out straight."

In the marbled Senate chamber, pages sat around the area below the raised desk of presiding officer Vice-President Spiro T. Agnew. Most of the ninety-nine were present. Old Karl Mundt, elderly Republican from South Dakota, was absent. He had been toppled more than a year before by a stroke, but his devoted wife, Mary, insisted that he remain a senator. Even President Nixon couldn't change her mind.

For the last time, Kennedy sat between Mansfield and Bobby Byrd. They watched swearing-in ceremonies; usually it was four senators at a time. Nobody talked. Back of the chamber, on either aisle, senators chatted about the upcoming presidential State of the Union message. Major points had been leaked. Nixon's proposed reforms of the Executive branch were equally kicked around. There were profound doubts that he could manage that one. Too many vested interests were involved, senior senators asserted knowledgeably. Nobody paid attention then to Kennedy. He had taken a major-league licking for a minor-league job. Two years before, he had entered this same chamber, wreathed in the toothy smile of triumph. Now he was a loser. The world's greatest deliberative body has no time for a loser, whatever his name happens to be.

It was ten years and a day after John F. Kennedy was inaugurated thirty-fifth President of the United States, in a blizzard that covered Washington in a white girdle, and the Kennedy years—dynasty, some still hoped—had begun. As Ted Kennedy now sat slumped in his chair, the family political fortunes were at their lowest ebb.

II

THE GREATEST
DELIBERATIVE BODY
IN THE WORLD

The ebb tide that eroded the political pinnings of the Kennedys also washed over the low state of the Senate. It was a remorseless coincidence of contemporary history. The role of the Senate and its stature had been going steadily downhill for years. Occasionally some giant personalities and minds arose to check the descent temporarily. When they vanished, the downward slide went even faster. With little understanding or help from its Senate, the nation began to grind its teeth in a national state of nerves.

There was Vietnam, the longest and most divisive conflict tearing the country apart since the Civil War. It triggered protests and defiance of political authority that didn't know how to cope with either the war or the dissent. Violent crime riddled communities. Life seemed to be held in utter disdain. Where once integration appeared as the only sensible solution for racial discontent, blacks and whites increasingly scorned it as a charade. A new generation come of age groped and griped in search of its rightful place in society. The ultimate question about the rights of man—woman, too, now—provoked recrimination and abuse rather than measured debate and consideration.

In a nation of "joiners," where everyone used to believe that he wanted to be liked, a great many people came to dislike and to be suspicious of everyone else. We had arrived at the worst of

times in a society regarded as the most affluent in the world. But
even the affluence was wearing thin. Unemployment rose; families
started shrinking from Depression memories of scrounging for
meals and shelter. The United States Senate, our great deliberative body, peered timidly at the problems mushrooming all around.
Except for a few voices, which tried to soothe by placating, the
Senate recoiled from coming to grips with the main problems.
Its factionalism, petty jealousies, and strident ambitions resembled
more post-Civil War vengeance and localism than national determination to confront realities of today.

Members urging reforms still clung to outmoded privileges.
More recent arrivals generally scoffed at the notion of the Senate
as an "exclusive club." Like huffy dissidents of the Union League
Club, they formed their own inner sanctums for like-minded
colleagues. In trying to present a fresh face, newcomers only
changed clubs. It was hypocrisy altered by cosmetics, rather than
by surgery. Consider what the pious modernists have done with
the Senate's pride and joy, the privilege of unlimited debate. We
have come to know the practice too often as filibuster. A minority
can kill a proposal by talking it into oblivion. It had often been
condemned as a defense mechanism of the South. Today, liberal
senators use the technique just as much and more. Rather than
dramatizing a controversial issue, long debate now inflates a
hot-air balloon floating aimlessly above urgent need for deliberation and decision.

When the chips were down, the new boys in the Senate almost
invariably sided with the veterans and traditionalists. They want
to preserve Senate prerogatives. Among the oldest and most
pernicious is the one called "senatorial courtesy." A member can
call an appointment to office "personally obnoxious." All colleagues will close ranks to defend the whim or visceral reaction.
They also will pretend to stand aloof if another senator goes off
on a rampage, destroying people and institutions. For five years
senators were generally scared stiff of Joseph R. McCarthy, Republican Senator from Wisconsin. Casually explaining their inac-
tion as a matter of "senatorial courtesy," they let him run amok.
Only when the Senate's interlocking system of preservation was
directly threatened did they turn on McCarthy. Colleagues re-

versed the Babbittry of courtesy on Joe McCarthy. The traumatic damage to the Senate lingers as a result, as does the still-smoking wreckage of the State Department.

These have been views of a select council, increasingly out of touch with the country. "Work within the system" was their palliative cry to all disjointed sections of the country. On paper or the speaker's platform it wasn't a bad idea. Unfortunately, few senators practiced what they preached. Theirs was an appeal to patience and fortitude. Yet we were in the 1970s when sound action and faster decision became obligatory. The Senate was never intended to live in a privileged vacuum or a do-nothing rut.

Alexander Hamilton, one of its creators, wanted an elite upper house. He thought of the Senate as a House of Lords with teeth. Men of property and breeding, Hamiltonians firmly believed, should be elected to the Senate. They would restrain the plebian House of Representatives, elected directly by the people, from reckless acts. The United States was a nation of four million people, principally agrarian. Illiteracy was common. Hamilton, who saw during the Revolutionary War what embattled farmers could do, wanted senators to be elected for life. After exhaustive argument, he agreed to six-year Senate terms, provided senators were elected by their respective legislatures, and not by the voters at large. Senators were so chosen until 1913. The Seventeenth Amendment to the Constitution stipulated that people of the states directly elect their own senators. But first the Constitution provided in Article I, Section 1 that:

All legislative powers herein granted shall be vested in a Congress of the United States, which shall consist of a Senate and House of Representatives.

Many incumbent senators today take the view that because the Senate was mentioned first in the Constitution they, therefore, enjoy total primacy. Section 3 of Article I says further:

The Senate of the United States shall be composed of two Senators from each state, chosen by the legislature thereof, for six years; and each senator shall have one vote.

Immediately after the first election, senators were divided into three classes. Seats of the first class would be vacated at the end of the second year; of the second class at the termination of the fourth year, and of the third, at the end of six years. In this way one-third of the senators would be chosen every second year. Vacancies by death or other causes would be filled by the governor of the state. All these points prevail, as still do, according to the Constitution:

No person shall be a senator who shall not have attained to the age of thirty years, and been nine years a citizen of the United States, and who shall not, when elected, be an inhabitant of that State for which he shall be chosen.

The Vice-President of the United States shall be President of the Senate, but shall have no vote, unless they be equally divided.

These are among the main constitutional provisions for the Senate. They are also expanded within the framework of the Executive branch, the Presidency. Electors, equivalent to the numbers of senators and members of the House of Representatives in a state, vote for President and Vice-President. All schoolchildren know that, in reality, we vote for electors pledged to a specific candidate. It is a step removed—a big one—from the direct vote for President. There have been some efforts in the last few years to have the Senate approve direct elections as a giant step forward toward a constitutional amendment. Noisy and crushing defeat of the sponsors of something so daring has been the Senate response.

Further, in provisions concerning the Executive in the Constitution, loom the advice and consent requirements by the Senate. They read:

He shall have power, by and with the advice and consent of the Senate, to make treaties, provided two-thirds of the senators present concur; and he shall nominate, and by and with the advice and consent of the Senate, shall appoint ambassadors, other public ministers and consuls, judges of the Supreme Court, and all other officers of the United States, whose appointments are not herein otherwise provided for, and which shall be established by law. . . .

A challenge to the Executive, especially on foreign affairs, is almost always mounted by the Senate. A nomination by the President to the Supreme Court has rarely been rebuffed. President Nixon chalked up a boomerang record by having two of his selections rejected within a few months of each other. It is principally on the conduct of foreign affairs and war-making powers that the Senate and the President have clashed since the United States became a world power and then a superpower. A Senate, justly suspicious of being hoodwinked and even deftly sidestepped by the Presidency, can make life miserable for the Executive branch.

The periods of World Wars I and II, with Presidents Woodrow Wilson and Franklin D. Roosevelt, were punctuated with stiff Senate challenges. Lyndon B. Johnson, once an effective Senate majority leader, ran into angry storms whipped up by old colleagues because of the war in Vietnam. The same treatment was meted out to Nixon, though he has been somewhat more fortunate. Nixon, also a former senator and vice-president, was installed in the White House from the minority party. Prudently, he began the painful extrication process from Vietnam. Nevertheless, he has been under steady criticism and attack from the Senate for not consulting with its members, especially those mainly devoted to determination of foreign issues.

The President, with his vast network of representatives at home and abroad furnishing him inside information, always is in a position to initiate and stimulate external conditions. It was Nixon's decision, predicated on months of preparation, that turned off an angry Senate—the world as well—with a secret mission, secretly carried out. The President dispatched his special security affairs adviser, former Harvard academician Dr. Henry Kissinger, on a trip to the mainland of China. Kissinger's nimble intelligence is an enigma to many, including Secretary of State William P. Rogers. Kissinger is the chief builder of affairs of state.

Two years before his secret mission, Kissinger helped the President map the path eastward in a state visit to Romania. The Senate knew little of the beginnings, nothing of the follow-through that took Kissinger to China for forty-nine hours with Premier Chou En-Lai. A Nixon visit to the "People's Republic of China" was arranged. It was unprecedented. An old hate-love by the United States for China, after it fell under Communist control in 1949, in a twinkling turned to starry-eyed wonder. What hath

Mao-tse Tung wrought? It was classic secret diplomacy, secretly arrived at.

Approval in the Senate of the whole clandestine operation, sort of Talleyrand with a dash of James Bond, rang out across the world. A gloomy critic of the exercise of Executive privilege, as opposed to consultation with the Senate, applauded and enthused. He was lean, oracular Senator J. William Fulbright, Democrat of Arkansas. Once a Rhodes scholar and loudly opposed in recent years to Executive wheeling-and-dealing, Fulbright thought the message to China was sound and precedent making. Here was a senator, chairman of the Foreign Relations Committee, applauding secrecy he condemned. He observed that the mission and upcoming presidential visit to China would help bring the Executive into closer liaison with the legislative, meaning his committee. His change of heart lasted only forty-eight hours.

Fulbright had, like all his critical colleagues, been totally out-maneuvered. Interestingly, they had nothing to say about the messenger—Kissinger. Fulbright led the critical pack in his dislike of Kissinger, who usually shrugged off their arrows aimed at him. Senator Fulbright epitomized the suspicions of encroachment of the Executive on their committees. His was the oldest in the Senate, by a few hours. Fulbright has held his committee chairmanship longer than any other senator in history. And the real clout in the Senate centers in its sixteen standing committees.

This all began in 1816, in the waning days of the second Madison Administration before Monroe took office. By resolution, the Senate voted to create committees on: Foreign Relations, Finance, and the Military and Militia. The military committee took its present name, Armed Services, in 1947 after assorted alterations over a hundred and fifty years. Finance divided into two in 1867, when the Appropriations Committee was established. With the creation of the first three Senate committees, subcommittees soon followed. After our Civil War, most other standing committees were formed by approval of the Senate.

Committee chairmen have the power to appoint subcommittees. They designate who shall be members, propose the kind of staffs required, and recommend the type of witnesses to be summoned. In the Senate, only two chairmen are below the age of sixty. The average age is around sixty-six. Being a senior senator and maintaining stamina in committee is the only way to become a chairman. Not a single Senate chairmanship of a standing committee is in the hands of an Easterner. The South has ten. More than half the heads of Senate committees come from smaller communities or the outright boondocks. Nobody from an urban center is chairman of a committee.

As the nation grew almost geometrically, so did the Senate's insistence on seniority in committees. The South was the chief benefactor. A senator from the region can be—usually is—re-elected until his will has been probated. One notable exception was the late Theodore Francis Green, the bachelor gentleman from Rhode Island. He retired at ninety-three, having been a Foreign Relations Committee chairman. Cruel jokes were played on him before he retired in 1961. Remarkably alert for his age, the "nineties" got him. Colleagues, with their idea of humor, introduced outsiders to him as senators. Green always shook hands warmly, called them by first names, and inquired into legislation supposedly on their desks.

The Constitution, in creating the Senate, kept states' rights very much in mind. Great courage and perseverance were required to keep national interests in the forefront. In 1789, when the first Senate was emplaced, it wanted to show its independence of the Executive. An opportunity was missed which was never to return. George Washington wanted to go a step further than the Constitution demanded in approving treaties. He believed the Senate should help in even shaping a draft treaty. Washington was negotiating a treaty with an Indian tribe. He met with the Senate, but they paid no attention to his pleas. Some mimicked him. Indignantly, Washington stalked off. It inevitably led Presidents to the device of "Executive Agreements." The Executive now avoids cantankerous senators and difficult treaty negotiations alike.

Most senators today work hard, or put in long hours. They are largely unable to concentrate on important issues for long. It may be that the demands on them of a bureaucratic nature are overly burdensome. It also may be that most senators are intellectually unequipped to grapple with the issues of importance that usually arise with a rush. The average senator wearily turns over the digging to a staff assistant. It was far different in the early days. The pace was more leisurely. A senator could—as did Henry Clay, Daniel Webster, and their colleagues—spend years on a single, transcendent issue confronting the nation.

It must have been fascinating, from contemporary accounts, to have witnessed senators in action when the move to Washington occurred in 1800. George Washington conceived of a "Federal City." When the government transferred from New York City to Philadelphia, awaiting the ultimate move to Washington, there were 130 clerks. There are 350,000 federal employees for the capital city today. Only one big business prevails, that of the government. That was so in its casual way when the Houses of Congress were first raised in the geographical center of the city, whose streets bogged down in thick mud in any rain. But in the old Supreme Court chamber of the Capitol, semicircular in dimension, great men debated in the Senate. During one particular golden period, senators like Clay, Webster, John C. Calhoun, Thomas Hart Benton, and Sam Houston debated the fate of the nation.

Their talents—for and against issues—were probably never again equalled. Calhoun was the articulate spokesman for the South. He also had been a presiding officer of the Senate as Vice-President to Andrew Jackson. His wife's snobbishness caused many official ladies to ostracize the wife of a Jackson Cabinet member. Mrs. Calhoun's old Magnolia decorum also irritated Jackson. To iron things out, Jackson fired his entire Cabinet. It had been the suggestion of Martin van Buren. Out went van Buren, too, but Calhoun was replaced as Vice-President by van Buren. He succeeded Jackson as President. Calhoun went back to the Senate, elected from South Carolina. He might have become President had he stayed with Jackson.

A contemporary some years earlier sought to rise above a wave of capriciousness in the Senate. John Quincy Adams defended the policies of President Thomas Jefferson. Adams's father, the second President, had been relentlessly opposed by Jefferson. It cost the elder Adams a second term. Senator Adams, to the horror of colleagues and the Massachusetts state legislature that elected him, went against prospering New England commercial interests. The issue was a Jeffersonian embargo, preventing British vessels from plying American waters. By supporting the President, John Quincy Adams became a pariah back home.

The Massachusetts legislature went further. It sought to snuff out his career. Nearly a year before the Senate term of Adams expired, the legislature elected a successor. John Quincy Adams resigned his seat. Publicly he continued all-out support to Jefferson. A proud, high-minded man of experience and learning at home and abroad, Adams came back to the political scene. He managed to win out for President over war hero Jackson. It was a wafer-thin triumph. Jackson had more electoral votes but not a majority. The House of Representatives voted John Quincy Adams the sixth President on its very first ballot.

But the Senate, his old stamping ground, opposed Adams. The new president refused to try patronage to bring recalcitrant senators around. Seed of special privilege, sown in the Senate, needed careful cultivation. Adams even declined mass firings at the top to please former colleagues. He had the temerity to treat friends and enemies from Senate committees as equals. Adams was not a politician. In admiration, though, Clay remarked that Adams had enough principle to spread around several Senates.

Andy Jackson was the all-around populist politician. He allayed outrage in the Senate when he became President. It was a time, however, when Calhoun and fellow Southerners were increasingly alarmed by the ever-growing population and industrialization of the North. The House of Representatives was acquiring far more Northern members than was the South.

Competition and tempers got cutthroat. Free states pitted their industrialization against agricultural slave states. Northern senators demanded additional patronage, more favors. The South countered by repeatedly spurning Northern behests. Times began getting tense. Calhoun, in eloquent appeals to the North for understanding and sympathy, often said: "The poor, poor South." It was an ironic echo of the "poor Austria" theme proclaimed by Metternich for the Hapsburg Empire. The phrase was revived nearly a hundred and fifty years later for a truncated, tiny Austrian republic.

To preserve the union was Clay's ambition. He was from the

Civil War. But the national interest was casually jettisoned in favor of ingrained vengeance, small-minded self-interest, and the greedy self-concern of corruption. In the generations of senators that followed Appomattox, until the arrival of the Twentieth Century, it was a rare personality that defended national preservation. One was Edmund G. Ross, of Kansas. Impeachment of President Andrew Johnson centered around the resolve of Ross. Few senators in office today can say much about the episode except that Johnson made it by a single vote.

Bent on interminable revenge against the South, Northern senators hankered after total prostration to prevail below the Mason-Dixon line. Carpetbaggers ran wild in the scorched areas. Pious abolitionist senators didn't mind taking fees and retainers from the legalized looters. They stacked their committees. Deaf ears were turned to appeals for compassion and rehabilitation. Johnson vetoed countless bills rammed through by the House with immediate Senate approval. Senators railed at Johnson as a wicked tyrant plotting to reduce their chamber to a pliant instrument of the White House. Members, fresh from pocketing their share of carpetbaggers' spoils, spoke piously of an organized attempt to throttle legitimate business interests.

Ross came into the Senate when it started to reach for Johnson's jugular. Soon the President was impeached by the House. It needed only two-thirds plus one vote of the Senate to sustain House action. Had it happened, the two-party system in this country might well have been abruptly terminated. Leading radical Republicans sought alternately to cajole and threaten Ross. He was on the fence. Even a young girl under his protection, Vinnie Ream, had a commission taken away. She was working on a monument of Lincoln.

Senator Ross was offered $25,000 to sweeten his vote for impeachment. He said, no. He defied his state legislature. In the end, his vote against sustaining impeachment kept Andrew Johnson in office. It was a great act. But Ross's name hardly evokes a murmur in the Senate now. You can count on one hand the number of senators who can relate his time in history.

The vicious assault on Johnson by the Senate also ushered in an age of wanton, damn-the-public irresponsibility. Senators repre-

union as a whole. In the winter of 1850, he supported Clay in a great compromise of free and slave states. Both senators were already in poor health. The great advocate of the South, Calhoun, was dying. Benton felt infirmity on him. Webster carried the day in the Senate with his espousal of the cause of union. In his last great Senate speech, Webster prevented secession from splitting the nation for another ten years. His prefatory words to the Senate might well, in today's context, be recalled: "Mr. President, I wish to speak today not as a Massachusetts man, nor as a Northern man, but as an American and a member of the Senate of the United States. . . . I speak today for the preservation of the Union. Hear me for my cause."

Firmly on the side of union with Clay and Webster stood rugged Thomas Hart Benton. His own state, Missouri, was a slaveholder. Benton, who had fought Andy Jackson back in Tennessee, never turned a hair at the angry demands from his own legislature. He was as fearless on the floor of the Senate to stand fast for what he believed was right as in his home state against a rising tide. After one antislavery speech, Senator Henry S. Foote, of Mississippi, rushed at him. At point-blank range, Foote drew a pistol. Benton threw open his coat and shouted: "Let the assassin shoot. He knows I am unarmed." Foote fled.

In the same vein, old hero Senator Sam Houston stood by Clay, Webster, and Benton. His onetime Texas adulators called him a traitor. The doughty old man, heedless of his own safety, toured wild-and-wooly Texas. His call: Union approval of the Clay-Webster compromise. He dared to attack Calhoun's position which the Texas Legislature that sent Sam Houston to the Senate had adopted. As Civil War steadily sputtered toward explosion, Sam Houston bade the Senate farewell. The great senators with whom he had actively associated himself were gone or dead. Of himself Houston had this to say: "I wish no prouder epitaph to mark the board or slab that may lie on my tomb than this—he was a patriot; he was devoted to the Union."

Physical courage cannot carry a senator. He needs moral bravery coupled with the incorruptibility that defies conflict of interest. Sounds like reaching for pie in the sky? The Senate actually boasted of men like these. Some arose after the hemorrhage of our border state of Kentucky. It was Clay, with his marvelous gift for debate and mastery of thought, who sought compromises in order to thwart all-or-nothing in both North and South. He incurred the wrath of Presidents and fellow senators. Jackson called him "the Judas of the West." Yet Calhoun, who fought him on the floor of the Senate, nevertheless remarked at the end of a denunciation: ". . . But by God, I love him." Not so generous was eccentric John Randolph of Virginia. Introspective and embittered, Randolph stood on the floor and said of Clay: "He shines and stinks like mackrel by moonlight." Thinking this was a good time to finish off Clay, another senator went into tortured and tedious debate. To Clay, he remonstrated: "You, sir, speak for the moment, I speak for posterity."

Up rose Clay, squelching the senator for good. "You are right, sir," he replied. "And apparently you are determined to speak until the arrival of your audience." Clay was elected to the Senate quite early in the nation's history, 1806. He stayed until 1851. We have had long-lived senators but none could match him in all-around talent except contemporaries like Daniel Webster, of Massachusetts, and Thomas Hart Benton, of Missouri. And Clay had been on the scene twenty years when these two senators arrived. There are many historians who insist that Webster was the most talented ever to sit in the Senate. He had talent, yet he also was possessed of a great flaw. Webster was one of the most corrupt men ever to become a senator. He saw absolutely nothing wrong in asking the Bank of the United States for his regular retainer.

A peremptory demand went out from Webster, for example, at a time when the Senate was actually debating the renewal of the bank's charter. Webster told the president of the bank: "My retainer has not been received or refreshed as usual." On another occasion business friends joined to pay off his debts so he could stay in office. Webster was never interested in amassing a personal fortune. But he lived high. He was always in debt and it never bothered him. He ostentatiously supported business interests in New England and was compensated handsomely. Webster believed in his advocacy—and expected to be paid accordingly.

Nevertheless, he was an outstanding lawyer, a magnificent orator and debater. Above all, Webster was a zealot about preserving the

sented railroads, insurance, utilities, minerals, and cotton. They were emissaries from separate states with special interests. The majority was bent on milking the country. Their avarice gave politics a bad name in America. It has largely endured. Schoolchildren no longer were attracted to great debates and intellectual duels that once was the hallmark of the Senate. They were turned off for a long time, beginning with the two administrations of Grant.

Bewildered and baffled by all the political shennanigans, senators found General Grant laughingly easy to handle and dominate. They demanded priority of place over Cabinet members at White House meals. Grant meekly acquiesced. It had never occurred before. Senators pointedly reminded him that they ran committees that could help him or kill him. Legislative demands often were read over the dinner table to the befuddled President by senators with their mouths full of steak. The floodgates were wide open for the fresh breed of senators.

In a precipitate rush, eleven new states were admitted to the Union. The move sent another twenty-two senators to the Capitol, as many as were in the original Congress. They were frequently escorted to their new posts by representatives of the special interests. Original lobbyists, pleading their own causes, boasted to any who cared to listen of "my senator." It has become more subtle today. Money that once went directly to a senator is usually assigned to an incumbent's committee handling re-election finances. Open greed in older times of the country at least spared the nation any pretense.

It also spawned the wheeler-dealer. One of the most notorious was Sam Ward, who was known to the political trade as "Wicked Sam." But they admired his methods and accomplishments. Wicked Sam claimed he could buy a senator between courses. He carried thick rolls of banknotes and bags of gold coin to back his offers. One of his specialties was serving lobster tails stewed in champagne.

Senatorial behavior outraged a minority traditionalist group. Their concept and reverence for the Senate was twisted into a roaring, money-changing barroom. Behavior was just like the no-holds-barred expansion into the Western lands. In the mid 1870s, a learned judge from Illinois could not contain himself at the sight of new senators coming into the chamber with their rich patrons, diamonds flashing from stickpins on cravats and from rings on fingers.

Senator David Davis exclaimed his disgust with this description of new colleagues: "The jackal; the vulture, the sheep-killing dog; the gorilla, the crocodile; the buzzard; the clucking old hen; the dove and the turkey gobbler." Glancing up at a hulking Westerner, beaming at a moneyed patron, Davis spoke of him to a trusted colleague. "A wolf, sir; a damned hungry, skulking, cowardly wolf." Their behavior so infuriated Davis that he served out his own term and shook the dust of Washington in relief.

Henry Adams has described his impressions. A Cabinet officer told Adams that he could never use tact with a congressman. Declared the Cabinet official: "A Congressman is a hog. You must hit him on the snout with a stick." Adams had noted that senators were more grotesque than any caricature could make them. So of the Cabinet officer, Adams demanded: "If a Congressman is a hog, what is a Senator?" The swashbuckling senators and their wealthy patrons paid no heed.

A railroad baron, Collis Huntington, notified three partners in the Southern Pacific what it would cost them all for a bill. Only $200,000, estimated Huntington. He added in a note to his associates: "This session will be composed of the hungriest set of men that ever got together. I stayed in Washington to fix up the Railroad Committee in the Senate." Another railroad tycoon was asked why he didn't become a senator. His amused reply: "Why should I bother? I've got enough Senators on the payroll now." Senate committees did a roaring business—for their patrons. A set of rules for the Senate, promulgated by demands to clean house, was adopted in 1884. They remain, with some amendments, guides to basic procedure today.

The rules had some immediate, premonitory effects. Money changers, so to say, were swept out of the senatorial temple. Lobbyists for special interests, grown accustomed to sitting even in closed committee sessions to make sure of their investment in a senator, got the idea. They retreated discreetly to their protégés' offices, to their own quarters, or to convenient restaurants to get full reports. Newspapers and periodicals laid down a barrage against overweening privilege. Cartoons and caricatures abounded. They depicted the special interests—a senator, propped up by his money-bags sponsor. It aroused public clamor, but indignation often fell into the silence of frustration.

A corresponding rise and fall in irritated outcry persists to this day. Lobbyists, plugging their special interests, are much more sophisticated and discreet. The art of persuasion is more likely to be geared to a senator's timidity than to his cupidity. In Washington there are very nearly as many lobbyists as ranking bureaucrats, regulatory agencies, and, of course, senators. A goodly number of persuaders are former senators and congressmen. They all know how to open doors. The list of lobbyists also has lengthened with the multiplication of activities and committees.

Public interest has become their special concern, along with those concentrating on special interest. Respectability has, thus, rubbed off on nearly all lobbyists. After all, industry wants to appear just as interested in ecology today as in a dedicated conservationist organization. Both sides can help a senator make headlines with researched knowledge, whether it be in machine tools, clean water and air, and registration to vote. Organized labor long ago learned how to compete with special interests of business for the favor of a senator. Both are quite up to date with their concern for pressing issues that can separately—frequently opposed —make or unmake a senator's mind. Lobbying today doesn't emphasize the potential cupidity of a senator. It's just his need to know—and be helpful.

Once, under the 1884 rules, the Senate tried to shift public heat against the Executive branch. Inside the committees, White House-proposed legislation came in for indecorous dissection. A principal and traditional pride of the Senate was its right to endless debate. Taken to the floor, that right could easily become converted into a filibuster to kill a proposal. With the introduction of the rules, the Senate drew together for mutual protection from the unfeeling harshness of the outside. It became a lace-curtain club, bent on showing its independence to stave off criticism.

The Senate's mulishness, in the interests of self-protection, drove Secretary of State John Hay up the wall of his antique office.

Ratification of a treaty requires two-thirds approval of voting senators. In the records only one percent of all treaties submitted have been so rejected. By the time members got through stomping on a treaty in committee, Hay compared its prospects to those of a bull in the ring.

"No one can say where the final blow will fall," lamented Hay. "One thing is certain. It will never leave the arena alive."

When the Senate blocked a treaty he sent up, President Theodore Roosevelt blew up. The lordly chamber, he fumed, was "wholly incompetent." He took it out later on Senator Ben (Pitchfork Ben) Tillman, of South Carolina. Tillman, old-fashioned in his regard for the Senate, met a colleague off the floor. They disagreed violently. Tillman beat the fellow senator to a slobbering pulp with his hands. Despite his contempt of the Senate, Teddy Roosevelt couldn't let the act go unnoticed. He showed presidential displeasure by disinviting Tillman to a state dinner.

It took special interests a little while to think up methods for making the new Senate lobbying rules more palatable to their tastes. Organized machine party politics held the solution. It pleased the sponsors of senators and made the officeholder easily accessible to his political mastermind back home. Nobody could seriously object to a home politician coming to talk sense to a senator he helped create and elect. The machines were always in contact with whatever special interest was most useful and eager to assist. Its manipulators calmed fears of total exclusion when the Seventeenth Amendment was adopted. Senators, from 1913 on, would be elected directly. The reform took 114 years. It didn't faze men like Boies Penrose, boss of Pennsylvania. He remarked mockingly to a reformer acquaintance after election to the Senate:

"Give me the people every time. Look at me! No legislature would ever have dared to elect me to the Senate, not even at Harrisburg [the state capital]. But the People, the dear People elected me by a bigger majority than my opponent's total vote by over half-a-million. You and your 'reformer' friends thought that direct election would turn men like me out of the Senate. Give me the People every time!"

It was interesting, of course, to hear Penrose on the floor refer to a colleague as the "Distinguished Senator. . . ." Having made so many at home, his contempt was blatant. Other machine chieftains tried hard to be more discreet. Their muscle was mighty until recently, when machines in many places began to crack up in the face of changing voter habits and ticket splitting. Yet the party organization—the machine—is still absolutely essential to the success of a candidate. In his state, an incumbent or an aspirant to the Senate usually is teamed with the nominee for governor or President. An independent or a maverick can run up a respectable vote. Rarely can he win without active machine assistance. And occasionally a senator gets the grudging cooperation of the organization even when he ignores it in Washington.

Today the machine concentrates on winning or keeping control of the governorship. It is in the State House, not the Senate, where meaningful patronage is located. The office of governor provides a power base from which influence and control can be extended throughout the state. That is why, until the era ushered in after World War II, governors—not senators—were wooed and cultivated as potential candidates for President. Television and instant communications have changed the preferences and priorities. A governor is more likely today to be regarded as a parochial character. The United States Senator has a national forum and easy access to national exposure on TV.

He still does not have the patronage—jobs, subsidies, and grants —that go with the governor's mansion. The machine, as always, handles the system of distribution in the state. In the past it also was tolerant of unorthodoxy by a senator provided he did not ignore special constituent needs, as wheat subsidies or highways. He acquired so much national prominence that the senator always was identified with the state that sent him to the Capitol. The provisos are much easier for senators to maintain today than they were in bygone days.

One such unique personality was Senator George W. Norris, a maverick Republican from Nebraska. He was not indifferent to his small state's economic problems. His supreme interest, however, turned on what he deemed was best for the nation, not Nebraska. It brought him into head-on conflict with several Presidents, starting with Woodrow Wilson. Shortly before we entered World War I in 1917, Norris led a group of Senate insurgents against a bill needed imperatively by Wilson. It would have armed our merchant ships against unlimited German warfare.

Standing alongside Norris was Robert (Fighting Bob) LaFollette, another unorthodox Republican, from Wisconsin. LaFollette was an early advocate of economic liberalism. With Norris he shared a passionate hatred of war. Popular sentiment leaned toward intervention. Neither senator believed the emotional appeal for intervention was good for the country. Both senators also deeply resented Wilson's push to steamroller the bill. Norris led a filibuster. His senatorial band of a dozen briefly blocked Wilson's bill. The President was so outraged that he cried:

"A little band of willful men, representing no opinion but their own, rendered the great government of the United States helpless and contemptible."

The Imperial German Government bailed out Wilson a few weeks later by resuming unrestricted submarine attacks on American shipping. In its fervor of the moment, the Senate also adopted its first cloture rule. The Norris filibuster was the main cause. By a two-thirds vote plus one, the Senate can throttle debate. It isn't all that easy to obtain. In the first ten years of the existence of cloture, it was invoked successfully only four times. For the next thirty-five years, it was virtually a dead letter.

During America's participation in World War I, the Senate went along with President Wilson. Norris voted in favor of the declaration of war. Once it was over, the Senate went back to challenging the President again. It rejected adherence to the Covenant of the League of Nations. Wilson, rudely rebuffed, lambasted his critics with:

"Outside of the United States the Senate does not amount to a damn. And inside the United States the Senate is mostly despised; they haven't had a thought down there in 50 years."

Senator Henry Cabot Lodge, Sr., of Massachusetts, backhanded Wilson this way: "We must be now—ever for Americanism and nationalism and against internationalism." His son, later a senator himself, in service repudiated the father's triumphant declaration. Henry Cabot Lodge, Jr., also served as chief United States representative to the United Nations and was twice Ambassador to Vietnam. The younger Lodge has since been pilloried for his tenure in Vietnam in essentially the same terms his father used against President Wilson.

Norris took no solace from his early opposition to the war. He concentrated on trying to redress domestic economic inequalities. It was his unyielding persistence that finally created the Tennessee Valley Authority (TVA). The Senator's political counselors in Nebraska were horrified. It didn't concern their state. Business and private power interests tried to put pressure on Norris. He shook them off and went a step further. In 1928, Norris charged that monopolies wrote the platform for Herbert Hoover. Senator Norris promptly endorsed Democrat Al Smith and the repeal of prohibition. In Nebraska he was told that he offended all good Republicans and the strong Anti-Saloon League.

Senatorial colleagues began making a point of deliberately shunning the company of the doughty old man. After he surmounted and survived the attacks, fellow senators saw a sparkle return to the chamber. They flocked around Senator Norris. His independence was envied. It has not been often in the last hundred years, remember, that an independent spirit could long survive as a senator. Being beholden, and adhering, to time-encrusted behavior patterns are important unwritten rules. These are folkways scarcely appropriate for grown men today.

Under the rules all remarks from the floor are technically addressed to the presiding officer: "Mr. President . . . ," the senator intones. A road block is immediately created. The speaker is prohibited from questioning the motives of a colleague or even to criticize another state. Even in the most heated of colloquies, senators are expected to call each other by title. Under the circumstances how can any member call the "Distinguished Senator from X" a liar? It is forbidden, to begin with, but starting with "Distinguished" nullifies any real cross-examination on the floor.

Senator Alben Barkley, Vice-President under Harry S. Truman, had a piece of valuable advice for a freshman. Said Barkley: "If you think a colleague is stupid, refer to him as the 'able, learned, and distinguished Senator.' If you know he is stupid, refer to him as the '*very* able, learned, and distinguished Senator.'" The *Congressional Record*, which five days a week publishes the florid remarks of senators from the floor, at a daily cost of around $17,000, is replete with these salutations. Senator Norris saw fit to write about his credo outside the *Record*. It is well worth a minute of any senator's time to study the comment, even if unpublished at the Capitol. Here is how Norris saw the role of a senator:

I would rather go down to my political grave with a clear conscience than ride in the chariot of victory as a Congressional stool pigeon, the slave, the servant, or the vassal of any man, whether he be the owner and manager of a legislative menagerie or the ruler of a great nation. I would rather lie in the silent grave, remembered by both friends and enemies as one who remained true to his faith and who never faltered in what he believed to be his duty, than to still live, old and aged and lacking the confidence of both factions.

Instead we have language day in and day out like this: "The Senator from Texas does not have any objection and the Senator from Texas wants the Senator from California to know that the Senator from Texas knew the Senator from California did not criticize him. . . ." You can substitute just about every other state and come up with the same approach. A freshman senator had better obey this study in punctilious behavior and also take a monastic vow of silence on anything else for a few months. If he starts by hectoring, senior members get upset. They control the committees. Someone new, full of fire and reform, learns a painful lesson. He is certain to be assigned by the Senate Steering Committee to the dreariest committees.

Should a newcomer take his complaints outside with easy access to TV, he becomes regarded as a show-biz senator. A good number of highly regarded senators are scarcely known outside the Capitol and their own states. They work in concentrated fashion on issues before their own committees and show calculated restraint toward publicity. Otherwise an upstart senator can be cut down at dinners, receptions, and over a cocktail. In Washington, social life is political. Factions for or against something stroke each other and disparage the other side. They incline to speak only to each other —and their hostess. This is the reward she earns to attract glittering names. Two old-timers at the professional hostess social game are in the age group of the more senior senators.

Enormously wealthy, Perle Mesta and Gwen Cafritz have for

years competed against each other. They are among the leading self-made ignoramuses of the capital.

A modest sign of reform is in the reluctance of younger senators to accept their invitations. It also has manifested itself by planting an oasis in the cultural desert that is the capital. The Kennedy Center for the Performing Arts is open now to music and the theater. To foreigners, and Americans returning from business stays abroad, Washington came to be called, "Bonn-by-the-Potomac." It amounts to an accurately snide comparison with the sleepy little capital of West Germany.

The United States Senate, however, is more concerned with its folkways than any performing folklore. Preservation of unlimited debate has induced, for example, more ingenious acrobatics than ideas to retread the privilege. Louisiana's former Democratic Senator Huey P. Long may have been the greatest modern specialist in the filibuster of interminable irrelevance. He once brought to the floor a wastepaper basket as a prop to demonstrate making potlikker. In 1935 the late Huey gathered himself together to launch an attack on the National Recovery Act (NRA). He wanted every senator summoned to listen to him.

Vice-President John Nance Garner, in the first two terms of Franklin D. Roosevelt, was an old bourbon-sipping friend of Long. His reply, as presiding officer of the Senate, was sharply to the point: "In the opinion of the chair, that would be cruel and unusual punishment as forbidden in the Bill of Rights." The Huey Long tradition was carried on by Senator Strom Thurmond, Republican of South Carolina. His twenty-four-hour anti-civil-rights speech was the longest on Senate record. Oregon maverick Wayne L. Morse indulged in a drawn-out liberal filibuster. He was incensed against what he charged was an oil giveaway bill. Morse used up twenty-three hours of Senate time. Statisticians still wonder if Morse didn't beat Thurmond's record. Thurmond went to the men's room; Morse never did.

On one of the startling occasions when the Senate invoked cloture to cut off a filibuster on a communications' bill, Morse and pocket-sized Senator John Pastore, wily veteran Democrat from Rhode Island, went at each other hot and heavy. Both are considered liberal, Morse more so. He also was opposed to cloture on the bill, which Pastore favored. They thrust their imposing mustaches perilously close to confrontation. Lips quivered. Pastore was heard to snarl at Morse: "Any time, anywhere, any place." A delicious possibility never became reality. In any other business, both men would have been well retired.

Morse was one of the Senate's most interesting anachronisms. Elected a Republican, he became fed up with Eisenhower and changed sides. Then he was re-elected as a Democrat. Morse and aged Democratic Senator Ernest Gruening, patriarch of of Alaska, were the only senators to vote in 1964 against the Tonkin Gulf Resolution. That gave LBJ the legal underpinning to wage war in Vietnam as he deemed appropriate. Morse and Gruening were beaten for re-election in 1968 despite their original opposition to Vietnam. Few fellow senators showed them any sympathy. Both Morse and Gruening had had the abrasive temerity to chide members for their dereliction and easy accommodation.

Moreover, the disposition of Morse to use the filibuster for liberal causes infuriated Southerners. Committee chairmanships and unlimited debate are great parliamentary weapons for defense of the South. Using a filibuster, as did Morse, went against the grain. He also invoked it to bring attention to a fruitless demand for cloture, requiring only a simple majority of attending senators. Southern senators—others from small states as well in the Midwest —detest cloture. The late Richard Russell summed up the feeling when he declared: "I'll vote to gag the Senate when the shrimp start whistling Dixie."

During the five years that Lyndon Johnson was Senate Majority Leader, he managed practical working arrangements on debates and votes. They were, in effect, compromises. He would summon intransigents of both sides on the matter of unlimited debate. The LBJ formula sounds cynical, directly simple, and workable: "You've got to work things out in the cloakroom and when you've got them worked out, you can debate a little before you vote." Ancient, recently deceased Carl Hayden, who represented Arizona from the time it entered the Union in 1912 until he retired in 1968, had an even simpler idea. "When you've got the votes," he said, "you needn't talk."

The Hayden "law" was one of consensus that nailed down committee chairmen. In turn, the chairmen badgered committee members. You cover a great deal of territory and Senate votes that way. In addition, the tradition of "senatorial courtesy" between senators is bridged without undignified debate and recrimination on the floor. The practice of courtesy has been distorted out of all proportion. It actually began as unwritten law when Washington was President. In its narrowest interpretation, "senatorial courtesy" means that the Chief Executive will consult about a federal nominee to or from a senator's state.

Washington's staff heard of the Senate's thin skin about courtesy. Somehow, they forgot to tell him. He nominated a Benjamin Fishbourne to be Naval Officer at the Port of Savannah. A Georgia senator, who didn't even know the poor man, objected to the appointment. It was "personally obnoxious" to the senator, a phrase that has come down through the years of the Republic. Mr. Fishbourne never got the appointment. Senators, no matter how they might detest the protesting colleague, close ranks solidly with him. The Senate publicly tweaked Andrew Jackson for the same miscalculation. He wanted Roger Taney to be Secretary of the Treasury. Some Senators objected and that was the end of the affair.

More recently, General Eisenhower felt the sting of outraged senators. Admiral Lewis L. Strauss (pronounced Straws) was nominated to be Secretary of Commerce. A group of senators cordially disliked Strauss on personal grounds and for his refusal or inability to communicate with them especially on the Dixon-Yates case. He was rejected. The widely celebrated case of the time, though, was the nomination of Mrs. Clare Booth Luce to be Ambassador to Brazil. A successful author, satiric wit, and wife of the founder of *Time-Life,* Mrs. Luce already had served as Ambassador to Italy. An incident in Rome, in which she was exposed to inhaling arsenic fumes unknowingly, set her diplomatic sights on another part of the world. It also gave her critics a needle. They referred to the story as "Arsenic and old Luce."

Mrs. Luce was just as merciless to her detractors. She militantly disliked Senator Morse, and vice versa. They confronted each other at testimony all ambassadorial appointees must give before the Foreign Relations Committee. Questions and answers became vitriolic. Then, Mrs. Luce committed the unpardonable—for senators, that is. She observed that Morse wasn't very bright, anyway, because he had been kicked in the head by a horse. Up ran the sacred banner of courtesy and it was affixed to Mrs. Luce as being "personally obnoxious" to Morse. His colleagues—at least half of whom on the committee hated him—rallied unanimously around the then senior Senator from Oregon. It put an end to the diplomatic career of Mrs. Luce.

The most sensational, and searing, case however, was that of Senator Joseph R. McCarthy, Republican of Wisconsin. Joe McCarthy used the Senate as a personal leather-lunged forum and pliant punching bag. His deliberate affronts to members lasted nearly five years until the Senate mustered enough courage to go after him. He was on the wings of a feckless hunt for Communists in government, in the armed forces, in schools, in all places of business high and low. At the height of his derring-do, McCarthy's words and feats were reported in all the media as dutifully as stenographers take down verbiage of senators on the floor.

He was a prominent TV personality. Joe McCarthy's picture, balding up top, with a sneering smile, was as familiar in those days as any big-time entertainer and quiz-show star. Right-wing lobbies adored him and contributed lavishly to projects and campaigns McCarthy advocated. He was supported by the father of the Kennedy clan, the late Joseph P. Kennedy. A Democratic associate counsel on McCarthy's committee for a while was the late Robert Kennedy. McCarthy simply cowed most of his fellow senators. On the floor and outside, they took McCarthy's insults and gibes in silence. Almost daily, any senator could have raised the issue of courtesy and McCarthy's being personally obnoxious. A ghastly scene on the Senate floor was enough.

McCarthy stood at his desk, piled high with documents and dossiers. He rattled off instances of subversion and betrayal. The data beside him were held as containing proof. Grandly, McCarthy offered colleagues the privilege there and then to look into any document to double-check his charges. One case stuck in the throat of elderly Democratic Senator Herbert H. Lehman, former Governor of New York and close friend and associate of FDR. It was a name and episode of which Lehman had personal knowledge.

Acting upon McCarthy's offer to let senators inspect the documents, slowly, Lehman walked down the aisle. He came close
to McCarthy. In his tracks, Lehman stared at the accusor. He
swivelled his eyes around a hushed chamber to see if any fellow
senator would support him. Nobody rose. McCarthy's smile, tense
at being challenged, turned to an open sneer. "Go back to your
seat, old man," he commanded. Lehman didn't reply. He looked
around the Senate again, searchingly. Colleagues lowered their
eyes. Dead silence. Lehman wheeled, turned his back on Joe
McCarthy. Looking dead ahead but seeing nothing, Lehman painfully returned to his desk. It took another two years and the
intervention of the Executive branch for the Senate to find Joe
McCarthy personally obnoxious.

Another Republican Senator, conservative Vermonter Ralph
Flanders, decided that McCarthy went beyond the bounds of
Senate propriety. There had been wild Army hearings before
McCarthy's subcommittee. Normally a Senate committee and sub-
committee are sacrosanct. Flanders laid down a resolution to the
effect that Joe McCarthy's inchoate antics brought disrepute to the
Senate. Like Flanders, many fellow senators who once supported
McCarthy had begun to worry that they could feel the knout.

The full Senate—or almost full—acted. Joe McCarthy was condemned by a vote of 67 to 22. Even then condemnation was the
most wishy-washy way the Senate could discharge its responsibility.
Being condemned is but a shade different from being outright
censured, like becoming a little pregnant. It had the desired effect.
McCarthy was racked by his peers forever. The Senate preserved
itself, but not its acquiescent abdication of responsibility. It cast an
image of high-mindedness that has done it profound discredit.
Take the case of seventy-six-year-old Senator Clinton P. Anderson,
once a Democratic crusader from New Mexico.

Anderson heads the Senate Committee on Aeronautical and
Space Sciences. Billions in appropriations are considered before
the panel. Great and controversial projects are its children, from
space shots to weather and communications' satellites. When
Anderson became a national name, he was a young newspaperman.
A former Senator, Albert Bacon Fall, was President Harding's

Secretary of the Interior. Fall was from the same state as Anderson and one of its first two senators.

This didn't make a particle of difference to Anderson when he learned about costly gifts going to Fall—courtesy of oil tycoon Harry Sinclair. Anderson wrote about the presents in the *Albuquerque Journal*. Hot on the trail, he learned that Fall sold the government's oil reserves in Teapot Dome to Sinclair. Fall stormed into the little newspaper office. "Who is the rotten son-of-a-bitch writing lies about me?" shouted the offended Interior Secretary. Calmly from his chair, Anderson replied: "I'm the son-of-a-bitch and I don't write lies."

Fall was convicted and sent to jail. Anderson went onward and upward. He went to the House of Representatives and served later as Truman's Secretary of Agriculture before grateful New Mexico elected him to the Senate. In the rarified atmosphere of the upper chamber, the people's old champion cozied up to the late Senator Robert Kerr, enormously wealthy and powerful. It was like the old, gummy get-rich-quick times all over. Kerr, a huge and brass-bound man, amassed a fortune of about $150 million out of oil and uranium. Quite a staggering feat for a boy who always said he was born in a log cabin.

Along came the poor crusader from New Mexico. He noted how Kerr always voted on oil and uranium legislation as a powerful member of the Finance Committee. It was a clear conflict of interest, but Kerr believed that what was good for the nation was good for him. Kerr also chaired the Space Committee that went, after his death, to Anderson. For steering a bill helpful to Kerr's interests, Senator Anderson got a lucrative percentage of Pinto Dome. This was in a next-door state, Arizona. It held natural gas from which helium is extracted. It was all legal, of course. Senator Anderson is quite a rich man, so different from the drudgery of the days of Teapot Dome. Senatorial courtesy prohibits asking questions about something that was approved as legal.

It didn't work out that way with the late Senator Thomas J. Dodd of Connecticut, who was accused of having misappropriated campaign funds to his own use, and was censured by the Senate. Once Dodd had zoomed skywards in the Senate. He was close to Truman and to LBJ. Dodd insisted that the moneys involved were personal gifts to him. His staff surreptitiously slipped from his office letters and documents that were published. In his own defense, Dodd challenged fellow senators. Most members, he thundered, did what he stood accused of committing. That was too much for the exercise of senatorial courtesy. For telling the truth and bringing the chamber into disrepute, Dodd was censured by the Senate by a vote of 92 to 5. It is interesting to note that both Senators McCarthy and Dodd died within a few years of their respective censures.

After the Dodd episode, senators self-righteously created an Ethics Committee. It is porous, indeed. At the height of the 1970 election season, news came out disclosing that Senator George Murphy, California Republican, had been drawing a $20,000 annual stipend from Technicolor, which also paid most of his Washington apartment rent and supplied him with credit cards. In private, Murphy explained to Ethics Committee Chairman John Stennis. Nothing wrong, decided Stennis. The public never knew what Stennis did. Murphy, old song-and-dance man, was beaten for re-election. He is active today as public relations counselor in Washington for Chiang Kai-shek's regime. Fees and expenses for a half year in 1971 for the stint ran to $220,000.

As Stennis found no wrongdoing with Murphy, there are senators who find it perfectly compatible to be interested in the oil business and vote on legislation concerning taxes for oil. Finance Committee Chairman Russell Long, Democrat from Louisiana, and the amiable son of Huey, has been doing it for years. Senators approve farm subsidies and have their own big agricultural interests. Members who are lawyers legislate in matters relating to railroads but see nothing contradictory in accepting from railroads legal fees that go to their old law firms.

Senators with stakes in papers and periodicals vote on postal rates that affect their own publications. The lecture circuit has become big and profitable for senators. They take fat fees from lecture sponsors directly affected by legislation requiring senatorial votes. Former Senator Eugene McCarthy, much sought after on the lecture circuit, bought a fancy house during his tenure. He paid upwards of $75,000 for the property. To critics of this kind of conflict of interest, personally incorruptible Barry Goldwater,

Republican from Arizona, defended his colleagues' extracurricular practices. He declared hotly: "By applying your logic, it would be impossible to find a person, short of a bum, who would not conceivably have a conflict of interest."

It could be that bums exist only outside the Senate. Consider Bobby Baker. He had never been a senator but at one time was more important than most. A gangling Carolinian, Baker was a protégé of LBJ and served some hair-raising years as secretary to the majority leader. He was convicted of tax evasion, conspiracy, and theft. After the New Year, in 1971, he went to the Federal Penitentiary at Lewisburg, Pennsylvania, to do time set at one to three years. Baker became a blockmate of convicted Teamster boss Jimmy Hoffa, who passed out word that the new inmate was an okay fellow.

Before he headed up to the Penitentiary, I chatted with Baker. He lamented the death of Senator Kerr, who was most fatherly and a financial tipster to the former Senate secretary. Baker wouldn't talk about LBJ except to say that he called to wish a Merry Christmas. But in his drawl, Baker's words were tinged with acid as he spoke about a prominent senator in the race for the Democratic nomination for President. Outraged, Baker recalled: "I took a check that was a contribution from some business interests in 1958. I deposited it to my own account so that it could be traced only to me. I even paid the tax on it as income to me. Then I gave the cash to the bastard. What did I get in return?"

Baker was overwhelmed by the ingratitude. The receiving Senator, Democrat Edmund S. Muskie of Maine, once had been profuse in his thanks. He told Baker to call him any time for anything. What happened? Baker got in a jam. He called the Senator. But he never got through to him nor ever received a call back. He wasn't the only senator, fumed Baker, ticking off a list for whom he'd done special favors and ferreted out contributions. Resignedly and philosophically, he observed wearily: "Now I'm the con and bad guy. Oh, they'll find guys who will take care of contributions. No problem. If they get into trouble, forget all the favors. You're on your own. There's always lots of others."

It was the primitive, unadulterated philospohy of the backroom wheeler-dealer. Bobby Baker knew his town, his principals, and the naked objectives of power. If anything, it is a more grasping scramble today than the quest ever was. Big money is the crass name of the game. Nickels and dimes, represented in little $5 and $10 contributions, are strictly for the publicists to show a popular groundswell for their men. It is a shoddy, promotional version of the Joe Frazier-Mohammed Ali, multimillion-dollar gate. Reruns of the 1970 elections will be staged on a vaster, costlier scale in the 1972 presidential circus.

The United States Senate, plus Nixon, provides us with all the main candidates. Theirs is a national forum now, played out in calculated casuistry. The majority of the candidates are Democratic senators. Small-time spectaculars before committees and personal appearances, like retreaded vaudeville shows, replaced steady and solid governmentship and legislations.

There even was the incredible thrust toward the presidential nomination by Oklahoma Senator Fred R. Harris (who has since withdrawn), because he was certain to be denied renomination to the Senate by his own state. Harris has been long on do-nothing accusations. His own record is a blur at best; a zero at worst. To match him has been the "switch to fight" by New York's formerly Republican Mayor John Vliet Lindsay, a pop politician. A bare minority winner as Mayor with an appalling record of accomplishment, Lindsay became a Democrat. In 1968, many of us watched him second the nomination of Vice-President Agnew. His TV good looks and fervor were at the disposal then of the party—Republican—as they will be now for the Democrats in triggering his ambitions.

All the aspirants have one trait in common: the scramble for the big money. Television has bred a pseudo science for measuring ambition. Fortunes, more than fame, are the essential ingredient. The incumbent President and the Senate have toyed with bills to limit the incredible costs involved in national and local elections. With a large degree of smugness, the Senate passed a bill presuming to put a lid on election spending. It was almost unanimous. Ah, but loopholes were inserted. The bill restricts, as originally written, presidential candidates of each party to $13.9 million for media spending. It's based on ten cents for each of 139 million voters eligible in 1972.

But an escalator clause was inserted. Worded carefully, it insures that the overall ceiling for national candidates will go up $2.8 million a year every year that the cost of living rises 1 percent or more. It begins with the 1971 increase over 1970. The ten-cent-a-voter limit puts a ceiling of a nickel on spending for TV and radio and the same for magazines, newspapers, and billboards. So the escalator clause provides that these figures will increase the same percentage as the Consumer Price Index did the year before, "rounded to the next highest cent."

A little simple arithmetic shows that the escalator leaves spending at six cents a voter in each category. This presidential year will enable each major party to spend an extra $2.8 million. Taking the same ratios—annually in the Price Index—the parties will be able by 1976 to spend $30 million each for the national ticket. The sophistry is patent and painful. As if the escape clause wasn't most convenient, opponents of even this leaky lid decry the effort to bring some balance into political life. It impinges, they argue, on their constitutional rights to spend and contribute where they like. The average voter, of the symbolic nickel-and-dime contribution, isn't even consulted. You get nowhere with his money. The special interests do with theirs. An incumbent or a candidate never forgets the real source.

On a sultry summer evening in Washington, a bloc of Democrats with ambitions to become President, were catching their breath in the air-conditioned comfort of Larry O'Brien's well-appointed pad. It was a year before the conventions. The Democratic campaign treasury was not only bare; it was debt ridden to the tune of $9 million. Getting credit would be quixotic. Utilities were demanding collateral and bonds to guarantee that even phone bills would be paid. The Republicans were smug as hell. Money was pouring in as if they had a license to print it. Indeed, in a few months Republicans would be squirreling away better than $40 million for 1972.

Democrats gathered around National Chairman O'Brien ran the gamut from pacesetter Ed Muskie to subsequent dropout Fred Harris. Money was on everyone's mind, especially O'Brien's. How to get it and keep a posture of reform too? O'Brien and his strategists, like lawyer Joseph Califano, had come up with a real score.

The problem was keeping it from leaking to outsiders, especially Republicans. The plan, as set up by O'Brien with key Democrats making recommendations and deletions, would put President Nixon smack on the public spot.

It called for a checkoff of $1 for everyone submitting a federal tax return. The United States Treasury would be called upon by Congress—Senate and House dominated by Democrats—to pony up a total of $20.4 million. Major parties could, if they wanted, collect around $8 million or so; a minor party, as George Wallace's, about $4 million. Any party could refuse, of course. It wouldn't look good if the Republicans did. A checkoff like this would have the public paying but reducing the frightful freight of a campaign which had cost everyone in 1968 more than $300 million.

The O'Brien strategy seemed masterly. To avoid a veto by the President, the checkoff would be tacked on as an amendment to a big tax-cut bill designed to get the American economy moving again. The Democrats proved they could keep their mouths shut where the money loomed. For four months, as the proposal was carefully broached to key senators, nothing leaked out. It was nothing short of amazing, in this community.

Surprise was the Democrats' big stick. The Republicans, belatedly aware of an opposition public-financing provision, were at first confused. Minority Leader Hugh Scott finally learned that Senate colleagues of the majority would tack the checkoff onto the Nixon tax-reduction bill. The bill had absolute White House priority.

Overnight, intrigue and maneuvers flowed like speeches between the White House and Senate. On strict party lines, the Democrats prevailed, 52 to 47. The White House stomped and stormed but could get only five Southern conservatives to defect. They lost two, in turn. The stage was set: The Senate tacked the $1 checkoff onto the tax bill already passed by the House.

Now it was in the astute political hands of veteran Wilbur Mills, chairman of the House's all-powerful Ways and Means Committee. Mills doesn't like being shoved around or mocked. The White House committed both mistakes and Mills was in an intramural power fight with President Nixon. Larry O'Brien was so pleased with the setup that he began making spending estimates.

On the other side, Scott warned the President to think in only the most drastic terms. It meant a veto of carefully nurtured tax credits, if necessary to wreck the checkoff.

Nixon summoned forthwith the tactician he admires most—Attorney General John Mitchell. At a strategy session, the President did most of the talking as Mitchell puffed or sucked at his pipe. Mitchell proposed the challenge or gamble—that Nixon say outright he would veto the whole program if the checkoff stayed on the bill in Mills's joint House-Senate committee decision.

In a brief lull at the White House strategy session, a Nixon staffer asked Mitchell why he was always on the pipe. "To help me from biting my tongue or tripping over it," snapped back the Attorney General. To the President he addressed a crucial question. What were the chances of the House passing the joint committee bill? Up for grabs, was the reply. Make it less even, shot back Mitchell.

All the muscle of the White House flexed and feinted for the countdown. Mills was besieged with calls from big business, demanding to know why he was pitting the future resuscitation of the economy against a partisan campaign plan. At the same time, pressure was applied to Southern Democrats who are normally inclined to go along with Mills. They began to wilt and were led to a cave-in by Representative Joe D. Waggoner, Jr., from an appropriately named community, Plain Dealing, Louisiana. Mills was alerted to the spin-offs. In the joint committee, he allowed as how they didn't have the numbers on the House floor to pass the checkoff. Mills doesn't like to lose either.

There wouldn't be any checkoff, his colleagues agreed, until the possibilities were re-examined for 1973. O'Brien was stunned. The White House was elated; so was big business, for the time being. Behind the scenes, though, specialists in the Treasury were unhappy. Why? Mills and his conferees agreed to grant tax deductions for small political contributions. It could pump $100 million from small contributors into politics, 1972—and it wouldn't be for Republicans. Even in retreat Mills can jab the daylights out of an opponent.

III

THE WORLD OF
THE SENATE

A seat in the United States Senate is longingly sought after today by a surprising number of people. The covetous run out the string of nearly every craft and profession in society: lawyers, up-and-coming businessmen, energetic young labor leaders, onetime career military officers, articulate and oft-abrasive Women's Liberation founders, college professors and even recent graduates, political reformers and standpatters, spokesmen for black communities and for other ethnic minorities. The list is as long as the multiple explanations for aspiring to a seat in the Senate, which Webster called the world's greatest deliberative body. It had been—in his day.

At $42,500 a year the salary is good but not glittering for one of a hundred senators who might challenge the President any time. Power is the magnet that is so attractive. All the fringe benefits of power revolve around the magnetic field of the Senate. Making a senator these days is big business. It is the business of professional politicians, great corporations, muscular labor, the military, scientists, antiwar activists—even the totally unselfish. They dearly want the power of the senator to maintain or make over conditions in their own image.

Take the incumbent senator. He—Mrs. Margaret Chase Smith, Maine Republican, is the only woman—wants to be re-elected if his frame is still warm. The opposition party hungrily wants his seat. In sheer numbers, having more senators than the other party

54

automatically provides control of all standing committees. It represents pure political power and is all important. An elected senator, even one appointed by his state's governor in case of vacancy by death or sudden resignation, quickly feels the touch inherent in one of the power elite. There also is enormous prestige with the office and perquisites which executives of mammoth corporations cannot command. More than ever is the tantalizing temptation before a senator to achieve national fame. About 20 percent of the Democratic senators began running for the 1972 presidential nomination nearly two years before elections.

In the quest for a seat in the Senate, bucking party organizations has become more fashionable. It can have practical—and disastrous—results. It contrives with another faction to dump the incumbent. Former Senator Charles E. Goodell, of New York, was purged just that way. His dissatisfied Republican party ganged up on him. It covertly but helpfully supported a smaller party candidate—James L. Buckley of the Conservatives. Goodell was retired to law work.

"You see it all happening," he remembered, sadly. "You know there are smilers with a knife. You don't know how many or who they all are. You try to fight back. You lose."

Goodell's experience crosses party lines. Reformers in the Democratic party try to fight the organization. They are usually persistent, dedicated, and well financed. But they create divisions in the party. The usual result to date: The opposition profits and the defeated party keeps up the fight for who gets control. Organization fighters try to get a shot at a Senate seat through direct primary fights. They have forced the use of more primaries. A state convention is always preferable to party leaders. Delegates can be controlled more easily. Discipline is enforced.

Nevertheless, most candidates, even when they show public gestures of independence, try to maintain good relations with party leaders. They still need them as organizers to the humblest level where votes are. Catching the eyes of the party chieftains requires background in some public service. Lawyers, by the nature of their profession, are in most frequent touch with the public. A goodly number have gone on to be elected as members of the House of Representatives. In five states being a senator is the most important elective post extant. We still have two senators and only one congressman-at-large from Alaska, Delaware, Nevada, Vermont, and Wyoming. For them, a senator's base of power must be rooted in the Senate. Localized and regional feelings of all smaller states are strong.

During this turbulent century only four states have been admitted to the Union. But the population has nearly trebled from 76 million back in 1900. With the population growth, we have had even speedier expansion of technology, industrialization, communication, and urbanization. By 1976, the population and all its built-in problems will be sixty times the size of the original republic! Besides new-generation dissent and discontent, we have racial unrest and urban disintegration. It was infinitely easier to be a senator at the turn of the century than presently or in the immediate future. A present-day senator or candidate, if unselfish, must concern himself with the bewildering conflicts of: the economy, racial minorities, national security, education, health and welfare, to name only some of the more important.

Even if he is selfish with an outsized ego, he has no real choice but to worry and research these issues. Most senators run pretty high on the ego counter. Otherwise, we would have far fewer believing they could make a good President. Yet the primary consideration—selfish as it may seem—for any senator is to try to stay in office. Every senator, from Clay to the late John F. Kennedy and LBJ, said so candidly. Remaining in office these days or running for it requires a money machine. Although only a minority of incumbents or hopefuls are rich, the number of hopefuls grows.

In this electronic era, a senator or an aspirant in a small state needs around $300,000. It can easily run to a couple of million, minimum, in a big state. TV time eats money as fast as guests wolf down handfuls of peanuts at a campaign party. Whether a senator is wealthy or of modest means, he quickly becomes indentured. In office, he can talk to audiences—for a price. This is the lecture circuit. Most senators make the effort. An average appearance is $1,500. Not bad. It can run as high as $5,000. The side money is most helpful. It enabled Democratic Senator George McGovern, of South Dakota, to launch his ambitions toward the presidency.

Obviously, talk-for-pay doesn't cover campaign expenses. It assists a senator to make ends meet. Importantly, it can give him prominence. For campaign and election purposes he needs big money. The dollar and ten-dollar contributions are great for publicity purposes. They can't make a dent in what is really needed. Tens of thousands at a clip are urgent. Here's where big business and big labor are so important. So are wealthy reformers, standpatters, and extreme conservatives. If labor has made substantial contributions, the senator so supported will be oriented toward labor. The same goes for business and for any collection of pressure groups and contributing individuals. Many senators try to hedge their bets by being nice to all sides. Sooner or later, they get into hot water. Rubbing large contributing interests the wrong way in favor of something else can doom a senator wanting to be re-elected.

The smoothest, most legal way for senators and competitors to lay their hands on big money has been through so-called "D.C. Committees." These are campaign committees set up in the District of Columbia. Money pours from all interested sources into their headquarters as water from a man-made hydroelectric plant into a dam. Because of the antiquated Corrupt Practices Act, adopted in 1925, the law is useless. There are more loopholes than restrictions in reporting who have contributed what to whom. The "D.C. Committees" also synchronize with fund-raising affairs in Washington, in home states—anywhere. There are dinners at $100 a plate; cocktails at $50 a glass, and handshaking receptions down to $25 a couple. Even the wealthy must get into the act to show that contributions come from everywhere. Lobbyists, big business—all pressure groups that festoon the Capitol—get into the ticket-buying act. By new law, this was supposed to end in April.

It gets so flagrant more often than not that rancorous Senate colleagues bad-mouth the riper cases. They showed their teeth recently at fund raisers for their senior Democrat from Indiana, piously shrewd Senator Vance Hartke. His junior Democratic colleague from the same state, Birch Bayh (pronounced "buy"), was riding presidential hopes. The Hartke testimonials, from Teamsters and steel groups, raised senate hackles to the sneering remark that Indiana has two senators: "Buy—and Bought." Hartke also has conceded that he got plenty of contribution help from a giant mail-order house and a radio station, among other sources.

His colleague, Bayh, permitted a wealthy industrialist to pick up the tabs for hotel stays in Florida. Winter relaxation, you know. He accepts free rides in labor-or-company-provided planes. This has become the norm, by the way, for the majority of senators. On contributions, the late Everett M. Dirksen, Republican Minority Leader, was as indifferent to charges as was Daniel Webster. Dirksen figured he had them coming to him as his due. His law offices in Peoria, Illinois, got big fees from companies and Dirksen used his share in the form of contributions to his war chest.

These are only samples of senatorial indulgences. More widespread instances will be examined later. The Senate Ethics Committee does little but serve as a protective agency unless challenged openly by an irate but unwise senator. It's always best, when the news comes out, for the senator to make a confidential, clean breast. Former Senator George Murphy, California Republican, did so with his Technicolor consultation income. He was cleared.

To help build up war chests, senators long have indulged in ramming through personal pieces of legislation, referred to by the legislative trade as "ship jumpers' " bills. They are aimed generally at saving Chinese seamen from being deported back to the mainland. It costs the poor Chinese about $2,000, half of which goes as a contribution to the senator and the other half to a lawyer. The all-time high in one year was churned out by liberal Democrat, Senator Gaylord Nelson, of Wisconsin. Under his name ninety-eight ship-jumpers' bills went through, all part of the office routine.

The personal perquisites that go with the office of a senator are hardly to be sneezed at. His staff depends on the size of his state or personal eccentricities. The smallest can command staff salaries of about $150,000 annually. For big states, it can run three times that total. A few, like Republican dean, Vermont's George D. Aiken, only dent a small percentage of the allowance. They employ tiny staffs, which are glaring exceptions. In a senator's home state, he also has a paid staff and free office. The senator's representative at home usually holds down a suite in a federal office building of the capital. Invariably, the top aide is an old political hand. He keeps his ear sharply attuned to local problems. The senator and his closest advisers in Washington are in daily communication with their man back home. They follow up his suggestions to help obtain federal contracts or subsidies for the state. Or, a worthy constituent needs help. The senator's office goes to work on the request.

A senator can get up to $5,000 annually in free telephone and telegraph allowances. Franking or free mail is nearly limitless. There also are a half dozen free round trips back home. Living in a far-away state can make this expensive. A senator, to keep his image before the constituents, had better go home more often than six times annually. It prompted dedicated freshman Republican Robert W. Packwood, of Oregon, to wonder whether the senate job was really worthwhile. Friends offered to raise a slush fund for him to take care of travel expenses and some entertainment. Packwood asked older senators about the ethics of the fund. They took him by the arm, so to speak, and told him, no. He would learn soon about legally getting extra free rides, they counseled.

Isn't it? Like all other senators, Packwood enjoys ludicrously low, no-examination life insurance. They all have good-sized office suites, although complaints about being cramped are daily grumbles. As chairmen or ranking members of committees, senators can call on extra office help. Heading a glamor subcommittee gives the senator powers of hiring and firing, big budgets that can go way beyond the annual million-dollar mark, and expense money associated with subcommittee tips and trips. Junkets to far-away places are available for members and their wives several times a year—everything free. These are in the interests of parliamentary conferences.

A little over 7 percent of the annual gross salary laid aside in a retirement fund can, in time, enable a senator to command a pension few company executives can expect. He can have countless other associated goodies, such as free parking space in an underground garage. His license plate is a guarantee against a parking ticket in town. Companies fall over themselves offering cut-rate services, from flowers to rented cars. Of course, the senator has to maintain two residences, one in the capital, the other back home. McGovern gave up his modest home in South Dakota for his luxurious D.C. house. It's a rare act.

Most senators grumble about the two homes. But they get a write-off of $3,000 on their income taxes if they need to maintain the two places. Taken at a glance, the senator's side benefits are as long as his arm. The real expenses of living put him in the top 5 percent of the country with his problems. His requirements to be a full-time senator are concerned principally with the recurrent problems of getting re-elected. For the nation this is where the most sensitive conditions prevail. A senator doesn't get elected, or try to, for the money he earns. That is by no means niggardly. He became a senator, never forget, for the power and the glory. Shying clear of all the conflicts of office that helped put him in office is our national concern.

Senators spend substantial sums—raised again by interested contributors—to test their popularity back home. In campaigns, polls are on a near-daily basis. Like politics, these can be an inexact science. Results, however, can show in microcosm feelings and frustrations of the times. So I asked fourteen knowledgeable people around Washington to answer a few questions. Interviewees were all trained or skilled observers, communicating with senators regularly. They included personalities in print and electronic journalism, business representatives of giant firms, and politicians. Respondents were of differing political ideologies. About half would like to think of themselves as "liberal." The other half, moderate to conservative.

Only five of the fourteen canvassed consented to have their names used. Thus, I decided to use none. The guidelines and questions were direct: Whom did each believe was a good or able senator? Was there any who could be called a supersenator, as a Clay or a Norris? What did each interviewee believe constituted a good or able senator? Experience of the respondents with the Senate was from six to forty years. First off: In the answers the unanimous response could not offer a supersenator. The results were shattering when it came to noting good or able senators.

Out of one hundred senators, the average number of "good" or "able" Senators came to seventeen. One respondent listed only nine as good or able. Another, whose name evokes near-household recognition, came up with thirty-four names. His was something of a hard-nosed first rule—the ability of the senator to keep getting re-elected. The trick is by no means confined to the South. He also agreed that a good and able senator measured first the national interest, with state and regional considerations a close second. Intertwined with his performance is the caliber and talent of the senator's staff. In all fourteen cards, only three names appeared on each one.

There was the liberal Democrat from Michigan, Senator Philip A. Hart. Another was a moderate Kentucky Republican, John Sherman Cooper. The third was conservative Republican, just retired, John J. Williams, of Delaware. Unanimous approval of Hart came as well from men who differ sharply with his politics. This also was true in the case of Cooper—many oppose his views on foreign affairs. Williams's conservatism had just as many opponents, but they all admired him for his integrity, dedication, and intelligence.

Next came "Scoop" Jackson, with twelve; and surprisingly, Birch Bayh, with ten. In his case it was surprising because he has many outspoken opponents of his ambitions and personality. In descending order were the late Richard Russell, nine; eight each for Majority Leader Mike Mansfield and Minority Leader Hugh Scott. Seven, or half the votes, were cast for Democrats Warren G. Magnuson, Washington; Sam J. Ervin, North Carolina, and Wyoming's Gale W. McGee. Liberal Republican Jacob K. Javits, of New York, also chalked up seven. Some freshman senators were in the seven league, too, with the caution that they were considered "comers." With one exception, they were all Republicans: Edward Brooke, of Massachusetts, the only black senator; Marlow W. Cook, Kentucky; Charles McC. Mathias, Jr., Maryland; and Robert W. Packwood, Oregon. The lone Democrat was bright, young Thomas Eagleton, of Missouri.

Falling just below were Southern stalwart John Stennis and one-armed World War II hero, Daniel K. Inouye, of Hawaii, both Democrats. They each got six votes and are as ideologically as wide apart as the distance between their states. Otherwise, the results were scattered. Interestingly, top names in the running for the Democratic nomination, like Muskie and Ted

Kennedy, received only two each. McGovern, first of the Democrats to announce, drew one. Iowa's Harold E. Hughes and former Vice-President Hubert H. Humphrey drew zero. Humphrey, it should be noted, returned as a senator from Minnesota only after the 1970 elections, which made him a brand-new boy in Senate terms all over again. There are certain to be demurrers from the unconsulted on the basis of this poll. It isn't likely, though, that they can come up with a bigger average, just some other names. Senate decline seems to be related to the dismal inadequacy to handle our size and problems.

Glibness has been largely substituted for deliberation, determination, and decision. Political chic—and accommodation with rising and falling fads—are criteria for the average senator rather than any skein of compelling national interests. The usual role of a senator in action today is that of an artful dodger. He divides his responsibilities with those of his chief aides. They are both administrative, who is No. 1, and legislative. An administrative aide is akin to a chief of staff or deputy senator. He was appointed, not elected. The daily business of being a senator, though, depends heavily on the talents and experience of the senator's assistants. They do most of the reading, attend to high and low visitors, and frequently think up most of the legislation. An effective administrative assistant can make or break a senator. There is normally more intrigue in the office than prevailed among the Grand Viziers of the Ottoman Empire.

The reason for all the intraoffice byplay is what the senator sought in the first place—power. Everyone in the senator's office acquires some feel for the power motive. It can be communicated in the personal secretary's dictation, clerks answering complaints and appeals for all kinds of aid and cooperation, right to the top aides shaping up the instruments of influence they want their senator to propose. There is interaction within the office. Jealousy of someone's more confidential access to the senator plays a big part. So does ambition in another assistant's belief that his plan is infinitely superior to another favored by the senator.

Most every working morning in Washington, all top aides meet with their senator. They go over issues of prime consideration—and headline quality. A vote on controversial legislation may be coming up that day. Aides provide pros and cons, always thinking of how the vote will look on the senator's record. They kick around ideas, be they war or peace. The senator is briefed on which assistant attended what hearings of compelling concern to the incumbent in office. A smart administrative aide can change his boss's mind. But he had better not convey the idea that he can knead the senator any which way. That gets around and it also puts his senator and himself in a bad light. In short, a senator and his staff comprise a separate legislature that tries to coordinate with ninety-nine others, or the most cooperative of the individual, inner senatorial legislatures.

All assistants must keep on top of important topics and pending or proposed legislation. The senator himself, these days, cannot be expected to come to grips with the avalanche of trivia as well as the needful and urgent issues. Staff people must sift the unimportant and make decisions on what is immediately essential. If their party is in or out of power at the White House, they also must establish some working liaison with the Executive branch. In many ways, it's like being in a baron's court during the days of many separate baronies in one country.

A sound senatorial assistant must study the system and master it. He makes the judgment of what calls to make, the kind of levers to push, shortcuts to take, and whom to trust. In time, the aide is part of permanency in the Senate. Senators—maybe his own—go. Presidents and Cabinets leave. Congressmen disappear. The staff system remains. A staffer, every so often, comes face to face with a get-rich-quick suggestion. It may be the offer of a straight cash bribe for a favor. That is, he'd influence his senator to do something for a special interest. Or, these days, a more sophisticated approach is to get on the "inside" of a pending business merger. Stock goes up, and makes up to a million fast. Some succumb, but not many. Power means more than money to most. Besides, staff assistants these days earn well, up to $38,500 annually, plus fringe benefits not too different from those enjoyed by their senator.

The incumbent senator, early in his career, learns how to get along. It has been the pragmatic advice passed on to members for generations. JFK commented casually on it before he ran for the presidency. He generally went along to get along. The practice helps immeasurably in obtaining cooperation for your own

legislation. Mavericks do occasionally turn up. They find themselves bogged down in noncooperation. A few, by persistence and
driving determination, make their style stick. Not many succeed.
Former Senator Paul H. Douglas, Democrat of Illinois, tried unsuccessfully to fight the system. He saw the end result this way:

> This bill is built up out of a whole system of mutual accommoda-
> tions in which the favors are widely distributed, with the implicit
> promise that no one will kick over the applecart; that if the Senators
> do not object to the bill as a whole, they will get "theirs." It is a
> process, if I may use an inelegant expression, of mutual back-scratching
> and mutual log-rolling.

Before he died, Everett Dirksen put the working senatorial
philosophy to me on this kind of working basis: "A man in the
Senate has just as much power as he has the sense to use. For this
very reason he has to be careful to use it properly or else he incurs
the wrath of his colleagues." Within this framework the Senate
exercises its own concept of flexibility. It's also commonly called
reciprocity. A classic case of modern flexibility-reciprocity is usually remembered by most senators today. It stems from a debate
in 1956. The issue was overacreage allotments for burley tobacco.
Senator William Langer, an unorthodox Republican of North
Dakota, and a border state regular Democrat from Kentucky,
Earle Clements, were doing the talking on the floor.

Langer: "We do not raise any tobacco in North Dakota but we
are interested in the tobacco situation in Kentucky, and I hope
the Senator will support us in securing assistance for the wheat
growers in our state."

Clements: "I think the Senator will find that my support will
be 100 percent."

It was this kind of accommodation, or flexibility, in the Senate,
to which Douglas objected so bitterly. There has been little change
in the you do something for me and I'll reciprocate since the
Langer-Clements colloquy. Rather than air it on the floor of the
Senate these days, the accommodation is worked out by trusted,
top staff aides—often on the phone—and quick conversations between the interested senators before they hasten onto the floor to
make their specific pitch. The aide, however, must be absolutely

sure of his senator's thinking. His word remains the coinage of interplay.

The senator's staff frequently comes to the point of thinking of him as "my man"—unidentified by name, which everyone else knows. Protection is built into the intimacy, often even fending off the senator's family so "my man" won't be distracted. Shielding a senator from many outside stresses and strains can produce uncomfortable situations. One senator's wife, hearing on the phone that her husband was almost always otherwise engaged, became suspicious. Cruel gossip, so common to Washington life, reached her ears. Her husband was playing around with a girl in his office, the rumor flew. That's why she was hardly ever able to reach the senator at the office.

Burned up at the gossip, the senator's wife waited until her good-looking husband left for an out-of-town speech. She summoned the staff women in the senator's office for a little get-together. Without naming names, she told them that the girls had better stop taking such special care of her husband. If they didn't, she said indignantly, she would fix them good. Anyone previously so involved had better resign. In a huff, two girls went off to other jobs.

The episode whipped through town. Washington dines out on juicy stories. It led some Senate wives to do a double take. The greater proportion of attractive, mini-skirted young girls work in committees. A Senate office can use only so many, usually three to about a half dozen. An important committee, with subcommittees attached, can have three to four times as many on the payroll. Senatorial husbands suddenly found themselves braced at home with questions about pretty little Miss So-and-So. Was she necessary? Were all those girls useful to the committee? It took a few weeks to make peace at home. But senators are past masters in the art of accommodation.

One Senate committee that has escaped girl problems through the years has been Foreign Relations. Affairs of state, especially as scrutinized by Senator Fulbright, have no time for handholding shennanigans. For the last twenty-five years or so, the White House has been doing its own thing on the "advise and consent" for treaties. The same attitude prevailed on making war and declaring one. It has been mainly the fault of the Senate. Starting in World War II and the subsequent bipartisan approach to external matters, the Senate was content to pass all the decision-making problems on to the presidency in this atomic age. The divisiveness of our conduct of the war in Vietnam got under Fulbright's skin in the late sixties. He couldn't, he declared, get an accurate count or a fill-in from the Pentagon, the White House, or the State Department.

So Fulbright, assisted by his experienced, knowledgeably bureaucratic committee director, Carl Marcy, created his own investigative agencies and foreign service. Marcy, a tall and professorial-appearing man, seems most reflective as he slowly pulls on his cigars. He is courted widely by diplomatic missions as a guest. Marcy has muscle with suggestions and recommendations to his chairman. It is Marcy who does the hiring and firing of the Fulbright foreign service specialists. He keeps his chairman apprised of trends and tendencies of the Executive branch. If staffers under his supervision come up with ideas and suspicions of hanky-panky anywhere in the world, Marcy dispatches them on missions. He tells Fulbright about the project, of course. Given the most active administrative aides in a senator's office, Marcy makes many more decisions. He is technically beholden to fifteen senators on the committee. But he is more beholden to one—the chairman.

Of the fifteen on this oldest of Senate standing committees, only six are Republicans. In the present, Ninety-second Congress, the membership of the Foreign Relations Committee is overwhelmingly receptive to Fulbright's views of the world. Senator Muskie came onto the committee after the 1970 elections. It's a fine forum to propound statesmanship—if Fulbright allows a member to get a little of the limelight. On the Republican side, Minority Leader Scott tries to do what he can for the Administration. He can't do much. Majority Leader Mansfield also is a member of the committee. Both can do more about up-coming Senate chamber business than Foreign Relations Committee activities. Fulbright runs a tight ship and Marcy is a faithful helmsman.

Marcy dispatches his troops to far-flung corners of the world. They research everything, from commitments to bases to governments. Few have ever been assigned abroad to draw a bead on a foreign problem and spent more than two weeks on the questions.

Marcy goes over their findings, verbally, upon return. Then they draft memoranda and reports as Marcy briefs his boss. Members of the committee get reports long after the chairman, Marcy, and concerned staffers have absorbed them. About 40 percent of the special assignments get a "secret" label. Some can be seen by senators only in the rococo offices of the committee in the Capitol Building.

As director of the staff, Marcy holds a curiously worded title: "Chief of Staff." It is a traditional one, but in the anti-Pentagon atmosphere of the committee, a title like Staff Director might be more appropriate. Marcy is unremittingly loyal to his chairman. He doesn't have the drawl, but quite often pronouncements from Marcy sound just like the sayings of Chairman Fulbright. The committee, as supervised by Marcy, has a beleaguered but confident air. Fulbright has precisely the same behavior pattern. It makes an outsider wonder about coincidences and imprints in history. But the Foreign Relations Committee has glamor. It suffers all other committees with the patience of instant wisdom.

The Senate and the House of Representatives often treat each other as foreign countries. Provisions in the Constitution, dividing and assigning responsibilities, helped make them that way. Traditions and the massive growth of government confirmed both houses of the legislative branch in jealous and zealous protective vigils over the prerogatives of their own sides. They team up in a spirit of cooperation when an opportunity is spotted to give the Executive branch, the President, a hard time. Their salaries are the same. A chief physician, with two assistants, looks after the health of both houses. He has urged elderly members to carry cardiac cards. Special equipment is stashed in strategic corners of the House and Senate to be used in emergencies.

Similarities between the two houses tend to vanish after primary common cause. A congressman, as a member of the House of Representatives is usually called, needs to reach the minimum age of twenty-five to be elected. He also runs for re-election every two years. Generally a congressman starts shaping up for re-election after only a little more than a year into his term. He feels, from the Constitution and practice, that he is more responsive to constituents than are senators. There are 435 congressmen as opposed to 100 senators. More importantly, as the Constitution clearly stipulates, the House of Representatives has the responsibility for originating all money bills.

Although both houses keep each other normally at arms' length, they must coordinate on legislation. It frequently can be difficult despite the fact that one-third of the Senate came up from the House. They work on differing wavelengths. Written and unwritten rules for each chamber abound for nearly every occasion. Curiously, a manual of rules compiled by Thomas Jefferson when he was Vice-President and presided over the Senate, has been excised by each house to suit itself. The House has lifted most of the Jefferson manual bodily.

It's only a brisk walk on the second floor of the Capitol to get from the Senate side to that of the House, and vice versa. But the direct route is strictly for tourists. Senators never go to the House unless it's for a special joint session such as the President's State of the Union message or for an address by a foreign dignitary. A congressman wouldn't think of voluntarily visiting the other side unless maybe invited to lunch. He is usually bothered by what he feels is the elitism or club veneer of the Senate. The relations become a condition of coexistence.

"It may well be the longest legislative walk in the world," Senator Jackson observed, in pondering House-Senate behavior patterns.

Jackson should know. He has been on Capitol Hill since 1941. He served twelve years in the House as a sharp young congressman. As a Democrat, he was elected to the Senate in 1952 despite the Eisenhower landslide. Another Senator, resourceful Republican Minority Leader Hugh Scott, served fourteen years in the House. His cautious view:

"They do their own thing in the House. They don't like to feel there is any upstaging by the Senate. We, in the Senate, do our own thing. When it's essential, we both get down to business."

Scott and Jackson know, firsthand, about the touchiness of House colleagues. At the same time they are keenly aware of how fellow senators sensitively regard their special status. While senators in the last five years have tried to create their own intramural factions, they draw together on what is deemed Senate business only. Cutting down the President to size has been, from the beginning of the Republic, a magnet attracting both houses. Between the legislative and Executive, the balance of power is constantly subject to the shifts of public and group support. The whole Congress has a latent inclination to kick the President around. It tries, if it can, to wrest away to itself the President's initiative. There has been an almost daily exercise in those tactics against President Nixon.

The House, supposedly more responsive to the electorate, has been stodgier than the Senate about reform. It's a matter of degree, of course. A basic reform finally prevailed only in 1971. In the new procedure congressmen's names are recorded on votes, especially on important amendments. It requires only twenty members to compel the identification method known as "tellers with clerk." This enables the folks back home to know just how their representatives voted. In the past, congressmen were identified on votes when nosy reporters collared them. Liberals claim credit for the reform. But many liberal congressmen hastily backed away from their election appeals to at least water down seniority rights. Veteran congressmen warned the loudest protesters to defend seniority or see themselves in meaningless committees. Ironically, some older hands suddenly saw their own seniority status threatened. They changed their minds overnight.

Both houses are fierce defenders of the rights of seniority. It's a little more in the House because there are four more standing committees—twenty—than in the Senate. Our legislative system, bear in mind, is a committee system. Its total power, coordinated, can make or break an administration. The country, too. Unfortunately, no matter the administration and its political slant, the committees have been out of step and out of tune with them. One of the most glaring committee anachronisms is the House and Senate's separate panels for the District of Columbia. They each are commonly called "The D.C. Committees."

The federal government, therefore, has had supreme say over the conduct of municipal affairs in the capital ever since 1878. It was then that the House and Senate delegated a committee each to run all local affairs. They took away home rule, demanded today by most District of Columbia residents. And appropriations had to be forthcoming from the generosity of the Congress. Only in 1961 was the privilege extended to D.C. residents to be eligible to vote for President. They were unable until then to vote for anyone. A decade later, as we began the seventies, was D.C. granted the right to elect a nonvoting member of Congress. By this time the population of the capital had become 71 percent black. The elected nonvoting congressman is Democrat Walter E. Fauntroy.

This city has a population bigger than a few states, Alaska included, but can only have a nonvoting congressman. Lately, Senator Robert Byrd, for years a symbol of congressional power over the District, said he changed his mind. Bob Byrd, suspected by blacks as a segregationist, now urges home rule. His senatorial colleagues have often voted home-rule legislation. The House always buried the bills. Byrd's fellow committee chairman of the House D.C. Committee may not, however, change his mind. He is tough old Congressman John L. McMillan, out of South Carolina. Home rule would end the life of his committee. No congressman or senator willingly puts a standing committee out of business. Eliminating one committee can eradicate others. What does seniority, so jealously hoarded, mean if you can't have committees?

As do Senate committee chairmen, the equivalents in the House have the power to appoint subcommittees. They can each call up bills for action, or call them in committee. It's easy to see that voters exercise a pretty limited influence on legislation. As public demand for reform increases with each session of Congress, so does it fade away with do-nothing compromise. Just as age and geographical distribution of Senate committee chairmanships resemble a regional old men's home, ages of House committee heads look like a dismal geriatrics' table. The average age is past sixty-five in the House. Committee chairmanships are held in fourteen of twenty by congressmen with Southern and Southwestern constituencies. So devoted are Senate and House committee chairmen to their specialized tasks that they have subdivided their own committees into subcommittees. Today we have more than three hundred!

The most important committee chairmanship has been held the last fifteen years by a courtly Democrat from Arkansas. He graduated from Harvard Law School, so is half Establishment. Tall, fit, Wilbur D. Mills at sixty-three could be the single most important man in both houses of Congress. He comes from a rural community to which he faithfully returns at each adjournment. Mills is chairman of the House Ways and Means Committee, oldest in Congress. It was established in 1789 as a shadow Congress. Mills's committee is the one that has the power of the purse. It raises money, or denies it. The Committee, fifteen Democrats and ten Republicans, also appoints congressmen to other committees or pointedly recommends them.

Mills could make or break an administration from the second Eisenhower term to the one conducted by Nixon. He has made little secret of his dislike for Nixon and the whole Nixon economic team. In the past, Mills was able to get along with Presidents. They needed him to get their legislative programs approved. Everybody yielded a little and worked out satisfactory compromises. With Nixon, he simply will not engage in hammering out a deal. Mills even substitutes his own programs—as in revenue sharing—and abandons the President's. He says publicly and bluntly that he cannot take seriously Nixon's fiscal policies. The chairman sees them stagnating the economy, creating more than 6-plus percent unemployment, and ushering in agonizing fiscal crises. Mills has made it abundantly plain that the state of the American economy is the major issue of the 1972 presidential elections.

As a result, Mills basks in a boomlet to make him the nominee of the Democrats in 1972. His civil rights record, like that of fellow Arkansan Senator Fulbright, won't get Mills far. But his stand on the economy is bound to provide him with some strong veto power with the more radical wing of the Democratic party. To the Nixon Administration Mills has been the immovable object on the path of its domestic programs. While he twisted the executive beak, Mills made a great point of compromising in areas of compatability with the Senate. That means money in raising federal revenues. Bills from his own committee often get amended in the Senate. In they go to a joint congressional conference committee.

A handful of senators and congressmen get together in the atmosphere of the smoke-filled room. Secrecy is tight even if smoking has been largely abandoned by conferees as hazardous to their health. They usually make hash of months of legislative preparation they don't like. The practice is particularly true with all money bills—and this is the guts of legislation. In the ancient citadel, commanded by Wilbur Mills, seven senators and nine congressmen devise the fateful decisions. Mills, of course, runs the show.

There have been complaints past and present about the dictatorial methods applied. They get stifled or lose steam. Former Senator Albert Gore, veteran Democrat of Tennessee, recently lamented the high-handed practice. He even went into some detail. He waited until he had been beaten in the 1970 elections and was out of office six months to bring this to the attention of the public. In a thirty-year congressional career, Gore never once attacked the system so as to educate the voter. Gore happens to be a favorite of the liberals. But he interacted with the process. His reasoning was conventional enough: better to try to get something rather than be cut out entirely.

This is the area in which committee chairmen work out the deals behind closed doors. Hand-picked senators and congressmen get together on loophole language. When it comes to bucking the Executive, arrangements emerge from conference rather quickly. The atavistic tendency of the legislative is thus at full boil when it comes to testing an Executive who is controversial, diffident, or weak. The basic interaction between both houses is similarly a tandem process. A senator or congressman introduces a bill. The clerk of his house gives the first reading. He sends it along then to the appropriate committee. It can be killed in committee, or the chairman may find it worthwhile to hold hearings. If the committee vote is favorable, the bill goes to a second reading. Here you can get a filibuster in the Senate. At most, debate would last two days in the House.

Successful, the bill receives a *pro forma* third reading. Passed in one house, the bill goes to the other for a vote. If beaten in the other house, it dies. Final passage sends a bill to the President. He can veto it. Back it goes to the house of origin. The President's veto can be overridden by a two-thirds vote in each house. Nevertheless, primary power can repose within committee and a chairman, depending on his relations with the Executive branch,

Committee chairmen of both houses have been alternately denounced as barons, petty keepers of the fief, and kings of Capitol Hill. Long before he became President, Woodrow Wilson in 1884 wrote:

"Power is nowhere concentrated; it is rather deliberately and of set policy scattered among many small chiefs. These petty barons, some of them not a little powerful, but none of them within reach of the full powers of rule, may at will exercise an almost despotic sway within their own shires."

It may, therefore, not be such pure coincidence that President Nixon constantly mentions Wilson as one of his greatest heroes and models. A painting of Wilson is on the wall prominently in the President's working area of the White House. There is another Wilson portrait in the presidential living quarters. None of the committee chairmen have responded to the prominence of the Wilson paintings nor to Nixon's deliberately regular references to Woodrow Wilson. In numbers, Nixon has both Houses of Congress against him. The Senate has fifty-five Democrats against forty-five Republicans. Yet about a dozen Republicans vote against Nixon on major issues. Southern Democrats often split. They sometimes favor the President but not automatically. Being in a majority party also means committee chairmanships.

Nixon's two immediate predecessors both had numbers with them in Congress. LBJ, riding into election on his own landslide victory in 1964, had the Congress eating out of his hand for two years. Although all three recent Presidents have been former senators, Johnson was also majority leader. He played his former colleagues like a musical ensemble, until discontent over the war in Vietnam provoked active opposition. John Kennedy had never been regarded as much of a senator by his colleagues. The Southerners were mighty upset about his activist role in civil rights. In his abbreviated tenure, Southern Democrats and most Republicans made legislative life miserable for JFK.

The friction struck by interaction is by no means confined to the legislative and the Executive. In the President's own official family, backbiting, feuds, and upstaging have been more evident in the Nixon Administration than in those of his two Democratic predecessors. In the White House itself, the President's principal doorkeeper, Bob Haldeman, tries to keep a lukewarm distance between even Nixon's legislative friends and Nixon. He is assisted in the preservation of distance by domestic affairs' overseer John Erlichman. They are both called, by White House friendlies, "The Prussian Guard."

In a wing where political counselors—the nuts and bolts political ramrods—are ensconced, a maze of Byzantine intrigue is constantly traced. Harry Dent, a Strom Thurmond protégé from South Carolina, keeps his eye on everyone else. It amuses sardonic Murray Chotiner, who brought Nixon into politics more than twenty-five years ago. Chotiner has been in and out of the White House as a political counselor. He is out presently, practicing law across the street from the White House and helping to shape the 1972 campaign. In and out of favor like a fever chart are old Nixon political friends with White House offices. They keep an eye on each other. Bob Finch, former Lieutenant Governor of California, watches Charles Colson, from Massachusetts. Colson keeps a watching brief on Finch and they both study Clark Mac-Gregor. He was a former congressman from Minnesota, beaten by Hubert Humphrey in 1970 for the Senate. MacGregor has liaison with Congress. It can be a heartbreaking but ultimately rewarding one in a political career.

Hardly anyone in the White House or Senate is deliberately unkind to two capable Cabinet officers. Their jobs are so immensely burdensome that they usually get sympathy and even public understanding. Secretary of Defense Melvin Laird, long-time congressman from Wisconsin, has a hectic time in an era where military spending is under constant assault. Having been the opposition critic of the Pentagon as a congressman, Laird knows his business. He has the misfortune to be in a slot always under fire. The seven-year term of a prominent predecessor, Robert McNamara, occasionally gets mixed up in congressional attacks, and Laird suffers. Generally he is hailed as a dedicated public servant.

So is Elliot Richardson, head of Health, Education and Welfare (HEW). He is a Boston Brahmin, so different from Laird. Richardson is photogenic where Laird can easily be a cartoonist's caricature with his high-domed and sloping forehead. As Under-secretary of State, Richardson's first assignment under Nixon, his perception and ability saved a battered department from going completely to pieces. When Finch showed that he was unable to master the intricacies of the sprawling, multibillion-dollar agency, Richardson was summoned as the fireman. In the miasma that is HEW today, Richardson receives unusually high marks for his grasp and conduct of the football into which his agency has been converted.

It isn't so with a third and important Cabinet member, who is the only Democrat high in the official family. Former Texas Governor, John Connally, is a big man on the scene. Connally was badly wounded in the same car with President Kennedy when the latter was shot to death. Large in physique and shrewd, Connally also is a protégé of LBJ. His appointment to replace a safe Republican banker shocked regular party members. Connally can help share the blame or credit for the economy in these elections. His ease at the epicenter of power irritates envious White House staffers and goads anti-Nixon Democrats in the Senate. But Connally never has gone out of his way to court popularity—only power.

The foregoing are only spot-selected names of nearly three hundred in the White House caravansary. Two men in Nixon's official family stand out above all others, though. They are envied, feared, and also hated. The two couldn't be more different. On one side is Dr. Henry Kissinger, the President's national security adviser. He counsels the President on foreign affairs and great power problems. Kissinger, the curly-haired German Jewish refugee boy, made good in the American power structure. His intellectual prowess is prodigious. He has an office and a 110-man special staff with a multimillion-dollar budget smack in the vitals of the White House. With the exception of ex-advertising message-maker Haldeman, Kissinger sees the President more often than anyone else. Maybe even Mrs. Nixon. Haldeman holds the door.

On the other side is pipe-smoking, affluent, municipal bonds lawyer John N. Mitchell. He could be in danger of being lesser known than his loquacious wife, Martha. She talks a blue streak on any subject and personality of timeliness. Mitchell says her mind is her own. Could be. But Mrs. Mitchell doesn't even bother to couch her dislikes in lawyerlike caveats. She will tell Senator Fulbright that she despises him. Or tick off anti-Nixon senators as "traitors." She has brought color—lurid as it sometimes can be—to somewhat of a faceless, colorless Administration. Her husband, the former Attorney General, is hard nosed. He is disposed to equate "liberals" with party-line Communist adherents. Mitchell was Nixon's campaign manager in 1968. He has resigned his post to do the same chore this time. Mitchell evokes an unsympathetic image with the younger generation.

Many senators, on a bipartisan level, feel the same way even if they are older. They see him as a younger J. Edgar Hoover. Mitchell, who headed up the Department of Justice, had been Hoover's titular boss. FBI Director Hoover, who has been in the same job almost fifty years, shares mutual admiration with Mitchell. Many senators, anti-Hoover, have found an open outlet in criticizing Mitchell. Few dare tangle directly with Hoover. Who knows what is in his raw information files? Mitchell, a straight political appointee, gets the brunt of congressional wrath rather than Hoover. His Justice Department committed a series of errors on preparation of cases, civil rights, and straight research into two Supreme Court appointees who were knocked out by the Senate.

Mitchell came into high-powered politics late in his career. He has tried to make up for lost time. Conservative to the core, Mitchell believes implicitly in the bold exercise of the inherent power of the Presidency. Therefore, he undertook with relish the government's controversial case against great newspapers in the episode of the purloined Pentagon papers. Mitchell also advocated the theory of inherent power in extending the use of wiretapping. A conservative North Carolina Democrat, Senator Sam Ervin, argues today that the extension of electronic eavesdropping violates the Constitution. And Ervin is a judge of the old school and a learned constitutionalist.

Mitchell's attitude is unflappable. He'll face withering fire, calmly puffing his pipe. His attitude is that of an urbane, detached lawyer, ever so cool against enemies who are legion. He rates high with the President. They are on the phone to each other a few times a day. But Mitchell gets into the Oval Office of the

White House only a few times a week. His Justice Department has commanded most of his waking interest. Planning the 1972 campaign also takes up most of Mitchell's working time. It's just the opposite with Kissinger. He is the mainspring of President Nixon's concern with all affairs external. Despite all demurrers and disclaimers, Kissinger is No. 1 to whom Nixon turns to sort out nagging issues of affairs of state.

The Senate, in particular Fulbright and fellow critics on his Foreign Affairs Committee, fret, fuss, and fume at Kissinger. He will courteously reject their flow of invitations to testify at hearings. No deal, says Kissinger firmly. He invokes Executive Privilege. This has been a prerogative of the Executive since the days of Washington. Kissinger briefs senators and congressmen all the time away from the Capitol. Most resent it and him. He knows so much more than they. Kissinger began his service to Nixon knowing much more about his specialty than any senator, anyway. What he learns daily—and advises the President—outrages senatorial demands on the right to know.

As Fulbright assembles calculated onslaughts against Executive Privilege and its war-making powers, he also invokes the "advise and consent" provision in the Constitution in behalf of the Senate. The constitutional stipulation has caused Presidents many times in the Twentieth Century to devise an "Executive Agreement" with a foreign country. It is not a treaty and does not have to be approved by the Senate. To have any meaning, however, it requires congressional approval. Attacks aside, the President usually gets it. Today, this infuriates critics even more. Critical senators flail at Kissinger. They contend that he is responsible for too many Executive Agreements. Kissinger ignores all attacks on him, be they personal or professional. He begins any given day with an intramural, official family quarrel on his hands.

The State Department thoroughly dislikes Kissinger. It's jealous of his role. The department is downgraded—has been for years. For a while Nixon's Secretary of State William P. Rogers didn't seem to mind second-class status. He had been a lawyer all his life, including Attorney General under Eisenhower. Rogers, an affable man, began to believe after eighteen months in the job that he wasn't taken seriously. Friendly senators told him that he was

simply honorific; that Kissinger ran the whole show. Rogers' annoyance grew. He confided it to Senator Stuart Symington, Missouri Democrat. Symington heads a subcommittee of Fulbright's
Foreign Relations Committee. It nearly always tries to nail Nixon's
skin to the nearest mast. Symington promptly let gossip-ridden
Washington know that Rogers was being treated as a joke. Everyone, observed Symington, was talking about Kissinger being the
real foreign specialist and Rogers the joke. Symington said this
was common knowledge. Where? On the cocktail circuit.

This particular cocktail *hors d'oeuvre* quickly became indigest-
ible. President Nixon made a public TV defense of his Secretary
of State. Kissinger stated there was only one Secretary. Rogers
decided to follow this up fast. He called a secret meeting. To it he
invited Kissinger and Richard C. Helms, experienced and able
director of the Central Intelligence Agency (CIA). Rogers, blown
up with new publicized importance, had an idea. He would be
going to the Middle East. The new Egyptian President, Anwar
Sadat, needed assistance in the direction of making the Suez Canal
operable again. He wanted to have Israel yield on major portions
of real estate it captured in the Six-Day War in 1967. Rogers saw
a good chance to get an Americanization of the key areas in the
Middle East. The Israelis would, in his judgment, have to make
the major concessions.

Helms said it was not his job to make policy, just to set down
facts and situations as he knew them. Rogers, he told the Secretary, seemed oblivious to Israeli determination to safeguard their
own security. Examine, he added, their recent history. In addition, Helms estimated that the Soviet Union would by no means
accede to an Americanization settlement. It had a stake of billions,
plus men and weaponry, in the area, along with an overall strategic
technique. Not so, sniffed Rogers. He would take it up personally
with the President. Kissinger, debating quietly with Rogers, said
that he couldn't accept the project. To him it smacked more of
publicity than reality. Rogers took it up with Nixon who, mean-
while, had heard individually from Kissinger and Helms.

All right, said the President, try it, but it probably wouldn't
work. Kissinger and Helms immediately prepared fallback positions as Rogers went off to the Middle East. He got along well

with Sadat. It went badly in Israel—right to a shouting match with tough old lady Premier Golda Meir. Sadat survived an attempted coup and rounded up his enemies. In came the Russians with a high-power team soon thereafter. Sadat signed a fifteen-year pact with them. The air went right out of the Rogers publicity balloon. Any Middle East deal, the Russians made clear, had to be worked out with them. As anticipated, the Administration returned to the Kissinger-Helms fallback position. It requires lots of secret discussion and negotiation. Memoranda is tightly guarded in this instance. Revelations in the press about our role in Vietnam had left a lingering bad taste in the national mouth.

The press has become an ex officio watchdog of government. When any branch goes off base, or seems to, the press blows the whistle. Its influence is unprecedented. In Washington the corps of journalists is unique in the world. There are about fifteen hundred, including a sizable bloc from abroad. They cannot make policy decisions. Quite a few fancy themselves, though, as shadow policy-makers. This can lead—sometimes does—to pomposity and self-anointment. Yet the role of the press in the United States is unparalleled. Just ask any foreigner here. Nowhere else where parliamentary democracy is exercised do journalists get belly-to-belly on a daily basis with the practitioners of power.

With the advent of television and its incredible development of national and international communication, the influence of the press is enormous. From the President to the Senate, down to the meanest corridors of power, declarations are synchronized to meet prime TV news time and newspaper deadlines. An agile President can use a TV press conference as an orchestra conductor. Indeed, the press conference has lately upset veterans in the media. They feel like props in a medicine show. But the use of "leaks," where information is deliberately fed to the media, has for generations been part of the safety valve between the press and government.

In recent years the leakage has been perfected to insure as much smoothness as goes into a space shot. The recognized arrangement—press and government—has been to let the government keep a few secrets. In turn, the media has made most of what was privileged information available to the public. Much of what has appeared, unfortunately, is never absorbed by the reader or viewer. The system was a live-and-let-live device. No one who has ever worked in American journalism at home or abroad deliberately kept himself out of this Rube Goldberg-like apparatus. The elaborate arrangement, retreaded in the nuclear epoch, has broken with the publication of the Pentagon Papers.

Consider the influences and world impact of the revelations in the documents. These were taken illegally from a staff study involving about forty people. It covered seven thousand pages in forty-seven volumes. It was a Department of Defense compilation of American involvement in Vietnam. The span went from the end of World War II until 1968. Though staggering in sheer mass, the documentation also was flawed. There was hardly anything from presidential papers; just as little from the State Department. A young political scientist, Dr. Daniel Ellsberg, was the source of the massive, unauthorized leak. He has admitted so publicly and passionately. In addition, Ellsberg declared that he had plenty of help in making Xerox copies for national distribution. For publication, he said that he gave all the data first to *The New York Times*.

Of more than passing interest was Ellsberg's having given about half the material to Senator Fulbright eighteen months earlier. Fulbright never let on that he had them. The Executive branch, with which Fulbright was at loggerheads, didn't know what Ellsberg turned over to the Senator. Yet some of the Fulbright staff was privy to a portion of the papers. Fellow senators on the Foreign Relations Committee never knew a thing about them. Fulbright, bitterly opposed to the war in Vietnam after his original supporting role, kept clawing at the government. In Executive, or private, hearings, Fulbright occasionally startled witnesses. He held out tidbits of information. Witnesses were perplexed. A few knew some aspects of the Pentagon study. They communicated their uneasiness to superiors, right to the White House. Fulbright was never questioned. Everyone else stayed mum.

Once Ellsberg had been part of policy planning and drafting on means of executing the war. It was afterwards that he became one of the historical review team. Ellsberg explained that he had become revolted at what was happening to our soldiers, our people, and to the Vietnamese. So he took it upon himself to "liberate" the papers. *The New York Times* had its own great in-house debate. Arguments, boiled to essentials, were: The documents, SECRET stamps removed by Ellsberg, were unauthorized. Insistence on publishing came from the editorial side of the great newspaper. The Vietnam war, undeclared but longest in American history, was getting to be as neuralgic and divisive as the Civil War.

Here, proponents of publishing insisted, was an opportunity to depict—even piecemeal, as were the Pentagon Papers—how we became involved in Vietnam. Then came the clincher: back in 1961 the *Times* got advance information on the Bay of Pigs. On consideration of national security, it didn't publish the news. For years thereafter, the late President Kennedy's remarks bit deeply at the paper. He was quoted as having mournfully observed that if only the paper had printed the leak, the nation might have been spared the fiasco. Kennedy's later suggestion to the *Times* that it remove a correspondent from Vietnam was rebuffed by the newspaper. The late President was furious over the reporter's stories.

The decision of *The New York Times* to publish set the Senate—House and White House, too—into the greatest national tizzy since World War II. When the *Times* was enjoined by the Justice Department to cease printing the papers, the documents appeared all over, in a nationwide string. The *Washington Post* was second. It was like Avis trying to be No. 1. The *Post* was enjoined, as were a few others. Ellsberg trumpeted his rejoicing. He claimed to have provided all the papers with the documents. His Xerox must have been red hot from use. Precociously, publications would not reveal their sources. On his own, Ellsberg took the blame—or credit. The newspapers and he insisted on the "people's right to know." They contended that Americans had been deceived into the splintering war in Asia.

Above all, the First Amendment to the Constitution was cited. It guarantees freedom of the press. The arguments in favor of the published leak sounded like a mixture of Sir Galahad, *The Front Page,* and a whiff of ham. It also was good business. Caught short, the Administration—not mentioned in the leak—had a lowered profile and less skilled hands to counter the newspapers. Their rebuttal was buckshot fired at massed cannon by Presidential Press

Secretary Ron Ziegler. He is a nice young fellow, peerless in saying nothing of substance. Communications Director Herb Klein, more experienced and older than Ziegler, has been a veteran editor in San Diego, California. Klein's name isn't taken seriously beside that of the gilded by-lines in the *Times* and others of the media.

As all expected, the case went to the United States Supreme Court. A six-to-three decision upheld publication of the Pentagon Papers. Despite newspaper acclaim, it was not a very famous victory. There will be lots to watch. Two justices, voting for publication, noted that prosecutions could ensue from violations of the Espionage Act. All nine justices voted and there were nine opinions. This is rare. It ultimately could all end in a frustrating deadlock. A junior justice, who opposed publication, predicted forebodingly: "The First Amendment, after all, is only part of an entire Constitution."

He may have had in mind what Jefferson wrote in his manual: ". . . that if our tranquillity is to be perpetually disturbed by newspaper defamation, it will not be possible to exercise our functions with the requisite coolness and deliberation. . . ."

Yet it was Jefferson, at the same time, who led the opposition to Federalist attempts to muzzle the press. It was the time of the Sedition Act in 1798 and an undeclared war raged with France. The Sedition Act passed Congress in the name of national security. A secret treaty with the recent oppressor, Great Britain, was leaked and published. The Sedition Act made it a federal crime to "paralyze the public arm, and weaken the efforts of government for the defense of the country." By its own terms, however, the act was due to expire with the election of 1800.

Because of his opposition, the number of newspapers in the young nation doubled in support of Jefferson. By election time, it seemed that there were not enough prisons available to hold all the writers, citizens, and politicians violating the Sedition Act. They all rallied to Jefferson, who made John Adams a one-term President. Documents like the secret treaty with Britain turned up everywhere. Deliberate leaks funneled in a steady stream to the Jefferson camp of newspapers and periodicals. People taking newspapers read accounts avidly and passed them on. We can trace the process of leakage to the press from the time of the Sedition Act to its contortions of today.

Presently, the whole system of leaks to the media is up for grabs. It probably will operate full blast again with some revised ground rules. Neither the branches of government nor the press can genuinely function without the leakage process. When the Senate finally got copies of the Pentagon Papers, Senator Allen J. Ellender, Democrat of Louisiana, was asked if his mates could keep secrets after reading the documents. His arch response: "You can't mumble something to a mirror in this town without it getting around in a few hours." Very much on his mind was an extraordinary senatorial performance twelve hours before. Freshman Democratic Senator Mike Gravel, from Alaska, who in two years disturbed his colleagues with wheeling-dealing and publicity grabbing, had received some of the Pentagon Papers that were leaked.

Gravel, ruffling his shiniest dove feathers for the public, wanted to read the data on the Senate floor. He had just staged a grandstand filibuster against continuation of the draft. Aware of the nature of his next theme, Gravel's colleagues refused him time. A quorum could not be assembled. Late at night, Gravel called into session the tiny subcommittee of Public Works which he chairs. He read from the secret papers for three and a half hours. It was a weird performance. The forty-one-year-old wept aloud. Copious tears ran down his darkly handsome face. His histrionics shocked the Senate. While many senators privately scoff at the idea of the Senate as a "Club"—even have their own competing factions as clubs within The Club—they ganged up on Gravel. In their eyes, he went after the limelight without asking anyone's concurrence. In a bipartisan spirit of outrage, some demanded disciplinary action. Majority Leader Mike Mansfield, anti-Vietnam to the core, was upset and uptight about the Gravel antics. He warned him to watch his language and behavior. Others quietly banded together to look into, on their own, Gravel's associations and sources of money. The junior Senator from Alaska faces some Arctic days ahead in the Senate.

Through all the tumult and recrimination, *The New York Times* stuck to a professional theme: that the Pentagon papers they published were the result of prodigious investigative reporting. The documents having been acquired over the transom, so to speak, it was a pompous claim to fresh fame. Few in the media have accomplished a tiny percentage of the investigative findings achieved, for example, by consumer advocate Ralph Nader. In their brash, muckraking manner Jack Anderson and his staff have done a consistent, no-favors, seven-day-week job. Sometimes their work is crude but often it is on the button.

Life magazine, through Bill Lambert, chopped up two senators for good. Lambert also compelled aged House Speaker John Mc-Cormack to retire sooner than he planned. McCormack's office was misused by a trusted aide—without the Speaker's knowledge—for influence peddling. The hard digging that goes hand-in-hand with investigative reporting is hardly the norm in Washington.

While the Senate snoozed—as did, indeed, the entire Congress—through a winter hibernation called "recess," the Nixon Adminis-tration was painfully wounded at yet another battle of the credi-bility gap. This time the culprit was Jack Anderson. With his staff of three and a worldly-wise executive assistant, Anderson is America's most widely syndicated columnist. He gets closer to the bone than anyone else in Washington. His peers, however, usu-ally have been condescending toward his column.

From a supersecret branch of the National Security Council, the Washington Special Action Group (WSAG), Anderson ob-tained documents stamped "secret sensitive." They dealt with the India-Pakistan war. Nixon sided with the Pakistanis, the Russians with India; we lost on all fronts.

But the papers Anderson published showed the White House making public gestures of neutrality and secretly supporting Pakistan in planning and policy. Henry Kissinger, the President's one-man foreign policy band in the White House, showed up as his con man. For three years Nixon had taken evasive action to avoid just this kind of pitched credibility battle. It had ruined Lyndon Johnson before him. And the country was on the verge of a new presidential year.

Specifically designed to wound the White House, the leaks were not offered to a critical senator. They went right to Anderson who could provide publicity almost instantly. Ironically, when Ander-son offered the first revelations for a TV spot, they were turned down. Why? Television newsmen thought there would be no interest. After they were printed, television went on a binge and made Anderson pretty much a household name.

The current timeliness of the Anderson Papers also was calculated to curtail Kissinger's foreign policy counsel. He had built up an in-house list of critics and enemies as big as any bureaucracy. In addition, there was an ugly whiff of anti-Semitism. Kissinger, bright as he is, had become a pushy little Jew to quite a few establishmentarians.

Here, then, was a chance to get even, and even put a crimp into Nixon's own re-election ambitions. The President always tried to show he enjoyed special skills and insights into foreign affairs. But the Anderson Papers—leaked without authority—peeled the varnish off this coat of many colors. They thrust the legal battle over publication of the Pentagon Papers into dull courtroom tilts. The public eye boggled at the Anderson Papers, instead.

With all its own resources and manpower, Congress and the Executive branch also like to dwell on their investigative prowess. So for the last twenty years and more the government and the Congress have employed outside "think" tanks for special missions. The Pentagon's inquiring cerebral capsule, at the cost of $25-$30 million a year, has been the Rand Corporation in California. Ellsberg once worked there and got access to the secret papers he littered nationally. The Senate farms out work to special think tanks, too. Fulbright's Foreign Relations Committee began several years ago with special surveys—at big fees.

Being investigative has gotten to be extremely chic today. It can also be attached to a house detective's work. Attorney General Mitchell's Justice Department moved like a massive house detective in conducting its case against release of the Pentagon papers. Maybe there wasn't enough time to prepare adequately. Moreover, the Pentagon data case will be around with us for some time to come. There was adequate lead time, though, to prepare cases against nonviolent protesters, sensitive busing and desegregation questions, and, of course, the thorny matter of wiretapping. Compassion appears to have become easily expendable.

Rightly or wrongly, the Justice Department today conveys an image, among the young particularly, of a hard-bitten gang of night riders. This is unfortunate for an ultrasensitive, image-conscious Administration as is Nixon's. Sour feeling toward the Justice Department has communicated itself into the Congress, where the Senate knocked off two Nixon nominations to the Supreme Court. The media cannot take too much solace from this development. Its reliability—as Vice-President Agnew quickly learned with his own brand of antimedia slugging—also has become questionable. Public feeling is volatile. The press often is as suspect as the politicians and equally old professions. One side, remember, has real power. That is government. The other only wields the influence of persuasion.

Vigilance, as practiced by the press, is hardly a substitute for power. Leadership is power, pure and simple. For at least six years we have seen the steady erosion of that leadership on the Executive and legislative levels. It has brought the country to the threshhold of a breakdown; nervous, anarchic, regional, or a ghastly amalgam of all three. The two-party system, badly sundered with George Wallace's special appeal in 1968, also is verging on collapse. There may well be third and fourth parties of some substance in the 1972 elections. Issues such as race and the Vietnam War placed great strains on the traditional system. We already have divided government. The Executive is Republican; the legislative, Democratic.

To the new voters—eighteen to twenty-one—being independent has the strongest appeal. The Twenty-sixth Amendment to the Constitution will enfranchise about 11 million youngsters in the upcoming elections. Add to that total another 14 million who come of age at twenty-one and it makes even a political professional's mind boggle. They constitute one-sixth of the total eligible vote. We may soon be confronted with as many parties as contested the first election of Lincoln in 1860, or more. Then we had four. Lincoln got the electoral vote. But the total was less than 40 percent of the popular votes cast. A new secession, away from the traditional parties, is gathering momentum. It could break the two-party system forever.

Profound change, a search for individual identity, and reassessment of values are abroad in the nation. None of our front-running aspirants show any special gifts for leadership in the winter of discontent. They have not proved to be capable of presiding over change that should be carried out in an orderly but thoughtful, albeit compassionate, manner. Change does not mean headlong plunge into an Orwellian depth, nor wanton destruction from which peeps a vestigial form of American Maoism. But young voters might not select candidates as do their parents. This is an unrealistic myth. Their majority choice consistently shows "independent," despite polls that conclude the young favor three or four to one Democrats over Republicans. Out of frustration with both major parties a bitter cry has emerged: "The Republicans can't win, but the Democrats can lose."

They want a new and elementary set of three R's which have nothing to do with the dear old golden school rules. The three R's can be listed as: rejuvenation, restructuring, and reform. These rules go to the marrow and meaning of American society. The glib, greening process can be too easily converted into lockstep shades of red or brown. Despite ills and malfunctions, ours is a highly developed society. Lots of the tracks have been torn up or distorted in the last generation. But human dignity remains a transcendent and precious resource. Under our present creaking, patched-up system, we are incapable of actually confronting 1976. It happens to be our bicentennial, the two hundredth anniversary of the signing of the Declaration of Independence.

We can no longer take casual refuge in the aspirations, precautions, and concerns laid down by the Founding Fathers. This nation sorely needs rebirth with some helpful midwifery counsel in the wisdom of the founders when the United States had a population of barely 4 million and was agricultural. The United States Senate, as its greatest national service, could provide the incubation. Just about everyone today clamoring to be President, including the incumbent Nixon, has been or is a United States senator. At the rate the Senate selfishly limped toward the last generation of the Twentieth Century, it will persist in inadequacy. Society will thus splinter further. We are on the verge of a new and terrible 1860. Take a look at the way the Senate behaved—the world's greatest deliberative body—as it lurched—kicking, screaming, and struggling—into the trenchant realities of the seventies of this century.

IV

THE SENATORS

Senators almost always go to great lengths to show the voters how frugally they live and how hard they work. It's a strain on them, because quite a few really mean it. They happen to be on the elderly side of an already aging Senate. Take an endearing spectacle most working mornings in one of the Senate cafeterias. Around 7:00 A.M. Majority Leader Mike Mansfield and Republican dean George Aiken take breakfast together. Aiken, the austere, seventy-nine-year-old from Vermont, usually chooses a fruit or vegetable juice, skimmed milk, and once in a while French toast. At most the tab is seventy-five cents. Dour but meticulously courteous Mansfield selects his breakfast with care. His milk is half-and-half, maybe some toast and a juice every other day. When he splurges, it's for scrambled eggs—not very often. Usual cost: forty-five cents. They carry their own trays to the cafeteria tables. Nobody can say what they really talk about. Eavesdroppers can only hear terse reflections on the weather and see-you-later salutations after the twenty-minute breakfast.

Mansfield, as majority leader, has a chauffeured limousine at his disposal. He uses it as sparingly as if he had to pay all the charges. Aiken lives in one of the service apartments around Capitol Hill; Mansfield not too far away. Their wives are unpretentious. The Aikens hardly ever go out evenings. For duty's sake, Mansfield and his wife attend occasional dinner parties, entertain rarely themselves. Of course, the Aikens and the Mansfields are older people and have set routines. But these two senators also have staff assistants who have sifted the mail, coordinated with

opposite numbers on legislative matters, drafted pertinent memoranda, and made the couple of dozen calls their bosses wouldn't
have time to make. Everything is set for them when they enter
their respective offices.

Neither senator was born rich, neither has amassed a fortune.
They have saved their money and have modest nest eggs. It is
vastly different from the lifestyles of many younger colleagues,
especially those on the hunt for the presidential nomination. Mc-
Govern and his wife have four pretty grown-up daughters and
an adult son. Their housing is expensive. Built in Japanese
style and decor, some of the ceilings are low enough to make
a visitor involuntarily bow his head. Ash trays are sometimes hard
to find; the McGoverns long ago kicked the cigarette habit. Almost
all McGovern's fellow senators have also given up cigarette smoking. Some, like Mansfield, will puff a pipe or take a cigar. The
McGoverns entertain handsomely. It's a big change from Avon,
South Dakota, where he was born. His car is a two-year-old popular
model, smaller than the one operated by front-runner Ed Muskie.

Although Muskie drives a Chrysler, his tan-colored suburban
home is modest by comparison with the McGoverns'. The Muskies
also have five children, three at home. Both they and the McGoverns have something else in common besides being Democrats and
in quest of the presidential nomination: They are grandparents,
too. There aren't many senators with really small children. Young
senators—just forty or hovering in that age group—either have
installed their families in the suburbs or keep them in the home
state. The schools in the suburbs are far better than those in the
District. If a senator is young and affluent, his children are in
private schools.

Muskie has simple tastes. He puts both red wine and white
on ice. Golf is a real avocation with him although he never went
into competition with Nixon or Agnew, other golfers about on a
par with him. The lanky junior Senator from Maine likes Chinese
food—the takeout variety. He is by no means an ostentatious host
or a demanding guest. A visitor at his office—it's difficult these days
to find him there—will see a desk lunch of a cheeseburger or some
eggs getting cold. Muskie makes a point of trying to keep his
private life just that—private. If you're running for President,

it isn't easy. His mother and four sisters in Maine are devotedly loyal. They don't see much of him. His spunky mother, who does her own housework at eighty and makes aprons for neighbors, doesn't care much for the idea that son Ed wants to be President. The apple of her eye is a younger son, Gene, a steelworker in California.

Simple in his tastes and lifestyle—his opponents like Mc-Govern openly say simpleminded as well—Muskie plays simplicity to the hilt. His press releases invariably point up his stature of 6 feet 4 inches as "Lincolnesque." That implies being a man of the people, too. His former bossman, former Vice-President now Senator again Humphrey, has a philosophical point of view about the 1968 Vice-Presidential running mate. Muskie has studiously ignored Humphrey, while always being coldly correct. An old pro like HHH, also an outgoing and emotional personality, resents being ignored. Long before the Democratic race became so scrambled, Humphrey wondered sadly why Muskie thought it necessary to cold-shoulder him.

"I know better than most what happens when the presidential bug bites," reflected Humphrey. "But a man doesn't have to put on airs that don't belong to him by pretending that dissociation is disavowal of a friend. I was—hope I still am—his friend."

Of course, Humphrey keeps hoping that he can himself catapult back into the race for the nomination. His backers with money, the larger majority in the New York area, have at his behest held off giving anyone else more than walking-around money. It may well be that this is HHH's greatest asset at the present: his yes or no on to whom to contribute. Humphrey has rather little in personal wealth. The Humphrey children are grown. His wife, blonde and hospitable Muriel, keeps their posh apartment near the Potomac amid the slums without any help. In the rolling countryside of Waverly, Minnesota, the Humphreys have a house that is solid but unpretentious. It's located in duck-hunting country and also good for bird-watching, which Humphrey likes. His drinking habits are ultramodest. He shares with Muskie a mania for picking up tourist gimcracks wherever he happens to land abroad, but he is way ahead of Muskie on the collectors' end. His eating problems have been solved by being most spare and by cutting down on his weight. HHH likes to be regarded as ultrafit and spry for a man of sixty, just a few years older than Muskie.

A collector of taste and acquired learning is Republican Minority Leader Hugh Scott of Pennsylvania. His wife and he have a charming house in Georgetown, loaded with Chinese art and furniture. He certainly was well in advance of the Administration change in taste to affairs Chinese. Scott, a pipe smoker, also wrote a good book on Oriental art. The Scotts are well off but not showy. There were sound investments in times that boomed—interestingly, under the Democrats. And a little inherited money came in handy. They have a married daughter, and the lovely art works are one day to be hers. Scott goes to about half the parties to which he is invited. He'll sip about one-third of a Scotch and soda. Food must be simple and broiled. Two sparse meals a day and lots of walking for exercise are musts for him. Scott is in his seventies.

A courteous and very wealthy Republican senator is John Sherman Cooper, of Kentucky. His wife Lorraine and he are generous hosts in their handsome and expensive red-brick Georgetown house. Cooper's hearing has faded badly since he passed the age of seventy. He has announced he will not run for re-election this year. Never loud, never excessive in remarks or temper, Cooper has been a quiet, hard-working senator. He rises early but has trouble getting glued together in the morning, puttering around the house and reading newspapers. Cooper also is the only senator who has a personally paid-for, chauffeur-driven limousine. From inheritances of his wife and his own, he can well afford the luxury.

The gentility of low-keyed wealth by a Cooper is thrust into the background by the boisterous opulence of Ted Kennedy and his blonde wife, Joan, at their estate in McLean, Virginia. They dispose of vast acreage—good for their three kids and all the Kennedy relatives from the nearby property of his late brother, Bob, and Bob's widow, Ethel. It's open house at big outdoor parties of the Ted Kennedys. They have more sleep-in servants than the entire Senate combined. But young and old unflagging supporters of Kennedy have never muttered an unkind word about their wealth and its political use—only about that of others. Lately, Joan

Kennedy has lent her splendid figure and minor talents to appear-ing on TV and playing the piano. The Senator eats sparingly in his Washington surroundings but wolfs down great gobs of sea-food and hamburgers at the family compound in Hyannis Port, Massachusetts. They spend money lavishly, but are parsimonious about wages for servants. It may be a reverse form of *noblesse oblige*. Interviews with servants indicate directly that the appli-cants should consider themselves fortunate to land a job with the sacred household.

Kennedy drives one of the older model family cars to the Senate. He has been behind the wheel only about a third of the time since Chappaquiddick. Younger members of his young staff often pick him up. Sometimes wife Joan ferries him to Capitol Hill on her way to an appointment. For a couple of years Kennedy let his hair grow long, curling around the collar in the back. These days, the cut is on the shorter side but trimmed to acceptable youth recognition. His clothes are tailored and he dresses with studied carelessness. Neckties are normally on the dark-hued side. In the mood of heavy preoccupation, Kennedy often sheds his jacket and carries it hooked in a finger over his right shoulder. He toys with food but has trouble keeping his weight down.

The leading food fancier in the Senate is Louisiana's eighty-one-year old Allen Ellender. On the death of Dick Russell, he moved into the first rank of makers and shakers. Ellender, a veteran of thirty-four years in the Senate, became not only chaiman of the powerful Appropriations Committee but also President Pro Tempore. When the Vice-President is away, Ellender presides over the Senate. That also entitles him to an extra privilege of rank, a chauffeured limousine. Only the Majority Leader and Speaker of the House are allotted these noticeable luxuries, courtesy of the taxpayer.

Ellender has been a widower more than twenty years; there are no bachelors in the Senate. He learned some of the culinary arts of Southern cooking while his wife was alive. In the ensuing years, he has made a real hobby of special Louisiana dishes. A consciously courteous man, Ellender lives simply. But he can be as much of a tyrant in the kitchen as he is toward old-fashioned Southern legis-lative prerogatives. Mention a picnic, though, and Ellender instantly offers his services. He can make the best, spiciest gumbo this side of Louisiana.

There isn't a tougher legislator around than Ellender on foreign-aid bills. He says repeatedly that he'd do everything within his power to reduce the program to the lowest possible level. That doesn't prevent him from taking more free junkets all over the world than any other senator or congressman. He does pick up new recipes, though. In addition, Ellender grinds out his own home movies. They are accompanied by rambling travelogues. After a trip to Moscow, Ellender showed movies he made. His most pertinent insight from that trip—free, of course, to the tax-payers who made it possible—was: "In a collective society the toilet paper is the same in all hotels."

His junior colleague from Louisiana, as everyone should know, is Russell Long, who drinks hard in spurts. At least Russell Long doesn't try to conceal his love for the businessman's point of view, especially the oil business. His father set up an interestingly named company, the "Win or Lose" oil concern. It was dissolved and reorganized as a family partnership. The firm today handles principally rent paid by big oil enterprises for the right to drill on land owned by Long. He is Senate Finance chairman and doesn't hesitate to admit to an identity of interest with oilmen. He is meticulous in trying to obtain every possible break for the industry, starting with oil depletion allowances.

In Washington, Long keeps an apartment in the Watergate. It is expensive living. Divorced and remarried, Long has a quiet home life. It's otherwise when he goes out. When he isn't quaffing, he can be exquisitely charming and thoughtful even under provocation. A few snorts and it's a vastly different ball game. Nobody can say what will happen, from a sudden blow to a towering rage punctuated by errant charges and suspicions. The image of his father, assassinated when he was a boy, seems to rise up on the occasions of anger, driving him even against old friends, who are forgiving.

A Southerner, wealthy by inheritance and astute investments, is power-conscious J. William Fulbright. The chairman of the Foreign Relations Committee and his wife, Betty, out of old Philadelphia mainline stock, always have a heavy social schedule.

Fulbright prefers the company of the mighty, and the rich. During the two terms Winthrop Rockefeller served as Republican Governor of Arkansas, Fulbright and he became fast friends. It certainly could not have been for this Rockefeller's brain power. He has the lowest intelligence by far of all the Rockefeller brothers.

When Senator Fulbright takes odd moments off from his specialized views on foreign affairs, his favorite entertainment generally centers around special interests: natural gas, textile manufacturing, and even cattle ranching that has become such a safe tax haven for the few who can afford the investment. The Fulbright house is in a grassy, tree-fringed, rich residential area of the District. Furnishings are a blend of old Philadelphia taste with contemporary Arkansan. It certainly is comfortable. The Senator and his lady are entertaining at home or out to dinner most every evening. He has three dinner jackets to match the heavy schedule.

Fulbright gets to his office around 9:00 A.M. on working days. He takes his coffee black, doesn't smoke, and appears fit and brisk in his middle sixties. His favor is sought by almost every foreign mission in Washington. Relations between the White House and Fulbright are almost as important to the President as, say, those between the United States and the Soviet Union. The President cannot totally ignore the chairman of the Senate Foreign Relations Committee; but he can limit the total number of protocol state dinners for foreign dignitaries to which he invites him. The cutback began in the last couple of years of the LBJ Administration. The invitations dropped sharply in the last few years.

A favorite topic of pro-labor, Northern, and Far Western senators is Fulbright's anti-civil-rights stand and his opposition to minimum wages. The most clearly outspoken has been Scoop Jackson. For years Jackson led floor fights for civil rights and labor coequality in Southern states such as Arkansas. He consistently refused to do a fashionable *mea culpa* for his stand on national security, including our role in the Far East. Jackson has caused gales of laughter by scathingly referring to Fulbright's "arrogance of ignorance." The reference is to Fulbright's irate description of presidential outlook as the arrogance of power.

From the beginning, Jackson and Fulbright were on opposite

sides of the fence on numerous issues, starting with the domestic. They have clashed regularly on foreign affairs. A voluntary witness, appearing recently before Fulbright's committee, wondered why the chairman couldn't get together with Jackson on Asian issues in the national interest. Before his distressed colleagues, in a poorly attended hearing, Fulbright burst out with: "I wouldn't think of it. Senator Jackson keeps trying to undercut me."

This is a question of semantics, too. With powerful chiefs of foreign missions, Fulbright is on a first-name basis. Jackson has a first-name relationship only with the ambassador from Israel. The two senators also look at the Middle East this way: Jackson is all-out for Israel; Fulbright looks with favor on the Arabs. The cleavage, although both are Democrats and today many Southern senators prefer Jackson, goes deeply into other issues. Jackson is a contender for the presidential nomination. A trial balloon lofted a couple of times for Fulbright as Secretary of State turned out quickly to be so much hot air.

Moreover, Jackson cannot afford gracious living as practiced by Fulbright. Mrs. Jackson—a lovely strawberry blonde and one of the prettiest young women in Washington—takes care of two small children herself, as well as a heavily mortgaged house in an upper-middle-class, tree-lined neighborhood of the District. Their son, touseled Peter, is not of school age. Anna Marie is eight years old and is the only senator's child to attend a public school in the District. The school is integrated—about 30 percent black— and the principal also is black. But the educational standard is high. Otherwise, as Scoop Jackson says, he'd see that any child of his would go elsewhere. He is opposed to busing kids if that means downgrading the level of education. Other senators, such as Muskie and McGovern, send their young children to private schools.

The Jacksons also maintain a small house in their home state of Washington, where they spend their summers. He gets about six hours' sleep a night while the Senate is in session. This is the norm for most senators. On the road, in the quest for the nomination, he is fortunate to get four hours' sleep and airplane catnaps. All the other active aspirants have the same problem—how to get some rest and appear fresh.

Jackson, along with the other competitors, also misses the daily swim in the Senate pool that has been his chief exercise. The Senate health center is more secret than a closed committee hearing. Senators strip, do their push-ups, get pummeled by a masseur, and swim in an Olympic-sized pool. The older members paddle solemnly and do their exercises a couple of hours daily. Being fit these days is a ritual. Some, like Fulbright, golf consistently, entailing lots of walking.

The most noticeable health fan is William Proxmire, Democrat from Wisconsin. He jogs at least seven miles a day, rain or shine. When he walks, the pace is swift.

The best all-around athlete in the Senate is probably Bayh, who was a fine college baseball player. In heretofore annual games at the Washington Senators' RFK Stadium, Bayh single-handedly has led the Democrats' hitting attack against the Republicans. Nevertheless, the Democrats have managed to lose consistently.

The most partisan, Strom Thurmond, is evenhanded in matters of health. A new father, as he approaches age seventy, Thurmond is all for both parties to be brimming with vigor. It's good politics, particularly in an era that accents youth. Thurmond can, and will, perform a spry headstand in his office.

In the Senate gym, a freshman senator is on equal terms with a naked senior member. They can take time off from the dumbbells to sit together and talk over knotty problems on which they disagree. There has been nothing like it since the days of senators dawdling at the Roman baths.

Tennis also has become a big avocation for a good third of the Senate. The most consistent player, who learned his way around a court in middle age, is pear-shaped Javits. He likes to show his agility as he moves into the late sixties. Younger members such as freshman Republican Lowell Weicker, Jr., of Connecticut, have been playing tennis since childhood. Weicker's enormously rich family had courts available for the children at home and abroad. An indifferent tennis player but an inveterate walker is another freshman Senator, James Buckley, Conservative of New York. Also wealthy, Buckley is Congress's No. 1 bird watcher. Patience and walking with a glide are vital to the hobby. Another rich Senator, Claiborne Pell, Rhode Island Democrat, is the top sailor.

The biggest single brigade of physical fitness addicts ever to grace the Senate were the ten freshmen who took office with the Ninety-second session. They all think highly of advice given by Dr. Paul Dudley White on how to avoid a heart attack. Suggested Dr. White: "The simplest, least expensive form of exercise is walking." Undisputed champion walker is Florida's amiable Sena-Chiles. He trudged 1,003 miles across his state in 1970 to interest the voters. It was a brisk pace—ninety-two days. His Republican colleague from Ohio, Robert Taft, was dismayed to learn his office was tucked away nearly half a mile from the Senate floor. It turned out, he says happily, to be a blessing. Taft walks back and forth several times a day. He also plays paddle tennis on weekends.

Young John V. Tunney, Democrat from California, plays strenuous tennis and handball and skis a lot. Evenings, he roughhouses with his three children at his soft-carpeted, luxury house. Democrat Adlai Stevenson, III—still called "Young Adlai"—keeps up an Illinois tradition. He is a modern-day rail-splitter, chopping down trees for firewood. Republican William E. Brock, 3d, of Tennessee runs and jogs. At forty, he beat a thirty-three-year-old aide in a sprint race. Maryland's Republican Senator J. Glenn Beall, Jr., may be the best golf player in the Senate. He plays steadily, with uncanny accuracy. Texan Democrat Lloyd M. Bentsen is a fierce tennis buff and player. He wears out colleagues who agree to play him. Back home, Bentsen is an inveterate deerstalker and hunter.

Senatorial living styles are as different, too, as their individual approaches to legislation. Bayh, for instance, has been making himself heard on full disclosure of personal assets. He claimed modest assets for himself: less than $200,000 all told. Yet his house is in a D.C. real-estate area regarded as prime. It takes at least $100,000 to own such a home even with a mortgage. Real-estate and interest rates run high for such luxury housing. Bayh doesn't lack for interested angels such as Miklos Sperling, Midwestern industrialist.

As an old athlete, Bayh stays away from all fattening foods. He must attend outdoor picnics, where the goodies can be tempting, from fish fries to hot dogs. Hosts and admirers thrust grease-dripping frankfurters at guests of honor. It's instructive to watch the guest senator's pained smile as he lifts the delicacy to his lips.

Last summer, I watched Muskie take tiny bites out of hot dogs off the grill. Each time he dropped one in a convenient bin, a host turned up with a fresh frank in a roll. There were seven before the perspiring candidate could get away.

A senator who doesn't have to watch the pennies and the household budget is Phil Hart. His wife is the daughter of Michigan's industrialist Walter Briggs. He once owned the Detroit Tigers baseball club. They have the largest family in the Senate—eight children. Their house sprawls in solid comfort, but the Harts hardly ever indulge in anything splashy. Jane Hart is busy with her own causes, and the Senator relaxes over additional office work. They eat in shifts—nobody knows when Mama and Papa will be home to sit down at regular meals.

Only a handful of senators still live in hotel suites. When sessions were shorter and schedules could be predicted, many lived at special rates in hotels. Most stay in apartments if the children are grown and away from home. Veterans like Magnuson keep a small suite in a hotel. His set-up could be lost in a corner of the vast apartment at the same hotel holding Perle Mesta and her social secretaries. A majority of Magnuson's senior associates live in older but capacious apartment buildings. The rooms are larger, and rents always have been more reasonable. Veteran senators prefer to maintain a low-lifestyle profile in Washington and do something more striking at home where voters can appreciate them better. Seeming to be a show-off in Washington remains a restraining factor. The inhibition no longer applies to the younger, wealthier, and new senators.

Young Adlai Stevenson and John Tunney bought lovely houses in fashionable residential areas. In a moment of speculation, Republican Minority Whip Bob Griffin, of Michigan, wondered why it was usually the avowedly richest who made the most noise in behalf of have-nots but accomplished little for them. He had his own answer: It doesn't cost them anything and their influence is limited. So, it sounds good. The notable exception is Griffin's senior colleague, Philip Hart. He can pilot basic legislative ideas because of his own seniority and concentration on just the duties of a senator. Wealthy as Hart is, his ambitions have never leaped upwards.

Rich or poor, most any senator—usually in private—will lament the lack of security. Hotels have discreet notices warning guests about straying around corners at night. Senators living in apartment houses find their neighbors' apartments were looted a night or two before, so they complain, and unscheduled police watches keep vigil. Some senators, with the wherewithal, decided against buying houses. Instead, like Russell Long, they moved into the Watergate Apartments, close to the Potomac, not far from the Kennedy Center for the Performing Arts.

As with any other high-rise, you can sniff in the corridors what's cooking for dinner next door. Lots of utility breakdowns occur but none were so flagrant as a daytime holdup in one of the wings. The Watergate has internal TV for security precautions, but anyone with a shave and a necktie can amble through the place. It also boasts of two prominently contrary occupants. One is Attorney General Mitchell and family in a seventh-floor duplex. The other is the Democratic National Committee on the street level. Any interested onlooker can watch the computer services of the committee as casually as a window shopper. Occupants of the Watergate, like Senators Javits and Alan Cranston, the California senior Democrat, often stop and look in the window for a moment or two.

Hard as senators try to show simplicity of manner, living, and feeling for people, none can match Ralph Nader. Many of them wish they could—at least in getting the quality volunteer help that comes Nader's way. The nation has heard of him constantly, either applauded or reviled, but Nader is difficult for most voters to fathom. He never has indicated that he wanted to run for public office. A one-suit man, who lives in a tiny, sparsely furnished room, he eats as little as Mahatma Ghandi and walks more than he rides. The last may be caused by all the failures he has found in autos, from makes out of General Motors to foreign imports.

Nader is outside the power structure but crusades fiercely. He stings senior senators and he defies comparison with any other citizen who wanted an even shake for the consumer. Any senator, no matter the size or quality of his staff, would give his eyeteeth to have even 10 percent of the young lawyers and researchers who flock to Nader. Himself a lawyer, Nader doesn't shun the limelight, though he has made of accessibility almost as much of a chore for curiosity seekers as has recluse Howard Hughes. But unlike Hughes, Nader revels in the rough-and-tumble of TV confrontation, particularly with congressional panels.

There have been lots of names and descriptions of Nader, depending on the point of view. He became a national personality with his book, *Unsafe at Any Speed*. General Motors settled a case out of court with Nader for nearly $500,000. The counter-Nader inquiries were so clumsy and high-handed they provided Nader with his real start. Usually called "consumer advocate," Nader has done infinitely more—such as reminding the nation of its conscience. Where Nader and his teams go—known as "Nader's Raiders"—they have emerged with fact-packed revelations. There isn't a single senatorial investigative staff that can come close to Nader in any field of consumer affairs today.

This skinny and intense man—younger than any senator but thirty-seven-year-old Tunney—has been able to finance work by using funds he received out of the settlement from GM. All fees obtained from TV and other outside appearances are pooled into projects headed by Nader. He also insists that for the best results and reforms his kind of work must be carried on from within what today is called "The System."

Self-styled revolutionaries have made a big business of demanding elimination of that same system. Many get $2,500 to $5,000 for a campus speech. Time limits go from a half hour to an hour. Do that three or four times a week and the orator is good for $10,000 weekly.

Where does the money go? Recipients of these mammoth fees have set up their own tax-free foundations, or diverted money into channels you have to chase in circles. The difference between Nader and them is reform, in his case, and hysterics in theirs. His teams painstakingly amassed a vast amount of data on key inequities in the economy. It emerged almost at the same time big labor such as the AFL-CIO independently urged the Administration to come to grips with the horrifying disorder of the American economy. When President Nixon made a midsummer dramatic Sunday evening announcement of great consequence to the economy at home and abroad, few senators had even glanced at either the Nader fact-finders or the union research.

Senators expect that their staff assistants will review any memoranda or report for them. An experienced aide won't go through anything voluminous. He expects no more than a two-page rundown on a given legislative proposal or research into conditions that must be remedied. Why? He makes similar proposals himself; the huge number of ideas and recommendations call for a bird's-eye view. It is even better if another aide provides the gist of an assessment by telephone. That normally carries urgency. Communication is thus swifty established between the informed aide and his senator. A report like Nader's simply cannot be boiled down to five hundred to six hundred words and make a significant contribution. It's hopeless to try it out in a few minutes' telephone conversation.

Yet any senator, particularly a senior member, expects staff assistants to have at their fingertips a lode of information that can be quickly digested. Men like Javits, Jackson, Hart, and Scott are uncannily fast readers. The aide in the legislative field or keyed into the beehive of committees has to steep himself in the work and its progress. Otherwise, his man can be caught in a silly question—and that won't help an assistant's future. He— lately some young women have been added to positions of more staff responsibility—becomes the senator's mouthpiece as well as his eyes and ears in a table of organization that can be as categorized as the Army's.

How else would the champion committee member of the Senate be able to manage it? Javits has undertaken seven committees and commissions, as well as nineteen subcommittee assignments. Just getting from one to the other could use up a good part of the working day. He will spot-check a half dozen at best. In he comes, say, to the Foreign Relations Committee. Rarely does he spend more than thirty minutes. But a staff assistant has been on hand before his arrival, and awaits the end of the session as Javits moves on. The procedure is essentially similar with other senators. They haven't, however, taken on as many of the assignments as has Javits. He likes to count them up whenever anyone cares to ask about his day's work.

Each senator is a member of at least two of the sixteen standing committees, and several of the sub-committees. A member also gets assignments to special, select, and joint committees and commissions. The Rules Committee parcels out the assignments. If a senator is chairman of a standing committee or a member of an important one, the chances are that most of his time at hearings will be concentrated on what is important. The assistants thus play an essential role in keeping a senator up to the minute where he cannot attend a hearing or appear briefly. Most administrative assistants become close to their bosses as a result of their chief responsibility. Many also socialize with them. The most prominent is Robert Hunter, Senator Long's administrative assistant. They will eat and drink together more than any other senatorial twosome. Theirs is an old friendship and mutually protective whenever one or the other may be under the weather.

The mass of detail that falls to a staff aide can be overwhelming enough to drive someone zealous to drink. That doesn't very often occur. What does happen is attrition. A senator who makes a fetish of collecting committees can grind assistants down to the raw nub. He or she must decide for the boss which hearing to attend, draft memos so he can sound knowledgeable, consult with committee people, and research the issues. At the same time an aide must ponder over stacks of mail on a special subject and decide to which ones the senator replies and how—with a draft. By the time the assistant is geared to the working procedures, the senator also may want a speech. The turnover in assistants is fairly rapid among demanding senators.

The minutiae are what really get them down. Playing assistant or deputy assistant senator doesn't compensate for the dreary, anonymous chores of detail. Freshmen senators invariably start off by saying they will attend to most all burdens personally. What happens? In earnest, perservering Fred Harris burned the desire to answer all letters himself. The resolve lasted about ten days. Mail, even from a small state, can swamp any individual, let alone a senator. It must be parceled out for replies. A senator usually handles personally one of fifty if he is most meticulous. A taste of trivia also can turn an earger freshman off.

At the beginning of this Ninety-second session, Senator Adlai Stevenson sat at the first meeting of a subcommittee he chaired. He was preened and eager. It was a session of a District subcommittee on Business, Commerce, and the Judiciary. Stevenson found himself plunged immediately into taking testimony for bills to simplify settlement of minor estates. Another detail that came his way included making it easier for minors to inherit small sums. There also was a requirement that gas meter inspectors place a paper seal over each meter they check. Worn down by this initial experience, Stevenson observed wearily:

"I've done a lot of presiding over routine hearings as a state legislator, but nothing as routine as what I find myself presiding over now as a United States senator. As a very new junior senator, it just amazes me that the Congress is dealing with bills of this nature."

That's why staff assistants are available for hire. Stevenson, from a large state, Illinois, can get a budget for a payroll up to about $300,000. Not bad for a freshman, but a senator always hunts for good assistants. They are in short supply. A senator from a small state could put together an office budget of $150,000 annually. Senior members from the more populous states can dispose of nearly $500,000 a year. Big, small, freshman, or intermediate, all keep looking for talent. An innovator or a perceptive brain can make or break a senator. An indifferent talent can keep him mediocre. About half the Senate prefers mediocrity in staff work. But there's no raiding other senator's staffs. It is an unwritten but rigid rule. If a colleague lets someone go, retires or dies, then it's different. Newcomers always make certain to have a few experienced hands with them as they enter office. They usually are hacks, thoroughly familiar with routine like bullpen catchers.

An average office staff will number around a half dozen young women. They can double as secretaries and handle routine cases —home state requests for federal jobs, Social Security problems, or federal funding for a small state project. Normally four to six higher powered senatorial assistants take care of the brainwork. They are responsible for learning of impending legislation, what amendments their senators should introduce, and for maintaining liaison with party leadership and the White House, when they can. Senators from big states often have staffs double the average. Ted Kennedy also has specialists he pays from his own resources. But the administrative assistant is on a more equal footing than any other aide. He will often confer alone with the boss after pumping other assistants. Many senators prefer talking only to their "AA"—as abbreviated—before heading off to other assignments in the morning. Full-scale meetings with all top assistants present are unusual.

An office staff can be crowded into a couple of rooms in the New Senate Office Building, opened in 1958. It is right behind the so-called Old Senate Office Building, set up in 1909. Both are linked by corridors or by little subway cars on the basement level. The new building is brighter, more functional, but has the disadvantage of small suites. Even in the old building, senators from more populous states complain about having their people and typewriters jammed tightly together. In the more rambling, old office installation a senator could have a suite as big as four large rooms. He also has the constant irritation of insect control. Cockroaches and beetles scuttle across the floor frequently in the middle of a high-level conference. The senator, though, always has his own well-appointed office, furnished with some of his mementoes and the building superintendent's garish taste.

His personal secretary, even in outside and crowded quarters, is pretty much Queen Bee of the inner sanctum. She must be endowed with the disposition of a minor-league angel to avoid intramural sniping. Most personal secretaries have their favorites. It helps stir up intrigues and backbiting, the like of which never flared in the small towns from which most of them come. Plots and counterplots, all aimed at gaining favor with the senator, swirl like dust-bowl storms. A young man on the make for another aide's job always makes pleasant accommodation, first, with the senator's private secretary.

The same practice of intrigue and plot is rife within subcommittees. In the committee itself, the director has been with the chairman a long time. He is practically impregnable. But there are juicy subcommittee operations. An agile young man or woman can be left alone, once the goal of a special job slot is attained. Moreover, subcommittees are subject to the most frequent change. A senator can retire or be defeated. Then the new subcommittee chairman institutes his own game plan with new players. Solemn promises are shelved almost immediately. Take the recent case of Birch Bayh becoming head of the subcommittee on Juvenile

Delinquency. It's made to order for headlines, because drugs and their fallout on society are among the priority issues before this subcommittee. Bayh took over from Tom Dodd a little earlier than usual. He promised Dodd he would keep most of the top staff intact. Once in control, Bayh wasted little time giving pink slips to all people he pledged to keep in jobs.

Office space is assigned by seniority and size of the state. Many senior senators from the smaller areas prefer to keep space in accordance with their size. It isn't so noticeably immodest. Maine and Vermont Republican Senators Mrs. Margaret Chase Smith and veteran George Aiken are shining examples of small staffs, working full speed, in small suites. New freshmen have become balkier about accommodation. They prefer the commodious arrangements of the old building but almost never get them unless the senator represents a big state like Texas. That's how Bentsen got his rooms. They adjoin those of Stevenson—big-state man, too. Collegial freshmen still grumble about the status symbols of those two compared with their own cramped suites.

By far the biggest accommodation status symbol in the Senate is the hideaway, a well-furnished room in the Capitol. Telephones, of course, are in these private sanctuaries. They are all close to the Senate floor. Strict seniority—coupled with a tinge of favoritism—prevails in allocating a hideaway. The Rules Committee decides distribution. Inside the private room, a senator can meet with people he doesn't want any staff member to see. Only his most trusted confidants know with whom he confers. The private secretary is informed that the senator can be reached at the special extension of the hideaway. Each room has a good ice-making refrigerator. Whisky and soft drinks are stored in a cupboard. A senator can come off the floor and get right to his hideaway—if he has one—mix a snort, and talk shop with contributors, assorted interest groups, or someone special.

There are about forty hideaways. Some are quite tiny. All are functional. The main Senate dining room can be called to bring cups and pots of coffee and sandwiches if the session stretches out. Most senators denied the sanctuary privilege because of seniority talk longingly of the days that might favor them. Freshmen, like John Tunney, wonder why they shouldn't all share. His tentative pleas have been so much wasted breath. The special visitors destined to meet the senator in his hideaway are escorted by the AA or another top assistant. One or two aides might stay on to refresh the host's memory after the visit has been completed. It is unique when the senator meets a privileged guest alone.

Staff assistants from the AA down provide their man with shadow and substance. They also enjoy the fruits of office. A trusted assistant can ask—and get—use of the hideaway on occasion to see someone in the senator's interests. He has fringe benefits proportional to those of his man. These run from low-cost life insurance, for which no physical exam is needed, to such items as pens and glasses sold at bargain rates in a grimy stationery shop. His salary can be higher than most any college professor's or newspaper editor's, but he gets cheap haircuts, in a special barbershop. The taxpayer pays the salaries of the barbers, who get tips depending on the senator's or the assistant's generosity. Many senators give a dollar. The average tip runs better than fifty cents.

Last mid-August caught a good number of staff assistants in the chair or waiting their turn. That was when Nixon sprang on the public the wage-price freeze and the whole series of sensational economic measures. The Senate had been on vacation recess about a week. Democratic candidates for the presidential nomination were on a "working holiday," rushing around the nation pointing up our economic fragility and suggesting their own remedies. Nixon, most contended, never would do a thing to correct the deplorable problem. So, he did, going much further in many instances than his critics ever dared suggest. The hapless staff assistants who had opted for vacations at a later date—a senatorial force always stays on hand in the office, recess or not—were showered with angry calls. In an hour eleven were tracked down in the barbers' chairs.

The questions were what any voter might ask. How did the freeze come about? Why didn't you (the assistant) have some knowledge of its making? The speeches you gave me are no damned good now. What can we say now? You and your contacts! That's how it ran. There is only one phone in the assistants' barbershop, so half-trimmed aides rushed back to their own offices. Their confidence in themselves was severely shaken, though it doesn't take them long to revive. Otherwise, they would land generally in psychiatric wards. A quick telephone call, often to someone on the same wavelength, can always produce a temporary explanation. The switch in Nixon's economic approaches was admittedly the most difficult top assistants had to interpret instantly. China? That had to be kept secret. But the economic turnover could divest a candidate of all his clothes. No senator likes to be caught naked outside the swimming pool.

They all returned for the autumn session, refreshed if not especially enlightened. This was the period before presidential primaries. Ideas, criticism, and ringing declarations were absolutely essential. Lapses of the major senatorial assistants had been forgiven by the principals, if barely remembered. These were the bodies and brains absolutely vital to the senator if he were to be heard or even casually noted. Dry-cleaned, so to speak, the Senate chamber under the dome of the Capitol seemed specially spruce. It always had been that way since this chamber opened in 1859. Cream-and-red marble constitute the main decor. Desks are of mahogany, arranged in four tiers facing the presiding officer in a semicircular arc. Looking down from the galleries, visitors will find Republicans seated on the right; Democrats on the left. From the press galleries, the scene is reversed. The presentation is presumably to rule out ideological speculation.

The walls of the chamber are of gold silk damask, intended to reflect an air of studied elegance and dignity. A major remodeling job was undertaken in the years 1949 through 1951. For the benefit of wandering tourists, a chandelier hangs outside the south entrance of the hall. Two bulbs are attached to the lower part. If a red light is on, it is a signal that the Senate is in rare executive—or private—session. A white light means regular open deliberations. The lighting system caused former Senator Douglas to muse: "One if by land, two if by sea . . . ."

From their desks the senators see arrayed before them, besides the presiding officer, the chief clerk, legislative clerk, parliamentarian and journal clerk. Ensconced behind these functionaries are the sergeant-at-arms and secretary of the Senate. All of them came in years ago, as protégés of powerful senators. Directly back of the Vice-President, when he presides, impassively sit the secretaries of the majority and minority leaders. They rush in and out, from and to special offices provided their senators, convenient to the chamber. Minority Leader Hugh Scott's office often becomes involved in tourist directions. Visitors every fortnight see long lines near the offices. The queues are from Senate staffs, waiting to collect their pay from the Disbursing Office. These are people who want their pay in crisp banknotes tucked in yellow envelopes. Others get their salaries deposited once a month in banks of their choice. Tourists, of course, become confused at the sight of the long lines.

Demonstrations in the galleries are supposed to be forbidden. In the last few years, young spectators particularly have been moved to roar approval or moan disappointment. Majority Leader Mansfield, irked by the unwarranted noise, threatens to clear the galleries. He hasn't done so yet. But he has thinned out the crowds of staff aides flocking back of senators' desks during votes of national interest and controversy. Noise is graveled down by the Vice-President or his substitute. The Vice-President's gavel is solid ivory. It was presented by the Vice-President of India to then Vice-President Nixon in 1954. A token of friendship for the United States, so to speak. Remembering the gift, conservative Texan Republican Senator John G. Tower recently observed sourly: "Maybe we ought to give it back to the Indian government. They might want it for the Russians." Tower had in mind the fifteen-year treaty between the Soviets and India.

The old gavel—ivory capped with silver—is seen but not used. It had been banged down too hard over the years, especially in the times of the great debates. When the Senate is in session, the old gavel can be seen in a place of honor on the rostrum. It was supposed to have graveled gabbling senators into silence when they first convened in 1789. Not so evident as the old gavel are busts of Vice-Presidents. Only twenty occupy niches in the upper wall, near the galleries. They represent Vice-Presidents from John Adams to Thomas A. Hendricks. Missing is a bust of Henry Wilson. It stares down in the Vice-President's office, just off from the Senate chamber. Wilson died suddenly in the Vice-President's room.

To summon senators to the chamber is a system of buzzer

rings. If they are in their offices, it could take a little time to respond, depending on a member's age. A single ring means yeas and nays on a vote. Every senator's office is equipped with the bell-buzzer system. It goes all the way to six rings and requires an alert aide to count accurately. If the summons is important enough, the party cloakroom will call members individually. Cloakrooms are situated beneath the galleries on the south side; Republicans have the east end and the Democrats are installed in the west end. Directly behind the Vice-President's rostrum, separated by a wall, is a narrow but long room known as the Senate Lobby. It has desks where secretaries often come to take fast dictation for an amendment. Wire service tickers also spew out news by teletype. This is very handy for most members who get behind with their own problems.

Early in the present, Ninety-second session, the Senate accepted a sensational reform. After more than a year of negotiation, arm-twisting, and promises, the first two girl pages were sworn into office. They joined thirty boys. A page must be between the ages of fourteen and seventeen. Boys are jacketless, in white shirts, black ties, and black trousers. Salaries run to $7,380 a year. Pages must attend high-school classes early in the morning. The first two girls—a third still waits her turn—found solicitude among senators the greatest delaying tactic. Senators like Gravel wanted to know what they would be required to wear: miniskirts? That wouldn't do because pages sit around below the rostrum to await senatorial commands.

Attire was straightened out with general agreement that the girls wear pants suits. It was a little more difficult to persuade senatorial fathers about security. Doughty John O. Pastore, for example, said: "These girls will be between the ages of fourteen and seventeen. They cannot be on the streets of Washington alone when it is dark." Senator Cooper was opposed for certain practical reasons. The proximity of crime to the Capitol disturbed him. So did: "The physical stamina required is very pressing. Pages have to run errands all over the Capitol. They have to carry books and packages and find us in the washrooms. I think a young lady would be at a disadvantage." It was spoken like the gentleman that Cooper is.

His colleagues, Jacob Javits and Charles Percy, who sponsored the first two girl pages, appreciated the concern. In these days of women's emancipation they also reminded him that a page might become a most distiguished citizen and ultimately take up political life. Efforts to accept girl pages required more time and effort than any debate over major legislation and its amendments in the Ninety-first and Ninety-second sessions. Javits sponsored seventeen-year-old Paulette Desell; Percy, Ellen McConnell, just turned sixteen. A third, sponsored by Fred Harris, is sixteen-year-old Julie Price. She is due soon to put on her pants suit. Their sponsoring senators are responsible for the girl pages' security. Some of the boys already have complained that this is bias—they say they fend for themselves on dark streets.

Security is a major problem on Capitol Hill, entrenched seat of our legislative arm. For one thing, as senators fondly point out: The whole thing belongs to the people. By the tens of thousands, tourists stroll through the houses of Congress on working days and vacations. They cannot be forbidden entry into anyone's office. Nor can they be frisked, nor airline bags searched. At least a dozen bomb threats a week come over the telephone to the Capitol Hill switchboard. They all are listed. Jim Powell, chief of the Hill police force, told me inquiry and sometimes an appeal to the FBI results in little or nothing. In this age of youthful dissidence and rebellion, bearded, ragged, and strangely garbed boys and girls are around the Hill and in the buildings all the time. It's even regarded as quaint to find some unruly youngsters in a lavatory, taking a sponge bath, with the liquid soap and paper towels.

It was hardly surprising, then, that in a series of nationwide bombings a major blast shook Capitol Hill. Around 1:00 A.M., March 1, 1971, with the great dome bathed in electric light, a call was taken at the switchboard by operator Norma J. Fullerton. She remembered the voice as low but audible, hard but businesslike. It was a male who said: "This building will blow up in thirty minutes. You will get many calls like this. Evacuate the building. This is in protest of the Nixon involvement in Laos." Chief Powell was immediately informed. At 1:32 A.M. a bomb exploded in the Senate wing of the Capitol. Nobody was hurt. But it did more damage than anything since the British raid of 1811.

A time bomb had been placed in an unmarked ground floor lavatory off a small corridor. Senator Aiken said it had been so little used that few senators knew of its existence. Whoever planted the bomb, though, knew his way around the building. The explosion occurred in an area rich in American history. It was deep in the original wing of the Capitol for which George Washington, in 1793, laid the cornerstone. The enclave once housed the Senate, the Congress, the Supreme Court, and the Library of Congress. The blast blew out windows in the Senate dining room—quickly repaired—and mangled six nearby rooms: the hideaway offices used by Senators John J. M. Sparkman, Everett Jordan, and J. Caleb Boggs; a hearing room of the Senate Appropriations Committee; a storeroom, and the Senate barbershop. Shattered glass was ankle deep. Structural damage was surprisingly light; the injury to the senatorial and national psyches was deep.

Early Senators Mansfield and Scott inspected the damage. They were saddened and horrified. Probably the most tasteless reaction came from McGovern, who called the act barbaric and added that blame must be ascribed to "our Vietnam madness." None of his dovish colleagues contrived the same linkup. The bombing was actually the second in the Capitol's history. A Senate reception room was superficially damaged in July 1915. Frank Holt, a Cornell instructor of German, planted that bomb. He was protesting United States arms sales of early World War I.

A national inquiry into the bombing of the Senate wing is still in force, still pretty empty-handed. The same night, after the explosion, a visitor came to Mrs. Alice Roosevelt Longworth. The dowager, octogenarian lady, possessed of one of the nimblest minds and rapier tongues in Washington, was shuffling some cards. It was poker night at her house for some old friends who hadn't yet arrived. The visitor breathlessly recounted late details of the explosion's aftermath. At the end of the account, Mrs. Longworth looked up and inquired archly: "Tell me, dear, did they get Bobby Byrd?" She riffled the cards again. The Senate went back to work. It couldn't be frightened. So its pace took on even more deliberate serenity and slowness of deliberation. Senators have their own style of being poker faced.

V

THE OPENING OF THE
NINETY-FIRST

Two years before, muted cheer was the prevailing note for the opening of the Ninety-first session of Congress. It was especially apparent in the Senate as one hundred senators from the fifty states shuffled into the chamber. A deliberately old-fashioned decor has been scrupulously maintained. Looking down from the galleries, visitors saw desks in banks of four rows facing the presiding officer on his desk-dais. Below him and to the right and left were the minions of the Senate: clerks, stenographers, majority and minority secretaries, and official reporters.

From the galleries you can hardly hear anyone speak below. Even official recording reporters go to within earshot of a senator's utterances. While a Senator may decry or deplore—even with passion—colleagues talk to each other, sign mail, and some work crossword puzzles with the aid of pocket dictionaries. A senator, as we all know, must be thirty years of age and a citizen of the United States. That's no worry. Everyone is well above thirty; being below forty-five is quite a feat. Other requirements are pretty vague, like being an inhabitant of the state when elected.

The smell of furniture oil permeated the great room. All the senatorial desks are cast in the mold used by predecessors in 1819. To keep up with the past, every desk has an inkwell, pen, and penholder—and a glass vial filled with sand to blot unruly ink. Tradition is an overriding consideration in the Senate. This day in January 1969 a new ball game was about to unfold. The Republicans had taken over the White House on Pennsylvania Avenue. Wintry sunshine sparkled outside. Tradition would again be observed. For a new President, there'd be at least ninety days of a watching brief. That means the Congress would not snipe or cannonade at the Administration. Give the new President, Richard M. Nixon, a chance to feel things out; enable his liaison men with both houses of Congress to get to know the principal names and games. One of the main pieces of business early in the session was a raise for all members of Congress. It would go from $30,000 a year to $42,500.

A few senators and some congressmen balked. They got but little mention in the press. The raises went through, as did doubling the President's pay from $100,000 a year to $200,000. Pretty good compensation all around, particularly for a senator, who also had other emoluments. Depending on the population of his state, he could have staff salaries and expenses up to another $400,000 annually. In keeping with tradition, senators from states like New York and California always complained about not having enough. Pity the poor fellows who go regularly by air back home. After five such trips, they pay their own way. Deduct taxes and pension allocations, it's rough. That's what many say. But few ever talk voluntarily about low-cost life insurance, virtually free medical care, and secretaries who often also serve as social factotums. Instead, they'll complain about the necessity of maintaining two residences—one in the capital, the other at home.

These homely problems were major themes of discussion on the floor and in the cloakrooms just off the chamber. Senator James B. Allen, Democrat of Alabama, ticked off improvements he intended to make in the Senate dining room. Bean soup has always been a touted specialty. Normally, GIs in combat would reject Senate bean soup as poor man's fare. It's simply low grade. Made with a special Southern recipe, mind you. The soup was probably Southerners' revenge for the post-Civil War carpetbagging. Allen, who headed up the dining committee, also was aware of a health problem. He kept it under wraps until some kitchen help died—of tuberculosis. Then, everyone who ever used any dining room or cafeteria was tested. The problem is still with us.

The honeymoon phase provided older Senate hands with an opportunity to gossip. It happens to be the biggest avocation of the Senate. Just a couple of months ago, Nixon barely scraped through. More veteran members knew him well. He'd been one of them, as an elected senator from California from 1950 to 1952. Then for eight years, as Vice-President to General Eisenhower, Nixon presided over the Senate. Up there this day sat Spiro Agnew, Nixon's Vice-President. He had a fresh haircut and wore a light blue necktie for the opener. Only yesterday, it seemed, "Triple-H," as some senatorial friends called Hubert Horatio Humphrey, sat in that spot.

He lost by 510,000 votes to Nixon. Irascible George Wallace, running as a third force from the South, made a good bit of difference between who was winner and who loser. During the campaign both major parties sought to get the other to loft a story about Wallace. It was Kafkaesque. Wallace had running with him for Vice-President retired General Curtis LeMay. For years LeMay ran our Strategic Air Force. When LeMay was being transferred from the European theater to the Pacific in World War II, he asked to see reports on morale out there.

There were an alarming number—to LeMay—of battle-fatigue cases. He forthwith ordered hospitals to return the patients to their bomber and fighter wings. Cases in Wallace's bomber wing were ordered back on active duty. Not Wallace, bipartisan accounts ran. He was one of the few regarded as requiring further treatment. Wallace was sent home. LeMay, who never heard of him during the war, was duly asked to run with Wallace. Neither of the two big parties ever had the guts to surface the account through a senator. A member of the Senate could ask for the records held in St. Louis, Missouri.

When the Ninety-first session opened, a few senators talked about the episode—and shrugged. Others looked stonily at Eugene McCarthy, tall and graying in a handsome way, from Minnesota. Early leader of an antiwar crusade against LBJ. McCarthy would grudgingly support Humphrey only at the very last minute. As an all-out supporter of Adlai Stevenson II, he placed him—tried to—in nomination in 1960. That was against John F. Kennedy. McCarthy never wasted an opportunity to mock Kennedy. He had a

more bitter feeling against Robert F. Kennedy. Late in the nominations sweepstakes of 1968, Bobby Kennedy took off on his own.
McCarthy always believed the Kennedy-mounted operation was
against him. Everything was so personal.

When Bobby Kennedy was murdered by an assassin in Los
Angeles only weeks before the conventions, McCarthy was un-
moved to make room for anyone else, above all fellow-Minnesotan
Humphrey. He owed his Senate seat to Humphrey. It didn't
matter. McCarthy made a halfhearted pitch in stormy Chicago.
He departed in a publicized huff when Hubert made it easily
on the first ballot. For months, there was not a word of encourage-
ment or of support for HHH from McCarthy.

"He made the difference," bitterly declared young Fred Harris,
from Oklahoma, about McCarthy's national silence.

Attractive and young in the ways of big ambitions, Harris said
what was on his mind before the big ambition got to him. By
the time the Ninety-first session of Congress rolled around, Harris
was smitten. Being in a presidential campaign as a young senator
distorts the image in the looking-glass mirror. Harris was already
thinking of himself. He buttoned his lip. Only partisan shots
against Republicans emerged. Humphrey was out. McCarthy,
weaving a mist of mysticism around his future, said he would not
run again—as senator. Between 1969 and the 1972 elections, Mc-
Carthy had some personal matters to settle.

Except for public discussion, they involved life at home. Mc-
Carthy and his wife of twenty-five years, Abigail, were about to
separate. She was devout in her Roman Catholic vows. Therefore,
no divorce, she said. Her husband suggested the same. He was
more taken with terrestrial temptation. Mutual friends living
in the large and well-scrubbed Dresden Apartments on Connecticut Avenue—a splendid address—were badly frightened by a
large stranger a few nights running. Late one night they entered
the back door to walk up to their apartment. A shadow, made
gigantically grotesque in the dim light, trod down heavily. They
braced themselves. The footsteps kept coming. Face to face, a
voice pitched low, said "Good evening." In relief, the huddled
couple answered, enthusiastically: "Good evening, Senator."

It was Gene McCarthy. A few months before, his enthused

young supporters were calling him fondly: "Clean Gene." He had been in the Dresden visiting a lady friend of some consequence in Washington. When he had the chance—and they were more frequent since the elections—McCarthy slipped up to New York. There he stayed with another prominent young woman. Some of his more lascivious-minded colleagues openly admired McCarthy's stamina. Others thought he acquired in Washington and New York extracurricular inspiration for his poetry.

Dispassionately, the Kennedy political network kept its own political score card. Names, telephone numbers, times, and dates. It was most professional. Another Kennedy, you see, had seized the staff of anointed leadership from his fallen brothers. Teddy decided, after discussions with advisers and the more voluble Democratic senators north of the Mason-Dixon line, to go after Russell Long. It wasn't much of a job to savor, that of the party whip. Fellow senators generally liked Russell if they didn't care about his own outlook on the world around him. He was most convivial. When on the wagon, Russ Long could be lucidly intelligent. He seemed to be chased by the ghost of his father. And he was caught absolutely short by Teddy.

It wasn't until he read an interview with Ted Kennedy that Long knew he faced a challenge. That almost never happened in the Senate before. Teddy talked to colleagues for votes. He didn't labor as long and hard as did Bobby Byrd two years later. But he had far more going for him. The last of the Kennedys in public office was a hard man to turn down. The drums of publicity about Ted Kennedy beat out a steady obligato. Here was a Kennedy senator who did his homework, a real man of the Senate. Long didn't have to hear the count. He was drubbed and went off on a bat. Teddy Kennedy listened to questions about his next move—that of going after the Democratic nomination for President.

He never said anything about it in public. His entourage and all the old Camelot crowd did. They had been around his late brothers, the assassinated President and Senator. Camelot had been a name in the Kennedy Administration they contrived. It conjured up all the beautiful people of King Arthur's Court. Beyond the imagery few paused to think how much of a fairy tale the Camelot of King Arthur had really been. Power was their bag and all felt they had Teddy safely snared. It looked that way quite clearly for some months. It was nearly four years to the next presidential elections. Positions had to be built, fields of fire cleared. Sizing up the new Nixon team was clearly the first priority.

Republican life habits came in for scrutiny. This community sets great store by who is seen with whom, who goes where, and what you choose for a place in which to live. Most Republicans shun Georgetown. In many ways, on the outside, it looks like something from Old London. Makes it chic and fashionable. The Kennedys—the President and Mrs. Jacqueline—made it swing for their friends a decade earlier. Republican higher-ups fancied a sprawling pile of gray masonry, fringing the Potomac. Called "The Watergate" after some old sluices that stood there in the dim past, rents are high and advertised security is so-so. Despite closed TV to spot intruders, robberies of some spectacular nature riddle the complex on occasion. Still, Attorney General John Newton Mitchell lived there with his loquacious blonde wife, Martha, and their teenage daughter. Many residents believed that you couldn't ask for more security than "good old John." He had been campaign director for Nixon in 1968. They had gotten to know the feel of each other in the New York law firm of Nixon, Mudge, Stern, Baldwin, and Todd, et al. It has been known to the irreverent as "Mudge & Sludge." Pipe-smoking, suburban-living Mitchell was an eminently successful municipal bond lawyer. That is a recondite but prized talent.

The Mitchells had a six-room apartment at the Watergate East. Georgetowners referred to all Watergate as "The Vatican Arms." The reason was obvious. Vatican money had been used in the buildings and development as an investment. Rents and coopera-tive apartment sales are among the highest in town. Not many blacks in a city that is 71 percent black could afford anything but carfare there to hold down jobs. Its location, though, to all gov-ernment branches of the arcane jungle of bureaucracy, is most convenient. It is the reason offered by New York's senior Re-publican Senator Jacob K. (Jack) Javits for living at The Water-gate. A great vote getter in New York and superliberal on many issues, Javits was kept at arms' length by the Republican Administration. He never attacked Nixon directly, only most of his major policies.

Javits, shrewd and an artful dodger in politics and business, is the Vicar of Bray to many colleagues in the Senate. He publicizes his poor origins—son of a janitor on New York's Lower East side. High legal fees as partner for many years with his older brother, Ben, have made him an affluent man. It is regular practice for a senator or a congressman to suggest a law firm to handle a thorny problem involving legalisms. Javits also is blessed with a good Senate staff. It can devour position papers and legislation. The Senator, in his mid-sixties, has the ability to absorb problems easily and superficially. He also is devoted, he likes to say, to foreign affairs. Hence, concern with NATO. Trips to the Continent Javits likes to use so he can then touch base in Israel.

His devotion to the survival of Israel also is spiced with some subjectivism. To that extent, he wanted his son, Joshua, to be ushered into Bar Mitzvah rites in an old synagogue in Jerusalem. Gritting its teeth to remain silent, the Israelis redecorated the synagogue for that purpose. Their personal views of Javits—especially those of the military—could be used in the underground press. In Washington, Javits also is a peripatetic partygoer. He always announces: "I don't drink," and takes a tomato juice. His wife, Marian, who is twenty years or so his junior, keeps saying she detests Washington. Rarely does she appear in town. They rough it in a luxury Park Avenue pad in New York City.

In this socializing community, something known for years as "Potomac Fever" is endemic. Being invited to some place or to someone with a name is the local version of head-hunting. Parties at the Mitchell's, therefore, are much coveted. They are, even if some of the invited profess total loathing for the hosts. Mitchell, the suave and hard-nosed lawyer, makes no effort to conceal how deeply he cherishes Martha. Democrats clamored upon installation of the Republican Administration just how dull things would be. Martha Mitchell, originally out of Pine Bluff, Arkansas, made it ring out with her remarks very early in the new game. By midterm of the Republican Administration, the sayings of Martha were about as broad as the sayings of Chairman Mao. They were much easier to understand, mind you.

The Watergate was divided into East and West, with a hotel,

shops, restaurants, and an outdoor swimming pool. A sauna is on the side. A Watergate North had been ready for occupancy, but takers have been few. Maybe some status-seekers feel something for the future. It has not affected residents like Senator Long or Chinese-born, Republican advocate, Mrs. Anna Chennault. Her cuisine is still the best in town, bar none. Balding, openhearted California Senator Alan Cranston, also lives in The Watergate. For him, like Javits, it's a matter of convenience. He could be rich, too. Elected in 1968 and in Washington as a liberal Democrat with a Republican President—from Cranston's home state— the Senator quickly made of himself a carbuncle on the California media.

"He needs an immediate brain transplant," a disgruntned *Los Angeles Times* correspondent told me after a session with Cranston.

Cranston always mentions his journalistic career. He worked for Hearst abroad for a while. The stint must have equipped him with bona fides for an activist liberal posture in politics. Mrs. Chennault studiously avoids neighbor Cranston. Not that she turns her back on Democrats. A very old and dear friend is Thomas (Tommy, the Cork) Corcoran, of FDR fame. A big-fee lawyer in town, Corcoran gets to almost all Mrs. Chennault's parties. So do upper echelons of the American military. Chief of Staff General William C. (Westy) Westmoreland is a favorite. His all-American looks, service in Vietnam, and mangled phraseology collectively may have unleashed these last few years' attack on the military. Westy can be earnest. It drives pro and anti-military senators up the wall. Eisenhower, some remember fondly, comparing Westy with Ike, was a paragon of lucidity.

A most special "Our Crowd" philosophy seemed at the onset of the Republican Administration to create its own segregation. The vast majority of the media looked down on Nixon and his entourage. Two members, high in the Administration, they could not divine. Therefore, they held them to be traitors of the philosophy of The Wrecking of the President. Both were highly regarded academicians, out of humble beginnings. There was, first of all, Dr. Henry Kissinger. Nixon brought him in as his adviser on National Security. Kissinger, out of Harvard and the Rockefeller Foundation, was steeped in foreign affairs. He also had been a refugee boy from Nazi Germany.

The day Nixon announced Kissinger's appointment, Henry was called a fink by anti-Administration critics. Not to his face, ever. This is only carried out at parties, restaurants, the cocktail clambakes, and in written commentaries intended to explain problems and people to the captive readerships and audiences. Kissinger, onetime noncom in the United States Army, was put on the pan by the upper-class bedpan holders of the State Department. Individually and collectively, he is more erudite and far more intelligent than anyone in State. The bedpan bit certainly goes double for the Secretary of State, William P. Rogers, lawyer by trade and sudden assessor of affairs foreign by appointment. He was a very old friend—certainly one of the oldest—of President Nixon. A big collector of memorabilia and souvenirs on jet trips to far-flung areas of the world, Rogers could be made for central casting in a film.

A close friend and golf-sharing duffer to Rogers has been Senator Fulbright. The statesman from Arkansas talks business between holes with the Secretary when they are together at Burning Tree Golf Club. The course is exclusively quiet. Costly, too. Rogers, the lawyer, learned lots about foreign entanglements from statesman Fulbright. The junior Senator from Arkansas—senior is crusty seventy-five-year-old crime fighter, John L. McClellan—holds chairmanship longer than any other of the Foreign Relations Committee. Within a year it would be more than ten years. Of course, Fulbright's stand on issues of civil rights have been totally abysmal. He always was opposed. Take minimum wage laws. Fulbright also wants lower wages, sort of coolie minimums.

As an innovator of bold and imaginative programs, Fulbright fled in 1954 for some months to England. He speaks the language and understands it tolerably well. The time was crucial. Federal troops were sent into Little Rock, Arkansas, to see that a Supreme Court decision on civil rights was enforced. It was a good time to look into what have become known as "Fulbright Scholarships." These are exchange swaps, underwritten by United States funds, for students at home and abroad. The idea originated with a group of Eastern professors. Fulbright was shrewd enough to seize on them. A real student of foreign affairs, he urged fellow senators early in 1965 to pass the Tonkin Gulf Resolution. It came after some American warships off the coast of Vietnam reported they had been attacked by North Vietnamese torpedo boats and driven off.

"Lyndon wants it; let him have it," reported Fulbright to his fellow senators, of President Johnson's desire.

Fulbright still thought that the new President might make him Secretary of State. Johnson, after all, following the 1960 elections, kind of suggested that President Kennedy was thinking about Fulbright. LBJ's views of Fulbright, at the best of times and relationships, never glistened. So sharp a politician, he knew full well that no Vice President-elect ever suggests aloud who the President should have as a Cabinet member. LBJ simply set the stage for Kennedy to ignore Fulbright. He gutted his ambitions then and there. Fulbright only became aware of the blighted romance when Johnson soon showed he had no intention of dumping Dean Rusk as Secretary of State. Then Fulbright, with acquired Mandarin mannerisms, went after LBJ, the American role in Vietnam, and generally United States foreign policies.

Not the least of Fulbright's pet peeves was American interest in Israel. The Senator would be among the first to cry out that he is a man without prejudices. This is practically out of his ghost-written *Old Myths and New Realities*. But he always was harsh and fairly intemperate in talking of "Zionists." The Russians, he asserted, had a point about the whiff of imperialism over Israel. More important, in his views, the Arabs were right to be most apprehensive.

"We have at least one Senator in your Congress who is for us," remarked the late Gamel Abdel Nasser, long-time master of Egypt. "He is your Senator Fulbright, a wise man, indeed."

Nasser said so several times. The remarks were twice in my hearing with other correspondents when he visited Yugoslavia. Thereupon, the observation made its way into Senate circles. Fulbright was hailed, with corresponding chortles by colleagues, as "the Senator from Cairo-Egypt." Rogers has listened attentively to old social friend Fulbright. They have seen eye to eye on the Middle East. Kissinger? Ah, he would wrap himself in Executive

Privilege and decline to testify before Fulbright, ready with TV cameras and lights. What more could you expect? Kissinger's leanings, as any man with common sense could see, were pro-Israel. A Jew, you know. It follows and is understandable. Not as first counselor, though, to the President in foreign affairs.

These convoluted reflections rose repeatedly in dinner conversations that Fulbright and his gracious, well-gowned wife attended. There was no bias intended, naturally. It was simply a question of keeping the nation informed. How could that happen if someone like Kissinger ducked perceptive interrogation before Fulbright's Committee on Foreign Relations? Fulbright ran his show like an ante-bellum plantation. If a member needed some help, say secretarial, and he happened to be anti-Fulbright and intelligent as Gale McGee, he'd wait weeks for someone to show up.

Some senators, who shared the essentials of Fulbright's anti-Vietnam postures, demurred frequently at his high-handed methods. Tall and gentlemanly John Sherman Cooper, of Kentucky, was one. Cooper, a Republican and getting on toward his seventy-first year, said he would not run again in 1972. A sensitive man, he seeks earnestly to soften bitter conclusions and assessments made by Fulbright. When Fulbright sent staff members off around the country to make speeches, Cooper often objected. The chairman sent people out in the full name of the committee, but usually didn't inform his fellow members of the assignments.

All these personal antics of Fulbright, his vinegary private comments and views, always got back to Kissinger. He ignored them. Kissinger carefully always briefed senators and congressmen in the White House or in his office. A briefing by Kissinger could always be counted on to bedazzle listeners. What Fulbright thought of him Kissinger ignored in the most courteous manner. His on-scene, intramural problem from the beginning was with Bill Rogers. That friction with the Secretary of State rose and fell like a fever.

Kissinger had an enormous advantage. He was right in the same building as the President of the United States. He worked harder, often fifteen hours a day. And Kissinger knew infinitely more about foreign affairs, especially relations with the Soviet Union, than Rogers could possibly learn. Rogers took counsel from senior

State Department officers. They had been downgraded really since John Foster Dulles. President Kennedy eviscerated the "pros" in the department. During his tenure, LBJ relied greatly on views from Dean Rusk. He paid no heed whatever to people below the Secretary. Moreover, like Kennedy, President Johnson had his own Kissinger—Professor Walt Whitman Rostow. The State Department had become gilded messengers. In policy matters, the military at the Pentagon had much more clout.

Kissinger also had an active assist from a strange quarter. Attorney General Mitchell was usually in his corner. Except for some private deluxe trips abroad, Mitchell wasn't known to have any knowledge or interest in foreign affairs. At President Nixon's behest, though, Mitchell sat at the table for the regular, revitalized meetings of the National Security Council. Kissinger always attended. Mitchell, puffing his pipe, made his views known. He almost always supported Kissinger. At least Mitchell grasped early in the Administration that Kissinger knew more than he in a specific field. In addition, Kissinger was hardly interested in most of the growing, gnawing, domestic issues.

That's where Patrick J. (Pat) Moynihan agonized. Out of Harvard's academic maze by way of New York's old Hell's Kitchen, gangling, talkative Pat Moynihan looked just like an Irish playwright's Irishman. Still in his early forties, Moynihan had been nearly ten years before an Assistant Secretary of Labor under President Kennedy. In the eyes of most of the media and the groping Camelot crowd, that made Moynihan even more of an apostate than Kissinger. As head of Urban Affairs for Nixon, Moynihan dealt with the most neuralgic domestic problems.

To begin with, there was the heartbreaker of the disintegrating and dilapidated cities. That ran hand in hand with the politics of race. Demands by blacks for racial equality, housing, welfare, equal employment, and overall coequality were on Moynihan's plate. To be sure, Cabinet posts existed to handle each of those major problems: Department of Health, Education, and Welfare. That was headed by Robert Finch, good-looking, youngish former Lieutenant Governor from California. Searching for "liberal-minded" top officials, all anti-Administration forces concluded he was one of theirs.

"I don't know why they think so," he once told me. "Maybe because I'm head of HEW."

Even Senator William Proxmire, antipollution, antimilitary-spending crusader from Wisconsin, believed the Georgetown myth. Not so young, rumpled Ralph Nader, self-made national ombudsman for the American consumer. He regarded Finch as a hack, with a fresher, younger face out of a California political machine that was Republican. Nader dislikes about an equal number of Democrats as he does Republicans. But he is loud and clear on this: Nader wants to work—and does—within the system. He has provided senators and congressmen with lots of ammunition to fire at concerns that lull an unsuspecting public with high-flown claims of goodies.

Perhaps more importantly, Nader has fired up young people with zeal to get a more equal break for the consumer public. There's hardly a senator who could command as spontaneous and dedicated a following as has Nader and his team for Responsive Law. That even went for young, blue-blooded Edward Cox, Nixon's new son-in-law. Cox's father, Colonel Howard Cox (Colonel by commission in a wartime Air Force) was first appalled by his son's choice of vocation. A Republican by tradition, wealthy by inheritance, and in the lawyer's format of John Mitchell, the elder Cox didn't know what Nader would be up to. Still, young Eddie would be marrying Tricia Nixon. She was the President's daughter. If she could scribble a congratulatory message to former Governor Lester Maddox, of ax-handle notoriety in Georgia, Eddie Cox could deal in his youth with a different type of crusader. Colonel Cox—who loves his title as would any oldtime Kentucky colonel—didn't much care for the likes of a Maddox, either. Too crude, you know.

It didn't matter to the skein of regulatory agencies that proliferate the United State Government how young Cox felt about Nader. Almost all of them, from the Interstate Commerce Commission (ICC) to the Federal Trade Commission (FTC), hated—and feared—the disheveled young man heading into his upper thirties. They became especially concerned when rumor swept that he might spring for high elective office. A senator, perhaps? Nader performs well on TV. He has lots of dramatic ham underneath that shy hide. Nader also is a kind of people's recluse. It is always difficult to reach him. You try all sorts of phone numbers, letters, and finally catch up to him at a party where he was wholly unexpected.

Lots of senators dislike him intensely. Any time a member of the most exclusive club in the world fastened onto a Nader idea, the offending senator came in for vicious criticism in the cloak-rooms or the hideaways in the Capitol. Thus, Senator Proxmire was nastily hailed as "Pissmire" by dignified colleagues. Liking Nader and taking an interest in what he sought in reform didn't help Pat Moynihan. It confirmed in suspicious views of many who entered the White House with Nixon that he was truly a knee-jerk liberal. Moynihan, who labored strenuously and intelligently, was marked for pariahdom as well by the Administration critics.

His remarks, supporting some views of the President, were pointed up as evidence of his treachery. Then, when he used a phrase about the politics of race meaning blacks, he was pilloried. It was taken out of context but will haunt Moynihan forever. "Benign neglect," he urged on the Administration. It was overly simplified on the outside. The most convincing phrase of the remark was that Administration strongmen approved it. How, the reasoning went, could Moynihan or anything he said be any good?

He had fallen for the Southern strategy all the way, Moynihan's dissectors hold today. They fasten easily on slogans, their own or anyone else's. Southern strategy was a theme drummed up by a Republican publicist. The entry of Senator Strom Thurmond's aide, Harry Dent, into the White House seemed to be the clincher. Thurmond, from South Carolina, was the old Dixiecrat turned Republican. At the convention in Miami in 1968, I saw him work overtime in behalf of Nixon. Certainly, Nixon had a political debt to old Strom. His top political advisers realized full well that no matter what strategy was applied to the South, they could lose all the marbles by turning away from the eight to ten most populous states.

So that strategy was total hogwash to Mitchell, the man with the most muscle where President Nixon was concerned. Every day he spoke on the phone with the President a couple, three times. He saw Republican politicians from all over the nation. Mitchell also made speeches, usually read from a text, unlike his spontaneous wife. But he spoke his feelings, too. To anti-Administration people, the Attorney General's observations were so much gall. They perhaps recoiled most from his defense of J. Edgar Hoover, in his mid-seventies and the only director—ever—of the Federal Bureau of Investigation.

Hoover has been the only ambulatory monument we have in Washington. For years there has been a sanctimonious demand to retire him. Senators have sworn publicly and privately at Mr. G-man. Nobody from the Kennedys on has entertained Hoover's dismissal seriously. They simply have refused to face up to what they believe could be political reactions and consequences. Mitchell genuinely has been fond of Hoover. He was, of course, Hoover's superior as Lord High Executioner in the Department of Justice. It might be that the old politics prevail on the Hoover matter. Whatever the new politics are supposed to be, no clear definition has yet emerged. John Mitchell, whether you like him or not, has become a pretty shrewd politician.

He arrived at the top, in a manner of speaking, through the original insistence of Nixon's most controversial, old political friend and counselor. On a gray, late winter's day in February 1968, Nixon met his old architect in politics at an airport. He was searching for someone to pull his organization together. Nixon could—and did—talk confidentially to Murray Chotiner. It was Chotiner who ran his campaign for Congress way back in 1946. Further, Chotiner destroyed Mrs. Helen Gahagan Douglas when Nixon ran and won a Senate seat. He tore up a resignation Nixon drafted in 1952, when General Eisenhower learned about a special fund for Nixon. Ike wanted to drop him. But Chotiner urged the Checkers speech on Nixon, which saved his career.

Out in the cold in Nixon's subsequent defeats for President against Kennedy and Governor against Pat Brown in California, Chotiner remained loyal and steadfast. His friends are few. His enemies inside and out of the Republican party are division numbers. Besides loyalty to the Nixon he launched on the national scene, Chotiner is shrewd and intelligent. He can be a party poop. His life is politics even though he has also been a fairly successful lawyer. If there was any man Nixon felt he could trust implicitly from way back, it was Chotiner.

Two years from the time of the winter's airport meeting, the

President observed that lots of people were writing books about the Administration. He was assessing with his political consultants assorted prospects across the country.

"Murray," said Nixon suddenly looking at Chotiner, "why don't you write a book?"

"If I did, Mr. President," replied Chotiner, a thin smile creasing rather full lips, "I'd probably go to jail."

That broke up the meeting in chuckles. Into his early sixties, Chotiner knows more about Nixon's political lives and thoughts than any man alive or dead. But he isn't giving much to anybody about The Man. Physically, Chotiner is hardly a dreamboat: short and on the flabby side with a round head adorned by a good shock of wavy black hair. His black eyes are lively and intelligent. Chotiner is a partisan but a most skilled practitioner in politics. Even the dimmest opposing senators have acknowledged his talents —and his quest for power behind the throne.

"If I have to lose, Murray," once remarked Senator Vance Hartke, the squat and shifty Democratic Senator from Indiana, "I must admit that I don't mind losing to you. You're a real pro."

"Senator," shot back Chotiner, caressing his glass of grapefruit juice—he never drinks hard stuff—"I'm not running against you."

"As far as I'm concerned," rejoined Hartke, "you certainly are."

Chotiner has the ear of the President. He has access almost as much—maybe more—than John Mitchell. Few know or see him in such two-way dialogues. But inside the White House, quite a number know about his accessibility and deeply resent it. Mitchell and Chotiner act out an accommodation of coexistence. Mitchell has reason to be responsive, anyway, to Chotiner.

In near-ear-to-ear conversation at the airport, Nixon said that he needed a campaign director sooner than later. Clotiner merely answered that he made such a suggestion a couple of months before.

"If there is even the slightest thought, Dick, that you might want me, forget it," said Chotiner. "You know how many people dislike, distrust, and would love to destroy me. You also know where I stand as far as supporting you—all the way.

"Now, I've been doing a little research. There is this prominent lawyer in your firm. I know that he has been a loyal Republican.

He is shrewd. He never has been in politics to any extent before. From all I can find out, he is the man to pull together an organization and run it properly. He's John Mitchell, you know."

"Yes, I've thought about him," said Nixon. "I didn't know whether inexperience would be a plus in this case. You're right."

Nixon went back, talked to Mitchell, and the association was formed. At the conventions in Miami, Florida, in 1968, Chotiner chafed. He felt that he was not being activated. Chotiner went to Nixon.

"I thought I could be useful," he said. "But I don't want to be a flunkey. If you ever need me, Dick, I'll be in California."

That same evening, Nixon, the candidate, talked to Mitchell.

"Get Chotiner back next week to work with you," Nixon directed.

Mitchell made the call. Chotiner came East, to New York, to National Republican Headquarters on Park Avenue. His office adjoined that of Mitchell. They conferred, sometimes on an hourly basis. Curiously, the media never knew of this and certainly made no mention of it. Chotiner was a powerhouse throughout the campaign. He stressed the need to beef up speeches, activities, when the leisurely pace of the Nixon drive began to dip toward the frantic rush of Humphrey's.

Chotiner realized what he had set out to do in 1946 in California—the making of a President of the United States. It was late in 1968 and assignments were being made by the President-elect in suites at the Hotel Pierre, a fancy, high-cost hostelry in midtown New York. Time was being marked for the Inaugural, in Washington. Nixon made his high-level appointments. There was Kissinger; and Representative Melvin Laird, out of Wisconsin, was appointed Secretary of Defense. Laird had for some years been the Republicans' specialist on the military. Serious and dedicated, Laird was also a cartoonist's dream character. His egg-shaped head was so much better to shoot at than his predecessors', but one. Robert McNamara, onetime whiz kid, wore hair neatly parted in the middle and looked like a choirmaster. His successor for a year or so—Clark Clifford—was endowed with wavy blond hair and fading good looks.

Others were appointed, of course. Mitchell went in as Attorney

General. Herb Klein, Nixon's long-time press adviser, took over a new spot. He was made Director of Communications. Affable and parochial, Klein had been editor of *The San Diego Union*, in a comfortable enclave of California. He ran herd, or was supposed to, over all government departments and their image makers. As Press Secretary, Nixon appointed a young man, quite young for his age of twenty-eight. He was Ron Ziegler. Background? Advertising and mainly promotion for Disneyland. Ziegler is an unusual sounding board. He speaks in cliches and most remarks, even on the slightest matters, sound like box-top blurbs. Laird made probably the shrewdest assessment to some of us once in Seattle:

"Ron's a nice young fellow," he declared. "I wish he didn't sound so much like yesterday's commercials."

Freshets of appointments came fast. One—that of Walter Hickle, from Alaska—to be Secretary of the Interior raised a furor in the Senate. Hickle elicited shouts of anger from latecomers to conservation, pollution, the environment. Senator Ed Muskie, the attenuated presidential aspirant from Maine, wondered solemnly about Hickle's qualifications. He thought that Hickle became rich plundering the Alaska environment. Muskie avoided ever talking about how his own campaign supporters poisoned Maine rivers with wastes from their factories. Democratic Senator Proxmire, whose reflexes are attuned to the environment, thundered against the Hickle appointment.

But about a year later, Proxmire apologized publicly for his hasty evaluation. As Washington's leading jogger—six miles to the Capitol and the same back home—Proxmire thought of the injustice of his earlier cracks about Hickle. That was because Nixon fired the Secretary of the Interior. Hickle wrote a letter protesting about the Administration's indifference to youth and its concern about our role in Vietnam. His letter, which leaked before it reached the White House, made all the environmental difference to Nixon's critics. Hickle became something of a miniature hero. So contended Proxmire. Come to think of it, Muskie never said anything about the incident.

The contender from Maine, like all his aspirant colleagues, was much too preoccupied with other personalities. They took a dim view of the keepers of the keys to the President's office. There were two, in particular. One was lawyer John Erlichman, from Seattle. He worked arduously for Nixon back in 1960. He was then in his early thirties. Work and devotion he showed in abundance, running around the nation in 1968. Erlichman, who lives simply in barbecue suburban style, was chief key keeper. His close associate, H. R. (Bob) Haldeman, was a California advertising man. A more experienced Ziegler, so to speak. They disposed great power.

Appointments with the President could be set or rejected through them. Memoranda might get all the way to their offices, and stopped. Erlichman and Haldeman, good and old friends, had it in their hands to unlatch the door if they felt it needful. With them as the President's personal secretary was Rose Mary Woods. She happens to be the most perfect of discreet secretaries. Yet when her apartment was rifled of jewelry, Rose Woods' belongings were toothcombed. Who knows? Inadvertently, she might have taken home memos or highly confidential state papers. Because of their zealotry and the dislike of their functions, the media promptly dubbed Erlichman and Haldeman "The Prussian Guard." To carry the analogy further, Mitchell was dubbed "The Iron Chancellor," although he hasn't a drop of German blood. Kissinger? Rather weakly, "Metternich," after the conniving Prince of Imperial Austria in the Nineteenth Century.

Republican senators complained bitterly about their isolation from the President. It was all the fault of the Erlichman-Haldeman double-team vigil. The late Everett Dirksen, oozing charm and bile from every pore across the Senate floor where he was minority leader nearly the first year of the Administration, complained. A Dirksen complaint could be a command. It helped pave the way for a new chairman of the Republican National Committee. At the same time, access to the Oval Room at the White House was made simpler—at least for the senior Senator from Illinois.

Ray Bliss, outgoing national chairman, had always been considered a nuts-and-bolts political personality. He had no imagination, no fire in the belly, as Republicans in the Senate declared solemnly, as if this was a new description. Most rallied around the huge figure presented by Rogers C. B. Morton. A rich man and a member of the House of Representatives, "Rog" looked as if he dripped power. He was a rock of whipped cream.

"Rog is just great," chortled Russ Long. "He'll need a pass to visit the White House just like any other rubberneck."

But Morton, whose older brother, Thruston, had served as a Republican Senator from Kentucky, could be difficult. Nixon thought that Murray Chotiner would be the best man to put in the No. 2 spot on the National Committee. He had the brains and the loyalty. Morton was the perfect façade. Morton bristled. Chotiner's detractors and enemies ticked off laundry lists of reasons why Morton should never have Chotiner on the Committee. Chotiner, they argued to a bewildered Morton, would run the Committee. What would Rog do?

Rog rallied the anti-Chotiner forces. Put it this way: they persuaded the new chairman to rally them. At the beginning of a new Administration in the White House, no President wants his own party to combat itself. Nixon called in Chotiner, told him that it was no go at the Committee. But he urged him to stick around Washington; that a place would be found for him. In time he would be back with the big team.

"That was the third time to my knowledge that Nixon let Murray down," somebody involved in the whole issue confided. "But the President told Murray he'd do anything for him. He also has said so in public. Politics cannot be fastidious. Murray knows."

Shortly thereafter, Chotiner was named counsel to the Special Trade Representative. The office is part of the Executive branch. Top man selected was Carl Gilbert. He had to be confirmed by the Senate. A sizable bloc of senators didn't care for Gilbert and his big business attachments. Chotiner was his counsel. He also maintained steady but regular access to The Man. And he used all his political experience to produce a resounding Senate confirmation for Gilbert. Chotiner was on the sidelines—still calling plays. In a year, he'd be inside the White House.

VI

THE WHITE HOUSE
WATCH

Neither the White House nor the Senate wasted much time preparing for the national presidential election of 1972. They both began the probing, persuasion, and pledge-making about the time all were installed. It was easy to go over some groundwork. The time for transition, or political honeymoon, provided all concerned with about three or more do-nothing months to fix beads on ambitions.

Despite the Democrats' lopsided Senate majority, 57 to 43, the party was shaky. Fresh memories of street riots in Chicago the previous summer sent shivers up most members' backs. The way some talked, an outsider might think that castaways like Jerry Rubin, Abbie Hoffman, and Dave Dellinger had seats and forums in the chamber. There were few new faces in the Ninety-first Congress, especially in the Senate. Talk of reform from some of the wing called Liberal crackled briefly. They appeared—and acknowledged when challenged—to mark time. Mid-term elections of 1970 were virtually upon the Congress. Senators who learned in the campaign just ended they could be well paid for a speech lined up talks. There was money on the mental and physical menopause circuit. Republicans tried to watch Nixon. Democrats watched each other. In full view of others, they hailed colleagues with deference due club members. Outside, it was different.

A diligent Senator, re-elected, seemed to get everyone's goat when he ticked off a point, hour after hour. He was angular, wealthy Claiborne Pell. After World War II, Pell joined the United States Foreign Service. He got to be a vice-consul. But Pell didn't appear to have the stamina nor the deft double talk to go places. He resigned and dabbled in worthy causes. He decided "liberalism" should be a workable commodity.

Out of tiny Rhode Island and its more plush watering holes, Pell also managed to confound wealthy, and by tradition, Republican, friends. His wife, Noella, was charming in many languages. Pell decided he owed the public something. He went into politics. Lots of the new rich do this, too. Campaigns cost big money. Pleasant, earnest, and persevering, Pell knocked off an organization candidate in the primaries. Wondrously, he beat the Republican opposition. His wife and he campaigned in Italian, French, and Portuguese. You need something extra in Rhode Island on your own.

Because of Pell's experience with the Foreign Service, he soon was appointed a member of the Foreign Relations Committee. Senator Fulbright always spots a prospective member shrewdly, particularly a Democrat. In his years with the Committee, Pell has never even smiled crookedly at Fulbright. A good man, though. Always compassionate, Clairborne Pell has the utmost difficulty holding an audience of his colleagues. Needless to say, few senators can hold more than two or three members on the floor. They always do better off it. Clairborne Pell got to be the champion room clearer of the Senate. It led to his bipartisan nickname—never to his face—of "Stillborn Pell."

Although fresh alarms and excursions caused deep tremors in the nation a few months earlier, the Senate didn't move. Its dowager dignity couldn't be split in public. Thus they talked of and sometimes railed at the politics of ecology, the politics of the economy, violence, and law and order; the big slogans took priority. Hence, dissension always elicited defense; disorder, no. Within all-encompassing violence revolved the war in Southeast Asia, draft resistance, and clod-hopping antics of the Pentagon. Corruption in the military escaped most notice until senators felt safe in pursuing just about everything that put an extra dent in the swollen military image. The revelations of the massacre at My Lai prised open most of what came later.

With the scorn that only a man of untold power possessed, George Meany looks on much of the Senate as incapable of being plumber's helpers. As an old plumber, Meany had credentials. He had lots more going as well. Long the president of the AFL-CIO, Meany and his chief lieutenants call the shots for 16 million members. That could represent 35-40 million votes. But no trade union leader can deliver votes en bloc any more. They can hand out tons of money to candidates of their choice, though. In addition, they can exercise key hidden persuaders such as wage negotiations and money settlements.

To date, Meany and his vast trade union have established and perpetuated foreign policy practices without deviations. His anti-Communist attitudes abroad have never been impaired. Actually, Meany and his lieutenants carry on in areas that cause the State Department to recoil. In his late seventies but in amazingly sound shape, Meany steamrollered opposition without turning any of the scant gray hairs still adorning his top. The AFL-CIO surveys its world at home and abroad with a figurative cold cigar poked out of eighth-floor headquarters. They overlook Lafayette Park and the White House.

Power is entrenched in the huge glass-and-marble building. Meany sits on the eighth floor. He smokes cheap cigars. They usually go cold. Mostly, he'll speak over or through the weed. The talks are usually brutally blunt. The late Walter Reuther, head of the Automobile Workers, couldn't get along with Meany. Ambition was the main barrier. Reuther's politics—"too damned soft," according to Meany—was another. Meany wasn't about to withdraw. Reuther took his own big union out of the AFL-CIO. Thereupon the idealistic auto workers' leader hooked up in an alliance with Jimmy Hoffa's Teamsters. Hoffa was in jail. But the Teamster funds were droolingly juicy to any ally.

After Meany and Reuther split, each maintained a "loyalty" hold on a range of senators, almost always Democrats. Except to the most avowedly anti-labor senators—Midwestern, some Southern —labor keeps channels open to senatorial friend and foe. For their part, many senators have to rely on labor contributions to stay in office. If it hadn't been for Meany, his shop stewards and contributions, Hubert Humphrey might have been a complete financial deadbeat when he ran against Nixon in 1968. He had enough trouble getting money. Contributions and active AFL-CIO work at the factory level also reduced drastically some significant pro-Wallace tendencies.

More often than not, when Meany decides that an issue should have all-our labor support, his assistants get into the act quickly. They know their way around Capitol Hill. Due bills are called in. Past favors are re-evoked. It is mighty tough for a decisive swing element in the Senate to refuse a Meany behest. Meany has only open contempt for what he calls soft-liners where Communists are concerned.

"To hell with the bleeding hearts who never went on a picket line when it counted," he told me. "That goes double for the jerks who are known as the 'radical chic.' Great line, that."

Meany despises Senator Fulbright. He makes no secret of it. Once I asked him why, when Fulbright was running for re-election in 1968, the AFL-CIO endorsed him. Over his cigar, Meany declared: "Who else was there? What we gave, we can take back. That creep, Fulbright, knows it. He doesn't care? We'll see."

In most recent memories, Meany was the only personality who carved Fulbright up in public session. At a session that lasted three and a half hours—quite long for one man's testimony— Meany began by telling Fulbright: "I'm here to straighten you out, Senator." Nobody talks like that publicly to Fulbright. Shaken by the power-motored witness, Fulbright wondered aloud if Meany was as rude to his associates as he'd been to the Senator from Arkansas.

"You're the one that's been rude," barked back Meany, staring at his dead cigar.

Because of his foreign policy statements and positions, the White House thought Meany could be cajoled into coming over to its side. The echelons, high and low, plus Secretary of Labor George Shultz, showed they didn't understand the gruff old labor leader one bit. Meany is a tiger on domestic economic matters. He wants a full share of the economy for all his members. Having thought that Meany was ripe for conversion, they invited him to dinner at the White House. The Democrats, Schultz thought, were shaking themselves to pieces. Republicans hugged themselves in delight.

What happened? Republican senators, White House planners, and outriders circulated stories that Meany was with them. Within a few hours, the old tiger snarled back, heard around the country.

"What the hell do these yokels know?" he roared. "They give a dinner and think it's a tremendous honor. We've got a stake in society. We're not selling out for a lousy steak at a dinner."

Or, as one of his chief aides remarked in a lower key: "Presidents and Senators come here to try and establish good relations." Later on, President Nixon did come to Meany. It didn't change his attitudes.

"I'll support him when I think he's right," mused Meany later. "He's not bad on foreign policy. He'd better get himself a new crew to deal with the economy."

A less politically minded man took a fearful beating from Meany. He was David Kennedy, a Midwest banker become Secretary of the Treasury. Mild of manner, and hesitant on hard-fact employment issues, Kennedy at a private meeting heard from Meany: "Go back and get your flunkies to tell you what I've said about inflation. You've just wasted half an hour of my time."

It was really only twenty minutes. Men in the Treasury had only boundless admiration for Meany in another sector—drugs. The Senate, with the opening of the Ninety-first Congress, held interminable hearings. Committees took testimony and put out ponderous reports. There was precise information given about drug peddling and addiction in the military. The Pentagon fought back. Only some isolated instances, it averred. That soon proved to be sheer ignorance or a cover-up. Meany got reports of peddling and usage at some factories.

"Get it stopped," he commanded. "Get the users fired. Get the peddlers arrested or strung up. I won't take excuses."

Agents in the Treasury, known around as T-men, applauded Meany. He got drug habits out of the factory but fast. Maybe users took it home. But T-men, laboring assiduously to plug holes in smuggling everything from marijuana to heroin, wished they had a Meany. They required tougher legislation. That took another year. Cooperation with foreign nations, even allies, was a must. Any hearty assent from foreign friends usually turned out to be vanishing ink.

"There hasn't been a President in my years as a labor official who didn't think he could use us," Meany reflected. "This one is no different. It's up to us to be on our toes. A White House dinner doesn't make us walk on air."

When the wage-price freeze shifted into Phase II of economic controls and boards, crusty George Meany was skeptical. Treasury Secretary Connally, Texas Democrat turned Nixon Cabinet principal, sneered at Meany, who took it to mean that this was President Nixon's point of view, too. The fight was on: Labor vs. the White House. He was getting senile—seventy-eight— scoffed assorted White House voices. Besides, they trumpeted that Meany was out of step with the working men and women. Behind his horn-rimmed glasses, Meany ran a shrewd rank-and-file labor assessment. He had been a top banana in labor for more than thirty years and head of the merged AFL-CIO since 1954. Labor was behind him, including the breakaway United Automobile Workers. Meany started slugging and he had almost all labor's clout and organization behind him. Nearly half the Senate fell in line, too.

So, about a year after he gave President Nixon the gift of a hardhat, Meany was out to jam it over the Administration's collective ears. He had something big going for him—continuity of great power. Nixon was trying to win his own again for four years. They confronted each other at a labor conference in Miami. Tired, after weeks of lectures and travel, Meany tried roughing up the President. It was an immediate public relations victory for Nixon. But it didn't last. Unemployment kept at 6 percent and Meany was labor's champion, not Nixon. The Miami confrontation got lost. Meany, an uncompromising anti-Communist, also ridiculed Nixon's foreign policy by jet approach. His trip to China, declared Meany, was a stunt by the No. 1 stunt man.

"He'll do anything to get re-elected," said Meany confidentially.

Yet Meany saw Nixon in a kindlier light, when he was private and philosophical. The President, he reflected, knew that labor was the glue holding American society together. Neither labor nor the White House had to love each other; they just had to understand one another. He figured Nixon did, but that Connally led others in being anti-labor. "He was always anti-labor, back to his first wheeling-dealing days in Texas politics," growled the old labor chieftain at his home. Meany had fallen ill. Blockage of a stomach valve affects his heart. Nixon sent him a box of cigars for Christmas, 1971. Meany liked the gesture. He would have liked it more if Nixon called to say best wishes.

Few outsiders know anything about Meany, the private man. He seems a cartoonist's joy—constant cigar, little formal education, and exceedingly tough, like a backroom pal even. He is all that, and lots more. Born in the Bronx, he was a plumber but flunked the first test to get out of apprenticeship. He lived with strikes and fought strikebreakers until American labor came into its own. Presidents and petty satraps here and abroad have courted him— or tried. Meany is amazingly well read with a certain catholicity of taste. Senators, indeed the Congress, long ago learned he could not be upstaged. He can have the finesse of a polished diplomat or the blockbusting impact of pro-football's best linebacker.

Meany will never shout when he becomes angry; he ignores the irritant with maybe a "drop dead" for good measure. He fell ill after the Miami match with Nixon. There was tentative shuffling in the hierarchy of the AFL-CIO. The old Emperor might be fading. Nobody, though, pitched his union card into the ring to challenge. Recovery has been slower than Meany, a restive man, figured. He spent more time than he wanted at his $75,000 red-brick, near two-acre home in suburban Maryland. His quiet but decisive wife, Regina, calmed him down when he got his Irish up.

Meany adores his three daughters and grandchildren. They turn up weekends. In the backyard, as he calls the garden, Meany has accumulated twenty years of leaves for fertilizer. Any and all gardening friends in labor and politics help themselves to the heap on Saturdays. At home, he indulges a hobby that few have ever known about. Meany plays an organ, cigar clamped between teeth and ham-sized hands on keys. But he plays remarkably well and sings pleasantly after removing the cigar. It can be melodic, sentimental, and very Irish. Not bad for an untutored man. He also has seventeen honorary university degrees. For someone who just managed to finish elementary school, not bad at all. His critics are totally unaware of Meany, the whole man.

Meany's point of view about an invitation to a White House

dinner is quite different from that of past and present White House invitation wanglers. They dearly love to see their names in small type the next morning when papers list guests. That goes for an inside group, men who have been friends with Nixon for many years. The steadiest invitation-holder, and the most mute publicly, has been Charles Gregory "Bebe" Rebozo. He can perhaps be described as Nixon's best friend, depending on the pecking order of the week. Rebozo is supposed to shy strictly away from politics. That's a mocking laugh. Rebozo is so apolitical that he maintains a private kind of hot line to senators. There never is the slightest indication or suggestion that the White House wanted Rebozo to advocate something.

But senators contacted always have been his guests in the past. So was Nixon. They became fast friends back in 1951. Rebozo, Florida born, made money the hard way. He has valuable stretches of property at Key Biscayne, in Florida. When Nixon was a senator in 1951, he was recommended to Rebozo. Former Senator George Smathers arranged the introductions. Today a Washington lawyer, Smathers also was a close friend of President Kennedy.

Of Cuban parentage, Rebozo apparently never displayed flashes of any Latin temperament. His style, especially with Nixon, has been to listen. Through the years, Nixon opened up to him on dozens of subjects. Rebozo heard but said nothing to anyone else. He got the President interested in some property at Key Biscayne. Nixon often divides time away from the White House between Key Biscayne and San Clemente, California. And Rebozo never says no when he gets a call from the White House to come to dinner. He always is ready and makes the command appearance.

A property owner close by Key Biscayne is Bronx-born Bob Abplanalp. He is big, new money that came from inventing the aerosol valve. Some time ago, Abplanalp invested in a private sanctuary. It's a 125-acre estate at Grand Cay in the Bahamas. Broad-beamed and patently delighted to be a personal friend of the President, Abplanalp has been protective. He has, however, gotten into some public activities which Rebozo shunned. It may be a form of self-fulfillment for a boy from the Bronx to serve on a few White House advisory commissions.

Nixon's personal friendship with outsiders—that is, unofficial people—created crosscurrents of envy and jealousy. It was never more glaringly evident than in the Senate. The President knew all the Republican senators. Many actively supported him in 1968. Fellow citizens are always solemnly told about the mammoth burdens imposed on the Presidency. That's supposed to account for so much of his isolation. A mystical quality, therefore, is created. Dirksen was one senator who knew all about the levers of power, and wouldn't be stopped if he wanted to see the President.

Majority Leader Mike Mansfield had breakfast with Nixon about once a week or so. He almost never got to argue with the President about issues his fellow Democrats debated and wanted brought home to the White House. In a way, Mansfield is like Rebozo—a good listener and most taciturn. He was opposed to the Administration's handling of the war in Vietnam. Further, he assailed Nixon's economic policies. Talk about it to Nixon, eyeball to eyeball? Never.

The presidential elections altered little in the Senate and House. A senator, appointed by his governor, created something of a stir. He was former Congressman Charles Goodell, from upper New York State. Governor Nelson Rockefeller, on-again, off-again national candidate, appointed Goodell to the Senate. It was after the tragic murder of Bobby Kennedy in a Los Angeles hotel. Possessed of a nondescript record in the House, Goodell also in 1964 supported Barry Goldwater's running mate, Bill Miller.

The appointment raised eyebrows, especially among moderate to liberal Republican senators. Goodell switched positions and public attitudes almost immediately upon appointment. He fluttered with the most notable of the doves. Worse, he began to assail a Republican President by name. That technique Javits, from New York, always carefully avoided. Javits never attacked the President personally and always stood by to volunteer as a conciliator-mediator. Nixon didn't care for him, either. Both men kept a studied silence toward each other. It was very different with Goodell.

High among those Goodell consulted about conduct of his senatorial office was Mayor John Vliet Lindsay of New York City.

They both had been in the House of Representatives. In those days, Goodell regarded Lindsay the way Goldwater does any one with liberal inclinations. Counsel from Lindsay made the difference with Goodell, the Senator. Without much thought for the feeling the White House had about maverick Republican Lindsay, Goodell was always on the side of the most rabid anti-Nixon Democrats. Within days of the installation of the new Senate, he also tangled with Vice-President Agnew. It provoked some of the spiciest name-calling in years. Remember, though, that Lindsay delivered the seconding speech in Agnew's behalf six months before at the conventions in Miami.

"I made a mistake," was the oversimplified explanation Lindsay gave me at a party.

That's pretty doubtful. Lindsay was playing a cagey political game. He thought he could sooner than later count on Agnew to come up with some assistance from his presiding perch. Agnew had once been a Rockefeller supporter. Lindsay and Rockefeller have about the same feeling for each other as Cain had for Abel. Lindsay had gotten downright neo-Byzantine. His advice to an appointed senator like Goodell assured an ultimate showdown with the White House. Moreover, it drew violent hostility from Agnew as a thank-you for the convention speech. Neither a bright legislator nor a lively wit, Goodell soon came to be considered, on a bipartisan basis, a patsy.

He complained about his treatment to Bryce Harlow. Short, dapper, and energetic, Harlow was the President's Assistant for Congressional Relations. During the Eisenhower years, Harlow had been in a similar role. At Goodell's request, they met. Goodell beefed about the flak showering on him from other Republicans and the White House. What had come over him? asked Harlow. Why had he changed 180 degrees?

"I feel this is what the people demand," replied Goodell. "This is an honorable change we all must make."

"What would you know about that?" shot back Harlow.

They had very little to talk about after that session.

Harlow had other, more nagging problems. After the Eisenhower Presidency he became an affluent lobbyist for one of the nation's mammoth soap pushers. When Nixon scraped into office,

Harlow was recalled to active duty. So well known was Harlow to Republican senators that they tried to see him and consult with him. Others on the liaison level in the White House were ignored to a large extent. Many were new to the assignment. Others deferred too noticeably. And some were so partisan on any given issue that they raised hackles on even very conservative Republican senators.

Devoted Nixonite Senator Robert Dole, Republican of Kansas, soon became annoyed with a breakdown in communications between the White House and Capitol Hill. At the time, he told me, it was "either God-awful or sloppy." Dole, a World War II hero as a very young officer, was in quest of power, as were the majority of his colleagues. He always remained unflinchingly loyal to Nixon. When nobody else would rise in the Senate chamber to defend the President from some partisan attack—because few were ever on the floor—Dole did it. A good extemporaneous speaker, by Senate standards, Dole also was meticulous about detail. At any opportunity, he challenged Fulbright. In his most senior parliamentary manner, Fulbright complained of Dole's brashness. He should keep his place as a fledgling senator, was the import of Fulbright's attitude.

Tongue in cheek, Dole would reply: "I'm so new at this, how could I understand what the Senator (Fulbright) demands?"

Off in the cloakroom of the Democrats, Fulbright stalked, livid with anger. Most colleagues, including those who supported him on Vietnam, were delighted with Fulbright's discomfiture. The world's most exclusive club revelled in using an old nickname that once was used for his first initial, "J." It was "Jinx."

While Dole dearly loved tilting with Fulbright, he was burned up about liaison with the White House. He sniffed at most of the advisers. More in sorrow, he thought they were letting down the Nixon Administration. Nixon's Presidency, said Dole, was one of the greatest in history. How could it be so many-splendored, I asked him one evening, if there was such a proliferation of boobs he saw on assorted echelons.

"You can't blame the President for each and every appointment," replied Dole. "Appointees make most appointments."

In a political sense, he had some right on his side. Patronage is a major problem to solve. Over the last dozen years, most major patronage jobs have come under civil service. A qualified Republican, let's say, had real trouble getting a patronage post. Dole also was miffed with the dilatory methods of Representative Rogers C. B. Morton. As the new GOP National Chairman, the towering Morton didn't seem to extend himself very much. Jobs that finally came up were often given to people in states that hadn't supported Nixon. Miserable liaison was a major part of the problem, Dole felt. It became Morton's fault. In two years' time, Bob Dole would have Morton's national chairmanship.

During the transition-honeymoon phase, general agreement prevailed among Republican senators and the White House that a Republican President's image needed to be polished brightly. Television was the most immediate outlet on a national scale. Those immediately entrusted with communications, like Herb Klein, were fully aware of the media's anti-Nixon propensities. But any incumbent President has a tremendous asset because he occupies the office. He can deliver himself of a few thousand well-chosen words to the public at prime times of his choice. The opposition simply cannot. For some time the debt-riddled, disorganized Democrats didn't respond. Then, as honeymooners began to close the chapter of a relatively idyllic period, Democrats began to chant for equal time. This is for free. Networks don't like it.

Quite a few advertising men were in important spots in the White House. Crew-cut Bob Haldeman, a keeper of the keys, was an exemplary product. Press Secretary Ron Ziegler was another. Almost every senator has a TV complex. He'll look for the cameras, usually talk *non-sequiturs*. But he treasures the few seconds on camera, as he'd husband blocs of votes. Very useful, too, in splicing film when a man runs for re-election. There is nothing like the Capitol rising behind the senator for background. Even a peasant behind a water buffalo has probably seen a postcard with a picture of the domed Capitol.

The wait-and-see phase was drawing to a close. Nixon had begun careful withdrawals of troops from Vietnam. Doves started to clamor that he wasn't moving fast enough. Reform-minded senators relapsed. They thought it would be best to attack problems like the filibuster rule next year. The Senate, mind you, has a rule for nearly every occasion. It makes for continuity and durability. While these issues were downgraded, a gathering storm—ethics—hovered over the Capitol.

Behind the neighborly façade of the presidential honeymoon, a full-time investigation was gathering momentum. Target: one of the country's most honored lawyers, presently an Associate Justice on the United States Supreme Court. Outwardly austere and surgical of mind, Abe Fortas had already been categorized as a new Louis D. Brandeis. Fortas, who rose to command a $200,000 annual income before joining the highest court, enjoyed and paid for the good and stimulating life.

He had helped to found the Washington law firm of Arnold, Fortas, and Porter. It was most prestigious. Thurman Arnold was FDR's Solicitor General and oft-used trouble-shooter. Merry Paul Porter was a big wheel in New Deal and Democratic politics. President Truman frequently turned to him for help. He wandered around the world to report on problems for the President. In 1947, after the Truman Doctrine, Porter personally looked at torn-up Greece. In the same fashion, Abe Fortas became a confidant of Lyndon B. Johnson.

They were both of humble origins. And both, using their wits in different albeit highly skilled ways, ascended to the top. Fortas owned a splendid Georgetown house, filled with tasteful, expensive paintings. He was a talented amateur musicologist and played the violin with tender understanding. Chamber music was a major relaxation for the eminent lawyer. His wife, the former Carolyn Eugenia Agger, was one of America's foremost tax lawyers. She also was in the firm. They shared a Rolls Royce and a costly summer home in Connecticut. The Fortas's tastes were mighty expensive. But they were not loud, but muted like inherited gentility. Fortas, as a man of prodigious intellect, was closest to LBJ.

He walked in and out of the White House at presidential behest as if there were swinging doors. His name was an open sesame anywhere. Fortas handled fat cat clients—who paid through the nose for his talented services—and underdogs. His advocacy of the poor and seemingly mistreated heaped honors on Fortas. The big fees were never publicly noticed or even cared about. Lawyers universally approved Fortas. They admired and respected his talents. His friend in the White House did, too.

On a searing Washington afternoon, July 29, 1965, LBJ asked Fortas to come by for a chat. They talked briefly of the world at large and Vietnam, in particular. Leaning forward in his rocker, LBJ burst out:

"I'm sending 50,000 men to Vietnam and I'm sending you to the Supreme Court."

Any other man would never have dreamed of putting an assignment to Fortas that way. But Fortas and LBJ understood each other to the smallest of minutiae. The great lawyer accepted on the spot and LBJ made the announcement. Fortas had been making gobs of money since he had left government service twenty years before. Going to the Supreme Court could be a crowning accomplishment. LBJ had something else up his long sleeve. In good time, he intended to name Fortas Chief Justice. Earl Warren, Eisenhower-appointed Chief Justice, was soon to retire. He had already bedevilled conservatives with his decisions, which they hadn't expected from an Eisenhower appointee.

Warren, filled in by LBJ, agreed with alacrity to the choice of a successor. It all seemed so rosy. Johnson was king of the hill after a smashing election triumph of his own less than a year earlier. Escalating in Vietnam was heartily approved. Appointment of Fortas drew such written and spoken praise, it seemed that the second coming of a majestic temporal figure was with us. Even as he stood by President Johnson announcing his appointment, Fortas was aware of another agreement he made. For some reason, he never told LBJ. It might have terminated the appointment. Abe Fortas had negotiated a fee of $20,000 a year for life and for the life of his wife from a foundation. It was the family foundation of Louis E. Wolfson.

Wolfson, a rangy, former football great, turned financier, was serving time in a Florida jail. He had been sentenced for selling unregistered securities. Many millions were involved. How did it leak out? Originally through Wolfson, who later testified before a Senate subcommittee on inhumane, degrading conditions in a Florida jail. At his appearance, I asked him about some of the events of the Fortas deal. A Wolfson reply that stuck: "Fortas new all about it. He understood the problem because of my name. He isn't a little boy, you know." Fortas was confirmed by he Senate and swiftly sworn into office. That was in October 965. He had received his first—and only—payment of $20,000. Fortas, who amassed a fortune and respect, got around to paying back the stipend while he was on the bench!

Moreover, while on the bench, Fortas was consulted several times by Wolfson. A bit sadly, Fortas insisted he never interceded in any manner or form for Wolfson. His observation never made an impact. What did was an investigation, undertaken about a year before. It was time, LBJ figured, to have Fortas replace Warren. The Senate Judiciary Committee, as headed by Democrat James O. Eastland, the corpulent Mississippi all-around pol, and Roman L. Hruska, square-faced Nebraska Republican, dithered. They frankly didn't care for anyone like Fortas. His ultra liberalism unsettled them. Besides, LBJ was a lame duck. Some sleuthing and details of Fortas's espousal of varying liberal causes cranked up an Eastland-Hruska coalition to stop this appointment.

A whispering campaign, at which this gossipy community has no peer, was launched. Fact became intertwined with vicious fiction. Fortas's antecedents were invoked smartly. He was a Jew. Nothing could be ascribed to a witch's brew concocted by Eastland-Hruska. Most senior senators are past masters with untraceable stilettoes. Venetian assassins, character and otherwise, could have learned from them. A suggestion is offered, off the record, nonattributable, of course, and away flies the story. Fortas was kind of pinko, the reports circulated; he also was awfully lax on morals.

Eastland and Hruska, in this instance, shone as pillars of society. Darling of the lily whites in the South and receiver of fat farm subsidies, Eastland emphasized security and saw subversion all around him. Hruska, proclaiming ethical standards of unimpaired purity and probity to match, happily accepted all testimonial dinners in his behalf. Firms in the Midwest ran to buy tables to Hruska meals. Morality was a gallant, streaming standard attached to the Hruska helmet. His wife and he own a string of movie houses in Nebraska. Some of the most prurient films in the country draw sell-out audiences in Hruska theaters. That marvelous old Roman and father of TVA, Senator George Norris, surely gyrated in his grave.

Opposition, naturally, began to stir about making Fortas Chief Justice. LBJ tried all the political tricks in his bag. They didn't get far. A few senators have since wondered if Bobby Baker might have made the difference. He was a Johnson protégé, out of the deep South. Baker became chief clerk of the Senate under LBJ's sure guidance. Conflict of interest charges stopped Baker back in early 1964. LBJ had nobody as deft at arm-twisting any more. The AFL-CIO tried to go to the rescue. It was too late. Opposition was breaking out all over the Senate. A sordid fight was certain if Fortas's name was sent up as nominee for Chief Justice. Still, there was no inkling of the matter that blew the Associate Justice out of the water a year later.

Some puzzling bits of background, though, emerged from the inquiries that had been made. They centered around talks with the Wolfson Foundation. Yet nothing circulated for public titillation. In early May 1969 the storm broke. An article in *Life* magazine reported ties that bound Fortas to Wolfson. The periodical, in heavy financial going, had turned to investigative reporting in depth to mend its listing fortunes. It has been far superior in its efforts and digging than all the bureaus, commentators, and Capitol watchers combined. Still, the magazine needed a tip-off. That came from within the White House and double-checked out of the Department of Justice where a new team only a few months before took control.

Released fury hit the Fortas fan. The House of Representatives forthwith began planning a full investigation. With accompanying glee, so did Eastland-Hruska and their Senate committee on the Judiciary. In between, Associate Justice William Douglas and his ties to a Las Vegas gambling-financed foundation turned up. The Eastland-Hruska team and many in the Congress had long been after Douglas's hide. He was regarded as a near-revolutionary by enemies. Besides, his marrying ways didn't sit well with so many sanctimonious legislators. They undoubtedly admired his ways with women in secret. To top it all off. Douglas was a pretty good friend of Fortas.

Most admirers of Fortas pleaded with him in the media, and

whenever they could establish direct contact, to call the whole ghastly episode a cooked-up lie. It was like the little boy of yore going up to Shoeless Joe Jackson during the Black Sox baseball scandal. Theirs was the anguish of liberals, libertarians, and the self-righteous. It added up to the little lad's appeal: "Say it ain't so, Joe." Well, it was so, with Abe. In a fit of high-minded and outraged public spirit, congressional leaders suggested they would try to impeach Fortas. Only one similar case of impeachment of a Supreme Court Justice was ever tried. That was in 1804 and the Senate acquitted Samuel Chase.

Abe Fortas chose to let everyone, including himself, off the hook. He resigned in a letter to Chief Justice Earl Warren, the jurist he once had been touted to succeed. Relief, even with Eastland-Hruska, was the order of the day. Fortas's old firm—the one he helped to found—refused to take him back. He went into private practice. The immediate aftermath of the Fortas affair reverberates around the capital. It brought to a head all the ethical shocks that undermine the swampy footing in the community. There was sadness that a brilliant mind had been trapped in the easy ways of influence, money, and power. Ethics was something bandied around like a shuttlecock.

Politicians had to raise hundreds of thousands to millions of dollars to stay with the electoral process. How could anyone remain in office without proving special treatment to generous donors? Senior officials need a business they can leave temporarily in order to serve as responsible public servants. Life-long officials, for example, yearn for the security of foundations and corporations after retirement. Investment tips, loans, contacts, agreements are all part of the technique to sustain men placed in office by the public. There have been all kinds of programs to reform this latter-day spoils system. They have gotten nowhere. A senator doesn't think twice about reporting $50,000 in fees for speeches written by a staff member. And he didn't even have to report that until 1969. The Fortas affair caused some self-examination. Not for too long, though.

Soon Associate Supreme Court Justice William J. Brennan discreetly disclosed that he had been a business partner with Fortas. It was a profitable real-estate combine. Other big-name people were in the partnership. Brennan gave up his realty interest and sold stock he owned. He had a 1.4 percent interest in an apartment complex called Concord Village at Arlington, Virginia, a suburb of the capital. Brennan's share was worth about $15,000.

Not so hasty, however, was Senator Abe Ribicoff, Democrat from Connecticut. Darkly handsome in a saturnine way, Ribicoff grabbed some national prominence at the uproarious Democratic convention in Chicago. On the platform he tangled with Mayor Richard Daley sitting just below him. Ribicoff didn't let his feelings for the downtrodden interfere with a fair profit. He was a partner in the housing deal. So were Mrs. Fortas, former Associate Justice Arthur Goldberg, and two top militantly liberal capital judges: Chief Judge David Bazelon of the Federal Circuit Court of Appeals and Judge J. Skelly Wright of the same court.

Such business ventures are absolutely legal. But they do raise a profound moral question. Would a potential lucrative deal be available to any of them had they not held those positions? Is a man a legislator, jurist, or public servant without fetters if he has these and similarly tempting prospects? The quality of profit is by no means strained in the Senate. In thunderous floor speeches, members have declaimed the need to close all loopholes. Even as he was agreeing, Senator Joseph M. Montoya, Democrat of New Mexico, had his name on a wad of what are known as "ship jumper" bills. These are private immigration bills designed to aid Chinese ship jumpers. Such bills ask that the alien be permanently admitted to the U.S. Often the grateful claimant winds up in a Chinese restaurant working for coolie wages. But he won't be sent back to mainland China.

Maybe with a fresh, mutual accommodation between the People's Republic of China and this country, the aliens admitted will be regarded differently. Anyway, the practice persisted, although slowed down. Between Montoya and reform-minded Senator Gaylord Nelson, Democrat of Wisconsin, they chalked up 121 ship-jumpers' bills in a year. Nelson and Montoya heatedly have denied knowledge of this type of sponsorship. Senate aides brought them to the floor.

It was probably a feeling of high-minded sacrifice that also led senators to sponsor those bills. Another Democratic senator who offered a mass of bills was Harrison A. Williams, of New Jersey. Against his name he had seventy bills in a year. In small lots ship-jumper bills have been sponsored by such sensitive senators as George McGovern, South Dakota Democrat. Lee Metcalf, another Democrat, from Montana, has more modest ambitions. They did not deter him from ship-jumper bills.

Because of objections from senatorial desk neighbors, Metcalf switched from whiskey to vodka. Too often his breath came on in an overpowering way. He also concealed paper cups behind hydrants and other conveniences on the way to the floor. When a special bill to fight crime was being voted on in the Senate, Metcalf —briefed in advance—was dozing. The alphabet reached the "M's" and his name was called.

"Nay," shouted Metcalf and rushed for the floor exit.

Appalled, colleagues rushed after him. He could change his vote. Disconsolately, the pursuers returned empty-handed. Wise old Sam Ervin, North Carolina Democrat and a most learned jurist on constitutional law, saw the Metcalf vote this wry way:

"Lee was the only one in the Senate to vote for crime."

A delegation of Indians from Montana reservations came to see Metcalf. They abruptly broke off their colloquy. Why? "He [Metcalf] better change his brand of firewater," said the spokesman for the delegation, rather disgustedly.

But usually senators become aroused when it is fashionable to be angry in public against a traditional pillar of untouchability. Racketeering and corruption, for example, can ultimately trigger an inquiry with untold political dividends for examining senators in this era of instant electronic communication. TV can do wonders for a senator with sagging fortunes but with some screen acumen.

For more than twenty years there had been recurring reports and even published accounts of PX pilferage abroad. Stories of post exchange conflict-of-interest bribes abounded in military installations on allied and other foreign soil. Officers in charge of PXs were occasionally transferred, resigned their commissions, and a few were even jailed. It was all carried out pretty *sub rosa*. No point in getting the public unnecessarily inflamed. Military appropriations accounted for the single biggest slice of the national budget. For more than a generation nearly every senator had been happily characterized by the Pentagon as "defense minded." The cohesiveness began to fall apart rapidly as the war in Vietnam dragged on and uproar replaced unity.

Corruption in the military suddenly provoked a searching, new look from a Senate subcommittee looking into racketeering in the military establishment. The most alarmed senators on the panel— so they appeared on TV—were the chairman, Abe Ribicoff, and his liberal Republican colleague from Illinois, Charles E. (Chuck) Percy. A young man who made good by heading a great corporation, Percy went after the accused like a converted zealot. Curiously, neither Percy nor his reform-driven chairman ever indicated much interest in the infectious problems a couple of years before. Corruption and bribery were a sickly part of the known scene for a long time. At hand, though, was the grisly massacre at My Lai. Macabre details were leaking out, making instant national headlines.

Almost to parallel these wretched revelations came a spate of accusations and testimony from the Ribicoff committee. It turned from misfeasance and misconduct in the $400 million PX system in Europe to carpetbagging in Vietnam. The military, reeling from an antimilitary wave washing over the country because of Vietnam, was pummeled to the ropes. Tales of hidden Swiss bank accounts opened with money from bribes came from witnesses. The accused used the Fifth Amendment in their defense as much as did Cosa Nostra and Mafia organizers in years gone by. After a session, a listening, spectator senator uttered a cry from the heart.

"Can't anyone here play this game straight?" he observed acidly.

He was John J. Williams, Republican from Delaware. Williams, feared and respected by his colleagues, was called "The Watchdog of the Senate." He was fiercely fair-minded and ferociously incorruptible. When he said years before that no senator should hold office after the age of sixty-five, he meant it.

Other senior fellow senators ignored Williams's appeal on a voluntary age limit of sixty-five. They ran the gamut, to tick off a few, from septuagenarian Southerners like John Stennis, out of Mississippi and life-long advocate of the military; Eastland, of Mississippi, to Louisiana's Allen Ellender, at eighty the oldest

man in the Senate. He succeeded Senator Russell as chairman of
the Appropriations Committee. Through his stamina, Ellender
proved seniority has its own rewards. The Republicans have their
own share of the geriatric circuit: George Aiken, of Vermont;
Mrs. Margaret Chase Smith from Maine, and John Sherman
Cooper, the Kentucky gentleman. When Aiken ran for re-election
in 1968, he spent less than $5—for postage.

Another senator decided that, at eighty, he had had enough.
Irascible Stephen M. Young, Democrat of Ohio, went home. A
veteran of two World Wars, he was triumphant in two uphill,
upset elections to the Senate. Young was a great letter writer. He
answered critics personally. He scrawled their names on the wall
of his office. When the reply was completed, Young drew a line
through the names on the wall. It was the only known graffiti work
in the United States Senate as we went into the last thirty years
of the Twentieth Century.

VII

A SENATE
FOR ALL SEASONS

Other handwriting, in a manner of speaking, appeared in large, bold letters all around the Capitol. Partisan politics in the Senate took shape. It was aimed directly at the Presidency. Most of the media, its advocacy showing objectively, took sides immediately with the time-on-target critics. Their complaints revolved around a retreaded phrase: "Credibility Gap." It had been eminently useful against the now-gone LBJ Administration. Cooperative in tandem were putative power brokers. They were known, often fawned upon, as "Assistant Senators." Some even graciously accepted the label of "Shadow Senators."

The public only rarely has heard of these people. They have been a vital adjunct to senators for generations. Lately their influence has become enormous. Quite a few managed to make it as the legislators behind the seat. They are administrative aides, legislative assistants, and staff directors of committees. Add on directors and staffs of Senate subcommittees and the taxpayer is confronted with an entrenched bloc of centurions. All told, ten thousand men and women are on Congress payrolls. The lion's share belongs to the Senate. It is, naturally, appropriate for the world's greatest deliberative body.

Investigators have been hired and fired by directors of these committees. Administrative aides to senators consult closely with heads of committees of which their boss man is chairman or a member. High in this setup, perhaps at the top of the senatorial anthill, stands the Senate Committee on Foreign Relations. As the public has learned from TV shots, interviews and conditioned reactions, Senator Fulbright has headed the committee longer than anyone else in Senate history. His right-hand man for as long has been Carl Marcy. An academic turned superbureaucrat, Marcy never has been known to contradict opinions and ideas of his mentor.

Marcy has supervised a separate State Department. It is of Fulbright's creation and works on his Arkansan time. When Fulbright was a strict orthodox Southern senator in domestic and foreign affairs—most of his public life—the committee followed his direction without question. After Fulbright adopted the orthodoxy of heterodoxy on foreign relations in opposition to the Presidency, his committee went along in loyal lockstep.

Much more fervor and dash were displayed with Fulbright's vast range of inquiries and diatribes. Zestfully, his committee tore into "the role of the Executive branch of government," meaning the President. They alternately nibbled and hacked away at alliances, bases, Executive privilege, commitments, and budgets. Executive privilege could be the heart of the matter where the Presidency is directly and vitally concerned.

Fulbright's and his staff's demands on Executive privilege may well be unconstitutional. Senator Ervin has suggested as much. He knows the law inside out. Using the war in Vietnam and general war weariness, Fulbright has airily ignored constitutional restrictions. He has made up his own as time goes by. His loaded questions always require replies that are tailored to Fulbright themes. Witnesses are usually unfortunate and badgered when they come under his fire. Fulbright pursues issues and answers just as did Joe McCarthy. The differences? Fulbright is on foreign issues and McCarthy went after communism. Fulbright also dresses better than did McCarthy.

His creased, sartorial splendor meant nothing to rumpled George Meany. The tough old AFL-CIO chieftain shook off the McCarthy-type bully-ragging tactics of Fulbright. Before an open committee hearing, which Fulbright tried futilely to keep private, the Senator kept breaking off lances in Meany's leathery hide. Fulbright, for example, insinuated that Meany's union got an LBJ payoff to help with foreign activities in return for support on Vietnam.

Roared Meany: "You feel that anyone who disagrees with you on foreign policy must have some ulterior motive. Who paid you for supporting our policy in Vietnam? . . . I have as much right to say that somebody paid you for . . . the Tonkin Gulf resolution as you have to say that Johnson [paid] me for supporting him in Vietnam."

Snapping down his dark outfielder's glasses for the TV cameras, Fulbright wondered if the AFL-CIO might not have engineered the assassination of Kenya's American-trained political heir apparent, Tom Mboya. But, too few Americans, Fulbright included, know the tangled political plights of West and East Africa. Mboya was an American labor protégé. His loss was keenly felt. Fulbright's twisted query had totally missed the point. Of course, Fulbright sounded more scholarly. His attitude on origins and ethnic backgrounds has caused considerable alarm.

As a Southern reactionary, Fulbright has always made it clear that we have no obligation to inferior races. Color them black for Africa, or yellow for Asia. In a similar vein, he has gone on the attack against Professor Edward Teller and Dr. Jerome Wigner, nuclear scientists who disagreed with him. They both came from central Europe. Both were Jews.

"Your background," I heard Fulbright tell Wigner condescendingly, "probably accounts for your feelings."

The subject was coexistence with the Soviet Union: Wigner paled with indignation. The import of Fulbright's reference was unmistakable. But that kind of tactic wouldn't work with so powerful a personality as Meany. Sure, said Meany, he'd like a peaceful accommodation. But remember the Soviet takeover again in Czechoslovakia. And how about Castro and the Soviet-sparked missile crisis in Cuba?

During the lengthy hearing, Marcy passed newspaper clippings and memos to Fulbright. In turn, the Chairman shot questions at Meany based on underlined notes from Marcy. Earlier, Marcy held a preparatory staff conference. Serious of mien behind horn-rimmed glasses and with a thick cigar in his right hand, the Foreign Relations Committee chief of staff went over possible questions and answers.

Exchanges like these are usual from the President's press secretary to committee directors on every level in the Capitol. Some are held daily. Most about three times weekly. Others once a week. Because the Senate's Foreign Relations Committee is one of the most prestigious, it is ensconced in the Capitol on the first floor. A huge committee meeting room dominates the office. Its decor is on the old-fashioned side in keeping with the Senate chamber's traditionalism.

A separate office, a smallish one with a big desk, contains the quarters of the chief of staff, just to the left of the conference table. A couple of small working desks at discreet ends of the main room are for secretaries and file cabinets. In other corners are cubicles, desks, and files for staff and special assistants. Aides who made names for themselves furnishing data to Fulbright when he launched assaults on the Presidency attended most Marcy-conducted staff meetings.

They have diversified talents. The most prominent speechmaker is Seth Tillman, who hails from MIT where he was a professor of political sciences. Tillman appeared at well-known forums in the name of the full committee. His addresses have been spiked with anti-Vietnam war rhetoric for at least five years. Most senators on the committee never knew that he was making a speech or on what until they read about it somewhere.

Walter Pincus, occasional itinerant newspaperman, did lots of investigative digging for the committee. He generally worked for Senator Symington, onetime pro-military apostle in charge of a Foreign Relations subcommittee looking into American commitments. United States bases and why they still existed from Thailand to Spain were Pincus's targets. He thought we shouldn't have any to speak of. Once Pincus brought back what was presumed to be a devastating report on our bases and commitments in Spain. It was an interesting screed—for someone who could barely order ham and eggs in Spanish. But Pincus had a distinct point of view. It was shared by his bosses.

A couple of former Foreign Service officers, with brief tenure there, wandered at times around Asia. When Southeast Asia flamed steadily in the news, that's where they went. One of their reports on Cambodia was in the main filed from Bangkok. That's perfectly correct except for one thing. They filed most of the commentary before they set foot in Cambodia. These men, a traveling duet and Fulbright's answer to happily forgotten Cohn and Schine (Roy Cohn and G. David Schine) are James Lowenstein and Richard Moose.

Another, a specialist on Latin America, has a well-earned reputation as a good digger and commentator. He is Pat Holt. His reports, for instance, on Bolivia, Venezuela, and Peru have been most perceptive. When the gist of one such report appeared in one of our bigger newspapers, Fulbright raised an enormous fuss. It had been marked "private" for Senate members and sent to their offices. Which of the fifteen leaked the information would be hard to learn. Only Fulbright can do the leaking for the committee. For him this is his special parish. Most secrets are ill kept in Washington, anyway. That may be why Kissinger is such a constant target. He's one of the few who can—and does—keep his mouth shut.

Another is lanky Richard M. (Dick) Helms. Director of the Central Intelligence Agency since mid-1966, Helms is the first intelligence career officer to head up the CIA. His agency has for many years been criticized, envied, and cut up by former insiders and many outsiders. As a major figure in providing assessments on world conditions where they affect this country, Helms sits on hush-hush committees. There he meets with the President, Kissinger, sometimes Secretary Rogers, and a host of personnal counselors to Nixon.

Fulbright has assiduously attempted to cultivate Helms. He wants to have Helms approve of any suggestion he may offer. Helms never has, for Fulbright or for any other senator. When called to appear before the Foreign Relations Committee, it is always in closed session. Fulbright at every session sought to induce the reserved but articulate fifty-eight-year-old Helms to come down even obliquely on his side of an argument. He has never made a snide remark about Helms. It is unique. The explanation may stem from this assessment I got from an old, still active associate of Helms:

"Fulbright tries to make Dick the meat in the sandwich. Helms is on home ground when he talks of things Fulbright tries to snag him on. He knows the techniques and the tactics of most. He sticks to the information as he acquires it. But Fulbright won't give up."

I believe I know what he means. Personally, I have known Helms nearly thirty years. His attitudes never altered. Helms has a puckish smile and a long, retentive memory. That's a lot longer than any senator has. Helms won't rap any senator or public official. If he ever puts his own experiences between covers, then we'll know. It did not inhibit Fulbright from archly suggesting to George Meany that secret CIA funds were being slipped to his organization for cooperation abroad. Meany blew Fulbright out of the water on that one, too. His organization didn't need government money to function abroad. Study of the union's expenditures showed how the AFL-CIO spent tens of millions of dollars. Would Fulbright review the accounts instead of relying on some clippings?

Meany could fight it out with Fulbright and do better than hold his own. With few exceptions junior senators and entrenched bureaucrats wouldn't risk a tangle, and didn't. It became quite clear after Fulbright renewed his attacks on foreign policies that he had a big hangup on the Pentagon. While Senator Russell was alive, Fulbright laid off. He showed mild annoyance. Once Russell became fatally ill, the foreign relations specialist from Arkansas tore into the military.

His objectives were neatly defined. The military sought clumsily to ferret out additional information as the My Lai massacre drew the goriest of headlines. Senators on the Foreign Relations Committee, as Democrat Frank Church, of Idaho, and Cooper, of Kentucky, urged resolutions and amendments on the Senate whittling down our commitments. Church, who had been a boy orator back home, tried to pass himself off as a latter-day William Borah. His concern, always at the ready when a camera crew appeared, didn't match natural political prudence. Church always hammered out compromise deals. They never went as far as his rhetorical outrage.

He always was a perfect yes-man to Fulbright's warnings about the military getting away with murder. In his zeal, Fulbright got caught out by another Southerner. He lashed out on the floor against Stennis. No traditional Southern courtesy there. Besides,

Stennis ran the Senate Armed Services Committee. He also conducted the panel that passed on senatorial ethics. The body never examined civil rights, of course. Thus, Fulbright one afternoon astounded Stennis. They both shared similar views on all domestic issues. But Fulbright, powering his fight with the military because of involvement in foreign affairs, was decidedly anti-ABM.

In Washingtonese, everything comes up with initials. ABM, of course, means antiballistic missile. The Administration, as had previous ones, asked for extended sites and deployment. Lobbies for each group mounted hot campaigns. Fulbright, on the side, even suggested to Senator William B. Spong, Jr., Democrat of Virginia, that he'd get him membership on the Fulbright committee. He would, provided Spong voted anti-ABM. Infuriated, Spong voted for it, as was his original intention. A couple of years later, he got a seat. A vacancy was there for a Southerner. Spong knew his politics, too.

Fulbright's temper got the better of him. When Stennis disagreed with Fulbright, the latter blew his top. He characterized senators who disagreed with him on the ABM as stooges for the Pentagon. A few years before, a senator making such charges on the floor would probably have been faced with a censure accusation. Not any more. Fulbright then apologized to Stennis. They shook hands. No hard feelings, you note, between old Southerners. Fulbright subsequently "edited" his thunderbolts for the *Congressional Record*. Senators can do that. They often do through aides who handle language better than do the senators.

The oncoming battle over the ABM vote was provocative to anti-ABM lobbyists. They counted on Ted Kennedy to be the spearhead. Some managed to slip in and see him for a few minutes. Their intentions and fervor were written on expressions. Out they came from Senator Kennedy's offices, hurt feelings patent.

"He hasn't even read most of the material," they complained.

Had they known their way around better, the lobbyists would have gotten straight to one of the office aides riding herd on the issue. The eager, new lobbyists learned quickly. Riding the Fulbright hobbyhorse paid dividends. He had a new plaything with which to belabor the Pentagon. It was the Green Beret case. A Green Beret wearer was a member of the Special Forces. They were specialists at counterinsurgency. Established by the late brothers Kennedy, the Army didn't much care for them. The Green Berets were a very elite, highly honed organization. In Vietnam a detail was accused of having liquidated a Vietnamese double agent. The military and the CIA were accused of all kinds of conspiracy. The hired agent, playing the dangerous game, became something of a hero to anti-Vietnam forces. When asked straight questions by our commanding officer in Vietnam, General Creighton (Shorty) Abrams, top Green Berets were evasive.

They were pilloried in the media. In addition, they were transferred from hairy assignments to back home. Between times, the men involved spent some time in the stockades in Vietnam. Once again Fulbright blew the episode into his own calculated weariness with the state of affairs the United States conducted. He got plenty of mileage, something he shrewdly conceived. Fulbright was as instrumental as any single personality in riddling the military organization. Church and he had just shown public indignation over commitments to Thailand. At least Church used the qualification of "rumor has it," when saying that we were ready to order troops to help Thailand in an emergency. Yet the indignation needed another look when releases were handed to the press as the TV cameras began to grind.

Ancient draft director General Lewis B. Hershey seemed to symbolize Selective Service resistance. The idea of the midseptuagenarian employing old-fashioned yardsticks to call up draftees crystallized Senate and much of the national opposition. Seeking once to get a clue to Hershey's possible retirement, easily annoyed Senator Tom Dodd talked to him in his office. The conversation soon heated the room. In his plodding manner, Hershey raised the dander of Dodd.

"I know what's wrong with the whole draft system," Dodd shouted angrily, to Hershey. "It's you!"

Not quite, but the infuriated remark was symbolic. At the top the Pentagon sheltered quite a few fools, political plotters, and cynically venal men. So does the United States Senate. But the military must come to the Senate—to the House, too—for money. Where senescent and overage men can play with power and insist on dignity, the military can do little to dissemble before its peers.

As the Senate generally shifted gears to go from a tabby cat relationship with the Pentagon to an irritated lion's growl of defiance, something new was added. American prisoners of war drew attention.

They were hapless servicemen shot down over North Vietnam or prisoners seized by Communist ground forces. About 1,300 were reported missing. Less than one hundred were heard from. All one hundred senators urged their release. But techniques varied. Fulbright, for example, thought they would all be released if we withdrew swiftly from Vietnam. At negotiations in Paris, North Vietnam and the Viet Cong (formally called the National Liberation Front) spurned requests for Red Cross inspection. Peace groups visited selected POWs and got letters from them. Some senators like McGovern took off to talk to the Communists in Paris. He returned from his efforts at humanitarian statemanship repeating the demands of the North Vietnamese.

Ambitious and annoyed senators, turning their backs on Nixon's phased withdrawal plans for our troops in Vietnam, stormed and raged on the floor about the war. A foremost critic, whose Democratic colleagues had by acquiescence handed him the presidential nomination for 1972, was hailed for a staff-written denunciation only a day before catastrophe intruded on his aspirations. Up near Martha's Vineyard, in a midnight drive, Ted Kennedy drove a car off a narrow bridge at Chappaquiddick into the gloomy waters below. Mary Jo Kopechne, a Kennedy campaign worker who lived with a couple of other girls in a rented Georgetown house on Olive Street, was trapped in the car and drowned. The episode had repercussions that may never cease.

Anti-Kennedy senators—there are lots even among those who profess outward amity and deference—exulted in a macabre fashion. Kennedyites, whether right or wrong, evoked the terrible background of two slain brothers. The dead girl and her small-town, Pennsylvania, stunned and grieving parents were nearly lost in the aftermath. Power pursuers, trailing any Kennedy banner, tried to retrieve their champion's fortunes. The family compound in Hyannis Port, not far from the tragedy, opened up for wordsmiths come to Ted's rescue.

Two priests, long friendly to the Kennedy family, flew down

to Pennsylvania to comfort the parents, frozen with grief. They arrived much faster than it took Senator Kennedy to summon help. Miss Kopechne had gone up for a long weekend with some other office girls, regarded as swingers in their political set. Sailing and al fresco picnics had been on the holiday agenda. All the girls were unmarried. Mrs. Joan Kennedy, Ted's wife, was not present. A Kennedy male cousin was with the rollicking weekend group. Another companion telephoned his father, who confided later that: "My son is behaving like an idiot."

The small crumb of comfort Ted Kennedy could have drawn from the tragic episode was that he got only second billing. A rocket to the moon, Apollo 11, was in orbit. Senators, invited to watch the lift-off, forgot the excitement of a moon landing. Ted Kennedy's plight was for them Topic No. 1. His political star seemed to have set under the water where the hapless girl lay in the car nine hours before the accident was reported.

Every tidbit of information and gossip senators could get their hands on was eagerly absorbed and retransmitted. Friendly senators sent their own versions to the White House. President Nixon, preparing for the first leg of a round-the-world trip, kept mum. Information, nevertheless, poured into willing ears and hands from Kennedy's own club members. One finished a note of sympathy to Kennedy, signed it with a flourish, and observed: "That should take care of the son-of-a-bitch."

As the helpers and advisers closeted with Kennedy, they had a breathing spell for piecing the *mea culpa* apology together. Man walked on the moon for the first time in a two-million-year history. A brief remark by a pioneer astronaut, Neil Armstrong, was heard clearly over the din of Kennedy interpretations.

"That's one small step for man," declared Armstrong, "one giant leap for mankind."

And it was all on TV, to which the nation and much of the world was riveted with dread fascination. The Senate's Committee on Aeronautical and Space Sciences lauded the astronauts. Their capsule was appropriately named *Eagle,* members of the committee noted happily. Armstrong, his companion, Edwin (Buz) Aldrin, and space pilot Michael Collins were duly remembered as heroes known to the committee. Except for a couple of mem-

bers of the committee, none of the others had more than a vague
idea of who they were. Senator Clinton P. Anderson, the ailing,
aging Democrat of New Mexico, who headed the committee, got
some astronaut names mixed up. That was undoubtedly due to
the excitement of the first moon-landing ever.

Everyone, or so it seemed, basked in the afterglow of the moon
landing. Senators especially preened themselves. They spoke
glowingly of the feat and what would come next in future Apollo
missions. In hushed comments, however, they also sighed that
there had to be cutbacks in appropriations to the program. Getting
a piece of the limelight barely covered senatorial eagerness for
news of Chappaquiddick. Of course, that meant the fate of Ted
Kennedy.

Without Ted's presence, the Steering Committee of the majority
completed assignments. Senators who might stir up something
of a fuss are given committee posts in which publicity is at zero
level. If it is a more prestigious assignment, then the chairman and
ranking members could keep a new man's mouth shut. Steering
Committee is an apt name. The minority has its own. In all
assignments, seniority is a big factor. The longer a senator holds
office the higher in committee rank he goes. Ours is a committee
system. A prickly bill, or proposed legislation, can be carried
around in a chairman's pocket just about forever. Eastland, Fulbright, and Stennis have been deft masters of their own pocket
veto.

The moon shot and Chappaquiddick covered the Senate with
weariness. In the early part of the Ninety-first session, it had accomplished little in the field of legislation. Only publicity-enticing hearings and declarations seemed to count. Infectious drug
usage and accounts of pushing were certain to be written about
and televised. The new politics was certainly an emerging episode,
as seen by the Senate. There was the politics of drugs, the politics
of the environment, the politics of welfare, and the politics of the
war in Southeast Asia. The Senate showed itself a most subjective
body. Not only had it begun to splinter, but most issues became
very subjective. Even presidential ambitions broke through.
Muskie and McGovern led the way, three years before even any
conventions.

It caused particular surprise, therefore, that a Nixon proposal for revenue sharing went down well at first sight. The program provided for $5 billion to be appropriated by 1976 to state and local governments. Every senator pretends at one time that he is in touch and in tune with his state. In the next breath, he usually says that he possesses only the most superficial knowledge of home-state problems. Senators knew full well, particularly from the industrialized states, how bankrupt local governments were. They needed money. The revenue-sharing idea of Nixon sounded all right. Within a few months many changed their minds. They either wanted something different—or their own programs. But most of all, at this point, they wanted a holiday.

Senator Ralph W. Yarborough, a liberal Democrat from Texas, showed how they yearned to go homeward for a bit. His frequent impassioned appeals to save rare birds in Texas went unheeded. In his lates sixties, appearing much younger with a shock of black hair, he spotted an opportunity. More than two senators were on the floor. Freshman Democratic Senator Eagleton, of Missouri, was temporarily in the chair. Talk was desultory. Yarborough was recognized. In a semi-kneeling position near his desk, Yarborough made his appeal.

As he gradually straightened up, Yarborough twitted and tooted what were birdcalls. In the chair, Eagleton was convulsed in silent laughter. The few senators on the floor talked to each other. They paid no attention to the clemency birdcalls from Yarborough. When he straightened up, Yarborough urged that the Senate place the birds whose calls he imitated on the endangered species list. Vanishing fast, some of these birds were in a Texas park called "The Big Thicket." Yarborough made a telling point. The Senate adjourned for a brief holiday. It also was Yarborough's last major performance. A year later he was beaten for the nomination in the primaries.

Almost casually, the frightening word "revolutionary" had been reinvigorated. The White House used it with reference to new programs. Many senators claimed to have employed the term originally and to have been the first to say "revolutionary." They all signified change and they really meant revolutionary. But revolutionary was more of a piece of swinging semantics. It enabled senators to say they were understanding of restless youth and that revolutionary methods in certain key areas of society were compatible with the system. Vice-President Agnew made some references to the term. He looked on it alternately kindly and with hostility. It depended on which of the media he was attacking.

Resting or junketing, not a single senator wondered why joblessness increased. It wasn't much of a jump from 3.4 percent to 3.6. Yet the major trade unions were understandably perturbed. They read lots more coming into the bland figure. The Nixon Administration was pledged to damping down the economy and simultaneously to curbing inflation. Instead of some holiday examination into the jobless development, Fulbright led suspicious senators in wondering why Kissinger briefed NATO allies in Paris on Nixon's world trip. Had the senators devoted a little more attention, they might have noted Nixon launching his first initiative in foreign affairs.

It came in a tumultuous reception accorded him on a visit to Communist-run Romania. For seven or eight years, Romania's regime had stopped marching in tune with airs played in Moscow. It was not like Tito's in Yugoslavia, where Marx is half Karl and half Groucho. But Romania and its pudgy Communist No. 1, Nicolae Ceaucescu, were a communications channel to hardnosed enemies of the United States, notably Communist China. The approaches to the "People's Republic of China," the official name, came from Nixon to Ceaucescu. Although publicly Nixon got around a year or so later to referring to Mainland China by the name it demands statesmen use, he employed the stilted label in talks to Ceaucescu. The United States-Romanian dialogue on the highest level was presidential personal diplomacy. Fulbright never grasped the importance. Secretary Rogers was confused. In the whole Senate only Senator Scoop Jackson drew the conclusions.

Jackson, a serious and thoughtful member of the world's most exclusive club, became so involved in assessing Soviet and Communist Chinese policies, that he paid little heed to gadfly harassment by a fellow Democrat. Normally, Jackson is sufficiently shrewd to watch these irritations and excise them. Crusader William Proxmire, the irritant who would grow to be a major thorn, also had indicated to Jackson that he might well compromise. It was over the SST—the supersonic transport plane—vital in the economy of Jackson's home state.

Bald, health fan, Yale graduate, Bill Proxmire made a name for himself in Wisconsin. He had succeeded the late Joe McCarthy. Every working day, Proxmire jogs the six miles to the Capitol. He jogs home, too. No drinking, no smoking are high in his personal habits. Proxmire looks and sounds like a square. Hailing as he did from the dairy state of Wisconsin and its touted open spaces, Proxmire also battened onto the main ecological issues of clean air and water. That brought him eager, young, and some older environmental amateur lobbyists. The SST, if put into service, would foul up the already impure air space. So they declared.

Proxmire agreed, and these voluntary ecological helpers pitched in and straightened out much of Proxmire's haphazard agenda. The crusading senator also discovered about 1969 that there was waste and overcharging, amounting to billions, in military orders. He charged hard after that objective. Proxmire was the original "Mr. Clean" in the sense that Muskie, and to a lesser extent McGovern, tried to show as their very own. Proxmire also was up on his state politics. Big business and industry could usually find a compromise formula with him on potentially difficult problems with factories.

Proxmire also derived some special little pleasures out of needling Muskie and McGovern about their open presidential ambitions. He had his own ambitions to nourish. Proxmire waited until the Democratic field was cluttered at home plate and first base. Then, he solemnly noted he could be a dark horse, but a viable one. That was something new; a viable dark horse. The manner in which Democratic senators, professing progressive liberalism, tried togetherness in public has been tinged with a streak of hypocrisy.

Nearly all made snide comments about the others, collectively or individually. From a half dozen came cynical comments, for instance, just after McGovern went house-hunting and wound up with an expensive pad. His tiny, most hospitable wife was overjoyed. The house was decked out entirely in Japanese decor. It had been owned by wealthy, liberal-prone Judge Bazelon, who also happens to be a very canny business man. The price of the house and furnishings was well above the $100,000 mark.

Where did old George McGovern manage even to find the down payment? Before the Senate he had been on a less than $10,000 annual salary in a small South Dakota college. The tongues of his colleagues wagged furiously. In 1968, McGovern really acted as a stand-in for Ted Kennedy at the conventions. *Ipso facto,* McGovern got a large, interest-free loan from the Kennedys. If the reports reached McGovern, he never acknowledged them.

A well-heeled Democratic senator who didn't worry about contributions much but sympathized with those who did was Joseph (Swinging Joe) Tydings, of Maryland. His stepfather had been Senator Millard Tydings, done in by a scurrilous Joe Mc-Carthy-type phony photograph circulated widely. Rich, and a close friend of the wealthy Kennedys, Senator Joe Tydings followed big horizons. His after-hour activities often mystified his colleagues and upset some of them. Like the fallen of the Camelot crowd, Tydings keenly appreciated the ladies. Most senators indulge in the pretense that a magisterial decorum hangs over them solemnly.

By sheer coincidence Tydings got trapped early one morning in one of the cluster of small apartment buildings around the Capitol. Lots of senators and congressmen rent little flats if their families stay in the home state. In Tydings' case, it was in nearby Maryland. A bright morning, at 7:15, on the fourth floor of 128 "C" Street, N.E., Senator Len B. Jordan, Republican of Idaho, was wrestling in the elevator with a young assailant. At seventy, Jordan, a rancher, was fit for his age. The elevator, going down, stopped at the fourth floor because someone punched the button. When the door opened, Jordan and his attacker spilled out. Jordan shouted for help. An official account told of how Tydings looked out his own door. Too late. The assailant fled.

What went around the Senate, though, was that Tydings had a look at the scene and quickly propelled a lady visitor down the back way. Jordan was something of a hero in a community where

the crime rate was zooming at a scary rate. Patrols of two uniformed policemen covered the Capitol, a big dog between them.
It was a common sight. Jordan, who had a big lump on his head,
said of the incident: "It's ridiculous that you have to live danger-
ously like this. This could happen to anyone in the city. You
always wonder whether it's going to be robbery or whether the
motive is something else."

The Tydings' role was swept under the rug. It was something
for senators only to mull over. Club ground rules, you know.
Tydings would become an ex-senator later, for other reasons and
defeat at the polls. The Senate showed concern for a much more
eminent member. He was Minority Leader Everett McKinley
Dirksen, deft veteran in the black art of the politically possible.
Dirksen had undergone surgery for a malignancy. Within a few
days of surgery at Walter Reed Army Hospital, he died at seventy-
three. The highly skilled Senator, whose flamboyant and theatrical
style drove adversaries to the wall with frustration, was the target
of many and the victim of none. Most of his years were spent as a
minority politician in the Congress. He did wonders with depleted
troops. In the course of a long career, Dirksen was attacked for
getting big legal fees for his old home-town law firm. Democratic
colleagues frequently suggested that he stashed away wads of cash
and had secret Swiss bank accounts. They leaked anonymous
stories to that effect regularly.

As it turned out, Dirksen's estate was modest. Certainly he accepted large contributions. Then, he placed his own candidates
in key posts within the Capitol bureaucracy. His style earned him
a description as the "Wizard of Ooze." Venality attributed to him
was confused with the Dirksen quest for power and to solidify
it. He knew all about monkey business in the Capitol and what
was going on all the time. Dirksen could alternately flay someone
intent on defying him. Within minutes, he could switch and use
the velvet glove. A crowning achievement was the Civil Rights
Law of 1964. It became law largely because Dirksen worked hard
for it. Many of his liberal senatorial enemies sneered at his efforts
and his close ties to a former Democratic President, LBJ.

They closed ranks, however, to praise Dirksen. Laudatory
comments spewed from senators who hated him. It was typical

of the sanctimony of the world's most exclusive club. Never speak ill of the dead, only of the living. They made an exception. Ho Chi-minh died. Senators didn't say anything about him. They just wondered about the war and the conduct of North Vietnamese negotiators in Paris.

For timing, a much more pertinent issue gripped the Senate. Clement Furman Haynsworth, Jr., had been nominated by President Nixon to the Supreme Court. Haynsworth, of Greenville, South Carolina, was chief judge of the Fourth Circuit Court of Appeals. Senator Strom Thurmond, of the same state and a key operative in Nixon's nomination, was jubilant over the selection. Nixon had earlier designated Warren E. Burger as Chief Justice. He was a battle-scarred thirteen-year veteran of the crime war in Washington. Burger, from Minnesota, had fought liberals on the United States Court of Appeals. He believed firmly there was some connection between court decisions and crime.

President Nixon, within months in office, found he had two Supreme Court vacancies. It was a rare occasion. Chief Justice Warren retired; Abe Fortas resigned. A law-and-order majority on the nine-man Supreme Court appeared in the making. Burger was confirmed by the Senate almost instantly. With the nomination of Haynsworth, little difficulty was foreseen. Under Attorney General Mitchell, the Department of Justice did a routine check on Haynsworth. It seemed in order. A conservative record but nothing untoward. That was not, however, what the AFL-CIO uncovered. Battle was joined.

Haynsworth testified before the Senate Judiciary Committee. Chairman Eastland was benevolent. Not so Birch Bayh. Young and in quest of a more national future, Bayh stung Haynsworth with accounts of antiunion attitudes. Stock buying and selling raised conflict of interest charges. The Haynsworth nomination flared into the first major personality fight between the Senate and the President. Eastland led other Southerners in fierce tirades about Northern views. It was Thurmond who remarked bitterly that "the North doesn't ever want a Southern Supreme Court judge." A civil war on regional, political lines took shape in the Senate.

Smack in the middle of the battle stood George Meany and his politically sharp cohorts. They were openly determined to have the Senate reject Haynsworth. The force of big trade union-ism and the derogatory facts it acquired on Haynsworth compelled on-the-fence senators to retreat. In twos and threes, Republicans reported back to the White House, their vote would be against Haynsworth. To retrieve some, underskilled White House trouble-shooters tried to put pressure on doubtfuls in the Senate. The boomerang echoed throughout the Capitol.

Normal Nixon-liner Len Jordan spoke of arm-twisting that he couldn't tolerate. Delaware's Senator Williams, the Senate's in-flexible archangel, turned his back on Haynsworth. When the news of Williams's intention reached the White House, presi-dential assistant Haldeman moaned: "Even if we win, we lose." Factional fights over the nomination broke out everywhere in the White House. Thurmond and his protégé there, Harry Dent, were on the sticky end. The morning of the vote Bayh came over to see Tom Dodd. There was a certain coalition of fifty-two Democratic and Republican votes against Haynsworth, he re-ported. More, he suggested, would be forthcoming.

Feeling good about his role, Bayh became sympathetically indulgent. He could guess, he observed, how Dodd felt about the censure vote against him a couple of years before. It seemed that Bayh had heard that back home in Indiana inquiries were being made about his bank accounts and investments. Bayh had voted censure for Dodd. Now, said Bayh, he understood those pressures. At the moment—only then—there was kindred kindness. Senators lap up that type of treacle. The vote, called "up and down," which means yes or no, was a rejection of Haynsworth and a stun-ning setback for Nixon. The tally showed 55 against, 45 in favor, as the galleries applauded loudly. Senators don't like noise, one way or another.

A breakdown revealed a few interesting votes. Freshman Mike Gravel, Democrat of Alaska and one of the youngest senators, voted to confirm Haynsworth. Well on his way to a public reputa-tion as a lithe young man with a big family, Gravel acquired the dubious description by his colleagues as "the boy in the market place." Otherwise, why would a Democratic senator from Alaska vote for Haynsworth? Gravel had been designated a "liberal." Ful-bright also voted for Haynsworth.

Senator Albert Gore, known as the "White Fox" Democrat

from Tennessee, voted against Haynsworth. Before his vote, Martha Mitchell tried to persuade him to vote for a fellow Southerner. The wife of the Attorney General had just launched into telephone talkathons. Her views, generally most partisan, were at least blunt. In a town that thrives on wavelengths of hypocrisy, her late phone calls and party remarks left nothing to the imagination. In Gore's case, she didn't reach the Senator. He was generally anti-Administration and antiwar. The vote against Haynsworth, declared Martha at a party as she looked over her cocktail, was "just like the country slapped him [Haynsworth] in the face." Martha Mitchell was making news and adoring every line. It happens to people in Washington.

The Senate reached the Haynsworth moment of decision with up-and-down antics and soul-searching. Few concrete legislative results emerged. Grudgingly, ninety-nine senators gave the public a glimpse of their private financial interests. More revealing details, as income tax returns, were not available for public view. The reports finally provided a brief peek into personal contributions over fifty dollars in the last half of 1968. Big first, indeed! They also listed honorariums and book royalties. Little could be learned from the lists. Senator Ellender was late. But there was no apprehension. Failure to file and late filing carried no penalties whatsoever.

Fund-raising dinners, at outsized prices, flourished as if there never had been and never would be accountings. Joe Tydings, disdainful of money, was feted at a civic center by 2,500 close friends. Tickets were $100 apiece. The net to the Tydings team was $150,000. If you don't have available funds, a money raiser is a sure way to stay in business. There were "Appreciation Dinners" about the same time for three other senators. A $100-a-plate deal raised money for Hartke. Curiously, the dinner was given in Chicago. Hartke is from Indiana. The righteous sarcasm could always be applied from one senator to another. But he was always, personally, clean.

Two other senators drawing $100 a head were Hruska and astute Hugh Scott, minority leader after the death of Dirksen. Although from Nebraska, Hruska's "appreciation" fiesta was also in Chicago. It drew heavily on a business and industrial clientele.

Scott's was a stand-up, grab-a-drink affair in Washington. An acquaintance who bought five tickets invited me. In the crush, I managed to corral two highballs. I don't think anybody did much better. Pretty good. A drink at $50 a copy.

The Senate, pursuing the practice of high-cost testimonials, censured Dodd for using testimonial funds for his own benefit. Under the Senate's loose and wobbly code of ethics, funds raised like these can cover expenses from extra printing to TV reports. Inevitably they must place the beneficiary in the debt of the donors. Most ticket buyers are wealthy. They have special axes to grind. Bet on that. In a non-election year fund raising can be big business.

All these testimonials, interestingly, took place after the Senate was rocked by a big interest-peddling case in the House. Speaker John McCormack discovered from *Life* magazine that his trusted aide for twenty-four years was in an interest-peddling racket. Dr. Martin Sweig, the aide, was known personally to many senators. Involved with Sweig and subsequently indicted with him was a shadowy figure also known a long time to many in the Senate. Nathan Voloshen had wheeled and dealed out of a sizable number of Senate offices as well as the Speaker's.

Financial disclosure obviously could not reach unethical conduct. Morality and probity are quite personal. The Senate, that great body, has left it up to constituents to do the disciplining if fund-raising gets out of hand. The spasm caused by the grubby Voloshen-Sweig affair didn't stick long with the Senate. Fund raisers took precedence. So did contributions.

Hope crept in timidly with the Senate as it began the second half of the Ninety-first Congress. President Nixon's first year had been very private, grumbled most senators in a bipartisan spirit. They all like to be invited to White House functions. Dinners are a special treat because Mrs. Senator wants to be seen at glittering state meals. Guest lists are treasured; so are photographs to be mass reproduced for the great unwashed of the electorate back home. Nearly all the hundred senators got into the White House one way or another. But not all managed coveted dinner invitations.

Senior members fell into some philosophical speculation. The

sixties that had become stifling the last few years meandered
into ways and means of surviving the seventies. A fresh social
season opened. Senators and their wives in the majority like to be
asked out. The sight of presidential adviser Kissinger at every
White House dinner, and where the action supposedly swirled,
bothered lots of members of the world's most exclusive club.
Kissinger got more invitations in a fortnight to coveted affairs
than most senators in a year. Their exalted positions entitled them
to more consideration. So it was really in the Senate that Kissinger
earned the reputation of being a swinger. That was rather curious
for a Jewish boy out of the hallowed halls of academe. Some of
us, bantering with him at one of the capital's thronged cocktail
parties, asked to what he attributed his merit as a swinger.
Kissinger stared out at the bewrinkled ladies about him and said:
"If they can be hostesses, I can be a swinger."

He was referring to Washington's two major mealtime monu-
ments: Mrs. Perle Mesta and Mrs. Gwen Cafritz. Both enormously
rich, both given to extravagantly bad taste, they compete ferociously to attract names to their tables. Mrs. Mesta is very ancient.
Mrs. Cafritz less so. Seeing Perle Mesta in a voguish pants suit
is a sight indeed. Richly caparisoned, Mrs. Cafritz would be
perfectly at home in a Transylvanian castle scene with Bela
Lugosi. Hot pants were just coming into style, but the modish,
elderly ladies sometimes tried wearing them. Gwen Cafritz in hot
pants left Perle Mesta rigid. Their competition was wearing thin.
Senior senators and people-about-town of a certain vintage still
paid court. To the younger set of senators, and even the shards
of Camelot, the old girls were like something out of Mme.
Tussaud's. Traditionalists still thought of them in a most kindly
and indulgent light.

They were sort of like a rule of the Senate, ex officio, of course.
In the Senate the real rules for working, accommodating, and
breathing were fixed. Tradition, you know. There was that
Golden Rule on the filibuster. That was Senate Rule 22. It limits
duration of debate. The Senate, in the second phase of the Ninety-
first Congress, spoke with many voices. Reformists demanded
change. The Golden Rule demanded a two-thirds majority
limiting prolonged debate. Since World War I, that happened

only forty-nine times! Debate, of course, can be curtailed by unanimous consent. Ask a few who have tried when a major bill was under consideration.

Standing rules have been worked out for the media, just as for anyone else in the Senate. Sanctions exist for noncompliance. There are rules for supervision—not of news but for arrangements to gather it. Taking pictures or broadcasting is forbidden in Senate chambers. On only a few defined occasions can this be broken. One is when the President delivers the State of the Union message. A few others occur when a world personality arrives to speak. Seniority preserves are far stricter in the Senate than in the House, which has its own built-in reservations. When challenged on seniority traditions, senators have declaimed that advancing age should not be discriminated against. Senators Eastland and Stennis, for example, are among the more prominent champions of this defense. So are they, too, on the Golden Rule of the filibuster.

The Vice-President's major responsibility is to break the votes in the Senate. Agnew didn't have many opportunities in his first year. Yet Agnew, as any Vice-President, can and did rule at many stages on parliamentary and procedural questions. The Senate, in its omniscience, can override Vice-Presidential rulings. It had been too preoccupied with national needling as a do-little, or do-nothing, Senate to worry much this time about scoring brownie points against Vice-Presidential rulings on procedure. Loyal Senate club member, Majority Leader Mansfield, felt it necessary to defend his colleagues as hard-working and dedicated to the legislative process. His warm defense produced sniper attacks from senators on foot dragging in the House.

Between the House and the Senate a perennial bone of contention is their different methods of amending bills. In a House bill, amendments must be germane to the bill itself. The Senate, so special, can—and does—tack on almost any sort of amendment. That includes House-passed bills. They cover riders not only totally unrelated to the original bill but often more important and controversial. In addition, processes for bringing Senate-approved bills and conference-committee recommendations to the House floor differ glaringly from those used by the Senate on House-passed bills and conference reports.

How this maze could be traversed in the sizzling seventies didn't much bother the traditionalists in the Senate. Even some of the more avowed reformists stuck to essential traditions where it served their specific aims. Take a report that attracted little note at the start of the seventies in the Senate. It had considerable bearing on what was to follow in an election year—the mid-terms of the new decade. Seven senators reported, with a straight face, that it cost them nothing to get elected in 1968. That presidential year there were thirty-four Senate seats at stake, nearly the third that come up every two years. The candidates for those thirty-four seats reported to the Senate combined campaign spending of $2,714,464. Yet total expenditures for California alone were reported to the state as $4,451,849.

Senator Alan Cranston, who won the California seat, was one of those informing the Senate that campaign costs for him were zero. The reasoning was in accord with the Corrupt Practices Act of 1925. A candidate must have personal knowledge of the exact amounts involved. Of course, he never does. Try that on your neighborly folk singer. The tradition of not-knowing was accepted modestly by senators of all political hues. Cranston, a liberal Democrat, was in the same see-nothing, know-nothing boat as Barry Goldwater. So was Senator George McGovern. In Pennsylvania, Republican Senator Richard S. Schweiker spent $664,614 in 1968, defeating incumbent Democrat Joseph S. Clark. The latter reported expenditures of $425,000 to the state. Winner and loser, amazingly, reported to the Senate spending a total of $6,236. Those D.C. committees will help a candidate all the time. Another of passing interest showed Democratic Senate loser in Ohio, John Gilligan, had no expenses. That was where the Senate was concerned. The state had his report of nearly $400,000. The candidate beating Gilligan, Republican William B. Saxbe, reported to the Senate that he had personal spending of about $21,000. His report in Ohio showed that Saxbe spent $769,614.

The hydra-headed hypocrisy of the Senate and its members unfortunately provoked torrents of cynicism from a usually lethargic public. It had the effect of sending a scare into the faceless and behind-the-scenes power brokers. They managed in Senate offices to have principals in both parties sound alarms over the high rise of being a candidate. Plans and programs to cut down the costs flew sonorously through committee hearings. Peppery little Senator John Pastore, senior Democrat from Rhode Island, began yet another inquiry into the high cost of TV campaigning. But thirty-five senators were gearing up for the 1970 elections. Double vision became the operative technique.

The tendency was imbued into their wives, who naturally peddled the lines their husbands prattled. Thus it became acceptable for wives of proclaimed liberal senators to speak out on anything from their concept of civil rights to welfare, ecology, and the war. But the biggest talker in town—and the most talked about—Martha Mitchell, was pilloried for tripping over her nonstop tongue. It was perfectly all right for Mrs. Philip Hart, wife of the liberal Democrat from Michigan. Mother of eight, a pilot, and enormously wealthy by inheritance, Jane Hart was outspoken on issues of interest to her. Plain Jane—or Janey to her friends—also was a demonstrator. Her opinions of Mrs. Mitchell were of meat-ax dimensions. That was for her friends. To the public, Janey Hart thought that Martha Mitchell should keep her mouth shut.

"She's a kook," said Janey of Martha.

"She's a creep," said Martha of Janey.

Both calloused-tongued ladies had their supporters all over town. But a good number, adhering to tradition, fanned themselves with disapproval. They believed that women with husbands in high places, including the Senate, should be discreet. Knowing their men quite well, they believed in the old French aphorism of power on the pillow. While Washington rocked with shock or outraged laughter, Martha Mitchell didn't let up one decibel. In a genteel way, Mrs. Betty Fulbright thought perhaps she should. A Martha call to the Fulbright home had been taken by Mme. Senator. Mrs. Mitchell was frequently upset with one stand or another adopted by Senator Fulbright.

"I wouldn't want to go into it," observed Mrs. Fulbright. "I just don't want to start a Kentucky feud."

Kentucky or otherwise, all the pro- and anti-Martha Mitchell wives sharpened their knitting needles, so to speak. Many, though, have made nonpartisan judgments and then tried to devour the adversary. Typical was Mrs. Birch Bayh.

"It's something each lady has to decide for herself," asserted Mrs. Bayh. "But I would personally lobby."

Lobbying? If you put the most modest touch on the wifely actions, they might better be termed persuasion. Senators aren't generally known as chasers. Too many are of the age where it's hard enough to do a full day's work. Others find libido in the constant quest for power. In a community so full of single, lonely girls, senators just don't maintain their fair share of love nests. There are even some sweet, old-fashioned romances.

An outstanding one is that of Mrs. Nancy Thurmond and her physically fit but aging husband, Strom. He is about forty years her senior. A former South Carolina beauty queen, Mrs. Thurmond recently gave birth to their first child, a daughter. Barnyard jokes passed around his distinguished colleagues referring to the old Confederate's stamina. But they couldn't fault Nancy. She'll speak out or stay silent, as her husband directs. Her explanation:

"Senator Thurmond is the servant of the people. He is very capable of handling the political affairs."

It was a convenient public posture. The majority of Senate wives ignore the thought. Take a flare-up of temper between Senator Norris Cotton, Republican senior Senator from New Hampshire, and Phil Hart. Usually soft-spoken but spontaneously liberal, Hart growled at Cotton over time spent on witnesses testifying before committees. Janey Hart, the mother figure of the liberal Hill wives, had been telling friends at parties that Cotton was one who symbolized everything wrong and reactionary with the Senate. When Cotton fumed at a Hart-chaired subcommittee, Hart roared back at him. It was over the Federal Power Commission and its aides. Janey Hart had taken a dim view about many of the commission's time-servers. After his anger disappeared, Hart clobbered Cotton. Reason? He was so much better prepared. Hart has the best all-around Senate office and subcommittee staffs in the Capitol. Janey Hart had her say via her senator husband.

An area where nearly all senators kept their wives' mouths shut pretty tightly was in crime. A number of wives felt strong social

motivations about concern for the caught criminal, his background and circumstances. But Washington had become the
capital of crime. Besides an incredible growth of the drug culture,
rape seemed rampant. So did armed robbery. The Congress adjourned not long before with passing of the President's major
anticrime bills. Day of adjournment was a day of particulars.
Washington reeled from a record high—for a single day—of eighty
robberies. Only then did anticrime bills being to get consideration
by the Senate. Sociological considerations were left in the kitchen.
Because Washington is more than two-thirds black in population,
the crime statistics reflected the proportional color imbalance. Yet
those in the Senate who prided themselves on being foremost
civil rights fighters were most prudent to eschew this condition in
lopsided votes for law and order.

They ducked and weaved in an individual case that required
carrying an appeal from a young black man all the way to the
top. Eddie M. Harrison had been jailed for gunning down a
gambler when he was very young. His sentence was life. While in
prison, he set about teaching inmates how to read and how to
learn various skills. Released temporarily on a technicality, pending appeal, Eddie's case seemed hopeless. He had been represented
early in the matter by a court hanger-on whose legal qualifications
were dubious. Letters went out from interested black personalities
in Washington to senators and congressmen. Some cautiously supported him in his good works in and out of jail. Nevertheless, he
seemed doomed to go back, for life, because nobody appeared to
have the courage to take the Harrison story all the way up to the
President. Only a presidential pardon now counted.

A friend of mine on the House Judiciary Committee asked me
to see Harrison. He turned out to be a bundle of energy, full of
life and absolutely frank about the killing in his youth. He showed
me copies of letters sent out in his behalf. One was from Senator
Ed Brooke, Massachusetts Republican and the only black man
in the Senate. Compassion and a plea from the heart were in
Brooke's letter.

"He said it wouldn't do for him to go to Attorney General
Mitchell," Harrison told me somberly. "Others have said the
same thing to me as Brooke. Not much time is left; with luck a

couple of weeks. Could you please try with your friends and contacts?"

It was an ironic situation. More blacks were in high posts in the Nixon Administration than in any previous one. They were frequently assailed by their fellow blacks in the Democratic ranks as Uncle Toms because they consented to try to work problems out within the Administration. I called Chotiner. He had just come into the White House as one of Nixon's main political counselors. We went over the Harrison case. Chotiner, who also is an experienced lawyer, said he would take it up with Mitchell. The next moring Chotiner also called Harrison's new lawyer to get more information. Not once did Chotiner or Mitchell ever ask for any political dividends. The young man's plight was made for it. Neither was there ever any publicity sought or acquired. Professional Mitchell-Chotiner haters might, of course, snort about "one good deed." But no senator—and there were many who had originally been approached—ever took the predicament of Harrison very far.

Mitchell and Chotiner did. President Nixon commuted Eddie Harrison's sentence. The only publicity was a story that Harrison gave in an interview following the act. He was mighty grateful and went right to work with the illiterate and other handicapped blacks.

Nevertheless, this incident did not deter Senator Brooke from later lamenting in public that Nixon was very lax in enforcing civil rights. Such more-in-sadness-than-in-anger remarks are better known as "regional realism." Another liberal, a Northern Democrat, shook up his soul mates. Senator Abe Ribicoff of Connecticut announced that he was on the side of Senator Stennis on the issue of federal school aid. The North, asserted Ribicoff, was superhypocritical. It criticized school desegregation in the South as too slow and evasive. Yet the North, declaimed Ribicoff, engaged in similar dodging tactics. He wanted it stopped all over the country. Stennis was elated. The South couldn't have a better champion in the North, was his view.

To the public the issue was shortened to *de facto* segregation. Cut off federal aid to all school districts that fail to desegregate, even though their racial imbalance is a product of residential patterns and not illegal. That means suburbs, overwhelmingly white. Ribicoff's stand provoked a storm of recrimination among senators on the liberal line. How dare he think of even sharing a Stennis view? was their outraged cry. Then, fellow senators began their own derogatory campaign against Ribicoff. He was inordinately vain. Just remember how he baited Mayor Daley in Chicago at the uproarious 1968 Democratic convention. Worse, Abe Ribicoff was taking a deliberate stand with the South to improve his own political chances. Why? He really wants to be the first Jew nominated for the Vice-Presidency in 1972.

Few of the senators who always upheld Ribicoff's abrasive and cocky mannerisms in the interests of sound liberalism had a good word for him. Snide ethnic remarks generated heat. It was paradoxical to hear some leading Southern senators magnanimously rebuke passers of those ethnic cracks. Not too long before, they had been sneering the same way at another Abe—Abe Fortas. Moreover, Ribicoff's "realism" was defended by the same club members when he quickly opposed nomination of another Southerner to the Supreme Court. Judge George Harrold Carswell was nominated to the Court by Nixon. After the bitterness of the Haynsworth tussle in the Senate, the Carswell nomination looked easy. He was a Democrat turned Republican, fifty years old, and seemed to have little either to distinguish him or to criticize him. From Tallahasse, Florida, Carswell was a member of the Fifth Circuit Court of Appeals. Six months before his nomination for the Supreme Court, the Senate approved Carswell by voice vote to the Fifth Circuit Court.

Civil rights leaders grumbled at the mention of Carswell. Disapproval seemed only skin deep. Eastland appeared confident that Carswell would ride through easily. So did Florida Republican leaders. Later they split violently and chopped each other up mercilessly. The Senate Judiciary Committee looked at another contest biliously. By default, Birch Bayh wearily agreed to undertake separate inquiry into Carswell. The AFL-CIO and civil rights leaders wanted it. The judicial drawing boards had the Carswell nomination symbolically. It appeared even more futile when the Judiciary Committee, by 13 to 4, approved Carswell's name to be taken to the Senate for a later vote. Thereupon, the AFL-CIO blasted Carswell as an insult to the nation. Chairman Eastland and colleague Thurmond—who tasted the acid of defeat with Haynsworth—made the rosiest of predictions. They figured Carswell would get Senate approval by at least two to one.

So smooth did the Carswell nomination loom that attention of senators was really riveted on President Nixon's first State of the Union message. It was a time when senators grudgingly moved to the House to hear the President address a joint session. There wouldn't be enough room for 100 senators and 435 representatives in the Senate chamber, anyway. A senator hardly ever gets to the House side on his own. It's kind of a legislative caste mark. They all applauded the President's thirty-five minute speech. He urged major fights against pollution and crime. Nixon's clean-water program called for $10 billion.

"Don't hold your breath," said Proxmire afterward. He knew his colleagues.

Of all the presidential references, a phrase stuck out, "a driving dream." It covered all aspects of peace, including new talks with Communist China and Nixon's "Guam Doctrine." That would keep treaty obligations in Asia without expanding the American presence. The language was impressive, thought former Vice-President Humphrey. But he was keeping his options open, intending to return soon to political battle. So, he added that specifics were vague. Senator Fulbright wasted no time. He wheeled into battle, as a breaker of Presidents. Fresh agendas were prepared for his Committee on Foreign Relations. Fulbright informed the media that a whole new series of hearings would be launched. He chose silence on a Nixon statement earlier that the massacre at My Lai "was abhorrent to the conscience of all the American people." Appropriate action, promised the President, would be taken in accordance with strict rules of military justice.

Fulbright, more than ever suspicious of what he deemed presidential whole hogging of foreign affairs, lined up witnesses. Only after some fates and slates were fixed, did he inform other members of the fifteen-man committee, nine Democrats and six Republicans. It was really fifteen because Senator Mundt had been felled by a stroke and was unable to function again. Briefly, Fulbright turned from his preoccupation with Asia to the state of

Europe. He whiplashed Ambassador Jacob D. Beam, a tall, stoop-shouldered career officer, our man in Moscow. Some of the questions he asked of Beam in a closed session went:

"Are you afraid to walk the streets of Moscow?"

Replied Beam: "No, sir, but. . . ."

Beam wanted to add comment about rising crime in the USSR.

Fulbright: "Are there campus disturbances?"

Beam: "No, Mr. Chairman, but. . . ."

He had hoped to discuss student-academician-intellectual ferment.

Chairman Fulbright had no time for explanations. Eager to get back to the concept of Executive privilege and the war in Southeast Asia, he also gave full marks to a resolution by Senator Mansfield. The majority leader also was a member of Fulbright's committee. He wanted to withdraw most of the force we had assigned to NATO, particularly in Germany. Mansfield, who helped create SEATO—anti-Communist alliance in Asia—had been important in keeping NATO in business for a time. Our allies weren't meeting obligations, Mansfield contended. Why should we bear the brunt? It was another withdrawal syndrome. Mansfield dangled the resolution as a potential stick. He said he would select his own time to introduce it into the Senate. Fulbright agreed with the import and tenor of the resolution.

Although Fulbright was steeped, at least by osmosis, in foreign affairs, he had shown little interest in or patience with Europe for some time. As far back as the summer of 1961, Fulbright on a TV news show program had talked about Germany. In responsible assessments, government and academic, Germany is the single most important security issue for the United States and the USSR. Fulbright said: "I don't understand why the East Germans don't close the border because I think they have a right to close it."

Twelve days later the East Germans went ahead and built the Berlin Wall. Fulbright's declaration revealed a distressing ignorance of the Four Power Statute for Greater Berlin. Neither the Russians nor the East Germans, under the statute, had any right to seal off one part of the city from the other. Yet Fulbright asked querulously: "So why is this a great concession?" The twists and

turns of Fulbright's thinking about foreign policy and its formula-
tion are bewildering and bizarre. About the time he delivered
himself of random thoughts on Berlin, Chairman Fulbright lectured at Cornell.

He argued for expansion of presidential authority to conduct
foreign affairs with a minimum of interference from Congress.
In a fast-changing and dangerous world of the sixties—menaced
by nuclear weapons—Fulbright said that the President should
have the power to deal with emergencies unfettered by legislative
restraints.

"It is my contention," Fulbright lectured, "that for the existing
requirement of foreign policy we [of Congress] have hobbled the
President by too niggardly a grant of power."

But the world of the seventies is not very different from the
world of the sixties. Fulbright started wanting to make Congress's
grant of power more niggardly than it had been. What made him
start on another tack, of course, was the war in Vietnam. In
addition, the idea of breaking the President appealed to Fulbright.
He firmly believed that his anti-LBJ position on the war was the
most important factor leading to President Johnson's withdrawal
from further political consideration in 1968. Liberals applauded
his position and forgave him all his reactionary Southern racist
inhibitions. Even his vote against a minimum wage bill was forgiven.

In the Senate, ethics and morality have largely become stan-
dardized synonyms for an oblong blur of expediency and hypocrisy. The agonizing war, longest in American history, and its
seeming interminability provided the impetus for a withdrawal
syndrome. It was like a sexual reflex. With the clamor to get out,
suddenly popped a rash of Senate inquiries into spreading tumors
in and all military undertakings. Corruption in servicemen's
clubs, profiteers, research programs, contractors and business got
the clouting back of the hand from newly startled senators.

War was always hell. This one in Vietnam and the rest of
Indo-China was more hellish, the critics contended, than any
other. Names began to be bandied like a publicity juggling act.
Lieutenant William Calley became notorious for his part in the
grotesque My Lai massacre. Senators also learned to use a name

like Captain Ernest Medina, Calley's superior. They got around
to higher ranks only much later. Resolutions and amendments
to bring us out of the war surfaced and spread. President Nixon's
withdrawal policy drew suspicions. The doubts floated even after
Senators Mansfield and Fulbright thought he was doing a good
job of it. Fulbright changed his mind again shortly. Except for
the briefest reflections, when the subject was raised by an outsider, most senators never bothered to come up with a retraining
program for returning veterans.

The political fad was to get out of the war. Somehow the
majority of the Senate ran away from the problem that at least
two million men had been sent out there and returned. To what?
Many stayed jobless. The national rate of unemployment veered
to 4 percent, highest since late 1967. Jobs for returning veterans?
It appeared that the work force which stayed at home took first
priority. Senators relapsed into normalcy for them. They went
after certain publicity-enticing abuses. Those malpractices had
been imbedded and malignant a long time. Whenever abuses
could be exposed and maybe corrected, it was good all around.
The fanfare generated by the probes seemed blatantly orches-
trated. In a wide-ranging series of hearings the Senate Permanent
Subcommittee on Investigations went after accused crooks, poltroons, and venal misfits. All the juicy parts were recorded in
living TV color.

Ever Republican loyalist at any cost, Senator Karl Mundt, who
would shortly suffer a crippling stroke, went into a frenzy of
charges. As the ranking minority member of the subcommittee,
Mundt disclosed violations of trust in the Army, unbelievable
black market operations in Vietnam, and kickbacks by touring
performers to people who booked them. The word "fragging," in
vicious use for several years in Vietnam, only came into senatorial
use long after the instant headlines of corruption. To "frag" means
to roll a fragmentation bomb into a sleeping noncom's or officer's
quarters. The victims are usually killed by their own men who
have come to hate them and their orders.

There was little mileage in demanding all-out inquiries into
fragging. More immediate, to follow political fashions, were senators who upheld the purpose of moratoriums against the war.

They felt buoyant, having taken the credit for another with-drawal—that of Lieutenant General Lewis B. Hershey, the seventy-six-year-old draft director. Soon, critical senators suggested, draft-age youngsters wouldn't find it necessary to march and chant: "Hell no, we won't go." Foreign observers got an insight into the developing political chic shift. At a dinner party given by rank-ing officials from India, Senator Gore lamented about "our Geth-semane" in Vietnam. His wife spoke somberly of prayer. The hosts smiled and clucked indulgently. Their ruling caste represented the most studied hypocrisy in the world under the guise of the pursuit of democracy.

Gore and some senior guests from Fulbright's Foreign Relations Committee nodded enthusiastic agreement with his personal attack on Vice-President Agnew. The public assaults on the media, often singling out newspapers, networks, and commentators, had just lifted Agnew into whiz-bang national prominence. He defended stoutly Nixon's Vietnam policies—withdrawals, too—and tore into critics in the media as "effete Eastern snobs." Alliteration was coming into Agnew's lexicon. Dissected, effete applied only to a few. So did Eastern. Snobs, not really. Anti-Nixon feeling among newspaper and TV people has been rampant a long time. It took his election to the Presidency to barb the attitude. In many cases, pamphleteering is actually what passes for reporting. There were also many common, even mawkish, scolds. But they weren't snobs. Almost all of them talked to each other and, quite frequently, about each other.

Vice-President Agnew was a much easier target than Nixon. He was much more accessible. As presiding officer of the Senate, he also had to deal in countless little and big ways with the delicate temperaments of the members. Ted Agnew is not a good poker player, which Nixon has been. He never tried to bluff at the table nor as Vice-President. Once regarded as a liberal Republican, in early 1968 when he supported Governor Nelson Rockefeller, Agnew became a red-baiting reactionary to Nixon haters as Vice-President.

Never a cunning politician nor an artful dodger, Agnew says his piece because he believes in it. As often as media representa-tives attacked him, he blasted right back. He held no personal rancor; indeed, Ted Agnew has been a pretty enjoyable, sociable companion over a highball. If he had been capable of nuances and pussyfooting, Agnew might well have enjoyed a better press. His world is fairly limited and he never had the benefits of high-level cerebral thought translated into education. He became a rare Republican governor in Maryland almost by accident. The Democratic candidate was too abhorrent. The kind of consensus accommodation, so dearly beloved by LBJ, made him acceptable to the South in the 1968 convention.

"Speero will do," was the laconic acceptance by Strom Thurmond.

Not among the Georgetown set, where Spiro is usually a four-letter word. His pithy partisanship also made of Agnew a sort of soul mate for many Southern Democrats. One who had special reason to be thankful was Russell Long, chairman of the Senate Finance Committee. Long has been an off-again, on-again big drinker. It makes him moody. He can be sharp as a new surgical instrument when sober. In his cups, he is hopeless—and helpless as well. Agnew felt compassionate toward Long. The Senator could become violent in his off-moments. He blew one night in a German-type restaurant, the "823," in downtown Washington. German music was playing and two policewomen from Connecticut were singing along with the tune. Long, roaring like a rancid muzhik on a weekend bender, told the women to shut up.

They paid him no attention. The ladies were in town for a training session of the Bureau of Narcotics and Dangerous Drugs. We were, you see, becoming most alarmed at the growth of what sociologists call the "drug culture." A Republican congressman from the Midwest was at a nearby table. He didn't know Long except from photographs. When the lady cops persisted in singing, Long cuffed them. Was it a slip of the hand, in demonstration? Definitely not, the aggrieved policewomen told Senator Dodd, as senior Senator from their home state.

Dodd was a good friend of Long, one of the few who voted against Dodd's censure. Word went to Bob Hunter, Long's veteran administrative aide. Hunter, a slender man, has an infinite capacity with strong waters. He had not been with Long at the restaurant. Hunter was not disloyal, never would be.

"He [Long] probably had a couple under his belt," said Hunter, with a few under his own buckle. "That's the way he is. At a World Series game, I sat next to him and I wound up black and blue. He gets excited. He's been working his heart out, you know."

Hunter, though, got Long to come down to Dodd's office. There, the junior Senator from Louisiana apologized to the lady policewomen and promised to pay all expenses—dry cleaning and the like. The ladies seemed to like the idea of so personal and high level an apology. Earlier they informed Dodd that Long hadn't brushed them and upset the beer; he punched them in a wild way. One policewoman confided that she had a plate in her head as the result of an old injury.

"If he hit that plate . . . ," she mused.

Agnew learned about the incident. He urged Long to make all apologies and restitution. And he kept the incident quiet. So did Dodd. The club can compose its differences on thorny personal problems.

Its inward look did not cover the worst inflationary bind in eighteen years. While the Senate pondered self-serving politics, members froze at the end of 1969 over cold statistics that showed Americans, the great electorate, paying almost six cents a dollar more for living costs than in 1951. An inflation-recession had hit the country. The White House, operating under its own economic game plan, wanted to take away lots of steam. Unemployment kept creeping up. Hold out, was the word from the Administration. Democratic senators laid low. Under the Democrats, inflation boomed. They couldn't point any accusing fingers at the Republicans. The party of the people—as Democrats like to call themselves—took the easy way out. Their senators did nothing.

Instead, Democratic senators, more peace-bent than ever, thrust cosmetic-changed images to the public on opposition to the war. A bloc of Republicans, mainly from the Eastern seaboard, joined them. A Far Western addition was Oregon's Senator Mark Hatfield, once a big Nixon man when he nurtured hopes of becoming Vice-President. Hatfield's peace proclamations only paralleled his publicized anxieties about how tough it was to stay a senator on the salary and emoluments. From Oregon, the senior Senator was beginning to encounter factional disputes back home. Less concerned with economics was Senator Fulbright. One week he had joined Mansfield in saying Nixon seemed to be doing all right with troop withdrawal.

By this time, the White House ceased to regard any declaration by Fulbright as anything but a delusion or a trap. In a fast reversal—Fulbright's footwork is often agile—he told TV that the President had to move more swiftly. Therefore, new hearings on Vietnam must be held. Fulbright has held more open hearings on the war than all committees combined. It provided him with a ready-made platform. Fulbright and his closer associates asked witnesses questions that were short speeches. But they were good for TV editing.

He ho-hummed when the President pinned brigadier general stars on Alexander Haig, a top Kissinger assistant. Nixon, having announced further withdrawal of forces from Southeast Asia, had telegrams of approval stacked high at the White House ceremony. White House factotum Bud Hopkins said he thought it was the biggest volume of wires he had seen in fifty years. Obviously, upstaging Fulbright also had become part of the Administration technique. Croesus-rich W. Averell Harriman didn't care for it. He was completely out in the cold in his approach to the age of eighty. Once elected governor, in a squeaker in New York, Harriman aspired to an elder statesman's role. Democratic Presidents had used him as Ambassador to the USSR in wartime, and globally, too. He had been a world trouble-shooter and the first American negotiator for the United States in Paris with Communists from Vietnam.

In a year, Harriman only managed meetings. He defended LBJ's position loyally. In came the Republicans, and Harriman moulted and became a dove. Mainly, Harriman was a mandarin. In dealings with states and regimes requiring United States aid, he asserted they had better follow his advice—or no help. This attitude was especially true with smaller nations in Asia and recorded with a wince by a ranking official accompanying him on these tours. Thus, he loudly proclaimed endorsement of antiwar moratoriums. Leading dovish Democratic senators also said the demonstrations seemed absolutely splendid.

During the summer of 1969, the New Mobilization Committee

to End the War in Vietnam, "New Mobe" for short, was established. It had cadres on nearly all campuses. A delegation met several times in Stockholm with representatives from North Vietnam and the Viet Cong. Their appeal was a refurbished call of the thirties, the Popular Front. It could embrace the whole spectrum from Liberals to Communists and Trotskyites. The plan was a Trotskyite conception.

It has been quite a coup for them. The Soviet Union, with assorted apparatuses, has never come within a light-year's shot at such organization. Liberal foes of the war didn't do their homework; they believed they could outmaneuver disciplined activists or simply ignored them in their own enthusiasm. Even National Republican Chairman, easy-going, hulking Rog Morton, thought it wasn't a bad idea. He kept quiet, though, when provided with names, numbers, and salaries. Liberals also were prepared to blame any outbreak of violence on the Administration. It was too easy for the power purveyors of the steering committee. They managed to attract droves of Senate staff members and secretaries to use the Capitol steps for discussion purposes.

Most senators were too preoccupied with other self-serving matter. The military was rebuffed by Nixon on chemical and biological warfare activities. All their recommendations were rejected by the President and Secretary of Defense Laird. To obtain a share of the spotlight, the Senate's Permanent Investigations Subcommittee redoubled attacks on military corruption. A retired Provost Marshal, ill-tempered and narrow Major General Turner, stood accused. He had finally been found out for some personal gun-running. Turner sold guns turned over to him by police authorities. His depredations at home and abroad had been long known. The Senate and the military grappled with eels before coming to a decision.

At the noncommissioned level, the Army's onetime Sergeant Major, William O. Woolridge, was accused at long last of easy ways with enlisted men's funds and facilities. In a spate of rectitude, senators assailed the military for failure to unearth these scandals. It was most convenient, too, to link up the sordid episodes with military behavior in Vietnam. Senators wrathfully heard about kickback rackets in Vietnam servicemen's clubs.

Corruption was breaking out all over and senators sprang up as insatiable guardians of the public trust. Almost as a by-product, ugly revelations accumulated with direct bearing on the Middle East in general and American Jews in particular.

Students with obvious Jewish-sounding names had been in the vanguard of the anti-Vietnam war demonstrations on streets and campuses. Many were leaders summoning strikes in colleges. Traditional Jewish deep regard for education and liberalism— fetters that bound in central Europe—caused beneath-the-surface but widespread ethnic jokes. These cracks were even more vicious than the prattle leading to so-called Polish jokes. Anti-Jewish remarks went from "My son, the revolutionary," to "My daughter, the bomber," and "My civil rights slumlord." The last butt went out among black militants.

A fresh and uncannily accurate term, "radical chic," encompassed many Jews who made it to the top financially and artistically in the East, particularly in and around New York. They contributed generously to the Black Panthers, for instance. In turn, the Panthers reviled them with epithets at parties sponsored by the chic. But the donors accepted because it was chic and this was a be-kind-to-the exploited kick. Hell, it was like playing out the last chapter in a Jewish novel.

A blacklash, however, started building up. It has by no means abated. And it was tough-minded Israelis, on fact-finding tours, who learned about the depth of the feeling. A specific "universal psychological terror" had replaced the nightmare of the so-recent events in Nazi Germany. Jewish merchants in smaller communities outside New York were learning, to their horror, about a stab-in-the-back theory from parents and returning, fed-up Vietnam veterans. Fortunately, no leadership appeared to coalesce frustration, fear, and hate. Nevertheless, in key metropolitan areas anti-Semitic obscenities were uttered by militant blacks as well as upper-class, so to say, WASPS.

When the findings were reported to senators regarded as sympathetic to Israel's posture toward the Arabs and the Soviet Union, little was relayed to echelons of power. Senator Javits, a Jew, sought to make light of the problem. Adopting his worldly manner, Hugh Scott pooh-poohed the phenomenon. So did Muskie, busy taking crash courses from Harriman in foreign affairs. Most went on a binge of emotionalism when craggy Israeli Premier Golda Meir arrived. Scoop Jackson kept his head. He sought to plumb the combustible Middle East condition in some detail. Presence of complex technical weaponry, wings of Soviet MIGs, and fifteen thousand picked Russian troops in Egypt convinced Jackson that Kremlin tactics were hardly kosher.

Fulbright was consistent. He had been that way since the state of Israel was founded in 1948. Too little heed had been paid, Fulbright claimed, to Arab fears and frustrations. Now an alarmist streak was building up in the President's assessments. In Fulbright's view we had too many commitments in Southeast Asia. The President's authority had to be curbed and congressional prerogatives restored. Javits, all out for Israel in his home state, New York, tried to strike a middle ground. It was a typically deft Javits approach: all things to all men. Few senators ever cared for Javits, fast on his feet on the Senate floor and nimble of memory. In their inimitable club manner, they dissembled publicly and cut him up privately.

Many jealously spoke of the great wealth he amassed as a law partner with his older brother, Benjamin, in the opulent law firm of Javits & Javits. A veteran member of the House or Senate, associated with a law firm past and present, can always steer business to the old office. Nothing illegal. The merest hint or suggestion suffices. The morality? It happens to be part of the system. Although many colleagues grumbled behind his back, a good senatorial turnout appeared for the Capitol Hill party Javits threw for big brother Ben. Congratulations flowed mellifluously. The Senator beamed. The poor boy from the Lower East side had become a power on the Hill. About a year later Ben Javits was accused of manipulating a big divorce. A New York court forbade him to practice for three years. One of the judges wrote sternly that brother Ben should have been disbarred. Senate exclusivity wrapped itself like a fetish comfort around Senator Javits. He couldn't be his brother's keeper, could he?

A flurry of activity, mistaken for performance, went through a preponderance of Senate offices. Lots of voters and public-minded organizations, like Ralph Nader's, generated heat on campaign expenses and contributions. Daily morning meetings with their top assistants were held by many senators. Ideas were thrashed out and some were even put on paper. First things first, though. The Senate approved legislation providing each member with an additional $23,652 annually. It was to go for hiring more staff, upping expense-paid trips back home, and similar expenses. Then senators got together on some proposals that would provide for reduced TV rates for candidates. To push the programs, several senators made startling admissions. Joe Tydings led all the rest. Without TV, he declared, he couldn't have been elected in 1964.

"The expenses of political campaigning," observed Tydings, "have tended to make political office the exclusive preserve of the wealthy."

Tydings, who roughed it on inherited millions, knew whereof he spoke. There were, of course, notable exceptions. Two original poor boys who made it to the Senate fell out. The dispute was over environmental control bills. Back of the quarrel was the quest for power and search for cash the chase entailed for Ed Muskie. Jackson, tough-minded on international security matters, had a more glittering domestic record than Muskie's. A few months earlier Jackson pushed through the Senate without debate an important bill. It established a national environment policy. Through the bill, a Board of Environmental Advisers was created in the Executive Office of the President. Muskie threatened to block it at a joint House-Senate conference where loopholes are inserted in legislation and adaptations are wedded. Already running undeclared for the presidential nomination, Muskie selfishly wanted his own version.

Years before, through perseverance, Jackson was responsible for a major conservation bill. He wrestled approval even while Muskie accepted without protest contributions from mills in Maine that cascaded pollutants into state streams. Environment and ecology had become national political attractions. Muskie tried to grab environment control as his very own. At the same time he began to coo softly on the obsessive issue of Vietnam. His attachment to the environment was somewhat strange for someone of humble origins. Obviously controls and specific strictures were required. But the resources that nourished the ambitions of a Muskie would be denied to the poor and the blacks if his legislation made it. A compromise was hammered out. From then on, Jackson and Muskie were really never in the same camp. A fallout would carve a painful piece out of Muskie for 1972.

The club became increasingly testy as the tumultuous decade of the sixties limped into history. A new generation eloquently advocated by the late President Kennedy was bound up in senatorial hot air, mutual recrimination, rudderlessness, and lassitude. The introductory phase of the Ninety-first Congress, ushering in the new Nixon Administration, could be better recorded in invisible ink. Symptomatic of its unease and uncertainty, the Senate ricocheted to the thunderbolts against continuance of the American role in Vietnam. As intensity rose in antiwar movements, so did senators seeing principally political advantages in turning the other cheek. Only a few years before, the vast bulk of the select hundred had been in favor.

Clubbiness, whatever the party label, fast melted into partisanship, and factional partisanship at that. Even in the sacred confines of the steam baths and swimming pools—emulation of the Romans—our senior legislators deliberately shunned others for their own groups. On the Senate floor, personal attacks became common where once they had been so rare as to elicit national shock. In such a vein, white-haired Marlow W. Cook, Republican of Kentucky, faced down Ted Kennedy. It was over an obscure appropriations measure. Kennedy, majority whip, had been pretty much an absentee Senator since the affair at Chappaquiddick. Cook, a skillful lawyer and a man who did his homework, was still a freshman. Kennedy said that Cook was trying to rush through a piece of legislation without giving colleagues adequate time. Coldly, Cook reminded Kennedy that if he spent more time in the Senate he would have had the opportunity to do his job. Red-faced, Kennedy muttered himself into silence that even recorders couldn't get on the spot.

By this time sympathy for Kennedy was hardly ever to be heard. His plight, however, was temporarily ignored when another Democratic senator acknowledged the first of a series of political payoffs, known in the trade as contributions. Hartke, heartily disliked by the majority of his fellow senators, disclosed belatedly that he accepted a voter registration contribution from Spiegel, Inc., the mammoth Chicago mail-order house. A Hartke D.C. committee got the contribution. It so happened that Hartke was a member of the Senate's Post Office Committee when the contribution came. A former member, ex-Senator Daniel B. Brewster, Democrat of Maryland, was indicted on federal bribery charges. Hartke naturally denied all wrongdoing. His colleagues, many of whom felt they were invulnerable, rejoiced. For them it was proof of the "Bought" nickname they attached to Hartke.

There was more to emerge in Hartke's political affairs. A good-sized group of Senate club members confidentially leaked reports and raw material on Hartke contributions to an inquiry growing out of some Spiegel business operations in the Capitol. One was an unpaid bill of four thousand dollars that an Indianapolis radio station wrote off. The station was deeply interested in license renewal. It got the renewal. Senators may have been most indiscreet— but these men were not intimidated.

VIII

RHETORIC AND REALITY

If a senator, no matter the rest of his record, was critical of something favored by the Nixon Administration, he was automatically in good standing with liberals in search of new heroes. That was evident with Fulbright's about-face on Vietnam. And now a new Southern champion turned up. He was bulky, canny old Judge Sam J. Ervin, Jr., Democrat of North Carolina. Despite disclaimers and modesty, Ervin was a lot more than a back-country jurist. His attachment to constitutional liberties was unquestioned. He was a senatorial pioneer with inquiries into the invasion of privacy. Ervin also employed his experience and knowledge in deep defense of traditional Southern positions on the entire civil rights panorama.

Castigated for long as a Claghorn from the South, Ervin became a hero. He was unqualifiedly opposed to "no-knock" provisions in a law. It was contained in a sweeping drug bill, passed unanimously by the Senate. A point permitted in the legislation only scraped through, 44 to 40. It allowed officers to enter a house without knocking to search for drugs. First they had to convince a magistrate that evidence would be destroyed if they knocked before entering. Ervin saw inequities in no-knock. It might be applied in a host of other circumstances besides the needful search for drugs. Overnight, Judge Ervin went from being a civil rights ogre to a defender of privacy.

Amused at the instant anointment accorded him by yesterday's vitriolic critics, Ervin, with his judicious smiles, commented: "I haven't changed. I stand strictly by the law and what I believe is a proper interpretation." Onetime critics tried to lionize him with a shower of invitations to feast and to speak. Old Judge Sam was too wise for matinee heroism. He never yearned for spotlights and publicity. New admirers he treated with old-fashioned Southern courtesy, just as he did when they called him dirty names. When Ervin pursued inquiries into the vast and neuralgic field of surveillance—from bugging to Army Intelligence spying on civilians—his critics hailed him as the nation's wisest senior citizen. They wanted him to sit in special judgment on about everything they saw going wrong in the country. But Ervin still didn't change. He simply weighed facts presented to him. And he still wasn't beholden to any special interest group.

His Southern colleague, adopted as an earlier hero, went, however, from one televised triumph to another. Senator Fulbright, never one to duck TV lights and cameras, went after Vice-President Agnew. Having taken on the President, Fulbright felt that his broad brush should lather the runner-up, too. He charged that Agnew made certain—unspecified—commitments on Asia on his trip. In itself, that made it essential for Agnew to testify before the Fulbright committee. The technique would be to drag in the Vice-President; then maybe even the President. Fulbright went all the way on questioning Executive privilege. Constitutionalist Ervin, by the way, was dubious whether this ploy of Fulbright's was constitutional. But it didn't matter to Fulbright. His media applause meter shot up. So did the pace of his attack on Agnew. The Vice-President, he suggested, was succumbing to arrogance of power.

Agnew had become the top target on prime time and space in all the media. The Vice-President didn't shrink from counter-attack and initiating new offensives. He defended Administration policies volubly and bluntly. Newspapers and TV networks and commentators Agnew singled out for attention. The money changers in the TV business got scared. They remain so. But they don't dare run away from Agnew targets either, although they have asked embattled correspondents to tone it down or even lay off for a while. TV officials in charge of revenue worry about licensing renewals from the Federal Communications Commission (FCC).

They can play airwave liberals until a dollar sign starts going out of joint.

Not only did Senator Fulbright try to put darts in Agnew, a whole slew of Democratic senators got into the act. They were led principally by Senators Muskie and McGovern. The senators not only sought favor with the media. They were after the presidential nomination first among Democrats. Charges of bias rang out from pro- and anti-Agnew media forces. Veteran broadcaster Howard K. Smith made efforts to put the whole political gunsmoke scenario in some kind of focus. A liberal of the old school—meaning all his life notwithstanding the fact that adversaries cut the Smith school off their lists in the mid-sixties—he criticized his colleagues on the air and in print for falsifying American political realities through biased reporting. Hardly a simpering admirer of Agnew, Smith also detected in the Vice-President's assaults a whiff of intimidation. He didn't like it. But he disliked even more the onslaughts of a Fulbright and the Senator's media acolytes. It's worth noting a few of Howard K. Smith's observations. Networks, he contended, are almost exclusively staffed by liberals.

"It evolved from the time when liberalism was a good thing and most intellectuals became highly liberal," observed Smith. "Most reporters are in an intellectual occupation. . . . Our tradition, since FDR, has been leftward."

And Smith, who describes himself as left-of-center, added: "Our liberal friends today have become dogmatic. They have a set of automatic reactions. They react the way political cartoonists do— with oversimplification. Oversimplify. Be sure you please your fellows because that's what's good. They're conventional. They're pleasing the *Washington Post,* they're pleasing *The New York Times,* and they're pleasing one another."

Some other Smith observations on the media: The Presidency: "The negative attitude which destroyed Lyndon Johnson is now waiting to be applied to Richard Nixon. Johnson was actually politically assassinated. They hate Richard Nixon irrationally."

The Vietnam war: "The networks have never given a complete picture of the war. For example: That terrible siege of Khe Sanh went on for five weeks before newsmen revealed that the South Vietnamese were fighting at our side. They had higher casualties.

And the Viet Cong's were 100 times ours. But we never told that. We just showed pictures day after day of the Americans getting the hell kicked out of them. That was enough to break America apart. That's also what it did."

In Washington, remember, TV, magazine, and the newspaper press are held in the highest regard. Some in the media are considered as, or even more, powerful than senators and Cabinet members. Society in Washington, or gelatinous fashion, exalts the press. That could be because there isn't anything else quite as glamorous as showing off some media names at a party. In Washington, you could hardly find someone from the arts. Performing acrobats turn up only once a season with the Barnum and Bailey Circus. Only tourists get involved with call girls. A he-man wants his dinner party, so many can hang on his golden opinions.

Therefore, very few arms of the vast electronic and varied press apparatus really ever come up with crackling accounts. Digging and investigative reporting is more talked about than accomplished. Often it shows up as a scolding lecture under the name of investigation. It has taken an outsider like Bill Lambert of *Life* magazine to expose poltroons and shoddy conflicts of interest in the arcane world of Washington. Jack Anderson and his team do most of the muck-raking. They come up with frequent breakthroughs. On a day-to-day basis, the Anderson accounts have been the most penetrating in journalism. Sometimes they have been crude and suggestive. Usually their sources are first-rate and astoundingly accurate. The column, run seven days a week, has gained in accuracy since one of the originators, Drew Pearson, died. He liked to play President, maybe a senior senator. Most of all, Pearson doted on glittering social events for which his name was on an invitation list. Anderson and his team couldn't care less.

Little of the background and byplay within the Senate appeared when the world's greatest deliberative body passed an eighteen-year-old test vote. By 62 to 21 a Senate amendment granting eighteen-year-olds the right to vote was approved. Senators Mansfield and Kennedy proposed the test amendment. James B. Allen, Democrat of Alabama, between reports of TB examinations in Senate dining rooms and mobile units, tried to water down and stymie the political test. He was more successful with the turnout by worried, regular Senate dining-room clients than with the out-come of the vote. Yet nearly a year elapsed before full approval came and with it steps to having eighteen-year-olds vote for all candidates including the President. Allen's recalcitrance tried the usually Southern sympathetic patience of Senator Long. Although Long also opposed the eighteen-year-old vote, he declared: "The will of the Senate is clear." Long wanted final action but had to hold his breath.

Many of his colleagues were sucking in their breath audibly over the Democratic party's debt from 1968—over $9 million—fresh revelations on costs for running for office, and a quest for a new party chairman. Senator Fred R. Harris, the young Oklahoma Democrat with a stunning American Indian wife, had withdrawn. Harris needed to mend home fences. Larry O'Brien, in the tradi-tion of Massachusetts last-hurrah politics, was playing hard to get. He had been chairman three times. After a brief fling with a New York brokerage firm that went broke, O'Brien set up his own public relations-consultants firm. Merry of mien, with twinkling eyes, and an original in the Irish Mafia, O'Brien had grown ac-customed to roughing it in posh style.

Politically, anti-war was a major Democratic party theme, except with Senator Jackson. O'Brien, staunch defender of the Kennedy and LBJ policies, added his lilting tones to the partisan outcry. He also joined in the assault on the mammoth size of the military budget. This had to be cynical. One of O'Brien's biggest accounts was Riker-Maxson. The firm's major business was in defense con-tracts. O'Brien also lamented for the poor and underprivileged. It was a standard party line. He lived in one of the highest rises of all in New York, near the United Nations. Bobby Kennedy once lived in the building, too. Getting an apartment there prac-tically requires references from J. P. Morgan & Company. But O'Brien always had been a good, loyal Democrat.

The party desperately needed his services. It was leaderless and broke. After saying no, no, and after a special meeting at which aged Jake Arvey, the old presidential political broker out of Chi-cago, also appealed, O'Brien made the sacrifice. He accepted the chairmanship. Mid-term elections were coming up, the party needed not only funds but a sense of unity and purpose. Old Larry was big about it. No salary, he said. Just expenses, that included transportation, an apartment in Washington, and such-like deductible items. Although the party was deeply in the hole, the Democrats kept their National Committee in the Watergate, by far one of the most expensive rentals in town. Maybe they wanted to keep an eye on all the Republicans resident in the place.

Neither O'Brien nor anybody else—unless Harriman unbelievably turned philanthropist—could make a dent in the party deficit. All he could hope to do was raise walking-around money. Candidates for re-election had to tap their own sources. Previous campaign debts could perhaps be settled for a few cents on the dollar. That was still a thankless job for Senator Gene McCarthy's managers. His outfit owed $1.4 million. Whopping debts can be run up easily with hotels, airlines, phone companies, car rental agencies, and bars. Profligate use of credit cards can run up, and did, astronomical sums. A loser always tries to settle on fifty cents or lower for every dollar owed.

Candidates never express themselves publicly about losing. They think of the nightmare in privacy and what stares them and their friends in the face. Some detailed reports of the presidential 1968 costs elicited cries of horror from Democratic senators and some Republicans. Running for federal office in 1968 was a record $70.1 million. The figure was a total for all levels. Senator Daniel K. Inouye, Democrat from Hawaii, after looking at the figures with disbelief and chagrin, observed that growing burdens for candidates resulted in the emergence of a new elite. These were people with money to burn or beholden to their armpits to special interests.

"The $100-a-plate dinner and the $500 campaign contributions are just signs of the times due to inflation," remarked Inouye gloomily. "People who were paying $10 about 20 years ago today are paying $100."

Freshman Republican Senator Charles McC. Mathias, Jr., of Maryland, agreed. He also had this to add: "The bigger contributor is always necessary the way the system has been working. Unless you have big chunks of money, you couldn't make the commitments for various media contracts."

Skyrocketing costs of campaigns and then of staying in office can bring grief to a political personality. Just when expenses were inducing bipartisan moans, Senator George Murphy took it on the chin. A great tap dancer and film star, who starred with child actress Shirley Temple, Murphy was the Republican from California. He had won in the 1964 landslide triumph of LBJ. Murphy, whose wife was confined to a wheelchair and who was himself the subsequent victim of a throat malignancy, won comfortably over pudgy Pierre Salinger. An appointed senator through vacancy by death, Salinger had been President Kennedy's press secretary. Amiable and most casual, Salinger might well have been the laziest candidate of the Twentieth Century. It counted against him in California despite the Johnson national sweep. Probably the perversity of Californians also mattered. Anyway, Salinger went into business. He wound up with an investment firm abroad whose principal assets came from the hoard Cuban dictator Fulgencio Batista stashed in Switzerland. Salinger always liked what money could buy even when he poor-mouthed it along Kennedy party lines.

Murphy needed money, too. When he came to Washington in 1965, he was able to supplement his Senate salary with an extra $20,000 annually. It was paid by Technicolor, Inc., in Hollywood. The right-wing, self-made mogul, Patrick J. Frawley, Jr., then owned nearly all of Technicolor. His firm also helped defray the $520-a-month pad Murphy needed. It installed a movie projection studio in the apartment. Moreover, company credit cards were issued to Murphy. Among other contracts, Technicolor had one at $3.5 million a year for the filming at Cape Kennedy, home of the space shots. Murphy contended that he signed his Technicolor deal before he entered the Senate. He added that he avoided anything that dealt with contract renewals. A senator can stay away. Just the fact that he is known to have close ties with an outfit is usually enough to renew almost anything.

Murphy's attachment to Technicolor became known five years after he was elected a senator, publicly known, that is. When the deal was revealed, the Senator went to talk to Senator Stennis. As chairman of the Select Committee on Standards and Conduct, Stennis reviewed the episode. Murphy was cleared of any wrongdoing and conflict of interest. The committee handles its problems with obvious great care and selectivity. Murphy felt compelled to fight for re-election. It created some heartaches in the White House. Bob Finch, recently reassigned from being a so-so Secretary of HEW, was one of the President's top counselors. He wanted to run for the Senate and had been a lieutenant governor of California. Murphy said he would be happy with one term and promised Finch the chance next time. So claimed Finch men. Not so, rejoined Murphy. More important, Governor Ronald Reagan didn't want Finch. Murphy thus was home free—to run again. Old hambone actors-turned-politicians have something in common. Reagan and Murphy had it. Representative John Tunney was the Democrats' choice. His father was an ultraconservative Democrat and former world heavyweight champion, Gene Tunney. His greatest assets were parental prominence, schoolhood attachments to Ted Kennedy, and lots of money. He was ultimately elected handily a United States senator, thus ending Murphy's political career.

So absorbed was the Senate with its burdens and personal problems that it hardly noticed the increase of unemployment. With the arrival of the seventies, joblessness zoomed to 3.9 percent. In a little while, the figure would jump to 4.4 percent. The 3.9 increase was the biggest rate rise in nine years. To add to the confusion—Nixon economists had said 4 percent was "comfortable"—the Pentagon piled on problems. It announced the closing down of 371 military bases at home and abroad. Defense Department payroll pared 93,900 employees, of whom nearly two-thirds were civilians. About a billion dollars were saved.

Senators in the forefront of demanding military cutbacks were the first to complain. Why? Usually because their states, like Senator Kennedy's, saw more civilians out of work and bases closed down. Their excuse or charges? Poor planning by the military. The Pentagon couldn't win. Its cutback program was temporarily obscured with an international happening of great significance. The military was not blamed for the coup d'état in Cambodia. This time the ineffable cloak-and-dagger of the CIA was held responsible.

Prince Sihanouk was bounced while abroad in the USSR. The people who assumed control had always been on his side. Cambodia, home of the Khmer people and one of the states of old Indo-China, had been used by North Vietnam as a sanctuary, barroom refresher, and supply station for Communist forces. Sihanouk played the willing dupe to all the intrigue and violations. One of his old top hands, General Lon Nol, a Buddhist mystic, became top man. Sihanouk, who loved the good life afforded even a neutralist of the royal blood, had even left his saxophone at home. He tooted the sweetest blues this side of the China Sea. When he played, all courtiers kept their heads touching the floor. Quite a feat. Watching once, some of us wondered who would outlast whom.

The predicament of Prince "Shnook," as he was known to many reporters, because of personal and political acrobatics, became an international quiz game. He was overthrown while in Moscow. Then, Sihanouk went to Peking where he holed up, courtesy of the regime of Mao Tse-tung. The Soviet Union and most of its bloc continued diplomatic relations with Cambodia. Sihanouk allied himself with Communist invaders of his own normally gentle but fiercely nationalistic Khmer people. North Vietnamese were on foreign soil in Cambodia. There they had supply lines and operational bases long due to the courtesy of Sihanouk, who proclaimed neutrality. Communist China played the most puzzling role of all. It provided Sihanouk with exile under vigil.

But the regime, breaking off Sino-United States talks in Warsaw, maintained contacts with Americans around the world. It remained for senators like Fulbright, Symington, McGovern, and their willing associates not so zeroed in on foreign affairs to shower doubt on American intentions. Encouraged by senatorial suspicions, antiwar demonstration hierarchies plotted new spectacles. It may have been the first time in American history that voices keened in behalf of an enemy victory. Viet Cong and North Vietnamese flags for some years had been held aloft by disciplinarians controlling marches bent on tenderizing and mashing up daily life. The stage was set for another round of tragedy and tawdry political traffic.

As a result, the fuse at the end of the dynamite-laden package of the Middle East sputtered again. Few senators, except for Jackson, called the danger to the attention of the nation. Behind the fresh problems created by a new Sihanouk-successor government in Cambodia, brush-fire exhibitions took the place of policy. French President Georges Pompidou, wily former Rothschild banker, was the target of militant Jewish-American demonstrations. General de Gaulle, Pompidou's predecessor, had switched to a pro-Arab posture. Pompidou urbanely subscribed to Gaullist policy. His tour sparked anti-French rallies. The Jewish Defense League, which never did much for Israel but was a narrow and parochial organization, sprang into the public eye. The nation by now had acquired demonstrators for and against the destruction of nearly everything.

United States senators—congressmen, too—listened coldly to Pompidou address a joint session. Most of them acted as if their constituencies were predicated on an Israeli, if not a Jewish vote. Showing the most studied displeasure was Javits. It was as if he was running again in New York. Of Javits's calculated fondness for Israel, you could turn around Ferenc Molnar's biting sarcasm which went: "If you have a Hungarian for a friend, you don't need enemies." Javits was vocally opposed to the United States role in Vietnam but all out to aid Israel. Selective commitments, sneered Fulbright, among others. The Israelis wrung their hands in despair. They didn't need troops, only hardware. And they needed Javits's partitioned view of world hotspots like a hole in the head. Javits was serene in his own view of the scene at home and abroad. He boasted that in New York any candidate should see him.

"Anyone in New York—Democrat or Republican," confided Javits, "who needs money for office better see me. I know how to get it."

The claim never bothered the people in the White House. Goodell, who took advice from Javits but went ultradovish, took a bad beating later in the year. President Nixon, who viewed Javits with correct but detached courtesy, became alarmed at the anti-French manifestations. The French are inordinately sensitive, the old legend runs. So, he turned up unexpectedly in New York for a huge and resplendent dinner for Pompidou. At least the right wines were served if only because Pompidou brought lots of vintages along with him. Many senators regarded Nixon's soothing gesture of Franco-American traditional amity as unnecessary, if not an outright affront. Again, most senators ignored the fact that only a minority of the Jewish vote in 1968 went to Nixon. His debt to American Jews—and all politicians owe political debts —was about nil. Many American Jews equated Israel with their own viewpoints. The Israelis disliked the idea, but believed it more discreet not to say so. Still, as with blacks, Nixon had more Jews in high office than nearly any other preceding Administration.

"Nixon's wasting his time trying to get them [Jews] to support him," was the phrase many senators used.

The club members were so engaged thinking in terms of publicity values on the Middle East, they sometimes lost sight of the increased Soviet role in Egypt and its application of Russian roulette. Even worse, bipartisan groups were getting lists together for a junket to Monaco. Our parliamentary club members love to see and be seen with royalty. Over in Monaco, ancient home of the Grimaldi freebooters, there was an American, a Princess and once a film star. The occasion was a meeting of the Inter-Parliamentary Union. Princess Grace, née Kelly, helps rule the principality with her pudgy Prince Ranier. The world-famous gambling casino was also in Monaco, at Monte Carlo. Senators angled for invitations as few would on major pieces of legislation. The trip was all expenses paid, too.

Briefly, however, they were upset. Since so few paid attention to a gathering storm affecting the vitals of the nation, they were virtually unprepared when it broke. The country's first-ever postal strike was launched. The main cause was pay or lack of it. Postal services ran at a huge loss and services over the years had been truncated. It was Nixon's most pressing domestic crisis yet. His Secretary of Labor George P. Shultz was getting nowhere with officials of the striking and underpaid mailmen. It was a wretched situation for postal employees. Other federal workers, particularly in the Senate, got regular raises. If the cost of living or inflation shot up, so did congressional salaries. The mailmen and fellow employees earned about the same as kitchen help and worked much harder. George Meany put it on the line, and went to work. At stake was a pay hike and postal reform. Senators, clamoring for a recess to ease the burdens of office, wanted to get back at the problem later.

Everyone in government had a formula. The President thought he'd have to use troops to sort out the mail if the strike got worse. Labor-supporting senators were unhappy about the temporary and unsatisfactory solution. But they wanted judgment deferred. Vacations were uppermost in mind. Wyoming's Senator McGee, chairman of the Senate's Post Office and Civil Service Committee, was down the line with Meany. But he saw and grasped the significant irritation of vacation-minded colleagues. A compromise interim solution was required. McGee, whose forte is really in foreign affairs, but Fulbright keeps him stifled as low man on that committee, worked to near exhaustion. He had to keep lines open to the White House, to Meany, who is a friend and supporter, and to his tuckered-out senatorial club members. The Senate's record by this time in the field of legislation was scraping a new bottom.

Out of McGee's tireless—and thankless—efforts came an assent to work out a solution away from headlines and TV lights. There was fortunate good nature on the part of the strikers and even the grumbling public. Although pressing, this was not a crisis engendered by students, the mad bombers of the New Left, and restless blacks, but by the very dependable corner of Middle America—the mailman. A solution, the only one possible, soon emerged in a White House agreement for a pay hike. Promised postal reform was in the works. Best of all, the senators got a recess. And a group led by Thurmond and Bayh, very bipartisan, took off for the fairyland of Princess Grace. Senate face was saved.

A refreshing recess over, the Senate proceeded to get red faced over the Carswell nomination to the Supreme Court. The White House wanted him badly. Haynsworth's defeat in the Senate four months before rankled deeply. Besides, Strom Thurmond had one more shot at a big appointment. What once appeared a shoo-in, the Carswell nomination took on the aspects of a fight to the death. Well, nearly. Prominent lawyers, retired and in active practice, sent an avalanche of testimony to the Hill deploring Carswell's lack of qualification. The AFL-CIO, its heaviest artillery wheeled into position, blasted at Nixon's nominee. George Meany, in this case as in many, had more troops in the Senate on his side. Combined White House and Justice Department inquiry into Haynsworth's history was inexplicably inadequate. That was especially so in view of the poor preparation in Haynsworth's case.

Senator Hruska, always an unqualified Administration supporter, gave the critics the opening they needed. While the fight moved to a national crescendo, Hruska delivered an incomparable thought. The President, observed Hruska majestically, had the right to name a mediocre judge to the Supreme Court if he wanted one like that. Hruska's Solomon-like words:

"Even if he [Carswell] were mediocre, there are a lot of mediocre judges and people and lawyers. They are entitled to a little representation, aren't they, and a little chance?"

Hruska's reflections promptly made up the minds of a good many fence sitters. One in particular was Marlow W. Cook, a freshman of Republican Kentucky. He had been a principal strategist for Haynsworth. Of Carswell, Senator Cook noted: "He couldn't carry Haynsworth's briefcase." Cook, a loyal Republican, showed then and there he would never be a simplistic party-line knee jerker. The most independent of all in the Senate, also a Republican and the only woman in the club, was outraged. It wasn't so much the mediocre comment of Hruska but the arm-twisting tried on Mrs. Margaret Chase Smith. The cool and handsome white-haired lady from Maine was furious over a White House attempt at hidden persuasion. Bryce Harlow suggested that she'd vote for Carswell. Word was promptly circulated to impress the undecided. Mrs. Smith, on almost any vote, never tips her hand in advance.

From the Senate floor at voting time, to cheers from a packed gallery, Mrs. Smith voted against Carswell. President Nixon personally got into the act at the last minute. He telephoned several senators—Tom Dodd included—to ask their help. They all voted against Carswell. But the Cook and Mrs. Smith "nays" were the crucial tallies. Carswell was rejected by the Senate 51 to 45. It was the first time in history that two presidential nominations to the Supreme Court were rebuffed. The episode did not, however, disappear into the dustbin of history. A glance at the pro- and anti-vote produced strange reactions. Senator Hiram Fong, Republican from Hawaii, voted for Haynsworth and against Carswell.

He objected to overexertion from White House liaison men. George Aiken, Republican dean and superdove, voted for both Haynsworth and Carswell. For unexplained causes, Senator Cooper favored Carswell but had opposed Haynesworth. All the media, only hours before, predicted a close vote but a Carswell triumph.

In the wee hours of the next morning Martha Mitchell had sprung full-blown into the Carswell case. She telephoned the *Arkansas Gazette,* in Little Rock. Furious that Fulbright voted against Carswell—the Senator was dutifully Southern for Haynsworth—Mrs. Mitchell told the *Gazette* in her Southern high dudgeon:

"I want you to crucify Fulbright and that's that."

The paper printed her comments. Martial Martha Mitchell got nearly as much attention as the vote itself. Her late-night telephone calls were fast becoming as famous as big TV talk shows. She also said of Fulbright: "He makes me so damned mad I can't stand it." Mrs. Mitchell accurately reflected White House and lots of Senate views on the statesman senator from Arkansas. One mustn't forget, though: Martha Mitchell figured, as a girl from Pine Bluff, Arkansas, that Fulbright had let his state down.

As senators incline after so bruising a clash, they tried to put balm on wounds, not meaning a word of it. Thus Birch Bayh, who got to handle the floor fight originally by default, wanted bygones with cigar-chewing Senate Judiciary chairman, James O. Eastland, Missouri Democrat. "Sure, sure," growled Eastland. To an aide, after Bayh ambled down the corridor, Eastland said: "Don't worry. We'll get him soon where the hairs are short." Then Eastland to Dodd, who said, sorry he couldn't help.

"I didn't expect you to," answered Eastland. "I told the White House not to bother you."

Later, Dodd observed: "He's a realist. But he never forgot that I helped lead the civil rights legislative fight."

The aftermath of the Carswell vote was the determining factor in a personal decision by Nixon to get the Senate membership sufficiently altered in the 1970 elections. It meant, after dillying, that the President would take an active role in the sleazy politics of it all. A political animal, he realized chances to shift the balance —it would take a triumph of seven seats while losing none—were negligible. He hoped that he could win enough to neutralize Republican senators who more often than not voted with Democratic liberals. The presidential thoughts were communicated to Senators Scott, Bob Dole, and Bob Griffin of Michigan. The latter, a hard worker and articulate, was beginning to make something of a name for himself in an assembly characterized mainly by self-made mediocrity. Although some senatorial aspirants of both parties declared early in the year, the challenge was flung down by Nixon after the Carswell rejection.

A persistent, thorny outsider stopped the Senate cold from casually rushing through another confirmation. The stormy case—known as the ITT caper—broke early in this election year. Jack Anderson again got the goods. He produced memos linking ITT to a promise of a hefty contribution to the Republican Convention. The promise was made just about the same time as the Justice Department settled an anti-trust suit in favor of ITT.

Acting Attorney General Richard Kleindienst, veteran Goldwater loyalist and chosen heir by John Mitchell, drew withering fire from the club and the media. The imposing Senate Committee on the Judiciary re-opened hearings on his confirmation at Kleindienst's request. (Translated from German, his name means "small favor.") Yet this same committee only a short time before had approved his appointment as Attorney General unanimously, 13 to 0. The case became a Senate circus.

When the anti-Anderson counter-attack came, the columnist calmly produced another stack of ITT memos. These associated ITT with a plot to prevent Marxist President Salvadore Allende from assuming power in Chile, where the giant conglomerate had huge investments. Anderson set the country on its ear—the Senate, too. He piled it on by providing the media with 80 pages of confidential ITT papers. Anderson was setting lots of firsts: distributing secret documents this way was unique. It whetted the public appetite and dismay. Demands for inquiry into big business/big government coziness stayed at a high pitch because of elections '72.

The President promptly ruled out selection of another Southern nominee. He'd choose a strict constructionist from outside the South. Why? Because the Senate "as it is presently constituted will not approve a man from the South who shares my views of strict construction of the Constitution." In the declaration, Nixon watchers and haters saw the seeds of destruction of what was called a Southern strategy. There never really was one except in the minds of a few writers. George Wallace split sentiments in 1968 in the South. His divisiveness permitted Nixon to slip through here and there, hardly everywhere. The strategy or political warfare was centered for 1970 in the North and the border states. Mid-Atlantic strategy for label creators?

Political due bills to Strom Thurmond ran the statute of limitations with the Carswell fiasco. Henceforth old Strom would be an essential case of benign neglect. His concepts of school busing and desegregation were mused upon publicly, and principally dumped in the ashcan by legal decisions. To wound Thurmond even more—pretty unintentionally by the White House—a Midwesterner was nominated to the Supreme Court. He was Federal Judge Harry Andrew Blackmun of Minnesota. A self-made jurist and well regarded, Blackmun also was a lifelong friend of Chief Justice Warren E. Burger, also of Minnesota. His hearings before the Judiciary Committee were perfunctory. The Senate approved Blackmun unanimously, 94 to 0. Thurmond was more than ever convinced of the late twentieth-century civil war against the South.

So was Martha Mitchell, who was the butt of an unforeseen slight. She had hired the wife of a TV education channel editor, Bill Woestendiek, a former magazine editor and newspaperman in the Southwest, to be her press secretary. Woestendiek's wife, Kay, also had been trained as, and worked as, an active newspaperwoman. Woestendiek, a quiet, earnest man, never wore his politics on his sleeve. He was liberally minded but didn't brandish it like a terrible swift sword. When he was hired for WETA—directed mainly by avowed Liberals—his private views were known. But he was fired in the most crass manner, only a few months after he came to Washington, because his wife took a job with Mrs. Mitchell. There was no question whatever about Woestendiek's professional competence. The station said he was dismissed because his wife took the job with Martha.

The criteria invoked had been deliberately one sided. In Washington quite a few wives of pronouncedly liberal commentators and political figures had so-called sensitive positions. Nobody ever dreamed of dumping them if their competence met professional standards. Amazingly, there was little indignation raised about the roof falling in on Bill Woestendiek. His wife was in the employ of Martha Mitchell. That was enough. It was kind of a reprisal by the association of marriage. Besides, nobody thought to ask Kay her political views. If they did, they might have been horrified to learn that she, too, was pretty anti-Administration.

Of all the liberal-minded senators none rose to Woestendiek's defense. They had to live with the media. If the media didn't cry out, why should a senator? Three of the foremost in the Senate told me so—bluntly and cynically. Yet there were senators like Muskie who repeatedly claimed that Nixon weighted the news in his favor. In their own ways so did senators, ranging from McGovern to Bayh, Hughes, Proxmire, Ted Kennedy, and Fulbright. Nearly all harbored presidential ambitions. Woestendiek's case was spiked, so to say. The media swiftly ignored the injustice against him and took an inward look. What came out was a loud and shrill complaint against the presidential press conference, as it appeared on TV.

The sessions lasted about thirty minutes. A President in command of all his buttons could orchestrate a press conference as he chose. Nixon's two immediate predecessors played the conferences like Hungarian fiddles. Why shouldn't Nixon? The President wasn't holding as many conferences as others did, was a common complaint. There was little chance to follow up questions. The complaints had validity, as far as they went. But few in the electronic and print press gave any thought about how many tried to be actors when questioning the President. Nor did many ask why the questions posed were too often speeches, or flaccid. There was ample room for self-criticism, but precious little emerged. At TV conferences, the press were spear carriers in a sort of beggar's opera. The senators they usually showered with praise were, of course, on their side. Led by Muskie, they forged away at the No. 1 press target, Vice-President Agnew. Everyone shot from the hip, except the television revenue officers who continued to worry about license renewal. An alternate target, studiously ignored hitherto, came under fire.

A good third of the Senate discreetly supported journalists in assailing the now-wayward Al Capp. But the humorist, fast on his feet, gave back every calumny thrown at him, and more. He taunted college audiences. The schools loved to have him back, often at $3,500 a crack. In the last few years he added two hundred newspapers. His strip appeared in a thousand papers with an estimated readership of sixty to ninety million. His more recent brand of satire and rhetoric struck a deeply responsive chord.

With dismay Capp's critics found they couldn't counter his immense upsurge in circulation, so they have adopted a no-see, no-hear Capp posture. Fulbright, whose poses helped make him one of the composites for Capp's Senator Phogbound, pretended to ignore comic strips. Of course, "Dogpatch" is the antsy rural community, presumably Southern, that Capp created. It is uncannily like the community that has sent Fulbright back to Congress for thirty years. Laboring mightily to make the Presidency bend to his will, Fulbright could only be bothered with humor and commentary that filled his particular perspective. He had returned to his drafting board with more vigor than ever. A somewhat favorable report on springtime conditions in Southeast Asia and continued withdrawal of troops Fulbright deliberately withheld from the rest of his committee. His own pocket veto got back to the White House. There always will be minority members of the committee who resent Fulbright's tactics. Braced privately why he didn't release the memorandum, Fulbright diffidently explained he was waiting for something more timely.

Thus he maneuvered to have "expert" witnesses by the drove appear before the Committee on Foreign Relations to support the Fulbright thesis. A prize was retired General James (Slim Jim) Gavin, a World War II paratroop hero. Briefly a Kennedy-appointed ambassador to France, namely de Gaulle, Gavin flopped as a diplomat. De Gaulle was icily courteous. Gavin spoke schoolboy French and was hardly a political mind in the supreme Gaullist view. Still, Gavin was a genuine war hero, although it was a war way back when. He had been a progenitor of vertical envelopment. The concept involves use of helicopters to transport troops to hot spots. Essentially, vertical envelopment as propounded first by Gavin was implemented in the war in Vietnam. Gavin never mentioned it. Instead he contented himself before

Fulbright with worrying aloud lest our role in Vietnam provoke a war with Communist China. As in European diplomacy, Gavin was totally unaware of Nixon's personal initiative in coming to some kind of workable accommodation with mainland China.

So obsessed was Fulbright with Southeast Asia that he paid little heed to the massive Soviet arms build-up in the Middle East. Even when the great Russian writer, Alexander Solzhenitsyn, wrote that the USSR was a "sick society" and assailed its narrow leaders, there was hardly a murmur from Fulbright and most senators, who had one-front external minds. None had bothered to note the wretched first anniversary of forcible Soviet reoccupation of Czechoslovakia. Few noticed the second as well. As for Soviet-dominated Eastern Europe, it was an irritation now. The Russian haste to install the most modern air-to-air missiles in Egypt, complete with Soviet technical crews, was all but forgotten in Fulbright's activities.

The introduction of Soviet interceptor planes, pilots, and missile crews was of the highest significance to the United States. It was the first time since the crisis in Cuba in the tumultuous autumn of 1962 that the Russians engaged in a calculated risk outside their own domain. To man the missile sites, the Soviets had to transport highly trained cadres. They introduced in this stage at least four thousand. Their total in the air and on the ground in Egypt had climbed to the fifteen thousand-man mark. Of the build-up Fulbright remarked: "I believe these [Soviet measures] are defensive." In the short strategic distances of the Middle East, what is offensive or defensive is quite moot. Strangely, we paid more attention to the Soviet carefully contrived "worldwide" commemorations for the one hundredth anniversary of the birth of Vladimir Ilyich Ulanov than to the newest missile crisis. The world knew the man so distinguished by the Soviet Union as Lenin.

Senators Symington, McGovern, Church, and Gore—augmented by Republicans Aiken, Javits, and Hatfield—pounded away at a request by the new Cambodian regime for arms. Fulbright announced that he'd be sending out his own investigators to Cambodia. That he did. They spoke to correspondents in Vietnam and Thailand. Before setting foot into Cambodia, the Fulbright-dispatched investigators filed the major part of their report from

Bangkok. That rheumy practice used to be known once in journalistic circles as "the magic-carpet dateline." The opposition to furnishing arms to Cambodia provoked scathing rebuttal from some critics of the Vietnam war, as well as from senators like McGee and Scott. Their contention? Since when was it wrong to try to rid yourself of foreign invading forces?

Fulbright and the mass of his committee, as usual, chose to hammer at the thought of sending any assistance to what they now sneeringly called a "client state." Thrust into the murky background of affairs of state was the menacing Soviet collection of modern-day firepower in the Middle East. Until the last few hours before the President addressed the nation on a tense TV program, few senators knew anything of a decision he had made. Since the Cambodian coup and the regime's desire to remove Communist forces from its soil, Nixon was urged to act. How? By sending in an American force from South Vietnam, with South Vietnamese, to try to eliminate sanctuaries Communist units held for themselves for eight years. Depending on senatorial points of view, the maneuver was either bold or beastly. It triggered a spate of irresponsible statements and recriminations inside the Senate.

If senators supported the President, colleagues wantonly accused them of being mindless warmongers. Senators who opposed vehemently were denounced as capons, near traitors, and wooden headed. The division was even nastier than confused and divided public feeling. Tons of mail and telegrams poured into the White House. The count ran better than six to one in favor of Nixon's move. Interestingly, many of these guided missives referred distinctly to his very recent pledge to withdraw another 150,000 men from Vietnam. The combined operation into Cambodia—illustrated on TV by the President with maps of Communist sanctuaries—would save, not cost, American lives. Emphasis on life-saving had become an article of faith. Every senator stressed the point; methods were apart. Only a couple of hours before Nixon announced a 150,000 withdrawal, all the media leaked first-hand information: that he would announce 50,000! They got the feed-box special from both Democratic and Republican senators.

An accurate estimate was furnished by Attorney General Mitchell, but only when Nixon began discussing new withdrawals.

Senators, especially those inclined to side wi Fulbright and the majority of his committee, were red with anger. Mitchell was an appointed Cabinet officer. He had never been elected to anything. How dare the President consult with him on these matters and hardly even inform the Senate! Mitchell had become recognized by members of the exclusive club as the most powerful personality in Washington, other than the President. He got CIA briefings, sat in on national and international affairs deliberations. Mitchell's role—and his wife's outbursts—even drew differing senators closer in a spirit of togetherness.

The affinity within the club prevailed on Norris Cotton, Republican and senior Senator from New Hampshire. A veteran, Cotton was weaned on the wheeling-dealing of the late Senator Styles Bridges' Republican machine. Conservative to the core, Cotton also was a buddy of publisher and polemicist, William Loeb. The Loeb newspaper in Manchester, New Hampshire, *The Union Leader,* had borrowed $3 million from the Teamsters Union. Jimmy Hoffa, as the Union power, gave assent. Loeb paid back the loan but he always defended Hoffa raucously, when the Teamster boss was in and out of jail. Cotton picked up a bale of "free Hoffa" signatures collected by Loeb. He had been soothed by Senator Scott and the White House, which then pigeonholed the batch of Hoffa petitions. An old member of the Senate club, who supported the Nixon Administration a little more than 50 percent of the time, explained some of the post-Cambodian wrath:

"There are a hundred egos here," he said. "It doesn't matter how ineffective or inefficient some are. The ego is big to be a Senator. We all congratulated ourselves when Mike [Mansfield] praised our work. It was part of the game; the system. Hell, what major legislation did we accomplish?"

Just before the Cambodian invasion disclosure, Mansfield hailed the Senate's work. He said cooperation was outstanding. The calendar, he marvelled, had been virtually cleared of all pending legislation. Majority Leader Mansfield ticked off roll call votes— 128 in this half of the session. It was a real numbers game. Rhetoric was hot, often high. The number of major bills that got through to the floor of the Senate you could put in the corner of your eye. Nevertheless, it was the Cambodian venture that became combustible. Students across the country, egged on by self-centered, self-designated revolutionaries, sputtered and sparked.

A Black Panther rally at hallowed Yale brought in paratroop security and measured signs of ugliness. But while national attention was fixed upon Yale an explosion in mid-America ripped through the nation. At Kent State University in Kent, Ohio, four students were killed and eleven wounded. National Guardsmen shot at demonstrating students. It was the bloodiest confrontation of the student turbulence spawned in the mid-sixties by the war in Vietnam. There was a stillness in the Senate. Rage, bereaved and to some extent channeled by campus organizers, coursed through colleges coast to coast. Protest demonstrations were hastily put together. The Senate, the nation's body of elected wisemen, issued via members on the floor or before TV statements that nobody remembered the following day. The ritual of primaries and intra-party contests was already on the body politic. Too bad, of course, about the corpses and the maimed. The electoral process and the power brokers were all cranked up.

In Ohio, home of Kent State University, campaigning for the primaries paused almost imperceptibly. As the first preliminary inquiry into the shootings were initiated, candidates for the Democratic and Republican nominations for United States Senate were appealing to voters. It was comic-tragic. A former astronaut, John Glenn, wanted the spot that cranky old Democratic Senator Stephen M. Young was vacating. So did the son of a late senator and grandson of a former President, Robert Taft, Jr., want the Republican designation. Glenn, who made passing references to the glories of the astronauts—Apollo 13 had been to the moon and back with casual notice, alas—was supported by Kennedy backers. Young wanted his campaign manager, Cleveland millionaire Howard Metzenbaum. Metzenbaum massaged the media with his commercials and won. Taft beat back Governor Jim Rhodes, whose administration reeked with blatant conflict-of-interest office-holders. Ambition and the pretense of normalcy were being served.

In the South there was no Southern strategy except that Senator Allen, staunch watchdog of the TB-ridden Senate dining rooms, opined that former Governor George C. Wallace would make it again in Alabama. He ultimately managed. Senatorial aspirants, not yet in the great hall, sucked their thumbs and scratched for political support. Adlai Stevenson III made peace with Mayor Daley, of Chicago. He would be the Democratic choice. Dirksen's successor, Senator Ralph T. Smith, proved a sterling cipher during his interim tenure. Eyes on challengers and vice versa, senators puffed up their importance with a delegation that talked to President Nixon. He promised them that in less than a couple of months—by July 1—all GIs would leave Cambodia. The United States units, pledged Nixon, would penetrate no deeper than nineteen miles into Cambodia without congressional consent. Mollified, if not satisfied, Senators Fulbright and Mansfield went after Secretary Rogers. He was accused of having produced a credibility gap. Although a high-priced lawyer by profession, Rogers hardly is the most articulate exponent of foreign policies. Fulbright delightedly tripped him up with gaps in private testimony. The Chairman—there was only one referred to so sarcastically by colleagues—still nibbled around the Presidency. He didn't dare carry the attack to its center.

Weightier events concerning foreign affairs offended the *amour propre* of some senators. At a fine dinner, crystal shining and dry wines pouring, the Italian Embassy beefed. Something along the lines of a personal injury, you see. It seems that the Fire Department had gotten a rush telephone call.

"This is the Guinea Embassy," was the accepted appeal. "There's a fire."

Off rushed the equipment, sirens screeching, to the Italian Embassy. It took a little time to explain that the African Republic of Guinea was somewhere else. Fortunately, physical damage was minor. But the affront to diplomatic dignity to the Embassy of Italy seemed much deeper. Italians collectively had in this country managed to have official references to the Mafia expunged. And this use of a coarse, antiquated epitet about people of Italian ancestry might have resulted in a smoky debacle. The Fire Department was so informed.

Fastidious senators, poring over environmental behavior and ecology, also looked around their turf and fumed at a couple of colleagues—in private. Two tobacco chewers and spitters were in the Senate. At least they were known. One was Herman E. Talmadge, Democrat of Georgia. He was very tidy and never missed the few cuspidors around. A Northern tobacco-chewer also turned up in the person of Republican Senator William Saxbe, of Ohio. Apparently he acquired the habit as a kid in his rural family homestead. Saxbe, however, was nearly as fastidious as his ecologically minded critics. Never a suspicious stain. Tobacco chewing wasn't considered these days good for a projection of any senatorial image. It conveyed the sense of despoilment. Saxbe was pretty big on the ecology and pollution. His personal habit was almost equated with a blast put on Muskie. A team of Ralph Nader's Raiders tried to blow him out of the water. They said he failed miserably in the field of air pollution. They could—and later did— go after the presidential aspirant from Maine on water pollution in his home state. Many Muskie contributors spoiled the streams. It's not easy to raise money and at the same time clobber a contributor.

IX

SENATE SHADOWBOXING

Huge antiwar demonstrations in the capital and on campuses did not accelerate the dilatory pace of the Senate. Members wrangled in committees. The more astute headline handlers were quick to pounce on testimony by doctors and psychiatrists that GIs in Vietnam went into battle in drug-induced fogs. It was deplorable, declared Senator McGovern. Indeed, it was. So was a carefully researched screed that showed the use of wanton terror and mass killing by Communists in Vietnam. Douglas Pike, an academic-type specialist in Vietnamese affairs and horrors, produced the booklet. It comprised only 125 pages. A solid section was devoted to Communist liquidation methods and massacres, as in Hue. Pike's revelations were never mentioned by Senators Fulbright, McGovern, Muskie, and bipartisan critics. Fulbright didn't even bother to ask Pike to testify before his committee.

A new emphasis was added because primary time, or politics as usual, was in progress around the country. Although President Nixon announced that he soon would approve a bill passed to give the vote to eighteen-year-olds, activities by students in some key primaries were painfully thin in response. A fresh hero—for a brief season—cast a roseate glow over critics of the Administration. He was hailed by Senator Proxmire for "courage." When Secretary of the Interior Walter Hickle had been questioned about his fitness for the office, Proxmire had been sharp in disapproval. But Hickel, a smallish, round man going bald, leaked a personal letter to Nixon. He complained that the Administration was turning its back on a great mass of youth and thereby contributing to anarchy and revolt.

Hickel also assailed Vice-President Agnew. The mousy, uncertain little man from Alaska was applauded by many in the media and by anti-Nixonites in the Senate. He had become a minor league St. George. Against all customary practice, he neglected to see that the President received his note of protest before making it public. One of his earnest and enthusiastic young subordinates drafted the letter. Hickel approved but did not specify that it must be private until after the President, to whom it was addressed, had read it. Observance of privileged communications had become antiquated. Leaks and full disclosures had become the rule of procedure in the Senate. Why not in other areas? Senator Fulbright, for instance, thought nothing of divulging secret transcripts when they involved his targets. Directly or through the cutting edge of the Symington subcommittee, Fulbright maintained his running gun fight against the Executive branch. With the Hickel breach of etiquette, there was quiet approval from Fulbright and most of the Democrats warming up for the 1972 presidential races.

Delighted that vapors rose in Nixon's own official family, Senators Muskie and McGovern felt that Hickel had come of age. Impatiently, both were getting set for nomination contests in 1972. Muskie, up for re-election to the Senate, looked into the distance. All he wanted was a whopping election win to show the esteem in which he is held back home. What that afterglow has to do with the suitability of an aspirant on a national scale makes no sense. Yet it has been a cardinal thesis of politicians that a big show at home will rally the country around anyone as the people's choice.

In keeping with another hoary legend, Muskie put together a staff and raised money separately for his presidential nomination effort. But he didn't formally declare for a long time. Never making a secret of his desires, McGovern did declare, more than fourteen months before the first primaries in New Hampshire. He also took the initiative in raising money for "peace candidates." It would be hard to fund a true "war candidate," unless he was in Egypt or Syria. Adding to the cacophony, political shapers like Professor John Kenneth Galbraith endorsed superpacifists. As a

pop economist and wandering minstrel of no-account diplomacy
for a couple of years, Galbraith returned to the United States to
wave his bells and pass around an elixir for tranquillity and coequality. Just about every primary candidate he supported in the
Democratic party was mercilessly battered. The best example was
in the state of Washington. Senator Scoop Jackson made chopped
onions of the Galbraith- and, yes, the Gene McCarthy-endorsed
candidate. Then Jackson went on to win re-election as senator
with a huge 87 percent of the total votes cast.

Galbraith's knowledge of politics in Washington—the state and
elsewhere—can be matched only by his knowledge of Soviet and
other external affairs. Nevertheless he trumpeted a call to defeat
Democrats like Jackson, and McGee in Wyoming, two of the most
able and intelligent men in the Senate. He also urged that even if
Republicans should win, that would be a good thing. Out of the
charred remains, Galbraith and those candidates he preferred
would build a party in the totemlike image of John Kenneth
Galbraith. Nothing like this happened when all the returns came
in later. McGovern, rather favored by the blinkered visionaries of
the Galbraith style, showed more prudence. He went after money,
first. That was how any campaign had to be waged. McGovern
wanted others to be beholden, too.

With "Dear Friend" letters, McGovern raised about $500,000
in behalf of liberal Senate Democrats. It didn't matter that one
on his list, Senator Ralph Yarborough, had already been badly
beaten by conservative Democrat Bentsen in Texas primaries. By
asking for money to help fellow liberals, McGovern also kept his
name before many thousands dunned for contributions. The lists
could be used many times. Muskie, trying to be a loner or above
the pack, didn't go for the gimmick. He spoke in behalf of candidates, but money he raised for his own fights. Financial disclosures
for senators in 1969—put out in mid-1970—reflected some lucrative
moonlighting, especially by Messrs. Muskie and McGovern.

These were the two top money earners in senatorial honoraria.
A total of seventy-five senators reported outside earnings, not in
stocks or bonds, but in speeches and writing, in the amount of
$640,662. Not bad when you consider about 90 percent of these
extracurricular efforts are undertaken by staff assistants. They are

paid by the Senate anyway. Muskie, No. 1 Democratic aspirant for 1972, earned $80,183. That was nearly double his $42,500 annual Senate pay. Second, as in the running, was McGovern with $63,501. No. 3 aggregated $38,800. He was Bayh. A senator who earned relatively little, $2,600, was Ted Kennedy. Why he even bothered to take any money puzzled people. Of course the top money raiser among Republicans was Vice-President Agnew. That was in the many millions—but for the party, not for himself. Side earnings for the Senate also revealed that top man among Republicans was Oregon's senior Senator, Hatfield. Poor Hatfield. He complained continuously of how the cost of office kept him broke and away too much from a young family. No doubt Hatfield obtained some surcease with extra earnings of $28,750. Of the first ten honoraria earners, seven were Democrats.

A quick breakdown of the sources of outside income in this special field disclosed that colleges and universities provided the best pay dirt. In 194 speaking engagements, forty-three Senators received $186,337. Others known as "interest groups" were headed by Jewish organizations. They paid more money for senator speakers than any other. The total was $29,250, and it went mainly to liberals. Muskie got the most for six speeches—$11,000. It is baffling why an "interest" group should want to pay any senator around $2,000 for a set piece. Proxmire, who was represented by a lecture agency, didn't disclose a total. But he said he never received more than $300 for any talk. Since he sometimes failed to recognize a staff-written job, he was most modest with good reason.

Other moonlighting senators receiving honoraria from assorted interests included Alabama Democrat John Sparkman. He earned $11,200, of which $7,200 came from interested banking groups. Sparkman, No. 2 on Fulbright's committee on Foreign Relations, paid more attention to the Banking Committee. He was chairman of that one. Most interests that could be ticked off on a list in Washington, D.C., had senators speak or write. To mention a few, there were labor and business; nine members of the Commerce Committee earned honoraria from broadcasting, utility, telephone, transportation, and maritime interests. It went on that dreary way down to an anti-ABM organization that paid Senator Gore $1,000. He was a critic. The honoraria in this field came from something called the Chicago Citizens Against ABM. All of this is almost like having an extra District of Columbia committee to which contributions can be made.

"The main ethical problem involved in honoraria arises when a group with legislative interests within a member's committee jurisdiction invites that member to speak for a fee," noted a 1970 report of the Bar of the City of New York.

A foundation-funded study center, criticized by some senators, didn't have trouble getting honoraria takers. Senator Cooper received $2,000 from the Center for Study of Democratic Institutions at Santa Barbara, California. He conducted a panel and gave a paper on Chinese-United States relations. Senator Fulbright reported receiving $1,500 from the Fund and Senator Church $1,250. All are members of the Committee on Foreign Relations. Supreme Court associate justices got senatorial lumps for being paid as chairmen of the executive committee while on the Court. A few senators accepting honoraria contributed all sums to charity. Most noteworthy in this respect was Senator Jackson. He has given every penny, since elected to the Senate in 1952, to charitable causes.

In a charmed circle of the Senate stood Margaret Chase Smith. As usual, she never accepts any honoraria. Mrs. Smith, who made history in the Senate with a gripping speech in 1950 against the late Senator Joe McCarthy, is in her early seventies. Her independence and probity have remained unquestioned even by fellow Republicans who would dearly love her to be more orthodox. A fresh rose in her left lapel daily, Senator Margaret Chase Smith was the epitome of the flowering of New England. Her "Declaration of Conscience" speech against McCarthy was marked by a dinner from her admirers on both sides of the Senate aisle. Twenty years to the day of her speech against the extremism of McCarthy, Senator Margaret Chase Smith appealed for civility in the country. It was an expression of behavior rapidly fading from American life. Characteristically, she warned bluntly that a new era of right-wing repression could occur in reaction to "antidemocratic arrogance and nihilism from the political extreme left."

Comparing the atmosphere prevalent with that of McCarthy's Communist-hunting days, Mrs. Smith told the Senate in her calm but incisive manner: "We had a national sickness then from which we recovered. We have now a national sickness from which I pray we will recover."

Dutiful and transitory lip service was accorded Senator Smith's appeal. Then colleagues and candidates went right back to wooing the elements she warned about. Civility meant to many being just a nice guy. As everyone believes, nice guys can't win.

Only after Margaret Chase Smith berated her colleagues in the Senate for absenteeism—even proposing a constitutional amendment for expulsion—did the citadel of male domination loosen up on a known but well-kept, in-house secret. It was a special, tender kind of winter-summer love story. Suddenly Mrs. Smith stayed away from the Senate after record consecutive appearances. At the Walter Reed Hospital bedside of her administrative aide, William Lewis, Jr., she kept a twenty-four hour vigil. He had been stricken with a heart attack. Mrs. Smith spent her seventy-fourth birthday at the hospital. Lewis was fifty-eight.

They had been affectionately together as a team for twenty-three years. Lewis was fresh from the Air Force, and Mrs. Smith, widowed, had her husband's seat in Congress. Their love and respect for each other has been profound. Lewis was hardly known in Maine. In the corridors of power in Washington, it was different. Lewis got the full measure of honor and regard as if he was an actual senator. Indeed, his skill and intelligence helped Mrs. Smith in many major ways. Her "Declaration of Conscience" speech against Joe McCarthy was Lewis's idea. His offer also made it possible for Senator Smith to be proposed and placed in nomination as the Republican candidate for President in 1964. She was the first woman in history to be so proposed.

A bachelor, Lewis is a highly educated man. He happens to be independently wealthy and is part Chicksaw Indian, from Oklahoma. His parents helped with Mrs. Smith's first election to the Senate and came to live in a suburb of Washington in a house William Lewis built for them. Mrs. Smith and Lewis moved in with them. After the elder Lewises died, the Senator stayed on in the house in a small downstairs apartment. Lewis moved out but not too far away.

Up for re-election this year, Mrs. Smith may not decide whether to run—one way or another—until very late. It will depend upon whether Lewis is up to being at her side again. But the United States Senate did not forget that she had knocked Senate members and their campaigning for President in an election year. As Mrs. Smith remarked acidly: "We were elected to serve as Senators. Anything wrong with that?" Many of her colleagues thought so and out came the love story.

This was the age of pandering to one extreme or another and of plutocratic politics. Getting up the money for candidacies, for television commercials, and getting an image mattered most. A case in point on opening up a limitless cash war chest was in New York State. A young Congressman, Richard Ottinger, compiled a wondrously inflated record in the House. Pushed in any direction, it puffed up like a windbag on another side. He lavished money from papa's plywood fortune on TV commercials. And he got the Democratic nomination. Ottinger was briefly outstanding because he got to be a candidate. So did Metzenbaum in Ohio. Incumbents weren't far behind in putting money in the media. Senator Hartke opted for a third term in Indiana. He had the money backing. Not too far removed from the affair at the bridge of Chappaquiddick, Teddy Kennedy announced again. It was a tribute to his stamina and his contempt for his electorate.

Harry Byrd, Jr., in Virginia, son of the elder Harry who for years ran Virginia as a Norman keep, bolted the Democratic party. A long time before, Rennie Davis bolted, too, from all parties. Davis was an aberration from Byrd country. Byrd would run as an Independent. In the Senate, reform Democrats made angry noises. They subsided when polls showed Byrd would beat the combination of Democratic and Republican candidates combined. He could come back into the Democratic fold and thus maintain all his committee seniority was the solemn assessment of his colleagues. They couldn't possibly beat Byrd, so they'd join him. The Republicans kept a huge distance from the Republican candidate for Byrd's seat. They hoped fervently—negotiated with Byrd—to see if he would join Republican ranks. Byrd stayed an Independent, as a most conservative Democrat. Rennie Davis disowned the whole bit for revolution and its rhetoric. In the midst of all the antics, a TV senator visited the real things. He was actor Hal Holbrook. On NBC he portrayed a freshman senator, but was unidentified as to party association. Holbrook came away saying he learned a lot. In a couple of days around freshman senators?

None of them showed any more than casual concern—for the *Record,* of course—about the steady decline of the economy. Stocks dipped to a seven-year low and would descend further to the mid-600s by the Dow Jones averages, which most little investors used as their own measurement. Our gross national product (GNP) had dipped. Prices were up and unemployment, at 4.8 percent, was getting close to 5 percent. In a short time joblessness would shoot past 6 percent. Not too long before, Senator Scott had sought to soothe the alarms of a recalcitrant George Meany and other labor leaders by asserting that 4 percent unemployment was livable until the economy was properly righted. The Senate skirted the periphery of these urgent domestic problems. Members stalled and pondered injustices, a combination of fancied and real ones. They did mighty little except to deliver committee speeches or floor oratory but accomplished nothing to remedy welfare, environment, transportation, and health care. Senators spoke a lot. But the Senate did not legislate.

The majority of the members watched the swelling of campus and other antiwar demonstrations, trying to figure out where the political payoff rested. Kent State's tragedy was a rallying point, but senators, in a gesture of high-mindedness, thought they would await the outcome of several investigations. A grievous incident, similar to Kent State's agony, exploded in Mississippi at Jackson State College. It was a school for blacks. A police barrage killed two black students, wounded seven others in the wake of stone-throwing and name-calling. The grisly episode elicited sad but brief reaction. It was a segregated sequence. Calls for coequality up at Yale drew a massive student body response. It was tied to the trial of Black Panthers for torturing and killing an informer. Yale's President, Dr. Kingman Brewster, lamented that he did not believe a black man could get a fair trial.

He was soon proved wrong, but his remark was as easily forgotten as it had been disproved. Brewster, curiously, had asked for consideration for a prominent post in the Nixon Administration when it took over. He was never tapped. Then he thought about running for the Senate. Brewster stayed at Yale when his overtures were rebuffed with silence. He had a forum at Yale. There was a goodly group of Yale alumni in the Senate. He had supporters and critics there. Senator Peter H. Dominick, Colorado Republican, out of Yale and Connecticut, believed Brewster was out of his league. Marine veteran Dominick, whose forebears founded the prestigious firm of Dominick & Dominick, was senatorial proof that an Ivy League education didn't make a senator. His attendance record was splendid, effectiveness near zero. Dominick was the Republicans' answer to Democratic Senator Pell. Both were most earnest, and bores. Their grasp of legislation lay in college textbooks they once studied hard to cram for exams.

Neither liberal Democrats like Pell nor conservative Republicans like Dominick ever understood the phenomenon that arose among laboring people—the hardhats. These are building and construction workers. They wear plastic helmets on the job to avoid getting brained if some piece of the building falls on them. Hardhats earn pretty good money. Their roots are in the lower middle class. All had seen penury firsthand during the Depression. They wanted a piece of affluence, had gotten a little in their own homes, a car, and in seeing that many of their children went to college. Quite a few resented the idea of blacks being inserted in their work ranks at equal pay. It wasn't a particular color bias; the real leveler was economic. And also hardhats were faithful taxpayers.

They resented bitterly antiwar demonstrations. Their loathing of young marchers prompted hardhats to teach the errant young a painful lesson. On occasion they beat them up. Many had been war veterans. What dissenters did was immoral and smacked of communism. The label "silent majority" appealed to the construction workers. As long as the economic factor stood in their favor, they were for country, flag, and their concept of the status quo. Only a handful of senators bothered to try to understand their gripes, their emotionalism and concerns. Most members of the eminent legislative club were puzzled. All Democrats seemed delighted because one of the first hardhat targets was New York's Mayor John Lindsay. He worried ambitious candidates lest he jump from being somewhat of a Republican to the Democratic fold. All Democrats were united—in keeping Lindsay out.

Deeply puzzled, the Republicans couldn't make out the hardhat emotions. It pleased the Administration when Agnew attacks against the media were echoed; when President Nixon's stand on Vietnam was applauded. It was a chance, Republican strategists saw, to get a good chunk of labor on their sides. The hardhats always had been Democrats. Nixon trouble-shooters encouraged visits to Washington from hardhat delegations. The President accepted a token hardhat as a gift. Something new seemed to have bubbled up to the political surface. It would not and could not last, two contrary personalities said. George Meany declared construction workers couldn't be for the Republicans—a question of economics. Senator Barry Goldwater, an implacable domestic foe of Meany, agreed. The mild-mannered Arizona Senator, controversial Republican candidate for President in 1964, no longer delivered fiery texts. He learned that being away from the Senate even one term meant starting over. Goldwater was preparing to go back to his beloved desert. He had gobs of sympathy for the frustrations of the hardhats. When the chips were down, he believed, they'd never line up for the Republicans.

Democratic senators, trying to accommodate all camels under the same tent, tried to woo hardhats. They were terrified at the thought of any deep split in labor. Those fancying themselves as ahead in a contest for the presidential nomination stuck principally to much more left-leaning groups. The snobbery was evident, a bone that stuck in the gorges of both hardhats and Meany. Instead, nearly all aspirants—again with the exception of Jackson—curried favor openly with a new, self-proclaimed lobbying organization called Common Cause. Lobbyists abound in Washington, for special interests from business to anti-Pentagon. Many have gobs of money to contribute, for expensive meals and presents and with interest-free loans to a needy but helpful senator. Common Cause shone with a special glamor. It was the latest in a long succession of do-right lobby operations.

There was a big difference, though. Its chairman was John Gardner. He looked as if he stepped out of an impeccable page of the Establishment. An Eastern Republican who had been Secre-

tary of HEW under LBJ, Gardner was a true man of distinction.
Respectability was the long suit of Common Cause. It could—and
did—raise vast amounts of money. The organization wanted to
adjust all ills afflicting this society, from ending the war to making
the poor better off. In this context, urban disrepair was a prime
remedial target for Common Cause. Senators like McGovern and
Muskie openly hankered after Common Cause. It leaned rather
longingly in a Democratic direction. Its high-powered literature
proclaimed seeking good for all Americans, no matter the party.
In a short time, Common Cause enlisted 115,000 members at a
minimum of $15 apiece. Pretty good takings. The cost of obtain-
ing seed money of $1,650,000 was only $250,000. Idealism, indeed,
in a big-spending age. Politicians got bug-eyed seeing all that
money come into Common Cause. Besides, the organization
claimed a steady recruitment of five thousand new members a
week. Those lists, man, are the lifeblood that can help fuel any
candidate.

Common Cause, as announced and advertised, was for everybody, when enticing members. But it acted as a lobby with a
fancy name. It was for ending the war in Vietnam now, opposed
the SST, and was against the ABM. Despite protests from so pure
a believer as Gardner, Common Cause got into the mucky political cockpit as an auxiliary to the four-wheel drives of Senators
McGovern, Hughes, Ted Kennedy, and others. One deliberate
exception was made: Senator Scoop Jackson. On major security
issues, he was opposed to Common Cause. Democrats who showed
sympathy with Common Cause drew approval. From the onset of
his organization's national appeal, Gardner personally never
showed preference for one Democrat over another. This was held
up as proof of nonpartisanship. More to the point, it was proof
that Gardner cherished ambitions for himself.

The first blush of idealism was easily corroded with wheeling
and dealing for Common Cause endorsement. Its trend was clearly
toward the left-wing of the Democratic party. Gardner's immediate counselors and advisers were unequivocally so motivated.
Which aspirant would get all-out recognition from Common Cause
was the power name of the game. Any anointed in this fashion
would have to reckon with Gardner and his ambitions. The sena-

tors who longed for the pie baked by Common Cause spent more time in the organization's pastry shop than they did on the Senate floor. Their part-time duty, between hunting support and contributions and senatorial tasks, took on all the aspects of new vaudeville. To lighten public groaning, senators tried to strike fresh blows for a maiden form of women's liberation in the selection of girl pages.

The Rules Committee, replete with stodgy, standpat traditionalists, stalled. There was nothing that said girl pages were beyond or outside consideration. And at the rate they were legislating in the Ninety-first Congress, young-girl watching would have been infinitely more positive. A few Southern and Midwestern senators were really horrified by the idea. Suppose, they conjectured with mock horror, girl pages turned up in hot pants! Javits stopped their grumbling by getting Strom Thurmond to agree to support introduction of the girl pages.

The politics of re-election and enhanced national prominence became No. 1 in reform Democratic senators' shibboleth of re-ordered priorities. Larry O'Brien, only briefly back as National Chairman, made threatening noises about leaving. He went after senators who had some congressional outriders. The peerless legislators in this case were interested only in raising money for the party. A big idea, so it seemed, struck them with moonbeams. Mansfield and Dan Inouye thought Sargent Shriver would be a sure fund-raiser. His hair had grown long to match the childish times, although he was past fifty. As a Kennedy-in-law and a potential candidate for governor of Maryland, Shriver seemed natural to counter Agnew's tours for Republican cash.

So mixed up were the Democrats in conflicting eagerness to get on the central platform that they ignored some basic facts of party life. Every presidential hopeful was primarily for himself. Chappaquiddick still held Ted Kennedy close to the water line, nationally. Bouncy and bold Maryland Governor Marvin Mandel had no intention whatever of walking away from re-election to please Shriver. He said so and added that he'd rub Shriver's nose in it. Moreover, O'Brien hadn't been consulted about this plan by Shriver. There was a total collapse of communications.

To seal a breakdown of new stirring in Democratic ranks, Mansfield and Inouye told O'Brien they never thought for a moment a Shriver drive could get off the ground without Larry's clearance. Shriver, who saw in the original program a new Kennedy-type momentum for his cause, told O'Brien that he'd never do anything without the National Chairman. In this situation O'Brien was boss. Shriver and he had been close working associates with the old Irish Mafia. It was different now. Shriver was on the make. He had no power base. The result was that Shriver backed down, made a sign of fealty to O'Brien, and withdrew from fund-raising activities except for himself. His poor showings in that area pleased party hopefuls, who promptly abandoned Shriver for good. This is known as realism in politics.

Another indication of realism showed in termination of the long love affair Chicanos (Mexican Americans) had with Democrats. In two key states, Texas and California, they complained about piddling contributions made to their political adherents by the Democrats. The Senate races in the two states didn't interest them as much as reapportionment, that was up to the state legislatures. Their vote for Governor Ronald Reagan in California, for example, was noteworthy. And down in Texas, Chicanos turned out Yarborough in the primaries. It wasn't that Mexican Americans liked Republicans more. They came to the conclusion that the Democrats took them totally for granted.

The political mid-term hunting season having been launched in earnest, the White House circulated its own messages. From the White House, Murray Chotiner had taken control of liaison with thirty-one states north of the Mason-Dixon line. His office in the East Wing adjoined that of Harry Dent. They cooperated, in antiseptic terms of a communique. Dent, a Thurmond protégé, stumbled in Virginia early in the game. Senator Harry Byrd listened to him and went his own way. Then Dent got entangled in a Florida swamp. He tried to mediate in a Carswell-led maneuver to get the Republican nomination for senator. The judge, beaten by the Senate for confirmation to the Supreme Court, went into politics. This was the fault of a flamboyant governor, Claude Kirk; and Republican Senator Edward J. Gurney. President Nixon had promised support to Congressman William C. Cramer. In his amateurism and bitterness over the defeat of Carswell, Dent didn't check all bases. Result: Republicans in Florida ate their own young and devoured Dent into the bargain.

All the scrambling and backbiting was like a factional Democratic death wish. Chotiner, onetime *enfant terrible* of Nixon strategy, skillfully moved into the powder path leading to dynamite charges. He stepped on the immediate danger by talking of how the White House saw upcoming mid-term Senate races. Rarely does Chotiner personally make views known. In the Dent debacle of the South, Chotiner urged immediate containment on President Nixon and Attorney General Mitchell. They agreed to let him carry the can—or divert growing speculation in intramural Republican squabbling inside the Senate and the White House.

Chotiner's views as presented publicly plugged leaks in the party dike for several months. It distracted attention from inner party quarrels and jealousies. He was quite careful about candidates running on strictly law-and-order issues. Had his subscription been followed, the Republicans would have done a lot better than they finally did. In addition, Chotiner refused to predict a gain of seven seats in the Senate. He knew more than nearly anyone in the strategic hierarchy how impossible that would be. Chotiner had consulted lengthily with senators who bore the Republican label but voted rather consistently with liberal Democrats. Of the thirty-five Senate seats up for election, twenty-five were in Democratic hands. Chotiner had carefully sized up prospects and possibilities. He paid lip service to incumbent Republican senators he knew couldn't win.

In private, Chotiner was fatalistic about Murphy in California. Unless Reagan won the governorship in a monumental landslide, he predicted, Murphy was utterly finished as a senator. California was home territory for Chotiner. He started there back in 1946 with Nixon. Party loyalty showed in Chotiner as a strong suit. Yet questioners never got him to talk much about New York. Chotiner was the nuts-and-bolts man in getting rid of Senator Goodell. There were active efforts in behalf of Conservative candidate James Buckley, brother of writer Bill. Chotiner managed to get teamwork in New York State, citadel of liberalism, to elect Buckley as a minority candidate. It may have been his single most sturdy effort. Chotiner worked like a surgeon with a patient. He ignored his legion of enemies and patched up a working operation in behalf of Buckley while keeping Goodell in the race. By staying in, Goodell siphoned off sympathy votes and liberals. They were desperately needed by Democrat Ottinger, the rich boy. Governor Nelson Rockefeller, the Hamlet hopeful if Nixon should once more withdraw, helped. He suggested regularly that Goodell remain a candidate. For the Republicans, that is. Rocky dangled a possible judgeship as maybe a booby prize. The double-play combination was Nixon to Chotiner to Rocky. Chotiner worked it all out.

All political masterminds, so taken with immediate campaigns, took lots of time out—and money, too—to figure how the eighteen-year-old vote would look. It was a matter of days now before President Nixon would sign it into law. This would give young people, probably around 11 million of them, the right to vote in the 1972 presidential elections. A legal problem had also to be worked out. Although eighteen-year-olds could vote for President, they still needed amendments by three-fourths of the states in order to cast ballots in local elections as well. But machinery was in motion for that step. The Senate approved a foregone conclusion in a benign way. Yet a large group of senators from both parties, in their sixties and above, began to speak seriously for the first time of retirement, maybe? Going on eighty, Louisiana's senior Democrat, Allen Ellender, scoffed at such wasteful talk. He was hale and sharp, he told worried colleagues. So were they all. This talk, if it got around, could be damaging if not self-defeating. Ellender may have had a point in perpetuity for himself in Louisiana. Not so much, though, for others from Northern and Midwestern states.

As a breather, senators relaxed with a second sports mishap to Vice-President Agnew, their presiding officer. Not long before, in a golf match, he had nearly brained his partner. Agnew also, was in favor of youth—theirs, he said, is a spirit of inquiry and concern—and he heartily approved lowering the voting age to eighteen. To show that he himself was still youthful, if not agile, Agnew teamed up in doubles with Peace Corps Director Joseph Blatchford. It was a benefit tennis match that pitted the duet against a doubles team starring Javits. The Senator played with a cracked rib. At sixty-six he tried hard to be on the young side. Agnew was in rare form. He hit a reporter on the knee with a ball sent flying into the press stand. With his trusty Rod Laver model aluminum racket, Agnew batted a ball against the back of Blatchford's head. After a time-out, Blatchford returned to the court with a motorcyclist's helmet on his head. Agnew's volleys and returns were thereafter shorn of steam and drama. His doubles team lost in straight sets, 6-1, 6-1.

The Vice-President seemed preoccupied. Indeed, he was bursting with a secret that caught the opposition and the media totally unaware. There was no advance leak of a massive White House shake-up and restructure. (If nothing else, it was proof that when secrecy is a top-level decision, it is strictly enforced.) HEW Secretary Bob Finch was being assigned to the White House. The $50 billion government conglomerate he supervised had been in heavy going. Predecessors, including John Gardner, thought of HEW, as set up, a man-eater. To take Finch's place, the new HEW Secretary was Elliot L. Richardson. Once an attorney general in Massachusetts, Richardson had been a potent voice as Under Secretary of State. Without him as No. 2, Secretary Rogers would have really amounted to no more than a name at the end of a cablegram. Richardson, handsome and articulate, had been an alcoholic, as had been several senators. They shared common hopes: to rehabilitate drunks.

In HEW Richardson was a compassionate, modern, Northeastern Republican. Finch had ups and down as Secretary of the sprawling agency. Mostly they were downs and getting worse. He never could get a real handle on the post and take charge. His heart really belonged, he believed, in the United States Senate. The opportunity to get there vanished. As an old friend, Nixon wanted him around, and being a White House counselor provided Finch with a patina of importance. He was still in his mid-forties. As a national political liaison, Finch could possibly recover to some day satisfy unrequited aspirations. A few senators, mainly Scott, were aware of impending changes. They kept quiet. Within four days, President Nixon had a second major Cabinet reshuffle. Again no advance leak tipped off the public.

Professorial Secretary of Labor George Shultz was appointed to a new White House creation. It was the Office of Management and Budget and incorporated the Budget Bureau. A Californian, James Hodgson, moved up from deputy to Shultz to Labor Secretary. George Meany ho-hummed the switches. He got along with Shultz as friendly enemies; his opinion of Hodgson was indifference. Meany never deals with No. 2 men. A new deputy to Shultz was Caspar Weinberger. He had been finance director of California and was chairman of the Federal Trade Commission, one of the many regulatory agencies that proliferate government. Consumer advocate Ralph Nader and his Raiders found the FTC pocked with special conflicts of interest, do-nothingism, and a patina of paternalism. Nader, in the case of Weinberger, found himself on a strange side. In the White House, enemies of the abrasive, often arrogant, Weinberger abounded.

The former director of the Bureau of the Budget, Robert Mayo, also became a White House counselor. The job in effect put him in cold storage. When the Senate heard about these shuffles, most floor work stopped. Then again members were rocked with a Nixon announcement. One of the two keepers of the keys to the President's own office, John Erlichman, had a new title. Erlichman became Executive Director of the Domestic Council staff. This was in addition to his duties as presidential assistant for domestic affairs. With crew-coifed Bob Haldeman, the two guardians to Nixon's portals gave rise to the Washingtonian crack, "The German Mafia." Neither, by the way, speaks more than pidgin German. Senators Muskie and Bayh have variously claimed credit for the crack as opposed, of course, to Kennedy's Irish Mafia. The German part was quickly spread to Kissinger, Shultz, and even John Mitchell.

Republican senators generally were miffed that they were kept in the dark. There was bipartisanship in that ignorance. Much of the time Democratic and Republican members depended on their leaders and whips for such information. Majority Leader Mansfield spelled it out for all one hundred. He saw the President about once a week, he said. But there were things you just couldn't ask the President—any President. Mansfield must still have remained in shock after his experience with LBJ. Minority Leader

Scott, a high-grade Orientalist on the side, wasn't disposed to share secret information with colleagues. His whip, Senator Griffin, tried to pile up points with a few tidbits as if they came from the presidential mouth.

Griffin, at forty-six, looked and acted as if he wanted a bigger horizon. The result was that liberal Republicans chewed him out at a special luncheon. They reminded Griffin that it was the liberals who got him the minority whip's post. In their view he was too busy undercutting Hugh Scott. One of the accusations held that Griffin went Nixon one better when he intemperately described student rioters as "bums." Griffin slugged them with: "They're worse than bums." Of course, Griffin had the unrewarding task of defending the Administration in key debates. The one that flamed over Cambodia was tough to wet down, let alone douse. The scolding administered, Griffin recognized some unpleasant truths. Republican conservatives preferred a Hruska or pint-sized Howard Baker, from Tennessee, over him. Therefore, he would not try to outconservative the conservatives. The cracks were papered over and Griffin returned to the floor on laundered good terms with fellow Republicans.

Both Scott and he had rough work ahead of them. Nixon sent to the Hill a revamped welfare proposal. He also outlined a new national health insurance plan for the poor. The President wanted to increase work incentives and supplant the Medicaid program. The trouble was that at least a dozen senators on both sides also had pet plans and schemes. While they might agree on some one point, their own plans diverged. Senator Ted Kennedy, therefore, espoused his own health insurance program. Muskie advocated something different in welfare. Their own bills of particulars meant committee testimony in vast volumes and time. In addition, a senator with a given program had to offer its advantages on the floor. The proposals loosed oratory that washed like waves over the Capitol. The main points of Nixon's program carried out to sea, only to be triumphantly borne back by his floor managers, Scott, Griffin, and Dole. Legislation lay inert.

Chatter-boxing took hold, a senatorial predilection anyway. Briefly out of a share of the limelight, Fulbright brought up foreign affairs primarily in the form of our role in South Vietnam.

A few events focused interest on another part of the world—the Middle East. In a testy manner, Fulbright permitted supporters of his stand in Vietnam to discuss Israel and the Arabs. The tide of United States withdrawal—isolationism, as the President and others termed it—was viewed in a different light in the Middle East. Senator doves or dove senators like McGovern, Hughes, Phil Hart, Eagleton, and Cranston pleaded with Nixon to sell jets to Israel. A McGovern letter to the President had a curious double standard, as it read:

"The night you announced that American troops were crossing the border into Cambodia, you spoke of the firmness displayed by President John F. Kennedy—a firmness backed by the entire nation when the Soviet Union attempted to place missiles in Cuba.

"It may well be that we now face in the Middle East a Soviet thrust that is equally ominous and provocative."

McGovern's letter summed up most dove feelings in the Senate, except for Fulbright. He even had Democratic senators critical of McGovern's views on Southeast Asia applauding him. For the doves this was close to saber rattling. It was debatable, though, how far they really wanted to go beyond rhetoric. Secretary Rogers had proposed a ninety-day cease-fire at the Suez Canal. Pro-Israel senators thought that Rogers ignored Israeli security in the proposal and was being overly indulgent to the USSR. The Russians kept on pushing planes and pilots and missiles into Egypt. In his incarnation as statesman-diplomat, Rogers got on first-name terms with Soviet Ambassador Anatoly Dobrynin. It was "Toly" and "Beel." Fulbright also was accorded the familiar treatment. He was another "Beel." The Russians must first have been bemused with this; then amused. It's a hell of a way to achieve diplomatic recognition.

McGovern's concept of foreign affairs and contemporary history was instant political capital. As Secretary of State, Rogers struggled for some recognition as an architect of affairs of state. Within the Administration, and to senators who had known him for twenty-odd years, Rogers was an amiable girl-stalker when his wife wasn't around. His avocation got him into trouble at Key Biscayne one evening when Nixon was down there for a weekend. Rogers turned up, ostensibly to discuss something global and vital. At the bar, he got taken with a pretty secretary. It became sticky and Rogers was persuaded to leave without his *tour d'horizon* on the highest level. As always, the episode quickly made its way into the Senate, as well as causing guffaws in the White House.

Events like the one at Key Biscayne never bothered Rogers. One asset he possessed for diplomacy was nearly unequalled. He could, if so desired, drink interminably. He never showed any ill effects. Potions seemed to help him over the rough spots in his Middle East plan for a cease-fire on the Suez. He was determined to make a crash effort despite evidence that the Russians were flying close support of the Egyptians. Indeed, Soviet pilots had already tangled with Israelis in dogfights. In early confrontations, the Russians lost three MIGs. What made up Rogers' mind apparently was a private White House poll. It showed that only 18 percent of those polled said yes to a question of United States intervention in the Middle East if the Soviets threatened the survival of Israel.

The poll was an outcome of the public at large being fed up with the long war and American casualties in Vietnam. American sympathies generally favored support to Israel. Eight Republican and Democratic senators, nearly all of whom were demanding total withdrawal from Vietnam, sent a letter to President Nixon. They urged him to send forthwith a batch of new fighter planes to Israel. Their inconsistency long had been keenly felt by the Israelis. All they could do was argue their own case for security and up-to-date hardware from the States. Of all foreigners, the Israelis knew better than any that demanding withdrawal from Southeast Asia and simultaneously appealing for aid to them was upside-down.

They stuck doggedly to their views, canvassing senators who were most sympathetic and the White House where many aides were indifferent. Never forget, American Jews hardly lifted a finger for Nixon and mainly favored Democrats. Lately, a large number were in the forefront of the demand to get out of Vietnam but help Israel. Because of the most efficient intelligence network in the world, Israel was able to back up its attitudes with precise information on the flow of Soviet supplies, technicians, and highly trained military men to Egypt. Spies in the skies in the form of globe-girdling satellites could never provide names, numbers, and on-the-spot strategy discussions between Russians and Egyptians. The Israelis could.

Probably the biggest factor in Israel's favor where Middle East power policy mattered in the White House was the President himself. He heard often from disenchanted assistants their jaundiced observations. In this area, to their discomfiture, Nixon frequently vetoed a go-slow or do-nothing approach to Israel. Here he was assisted considerably by Senator Scott. The minority leader was a shrewd questioner at briefings. He found sound bipartisan cooperation with Scoop Jackson, who was most gloomy on Soviet intrusions and intentions in the Middle East. Several senators who sought active interest at the Pentagon in behalf of Israel were surprised and shocked. The Air Force echelon was pro-Israel. Not so the Army except for scattered cases. Why? The most plausible explanation goes to long-time stereotyped bias about fighting qualities of Jews. It combined with resentment that senators urging aid to Israel were the same legislators knocking the Defense Department and demanding immediate withdrawal from Vietnam.

Senators Proxmire and McGovern were two cases in point for offended Army brass. Proxmire, besides being a sibilant dove, was constantly after the military organization for being overbudgeted, wasteful, and quite a bit outdated and useless. McGovern, all for aid to Israel, was No. 1 in the Senate to lambaste the military for its role in Vietnam and for the way it burrowed into American life. He took to the Senate floor and was so angry that he attacked Scott while he belabored the American Legion, the Veterans of Foreign Wars, and the Administration. The Veterans' president had issued statements specifically critical of Senators Church, Cooper, Fulbright, and McGovern. The vets were escorted to the Senate press gallery by Senator Scott. McGovern said he was a member of both veterans' organizations. But how dare their leaders say they spoke for six million? They by no means represented him, McGovern declared. He demanded that they stop playing politics. Moreover, McGovern added for good measure, the Administration was using escaped and released

POWs to defend the United States position in Vietnam. This was, cried McGovern, no way to use these men.

The McGovern position was spuriously pious on both counts. To enhance his position, he used veterans when they were speaking up for McGovern's positions. He also, when drafting an antiwar resolution, forgot to include references to POW release. They were hastily inserted at the last minute. Our POWs in the hands of the Communists in Vietnam constituted a very skittish issue. Fulbright, smartly ignoring the veterans' organizations, took up the cudgels for McGovern. He launched his attack on the Pentagon. The high cost of Pentagon "propaganda" was his ammunition. Only a few years before—and for at least a dozen years—Fulbright was an unqualified admirer of the Pentagon and everything it did. He was even for a long time something of a mad bomber, before Goldwater became the butt of the sick crack, "Nuke 'em." It meant, of course, use nuclear weapons. Fulbright was a "Nuke 'em" archetype before the phrase was ever attributed to Goldwater.

The chairman of the Foreign Relations Committee socked it to the Pentagon. In preparation, he was host at a reception—thin coffee served—for Swedish Prime Minister Olaf Palme. In other official quarters Palme was not in good odor. He had in Stockholm marched in anti-Vietnam war demonstrations. He also held off saying much when anti-United States demonstrators howled "Nigger" at our ambassador, Jerome (Brud) Holland. An all-American end from Cornell and a highly regarded educator, Holland conducted himself with admirable restraint and great dignity. The epithet slung at him provoked indignation in most quarters of the Senate and the White House. It didn't move Fulbright. He always behaved like an old-fashioned redneck at election time in Arkansas.

The Pentagon was much more to the point of his attack. Folks in Arkansas don't concern themselves much about the lore of Washington. Stripped of regular consultation with retired writer and columnist Walter Lippmann, Fulbright's staff-written prose had become lumpy. Lippmann had fed ideas and helped draft declarations for Fulbright. But Lippmann had been in retirement for some years. His articulate albeit arguable prose was missing.

Sounding too much like a common or mawkish scold, Fulbright was urged by his staff and pliant colleagues of his committee to spread the action to the Pentagon. There was new book material in it, too. He picked out some soft spots. The Defense budget was around $76 billion, about double what it had been in 1959. Yet, thundered Fulbright, Pentagon public relations in that time went up fifteenfold to over $40 million.

The propaganda costs were outlandish, in Fulbright's view. Although Chairman Fulbright didn't talk about it, his one-man band on the Foreign Relations Committee had increased in cost and salaries about six times in that period. As noted, only friendlies could get help from his committee when needed. Fulbright pressed the assault on the Pentagon, and enthusiasts in electronic and print journalism applauded. He received analyses in depth. Reporters covering the Pentagon wondered. They knew firsthand the frailties of the Pentagon's public relations efforts. Nearly all had written and said unkind things about them. Their observations attracted the briefest of notices in their own newspapers. But Fulbright, with his stature, grabbed a spotlight. The chairman's sayings were duly taped, of course, and compiled. A new Fulbright book, courtesy of staff ghosts paid by the taxpayer, was in progress. So was a TV documentary predicated mainly on his book, Fulbright was pleased to impart to anyone who cared to listen. The junior Senator from Arkansas—don't forget sleuth John L. McClellan is senior, because he won't let you—had widened his attack.

X

SEARCHING FOR A FUTURE

Wherever it turned, the military kept getting bogged down in the Senate. The dean, ailing and old Richard Russell, was hospitalized more and more often. Stennis, the Pentagon's active pen pal, tried hard to minimize attacks with his mastery of parliamentarian magic. The senatorial penchant for following political fads gained ground. Many, for example, saw more instant horror in GI drug usage in Vietnam than in tackling the spread at home. Their shrill argument: if we hadn't been in Vietnam, then our boys would never have fallen into this dread practice that enriched corrupt South Vietnamese. The infection these unfortunate soldiers absorbed was communicated back home. *Ipso facto,* drug use and peddling flourished because of a senseless war. Some feeble attempts to get into deep studies of the problem were initiated. It remained for the federal and state agencies to try to roll the vicious issues back.

By this time a fairly solid bloc of a couple of dozen senators was demanding getting out of all Indo-China. They sounded like Cato, the Elder, always insisting at the conclusion of any speech, that Carthage must be destroyed. In the United States Senate it often sounded strange when a senator made his out-of-Indo-China appeal at the end of praise for some old city hall fogey who had died, or for a clean-water bill. The Senate was locked in a fight with President Nixon. His troops on the Republican side looked thin, even shattered. If it hadn't been for Democrats—North and South—Nixon might well have been kept at bay in the citadel of the White House. Our entry into Cambodia led to long debate and little else. Other legislation simply stuck in a host of committees. There was little use in trying to act.

At one point, Senator Cotton felt so frustrated that he stormed around the floor. When, oh, when, he pleaded, would his colleagues get around to an appropriations bill for educational projects? Cotton, the ultraconservative, making such demands! About $1.5 billion was being held up while his colleagues pondered the demerits of Cambodia. A couple of months after Cotton's anger exploded, the appropriation was passed. Time it all took? Around eleven months. Senators are pretty incapable, remember, of dealing with more than one complicated issue at a time. Hostility to Nixon over Cambodia produced a refurbished amendment, known to the trade as "Cooper-Church."

Its authors were Senators John Sherman Cooper, gentlemanly Republican from Kentucky, and Idaho's whiz-kid orator turned middle aged, Democrat Frank Church. Both were veteran members in good standing on Fulbright's committee on Foreign Relations. They wanted a test of strength with the President. It could lead, guessed the voluble Church, to a possible new relationship between the legislature and the Executive. There always are senators trying to show themselves as special guardians against erosion tactics from the Presidency. It depends on the strength and tactical talents of a given President to thwart Senators. The Cooper-Church amendment was, for all the advertised thunder, the mildest of several that also aimed at cutting off funds for operations in Cambodia.

Trying to lift the senatorial siege of Nixon, another amendment was offered. Precious little other work but oratory and paper approvals or denunciations showed for weeks from the Senate in this period. Senator Bobby Byrd had an amendment that would have authorized the President to send United States troops back into Cambodia after the pledged withdrawal date. It was so worded that if the President believed sending troops back to protect Americans in South Vietnam was necessary, he needn't consult the Congress. There was lots of action between the White House and the Hill. Sick senators, if they could move, had planes waiting to take them to vote. Propaganda—or public relations—on both sides of this question ran into big money. You probably could have paid the annual salaries of a group of senators and all their staffs.

For the White House it was a bad rebuff. Bobby Byrd's amendment was beaten 52 to 47. There were thirteen Republican opposing votes. Byrd, who prided himself on being a sound calculating machine, told friends on Pennsylvania Avenue: "You people don't know how to count, especially where your own [amendments] are involved." He had been assured that the amendment would scrape through. Four Republican votes counted as "sure" wound up in the no column. Although called a "major blow" in foreign policy by Nixon critics, the impact was lost on the public. Fresh resolutions and convoluted amendments on the same topic were stacked knee-high for further consideration.

Nixon had stolen a march on the out-now forces in the Senate. He reported on TV that 50,000 of the 150,000 troops he promised to pull out would be withdrawn in a few months. About a month before mid-term elections. The rest were due out six months later. His declaration that the Cambodia drive was most successful got lost in the shuffle. It was interesting how all the heat engendered in the Senate on amendments and resolutions against the war, or about Cambodia particularly, sustained the steam of yesterday's editorial. So engrossed was the Senate in Indo-China that few members paid attention to persistent crackdowns on intellectual dissent in the Soviet Union.

The noted author Andrei Amalrik was arrested. He had written questioningly a book entitled *Will the Soviet Union Survive Until 1984?* It was a piquant date, lost undoubtedly on all but the most literate of our senators. Other dissidents in the USSR rallied to the author's defense. They didn't have the benefit of bail bondsmen. Hardly a murmur came from Chairman Fulbright on the Amalrik case, or the patent dissatisfaction among intellectuals in the USSR. An old acquaintance, Ambassador Dobrynin, left a party after a friendly chat with "Beel." Asked by a couple of guests about the Amalrik arrest, Dobrynin replied tersely, "lies, all lies." He himself was quite supreme in that field— lying. In 1962, as the Cuban missile crisis grew ominous, Dobrynin lied to President Kennedy. His immediate boss, Andrei Gromoyko, also lied. They said there was nothing to the "rumors" of Soviet missiles being slipped into Cuba. Kennedy, of course, had the latest air photos.

That was to war critics in the Senate old hat and past history. They preferred to return to the cockpit of Southeast Asia. Silly and slippery tactics were employed in what had become something of a parchesi game. Senior Republican Senator Gordon Allott, a colorless but earnest drudge from Colorado, tried to be foxy. He introduced another amendment authored by Senators McGovern and Hatfield to end the war. Why? Said Allott seriously: "I'm hoping the Senate will reject it." The amendment got twisted out of shape subsequently and then rose mockingly again during the Ninety-second session of the Congress. Hatfield, his dander up because of rebuffs from the White House that began with a rejection of his bid to be Vice-President, had a new political idea. It was a lulu.

On TV, Hatfield whacked away at Nixon for steering the country wrong, internationally, economically, and domestically. He suggested that Nixon might withdraw from the 1972 race or be dumped by the party. In favor of whom? Governor Ronald Reagan. The superliberal Republican Senator from Oregon, in effect, loosed the first dump-Nixon boomlet. He also advocated sinking Agnew without a trace. A former governor of Oregon, Hatfield nominated Nixon for President in 1960. He was a freshman senator and would be running for re-election in the Presidential test of 1972. So far had he fallen from upper-level Republican grace that John Mitchell was moved to remark: "Hatfield will be no loss even if a Democrat makes it. And I almost never want to see a Democrat win." A dump-Hatfield movement began and the quest was on for a suitable primary opponent against him.

Polls aimed at testing potential candidates or feelings about the war or about prices took a fresh, hard grip on senators. Everyone running for office was in the act, bidding and outbidding. Political consultancy—a fancy name that was rather like calling Britain's bettingshop owners turf accountants—got its biggest vogue ever. Money poured out to pollsters-consultants as if the dollar sign had little value. The fashion swamped Britain's jack-in-the-box Labor Prime Minister, James Harold Wilson. He retained polling consultants. It may have been the worst innovation in a splendid, sensible, British campaign and election process. Much of Britain's media followed the innovative leader with polls. They were contrived hastily, as local subsidiaries of the American form.

Regular reports, just like our samplings, showed Wilson home free in a third straight successful bid to be Prime Minister. Wilson even took to showing ersatz pity on bachelor Conservative leader Edward (Ted) Heath. But the British voters not only baffled the polls, they made them purposeless. Over there, anyway. English men and women recoil from even census takers, let alone pollsters. In addition, eighteen-year-olds voted for the first time. They behaved like their elders. So Wilson, his party, and the new-look pollsters-consultants took a drubbing. A swing to the Conservatives was about 5 percent. Polls, therefore, were off by around 10 percent. Never again, apologized the media to readers and listeners. Republicans, especially senators like Scott and Dole, touted the results as a kind of Anglo-American trend.

Theirs was obviously intended as a propaganda point. It couldn't have been more wrong. The Republicans, instead of just cutting down on polls-consultancies, built them up even more. So did the Democrats, crying poor mouth, but every senatorial candidate was spending vast sums on himself as if there were no tomorrow. Chairman Fulbright looked at the results with reflective solemnity. As an old Rhodes scholar and architect of the Fulbright exchange scholarships—adapted from the original concepts from United States and British academics without credit— the Chairman said the British were usually so wonderfully sensible. He wasn't going into their politics particularly but their postwar shrinkage and trends to look homeward. He was on an old Fulbright favorite: the United States couldn't be the world's policeman. We hadn't been, of course, in the East Berlin uprisings, the Hungarian revolution, the Six-Day War, and many other neuralgic episodes.

History was too often cluttered with facts, and Fulbright chose his own to press an argument and a case. He thought of British "withdrawal" in terms of the Tonkin Gulf Resolution. He had, remember, pressed the resolution to overwhelming passage on August 7, 1964. "Lyndon [LBJ] wanted it," Fulbright chortled at the time. Only Democratic Senators Wayne Morse, of Oregon, and Ernest Gruening, Alaska's senior citizen, opposed the resolution, and they did so vehemently. Both lost out in 1968. Their fellow senators, becoming later doves and peace pigeons, were led by McGovern. He prided himself, in a bid for the presidential nomination, on having been one of the earliest war critics. Others in the pack were Muskie, Church, and Cooper. They all were members, too, of Fulbright's Foreign Relations Committee.

Fulbright, an original floor manager for Tonkin Gulf, started active resistance a few years later when breaking of the President got to him. Six years after the resolution was overwhelmingly approved, it was renounced by the Senate. A weird alliance of ornithological beaks—hawks and doves—voted 81 to 10 for repeal. Ironically, Fulbright was in this instance one of the ten against repeal. How come? He declared angrily that the vote was forced the wrong way, by the wrong people, for the wrong reason. Quite simply, Fulbright was outmaneuvered. Senator Bob Dole, one of the staunchest of Nixon supporters, proposed repeal. The Tonkin repealer, Fulbright complained, was already on the Senate calendar for a later vote. Stennis, jealous of chairmanship prerogatives, stood foursquare and Southern with Fulbright. Tongue in cheek, Dole said repeal in any case would not tie the President's hands in Asia.

Both Dole and Allott, with his unusual earlier proposal, had clearly left the Fulbright ranks puzzled and flat-footed. Exploded Fulbright: "I think it's very unfortunate for one member to appropriate another member's bill. It's not very different from appropriating the neighbor's cow." Colleagues guffawed in the cloakrooms over Fulbright's annoyance. It didn't seem so serious, after all the fuss, to hear them shoot darts at the chairman. They were earlier than most in their espousal of working longer hours. Majority Leader Mansfield, in his most leathery and mournful presentation, initiated night sessions. After spending most of the early afternoon on multifarious debating points, they tackled unfinished business beginning at 5 P.M. They didn't make much headway. Lots of horseplay, heavy eating and drinking were the night orders.

The night of the Tonkin Gulf repealer, Mansfield took to

national TV to attack Nixon's most recent economic message. He declared that the Administration's priorities were distorted. His theme was to concentrate on all the ills at home. As Majority Leader, Mansfield was asked to carry the load. It could not have been a worse choice. He was a poor but willing performer. Republican opponents were delighted. Said Dole: "Let's have Mike make all the appearances for the Democrats. We'll offer to pay." The Mansfield appeal had one of the lower viewer reactions of the time. It may have been due to a growing combination of national boredom, impatience to begin plain politicking for reelection, or preference to shoot-outs that made Mansfield a TV teeny.

Moreover, the McGovern-Hatfield amendment to end the war attracted drums even as scorecards were tallied on Tonkin Gulf. Nixon pulled the rug rather smartly out of that tactic. The Administration announced that the last of our troops in Cambodia were pulled out. And at that juncture, the Senate barred an immediate vote on the end-the-war amendment. The business of running the nation via Senate legislation would have been at a dead end had the House of Representatives also dawdled. The House, at least, did a little more. Thus it sanctimoniously excluded night sessions. Reviewing the shambles, Senator McGee observed sadly: "I'll bet that only a few noticed that Dubcek was expelled." He referred to the ouster from the Czechoslovak Communist party of Alexander Dubcek, its onetime leader and reformer. Dubcek's forcible descent into the ideological sewer of no-man came nearly two years after the Soviet occupation of his country. Senators were too busy to notice.

President Nixon signed the bill extending the voting rights law for five years. He lowered the voting age to eighteen on all federal, state, and local elections. The President had some misgivings. He asked the Attorney General to move for a swift test of the act's constitutionality. That was up to the United States Supreme Court. Nixon long favored a vote for eighteen-year-olds. But he thought it might require a constitutional amendment. This he asked Congress to approve, pending court action. The majority of the Senators figured a court decision would approve and they spent their waking moments calculating ways and means of picking up eighteen-year-old votes in 1972. There were two side attractions for the club members. A grand jury in Baltimore charged a contractor conspired with others to defraud the government.

Senator Russ Long was named in the alleged conspiracy as playing a role but was not specifically charged with any wrongdoing. The case involved a claim for extra expenses amounting to $5 million from the government. Named the same way as Senator Long was Representative Hale Boggs, Democrat of Louisiana, the House whip. Congressional roles are always hazy. They may be a wink of the eye or a nod of the head to someone vitally concerned. A gesture, of course, can always be misinterpreted, but significance can be clear if you are around the marble halls any length of time. Proving a conflict is quite a different matter. Senators knowing Long's abiding interest in good oil depletion allowances and other business matters, were most interested in the case. The vast majority winked and nodded in many instances themselves. They all were relieved. The case against the contractor was later quashed by the Attorney General. Democratic senators could happily point to the heavy hitting of Senator Bayh in a baseball game against the Republicans. He bashed two triples. Goodell kept popping up. But the Republicans won, six to four.

Incumbent senators were showing their restlessness, however. Against the din of the rhetoric for and against our commitments in Southeast Asia, more primaries and impending campaigns were at hand. Even a revelation that the South Vietnamese kept prisoners in so-called "tiger cages" on Conson Island drew little notice. The real outcry had to await the election results. And Mansfield delivered something of a funereal review on candidacies for President in 1972. The Democrats, he declared lugubriously, hadn't yet come forward with a "candidate of the stature" to beat President Nixon in 1972. Some months later, Mansfield made amends. But his pessimism of the day had Larry O'Brien reaching for nonfilter cigarettes. McGovern, Muskie, and Bayh—whose hopes were transparent—were aghast. Mansfield had loused up the scenario. He should have said the Democrats had many candidates who could beat hell out of Nixon. Be neutral, senatorial hopefuls begged Mansfield, but please don't knock Democrats any more. Mansfield didn't.

All the tribal rituals for political fund-raising caused incantations by partisans. Parties, receptions, and D.C. Committees began to flower like marijuana weeds in an abandoned lot. Candidates and incumbents for the Senate flapped their wings in real or contrived concern. The White House let it be known distinctly that President Nixon would help all Republicans everywhere. One exception—New York and Goodell. It was a rare gesture for an incumbent President. The decision, said Scott, occupied with his own re-election tremors in Pennsylvania, was the President's. Staking ephemeral prestige of the Presidency in a political campaign so overtly wasn't supposed to look good.

Democrats thought it was just so much open warfare. It was. Vice-President Agnew had been the cannoneer for just about the entire career of the new Administration. With Agnew a sure-fire fund raiser wherever he went, the Republicans had money to burn. And burn a lot they did. The Democrats, saddled with a National Committee debt, had for some time looked to raising substance, each for his own. Down to Tennessee returned Senator Gore. Agnew and Gore even despised each other personally. Politics needn't have mattered in this case. Against Gore, the Republicans were running a well-educated, rich Congressman, William Brock, III. His money came from family candy manufacturing. Brock had a platitudinous partisan view of the world. So did Gore. It was a good match. Either way, Tennessee couldn't gain. Gore literally began riding a white horse. Brock drove his own car and hustled the voting folks. Gore's trouble was immediately evident. He rarely went home except at election time. The white horse, mane flying, hardly made a hit in mule country.

In a much more sophisticated manner, Washington fund raisers took to posh homes, well-appointed hotels, and some estates. Ethel Kennedy wasn't there but made available Hickory Hill. This was an expensive piece of Virginia real estate bought by her late husband. There were lots of rooms and suites for the eleven Kennedy children and servants to match. It was a good setting for a man of the people in the person of former Governor Philip Hoff of Vermont. He was going after the seat held by Senator Winston L. Prouty. In two terms, Prouty worked hard to achieve a record of shining mediocrity. Into the bargain, he was a terrible speaker. It looked good at the beginning for Hoff. To his party at Hickory Hill flocked about a thousand couples. Price: $24 a couple. Just for openers. Hoff's sponsors tried to hire a parking lot from the CIA for the crowd. It was an incredible piece of arrogance. The CIA is part of the government, Democrat or Republican. They didn't get the lot, but they suggested there could be trouble as a result for the agency.

A cutthroat scramble began in Democratic ranks for contributors. Too often, candidates found they were tapping the same sources other party colleagues wanted to milk. This was a year, though, of every man for himself. No more loans, if possible. Hubert Humphrey had been over that potholed road in 1968. One of his main cash contributors that presidential year had been the wife of an ex-convict, John (Jake the Barber) Factor. It was Mrs. Factor, now dead, who contributed $20,000 to President Kennedy's campaign. Nixon's campaign got a little less. Barber received a presidential pardon in 1962. That cleared his record of a mail fraud conviction. Factor became a citizen. In 1968, Mrs. Factor gave assorted Humphrey committees $100,000 in cash and an additional $240,000 in unsecured loans. It was different with old money. Stewart R. Mott, son of a long-time director of General Motors, made an offer to Humphrey. Young and very dovish, Mott's father controlled a fortune of $500 million. The young Mott listed himself as a "philanthropist."

Mott, a Gene McCarthy adherent, informed Humphrey that his friends and he could help financially. There was a big hook in the suggestion. Saying that his team could raise $1 million promptly and raise two or three times the amount thereafter, Mott wanted to know how Humphrey would stand on issues like Vietnam. Horrified, some associates repudiated the move, and that ended Mott's attachment to Humphrey. Perhaps headstrong in his views and intentions because of youthful zeal, Mott was hardly unusual in his approach. The sum proposed was. But it shows in basic brutal form what a big contributor can mean even if he doesn't say it on paper. The Republicans, too, have these contributors in spades. One supercontributor was insurance tycoon W. Clement Stone. He said he gave the Nixon campaign $200,000. Through various associates, the figure was stated as over $500,000. All legal. Morality?

Devotions of love can come from the very rich and detached. For her stepson's abortive 1968 zig-zag reach for the Presidential nominations, Mrs. John D. Rockefeller, Jr., contributed $1,482,-625. Since the law forbids more than $4,000 to a single candidate or committee, Mrs. Rockefeller was subject to a tax of around $900,000. Hardly a trifling sum, even if you have a job. All these personalities were deeply involved with contributions and candidates for the 1970 mid-terms. For one thing, Governor Rockefeller was up for a fourth term in New York. Stone didn't have to be found in a retreat. He said bluntly that he intended to help President Nixon and all Republicans supporting the President as far as the law permitted. In itself that was a promise that could help national urban development. Moreover, all the superdonors were cranking up for the preliminaries and the main campaign races of 1972. Candidates are not the only ones who start early and spend big.

Individual Senate races, except for his own, never concerned Senator Fulbright. He seethed openly after Bob Dole outmaneuvered him on the Gulf of Tonkin repealer. Fulbright wanted it nailed down his own way. So he had senators on his side with regard to Vietnam reincarnate a Fulbright special to rescind the resolution. Senator Charles McC. Mathias, Jr., Republican of Maryland, obliged. A freshman who beat Brewster, in difficulty for conflicts of interest, Mathias was trying to be an unorthodox Republican. He had become one of about a dozen Republican senators who more often than not bucked the White House. The Mathias proposal easily passed in the Senate. On this occasion, Stennis could not resist a barb at his colleague. No Southern courtesy involved.

The two senators had fallen out a good deal in the last few months. They patched up a few ruptures, such as Stennis's support for Fulbright with the Dole dodge on Tonkin Gulf. Now Stennis, on the floor of the Senate as most colleagues were still in their high-backed chairs, couldn't resist a dig. He reproved Fulbright for repudiating his own offspring—Tonkin Gulf of 1964. Up sprung Fulbright.

"Lyndon Johnson was the father," Fulbright objected. "I was

the midwife of an illegitimate child. I repudiate any suggestion that I was the father."

His chagrin provoked the majority of his colleagues to private mirth. In the cloakrooms, their private Hill hideaways and offices, they were in near unanimity. "Bill got his ass scorched good and proper," a Southern senator exulted as he plucked ice out of a bucket to fix a drink for us both. "Fulbright never had to be as active as he was in 1964 for the Tonkin Gulf measure," a ranking member of his own committee told me. "He was eager, so eager to please Lyndon. Fulbright ran around with that resolution, with gusto. Yes, sir. With gusto." Some of the others mused about the spectacle the Senate caused during weeks of debate. Birch Bayh had been careless. He walked out on a vote, having opposed alphabetically, expecting its defeat. It won. Symington, confused, voted for paying third-country Asian forces in Vietnam. His subcommittee had vigorously denounced the practice. He hadn't understood the motion. On a key vote Minnesota's Democratic Senator Walter F. Mondale could not be found. The Senate's image needed more than an image maker.

A testy voice from Arkansas tried to be heard. It belonged to the senior Democratic Senator John L. McClellan. Overshadowed as he had been for some time by colleague Fulbright, McClellan wanted a fresh forum. As chairman of the Senate Permanent Investigations Subcommittee, he was rockribbed on the issues of law and order. His inquiries into fields or organized crime gave him a little privileged status. On most issues McClellan was a predictable son of the South. In his seventies, he, too, was preparing for the campaign of 1972—getting himself re-elected. Criminal bombings, asserted McClellan, were terrorizing the nation. He wanted to get to the bottom of vandalism and menaces to life. It was praiseworthy. But it got little publicity.

Fellow Southern Senator Ervin got the attention. He was on the rampage against President Nixon's bill to fight crime in the capital. Ervin, cherished by liberals when his analysis of constitutionality squared with theirs, was at his fiery best. He employed features of the filibuster that emptied the chamber of colleagues. And in nearly five hours of a monologue, Ervin invoked everything from the deity to football. His main bugbear was the "no-knock" provision. Amazingly, Ervin's ally in the floor fight was Senator Goodell. They couldn't be more different on almost any other issue. In his own right, however, Ervin was something of a Clarence Darrow. Goodell sounded like a hanger-on and an ambulance chaser. Judge Sam, as he was often called by fellow senators, wore out their tolerance. Senators Mansfield and Scott got the troops ready for the vote.

Everyone in the Senate knew Ervin's opposition to no-knock. This was the final omnibus version. The House and the Senate, behind the usual closed doors, put all the pieces together. So Ervin's harangue didn't please his mates. "Judge Sam isn't even getting any exercise out of this," grumped a Southern neighbor. "I'd bet even he would see it another way if someone jumped the old guy in the street." Senator McClellan paced in and out of his committee-hearing room. He was clearly miffed that Ervin's show got him onto the back pages. When vote time came, he was against Ervin, as was a heavy majority of the Senate. Law-and-order was clearly a burgeoning issue. The time was close to mid-term campaigning. Veteran Senator McClellan was lost again. Nixon loyalist senators pressed the declarations of alarm as expressed by Attorney General Mitchell. The theme—law-and-order—would be big.

A Republican senator, with long experience and cutting shrewdness, worried about the handling of the issue. "Administration people are making this all too strident," he said over dinner. "They are paying no heed to the minorities. In this case, the minorities are as concerned as anyone else. If the Administration keeps doing law-and-order this way, they could make it divisive, not meaningful." Officers of various minority groups like the National Urban League were distressed, but they sought to persuade, not attack. There was praise, for example, by executive director Whitney M. Young, Jr., for Nixon's strategy of negotiation. He said pointedly that he would not call the Administration antiblack. Further, Young hailed what he called actions favorable to minority groups. His private apprehensions Young and his colleagues pursued privately. It did not evoke favor from black militants or white anti-Nixonites.

Instead, the crisis problems that needed continuity on the home front were put on the shelf. The feud about conduct of the war had instant grab. Senators, therefore, returned to phases of debate about Vietnam. Legislation was stashed in cupboards, so to speak, while critics tried to pile up points, and supporters caught punches in the air. Mimeograph machines ran overtime. Senators adjusted color-useful TV neckties and hunted the cameras to speak for or against. Repeat television films sounded more exciting than senators droning on with their warmed-over set pieces. Majority Leader Mansfield varied the diet. He got more signatures for his resolution asking for a big cut in our NATO forces in Europe. The importance in his move—unnoticed and virtually unheeded at the time—was that Mansfield went over the top. More than half the hundred senators put their names to the resolution. Quietly Mansfield put the draft aside, as he had been doing since 1965.

"Its proper time will come," he confided in the manner of the quiet stoic the Majority Leader made his public trademark.

Then Mansfield, like the rest of his colleagues, returned to our role in Vietnam. He was ruffled, as were fellow Senators Fulbright, McGovern, Hatfield, and other critics, when President Nixon held an hour-long TV dialogue with three network commentators on foreign affairs. Senator Cooper, also a critic on Vietnam, showed the most gentle evenhandedness. The President, observed Cooper, had every right to conduct the unprecedented show. Nixon had a special talent—as in televised press conferences—to show himself in command. In the unique discussion program, three of the nation's most skilled commentators fired questions. So absorbed were they all with Southeast Asia that only eight minutes near the end were other matters introduced. And it was Nixon who brought up the Middle East. The questioners—Eric Sevareid of CBS, John Chancellor, NBC, and Howard Smith, ABC—got the back of the media's hand for their performance. They should have bored in and speared the President, was the gist of intramural criticism.

As Senator Mansfield long noted, it is very difficult to try to poleax any President in private or public. An urbane and highly intelligent man who knew just what that meant was David K. E. Bruce. He had served during World War II as second-in-command of OSS. Later Bruce served as ambassador under Democratic and Republican administrations to France, West Germany, and Britain. When he yearned, edging toward seventy, to retire, LBJ persuaded him to stay on in London. Bruce had promised his attractive and thoughtful wife, Evangeline, that he would retire. Wryly, he conceded that you can't say no to a President. Nixon brought him out of brief retirement to become our chief negotiator with the North Vietnamese and their Communist allies in Paris. We had been without a No. 1 for about six months after Henry Cabot Lodge left.

Bruce, a formidably keen mind, was lauded by Senator Fulbright. It didn't last long. He thought that Bruce had been led down the garden path by the President. The thing to remember in that context is Bruce's sense of independence and attachment to public responsibility. He never has played dummy to anybody's ventriloquist. Fulbright and Symington renewed their harshest assaults on the President and his policies. An intra-Senate simmering feud diverted Fulbright's attention for a while. It was, as often occurs, a matter of jurisdiction. Fulbright, assisted by Symington, tried to move in on areas of the Armed Services Committee. That was run by Senator Stennis. Mrs. Margaret Chase Smith, ranking Republican on Armed Services, had been charging that Fulbright's committee dodged around trying to exceed its authority.

She was actively joined in the checkmate to Fulbright in this instance by fellow Senators Jackson and Dominick. Fulbright's hearings before his Foreign Relations Committee aimed at overseeing American military policy in Vietnam. The clash reached the point where Mrs. Smith said she would introduce a resolution providing for investigation of committees that exceed their jurisdiction. In short, she threatened to investigate Fulbright's committee and the way he ran it. Only a powerful and popular senator would ever dare suggest so radical and penetrating a countermove. Mrs. Smith also disposed of some powerful allies who resented—even hated and despised—Fulbright. He backed off. But he didn't stop trying back doors and windows. Fulbright used the convenience of the Symington subcommittee to beat the military on its pointy head. In this area staff members were dispatched to collate statistics to match given arguments. A few years back, Fulbright and Symington used the same tactics to help build up the brass and their budget appeals on the theme of security. At this stage, Senators Symington and Fulbright spoke harshly about the military's "aggrandizement." If there were such, they were as responsible as any two senators for creating the condition.

Into the attack on the military swung Senator Proxmire. He had better credentials than his two colleagues. Proxmire never liked the way the military budgeted and spent. For years he had attacked waste and useless spending by the Pentagon. A fresh assault by such eminent senators as the two on Foreign Relations provided Proxmire with a newer front. He weighed in with a claim that the Pentagon spent more than $2 billion on a secret electronic detection system. The only trouble, Proxmire told a near-empty chamber, was that the system couldn't tell the difference between enemy soldiers and innocent civilians. Water buffaloes, too.

He was withering in his onslaught. The whole detection program dated back to former Defense Secretary Robert McNamara's scheme. It didn't matter to Proxmire whether his targets were Democrats or Republicans. McNamara, he asserted with deep sarcasm, planned to build an electronic wall across Vietnam that would eventually cost $20 billion. That sum would be twice what was being spent on the ABM and four times the amount Proxmire contended had already been spent on the C-5A airplane. The C-5A had already been battered as a terrible turkey. To Proxmire the electronic detection program was a "classic example of the Pentagon's foot-in-the-door technique."

"Small sums spents for research and development," thundered Proxmire, "are escalated into billions for new weapons systems which have never received a detailed and critical review by Congress as a whole."

Unlike Fulbright and Symington, Proxmire exercised rhetorical reason in his queries. He did not suggest that a research program was necessarily a bad investment. But he wanted the project carefully studied before committing more money for additional development. That procedure didn't go with Fulbright. If he pointed at a target he wanted it eliminated. In such a spirit he went ahead amassing material to use in a new book taking the Pentagon apart. His diplomacy, Senate style, was deeply rooted in hypocrisy. Years before they started to take on a President, the Pentagon, and the State Department because of Asia, Fulbright-Symington were aware of our operations in Laos. They called it the "hidden war" when they mounted their attacks. Yet they both heard and approved testimony about the use of mountain tribes as troops and about bombing raids on Communist-held positions from United States airbases. Moreover, Senator Ted Kennedy was fully aware of the use of the Agency for Internal Development (AID) in many Laotian projects by the CIA. He was present when his brothers were alive and approved plans. As a senator, for years Kennedy listened, discussed, and gave assent to the programs. When he thought it politically fashionable to attack, he went after AID as a CIA cover in Laos.

For a long time Fulbright tried every dodge he knew to get the CIA over on his side of the fence. His relations with Richard M. Helms, the only career man to make it to director, were cordial and correct—for a while. They remained cordial but went askew when in executive, or secret, session Fulbright asked Helms about the "cover" of agents. In the special world in which the CIA must operate, only one man can ask about a "cover" or identity. He is the President. No President, however, has ever asked for it as long as the agency has been in existence. Fulbright didn't get his wish. Still, he kept trying to persuade Helms to see situations as he did.

By exposing agreements with other Asian nations such as Thailand and the Philippines, Fulbright deliberately sought to undermine, not just American policy but those of the allied countries. He had been privy to the negotiations, had approved them, and then made them public at a time of his own choosing. It was real kiss-and-tell. Fulbright and his adherents in the Senate argued that the method was justified to keep the public informed. Therefore, they would be held up as guardians against new Vietnams. What then was the purpose in using off-the-record comments and information which these same senators expected others in government and journalism to honor? Walter Lipp-

mann, the godfather of Fulbright's present-day policies to break
the President, had this to say in 1954 in his book, *The Public
Philosophy*: "In the final acts of the state the issues are war and
peace, security and solvency, order and insurrection. In these final
acts the executive power cannot be exercised by the representative
assembly."

The antics and acrobatics of many foreign-policy planning
senators caused Thailand's Foreign Minister Thanat Khoman
to suggest that we were on the verge of a national mental breakdown. In rebuttal, Khoman was accused of arranging "bribery"
for his country so that we could install bases there. A most worldly
man and as good a foreign friend as we had—highly educated and
intellectual, too—Khoman could only shake his head sadly and
refer again to our need perhaps for a national headshrinker. At
the time he also was studying an absurd exercise into real politics
by one of Fulbright's faithful committee members, Senator Pell.

"I submit that our national interest would best be served,"
said Pell, "by a unified Vietnam even if under Communist rule
as it would then serve as a relatively firm barrier to Chinese expansion."

An avid student of foreign affairs, Pell hadn't a clue that this
Administration throughout the world was in private contact with
Communist Chinese sources. Had he taken the time to make a
few discreet inquiries, he would have learned what President
Nixon's personal diplomacy and overtures toward mainland China
constituted. Pell provoked criticism for his initiatives. His horrible
Senate nickname was invoked profusely, "Stillborn." He was at it
again and even mentor Fulbright ignored Pell's entry into the
swampy arena of external affairs. It was abandoned at a convenient time. The United Nations was marking its twenty-fifth
year and most everyone got into the ritual of hailing its existence.
That may have been relief because the UN had lasted longer than
the ill-fated League of Nations.

The President provided a testimonial black-tie dinner. Guest
of honor was UN Secretary-General U Thant, who had been for
years openly critical of the United States role in Vietnam. A
good number of senators had assailed him in the recent past as a
"One-man Troika." Senators also gave Thant lunch at the New

Senate Office Building. Bells and buzzers summoned the hosts to vote for repeal of the Tonkin Gulf resolution. Off went Senators Fulbright, McGovern, Pell, Percy, McGovern, and Yarborough. They rushed back to hear Thant's speech. In the middle they buzzed off again—this time to vote funds for expansion of UN headquarters in New York. The senators never asked Thant why he hadn't in his capacity pleaded with the Burmese regime to release former Premier U Nu when he was in jail. It was U Nu who sent Thant to the UN.

In fairness, other pressing social business may have prompted senatorial forgetfulness on that point. Two young members of Great Britain's royal family were due to arrive in Washington for a red-carpet welcome. Prince Charles, heir to the throne, and his leggy sister, nineteen-year-old Princess Anne, came to town for a few days. The scramble to get on invitation lists was infinitely more tempestuous than wheedling seats for an opening World Series game. Senators spent more time on the phone and in person over at the White House than on any item of legislation. Their wives wanted to go, so they explained. Those with children about the age of the royal youngster and the Nixon daughters campaigned for tickets to a White House dinner dance as if they were running for re-election.

Tricia Nixon, elder of the daughters, came to a state dinner on the arm of Prince Charles, his hair piled high and long on his head. Different from many of the crew cuts around the White House, anyway. For the young set, Julie Nixon Eisenhower was there as an assistant hostess. Beside her hovered her young husband, David Eisenhower, grandson of the Supreme Commander and former President under whom Nixon served two terms as Vice-President. The days and nights were full. The Senate paid little attention to anything else but the visit. A student wanted to invite Prince Charles over for a beer. He couldn't get through. The Prince had lots of difficulty, due to pinpointed scheduling, getting to a men's room. It was most fortunate for the Senate the royal visit lasted only three days. Getting back to normal business and affairs of state was cheerless and somewhat nasty.

The easiest transition from the make-believe ballroom to a symbolic picture of a shirt-sleeved, embattled hundred was to

work over a punch-drunk Pentagon. The doughtiest of military
supporters could always speculate whether this massive budget
of better than $75 billion could be pared. It had come to be the
worst of times for the military. Secretary of Defense Laird proved
to be on the whole perhaps the ablest Cabinet officer Nixon had.
He did his homework and had been a Republican watchdog of
the Pentagon for years as a congressman. This period—the Age
of Aquarius—was unhappy for anything military. The long war
in Vietnam helped create the image of the military ogre. Politicians, as embodied in the Senate, decried what they called
"militarism." It was a big spread—from the draft to bases, appropriations, research, security, war, to kitchen coffee canisters.

Priests, doctors, and lawyers encouraged draft evasion. Military
recruiters grew accustomed to being driven from college campuses. ROTC buildings were burned or bombed. Ignored in the
uproar as Senate critics waded into the Pentagon was a doctrine
for economy. Civilian accountants and managers lopped off billions from military requests even before they got to the Senate.
Divisions of troops were disbanded. The programming called
for 2.9 million men in the armed forces by the summer of 1971.
It was a decline of 600,000 in three years. Promotion lists were
curtailed. Servicemen by the thousands were returned to civilian
life long before enlistment terms expired. The Marines, our elite
unit, in 1969 discharged 47,000 combat-experienced troops twelve
to twenty months early. On the same basis, 57,000 went out in
1971. The Pentagon said with a wan, collective smile that its
morale stayed high and that it understood the politics of military
criticism. Maybe.

Its most persistent congressional critic, Senator Proxmire, went
after parts of proposed military budgeted spending. Nearly $1.5
billion more was earmarked for the Safeguard antiballistic missile.
Proxmire was anti-ABM. At this point, Proxmire was against
the military procurement authorization for fiscal 1971, which
amounted to $19.2 billion. He attacked waste and compounded
waste in military spending. He called attention to the multiple-
warhead weapons, Minuteman II and III. They were Air Force
intercontinental ballistics missiles (ICBMs). Proxmire, arranging
his thoughts as he jogged in the streets to and from work, hit a

particularly sensitive nerve on Minuteman III. A collection of senators wanted to halt deployment pending the outcome of SALT negotiations.

Senator Jackson urged a go-ahead on the ABM system. If we didn't, Jackson predicted: "By the mid-1970s the Soviets may be in a position to destroy all but a few tens of our Minuteman missile force." Senators Hart and Cooper said Jackson was wrong. They conducted their dialogue with civility and lack of rancor. Not so Senator Fulbright. By this time Fulbright made no secret that he destested almost anything Jackson defended or supported. A Northern senator, also opposed to Jackson on the ABM deployment, saw Fulbright's anti-Jackson positions this way: "He has never forgiven Jackson for being so active on civil rights. And Jackson never forgot or forgave Fulbright's obstructionism." Fulbright and Symington found the controversy useful as a springboard to go again after defense spending and bases abroad. This was to show that they couldn't be thwarted by Senator Margaret Chase Smith.

Secretary Laird tried soothing tactics. He declared that future defense contracts would be negotiated on a fly before bases would be bought. This would be designed to prevent massive losses to taxpayers because of cost overruns. The old procurement system had been developed by former Secretary McNamara. It had been thoroughly approved by Fulbright. Proxmire, ever vigilant against waste, had accepted the McNamara plan with some grumbling. It all had become suspicious now that slugging the military was fashionable. Yet the sudden zealotry shown against excess Pentagon spending all had been laid out long before in cold statistics. Admiral Hyman Rickover, unparalleled cutter of red tape within the military establishment, had done the research. It followed his arduous fight to get Navy funds with which to build our first atomic submarine. He learned how contractors often overcharged the government and tampered with the books to conceal padding from the taxpayers.

The no-nonsense Rickover uncovered all the malpractices in the sixties. He brought them to many senators. They, in effect, said how awful. Then they did nothing about the sorry series of affairs. Only through the persistence of Rickover was a combination of red tape, bureaucratic dodoism, and political pressure overcome. The Senate at long last, years after Rickover began to compile his statistics, voted approval. It authorized the Comptroller General and a blue-ribbon board to set up a uniform accounting system for defense contractors. Critics of excess defense spending, led by Proxmire, had never taken time before to get into the meat of the issue as revealed by Rickover. His vindication on this issue, too, only resulted from a new trend against the Pentagon. It was totally political, something Rickover abhorred. Satisfaction of Senate critics over the new panel and its responsibilities just about buried a Defense Department revelation. The lottery draft had been instituted and the new Selective Service Director Curtis Tarr had something important to impart to draft-age youngsters of the country.

The final four months of 1970 would see the lowest total of inductees in years. In all, the total drafted for the year would come to 163,500. It was the lowest since 1964 when 107,500 were drafted. That happened before the first landing of United States combat units in Vietnam. The disclosure should have pleased the main body of the Senate, since it was so concerned about military spending and the war. Defense cuts were the in thing, politically. Troop withdrawals by the Administration and reduced draft calls were conveniently ignored by the Senate. Instead members—led by Fulbright—wondered publicly if the President was undercutting his own Secretary of State. Rogers had been trying to get a ninety-day cease-fire agreement in the Middle East. There had been a huge Soviet build-up in Egypt. The Israelis, after stormy discussions, accepted.

Within hours of acceptance by all sides in the Middle East, the Egyptians violated the truce. They pushed missile sites forward. Israeli information pinpointed the moves. Senator Jackson complained. In an aside, Fulbright murmured: "Don't just believe every piece of Israeli propaganda." Coldly, Jackson ticked off: 1,400 tanks the Russians supplied President Nasser since the Six-Day War. He mentioned the overhaul of the whole Syrian military establishment by the Russians. Something like a shopping list of hardware and Soviet forces in the Middle East came from Jackson. Fulbright paid little attention. Only Senator McGee asked such questions in the Foreign Relations Committee. Jackson didn't even belong. On the Middle East, Secretary of State Rogers and Senator Fulbright had a meeting of the minds.

More to the mid-term political point—election time could be tasted if not savored—the Senate passed the no-knock crime bill for the District. The vote was 54 to 33. Chief sponsor Senator Tydings had alienated liberal friends and supporters with the bill. He was enthused: it would help reduce the level of crime and violence in the capital, hailed Tydings. In liberal eyes on this issue, Tydings was a fink. North Carolina's conservative constitutionalist Senator Ervin was a hero many times over. A clamor was raised to appoint Judge Sam on all kinds of investigative panels. He declined. Out on the coast, in San Clemente, California, President Nixon got the bill. He had established a Summer White House in his native state. It had taken a year of debate for passage. Nixon signed the no-knock bill but couldn't resist a crack at the Senate.

"This bill is evidence of the poorest batting average of the 91st Congress in terms of legislation submitted and not acted upon," said the President. "It's time for Congress to have a better than one-for-13 batting average."

In that vein, President Nixon, lawyer by profession, became an unvarnished advocate. Angrily, he soon said that cult leader Charles Manson was "guilty," directly or indirectly, of eight murders. The macabre Manson case was being tried in Los Angeles. Defense counsel immediately moved for a mistrial. It was denied. The White House hastily put out a statement denying the President intended to speculate on Manson's guilt or innocence. So grisly were the murders charged to Manson and his mates that the uproar Nixon's remarks caused subsided as swiftly as raised. Months later, Nixon, when asked about the remark, said he was wrong to have made it. In politics, it's still useful to say you've been wrong sometimes. Look at all the senators who use *mea culpa* on Vietnam today.

Senators also were mollified that United States judges supplied data on outside income. They had been aggrieved when their honoraria and other assets had been for the first time disclosed earlier. The reports had been ordered in the wake of criticism of the Fortas episode and then Judge Haynsworth. Income from all "extra-judicial services" was listed. But nothing was required or listed about income from stocks, bonds, real estate, or other business holdings. The survey covered 220 judges, including the Supreme Court. One name that caught most Senate attention was that of Associate Supreme Court Justice William O. Douglas.

The House of Representatives, egged on by Douglas haters in the Senate, was looking into impeachment possibilities. His report showed that for the first six months of 1970 he received $20,568.10. That was for off-the-bench work on lectures, articles, and books. The sum was in line with top extra-income earners in the Senate. They were among the leading Douglas defenders against accusations that the Justice was a latter-day rogue and revolutionary. Nearly everyone in the Senate and aspirants for their jobs were very money conscious.

XI

BATTLE FOR THE BUCK
AND JOBS

Time for decision moved remorselessly in on the Senate. Campaigning and the wherewithal to campaign was an absolute factor in the job. Still there were social amenities to be observed by all senators. They couldn't have turned up at a more taxing time. There was the pride of senior Republican Senator Milton R. Young, of North Dakota. He had been a senator since 1945 and was a hale seventy-four. Besides, he never let anyone forget that in 1968 he ran up a bigger proportional vote than any other Republican senator who was opposed. Quite an achievement. It ranked with his tireless sponsorship for the restoration of Ford's Theater. Every senator probably knew that Lincoln was shot there by John Wilkes Booth. The first showing in the restored theater had been memorable. It was an indoor sound-and-light program. Booth's words after he shot Lincoln—"Sic semper tyrannis"—were left out. Young got a full turnout. It may well have been his greatest moment as a senator.

Then the running senators turned as doggedly as they could to their own problems. It should be noted that the club's members had been doing just that for many years, more so than ever recently. A little lighthearted by-play distracted them briefly. That was unfortunate. Former Vice-President Hubert Humphrey, the Democrats' nominee for President in 1968, was upset. A senator for many years, he was running for the Senate again. It was the seat Gene McCarthy had decided to vacate. But Humphrey's old friend and personal physician, Dr. Edgar F. Berman, was in a jam. Berman, a little buzzsaw of a man, got fed up with cross-currents of women's liberation. That got him into trouble with members of the Committee on National Priorities of the Democratic Policy Council.

Berman challenged Representative Patsy Mink, Democrat from Hawaii, over women's suitability for important jobs. In short, Berman didn't want the Democrats or anybody else to be run on a menstrual cycle. He offended, therefore, women's liberation zealots, and what appeared to alarmed party strategists, voters. Berman talked out of turn and it had to be taken out of his hide. Democratic senators in the North pretended to be staggered. Republican senators were gleeful. (Women's Liberation hardly turned any of them on.) Humphrey, agonized, talked to his old buddy. Maliciously, senators saw Humphrey's penchant for non-stop talking responsible for Dr. Berman's plight. A prominent senator couldn't resist talking, over a Scotch on the rocks, about Women's Liberation. "Take this Betty Friedan," the senator said, stirring the drink with a forefinger. "I bet if you undressed her, you'd find she was covered with hair." Attacked by feminists all around the Democratic National Committee, Dr. Berman resigned from the Council.

Senators forced themselves to turn to weightier issues. George Meany warned that the Nixon game plan for overcoming inflation wasn't working out. Worse, Meany saw a rise in unemployment. He recommended measures that hinted broadly of controls. He wasn't prepared to push wage and price controls but perhaps they were needed. There were 4.7 million Americans out of work. Curtailing defense contracts could add another 2 million, asserted Meany, inside a year. Retraining veterans from Vietnam? What jobs, what retraining, with no jobs available? Meany sneered at the President's Council of Economic Advisers. Only talk, he observed, no real action. When Meany spoke, though, the Senate listened intently. A minimum of a third go along with him regularly. On domestic affairs and employment, he had the muscle—better than half the Senate.

Meany's economics remained very much in senatorial considerations. There were even some who equated it with their own money problems. The slump was crippling quite a few fund-raising efforts. It was an uneven pattern. With workers in states hard hit by lost overtime and layoffs, as Michigan and the state of Washington, the $5 and $10 donors, begged off. All candidates, especially senators, like to point with pride at the number of "little people" who showed their support. Those same little people, alas, usually could not come up with enough cash in time to pay a week's TV bills. What is known in the political trade as "big money" didn't dry up or contribute cut-rate. At worst it was only a little slower in coming in than in the past. Main game senators and candidates weren't hurting. They were just eager to get the adjournment to devote full time to electioneering. Majority Leader Mansfield was also up for re-election. But he was in no hurry. A scuba diver was the Republican sacrifice against him in Montana. Republicans, as usual, were getting the lion's share of contributions. But Mansfield had no problems.

He also had a car and driver that go with the job of Majority Leader. They are furnished by the government. Other senators hunted for automobile bargains. They didn't have the class—or the money—of Senator Cooper. His big chauffeur-driven limousine was paid for out of his own funds. The driver didn't care to move around in snow and slush, though. In those inclement conditions I frequently shared a taxi with Cooper to Georgetown. He must have made the trip, Capitol Hill to home, countless times. He always asked how much it was. Then he added a quarter tip. At least nineteen Senate and House members did better with vehicles. They got low-cost autos from the Ford Motor Co. Good deal. Luxury Lincoln Continentals were rented for $750 a year.

General Motors also competed. The firm rented thirty-three super-Cadillacs at a little more per annum. To especially picky members, Ford also rented Thunderbirds at $750 annually. A Mercury cost $600. To an average citizen a Continental could be rented for $290 a month. That worked out to just under $3,500 a year. The motor concerns provided the bargains in the interests of prestige. It so happened that most beneficiaries were committee chairmen or ranking members. Among the committees concerned were those responsible for auto safety, consumer, highway, and tax matters of interest to the auto industry. You could not get a car unless you asked.

Leasing Continentals were Democratic chairmen Senators Long, Finance, and Eastland, Judiciary. Their Republican colleagues in the Continental class were Cotton, senior minority member of Commerce; Prouty, District of Columbia Committee, and the ineffable Hruska, top minority in Judiciary.

Minority whip Senator Griffin had a leased Continental. On the Thunderbird class were Senators Allen Bible, Democrat of Nevada, who was chairman of the Small Business Committee. Driving Chryslers under special leases from $900 to $1,800 annually were Senators Clinton Anderson, Democrat, New Mexico, chairman of Space; Gordon Allott, Republican of Colorado, and senior of Interior; and Frank Moss, Democrat of Utah, chairman of the Commerce Consumer Subcommittee. Moss was very big against cigarette smoking and tobacco advertising. His efforts took cigarette ads off TV. Tobacco interests never forgave. A congressman, Democratic whip Hale Boggs, of Louisianna, defended the practice. It saved the taxpayer money, by golly. Only a few top leaders of the Senate and House had officially provided cars.

Being a senator was obviously a costly matter. Getting up steam for candidates made some lose sight of a few existing statutes. Florida Republican Senator Edward J. Gurney got himself temporarily into conflict with federal election laws. He signed a series of letters on Senate stationery, seeking funds for Judge Carswell. The senator had gotten himself involved in an internecine Republican fight for the nomination to a seat held by retiring Democrat, Spessard L. Holland. President Nixon backed Congressman Cramer, who charged other colleagues with a double-cross. It was as much a part of the game plan as obtaining the seat yourself. Carswell got licked in the primaries, but the party wounds never healed in the elections.

Anyway, the United States Code provides for a maximum penalty of a $5,000 fine and three years in jail for officials, including senators, who: "Receive money or anything of value for any political purpose in any room or building occupied in the official discharge of official duties." If that law was pressed to the letter, it could take care of two-thirds of the Senate. Gurney said it was a "slip-up." It was probably a valid explanation. Senators are much warier under normal conditions. In a related situation, Republican Senators Goldwater and Baker had fund-raising letters go to members of Congress and their employees. It was a violation. Chalk those slips up to inexperienced employees in the senatorial offices who were eager to make an early showing for their bosses.

That kind of mishap annoyed Senator Strom Thurmond. An impeccable spokesman for the Confederacy, he had become jaded with the Administration. Having skillfully assisted putting Nixon across for the nomination, Strom began feeling that he was out in the cold. True, Nixon nominated two Southerners—Haynsworth and Carswell—for the Supreme Court. They both were rejected by Thurmond's fellow club members. Still, Thurmond felt that not enough was done for his beloved South by the Administration. Moreover, his politician's antenna was attuned to strange noises in his home state, South Carolina. Thurmond, for the first time in his career, could have his hands full in winning in 1972. He went on the attack.

Nixon had become so unpopular in the South, especially in South Carolina, that Thurmond didn't want the President to campaign for him. Since the President would be out campaigning for himself, he might not want to go to South Carolina in any case. Thurmond also didn't like lots of Nixon's White House aides. Why? He declared there were too many "liberal and ultra-liberal" advisers around the President. Finch was a name Thurmond took special care to mention. In some bewilderment at a party, Finch wondered where he got all this "liberal" appellation. He mentioned that he had been campaign manager for Senator George Murphy in 1964. His tenure at HEW had led to assaults from liberals on his record. The media, that mass mystery, was undoubtedly responsible for so characterizing him. Finch said so. Perhaps he did, tongue in cheek.

With Thurmond threatening to go it alone—super-Dixiecrat style—a little respite came to the Capitol and the weary, wrangling senators. A few did recall, with staff help, that twenty-five years before, Hiroshima had happened. A few days later Nagasaki was atom bombed. The perspectives of modern military technology opened in hydra-headed form for all life on the planet. Hiroshima was a lesson in human horror. Nuclear weapons were not again used. They were developed and stored, and scientific controversy raged. Not only were the Soviet Union and the United States involved in mutual deterrents, but the regime of Mao Tse-tung was well along the path of nuclear terror development. Countries like France and Britain had nuclear bombs. Sweden could make one; so could Israel. A wise Austrian neutral, Chancellor Bruno Kreisky, asked one afternoon whether the world was waiting to buy A-bombs at the Five and Ten. He had just visited where the Russians and Americans in Vienna were at SALT talks. Like the Hiroshima anniversary, nobody noticed that the International Atomic Energy Agency (IAEA) had been cited by the world in Vienna. It was in its fifteenth year with no major breakthrough.

More realistic to senators as they backed away in the main from the power and pain of fissionable matters was a special events National Clown Week. Painted and caparisoned, a group of clowns came to the Senate to ask whatever did happen to commemorate the week. It turned out the resolution hadn't been passed. Senator McClellan, chairman of the Judiciary Committee's Subcommittee on Federal Charters, Holidays, and Celebrations, met with the clowns. He told them he was unable to convene a quorum of the subcommittee. The only other member, Senator Hruska, was sick. That's how most quorums crumble in the Senate. The clowns left McClellan and took an elevator down in the New Senate Office Building. It stopped on the second floor. A senator's administrative assistant entered. He looked at the clowns and in mock salute greeted them: "The Foreign Relations Committee, I presume."

Senator Fulbright presumed not to notice the gag that made the rounds of the Senate as rapidly as co-sponsoring a resolution with high intentions of no meaning. His sardonic humor was at its saltiest. The State Department accused the Foreign Relations Committee of leaking secret information. It was over a Spanish bases agreement. Fulbright wanted the accord submitted as a treaty to the Senate. Terms of the deal were divulged before any decision. Fulbright was the culprit, according to the White House, whose authority in this matter he challenged. The Senator had earned the reputation among his colleagues as "the biggest leak around." Only when it suited his purposes, of course. It was an awesome reputation, however. Senators are the leakiest legislators in the world, except for their own personal affairs.

"They leak it in Spain; they declassify what they want," said Fulbright rather defensively. "They leak whatever they think helps their own interests."

The self-serving declaration sealed a White House resolve. The Spanish bases agreement was not sent to the Senate—if ever there was a thought of it—as a treaty. It was renewed with a NATO acquiescence that Spain was in the classification of a backdoor ally if attacked. Fulbright and his supporters in the Senate assailed the accommodation but got nowhere. Continuing his assault on the Executive, Fulbright called access to TV vital to the staying power of Congress. He wanted the same automatic access to network television the President enjoyed through informal courtesy of the broadcasting industry.

As a personality he tried every trick in the political book to command television time. Fulbright argued parliamentarianism and expertise. He proposed to legislate Congress's right of access to the TV channels. And Fulbright was immediately challenged by the commercial networks that his project was an invasion of journalistic freedom. The rebuttal didn't faze Fulbright. Unless the access was granted, the balance in American government would be effectively destroyed.

"Communication is power," said Fulbright, "and exclusive access to it is dangerous, unchecked power."

The Chairman never mentioned that he always had access whenever there was something on his mind to propose before camera and soundtrack. Off camera, as with any senator, Fulbright has the freedom of access to the Senate floor. A senator could indulge in accusations, recriminations, and fiery oratory without fear of condemnation in court. That was privilege, too. Fulbright used the forum to lash out at Vice-President Agnew. The Vice-President, as presiding officer, was sitting smilingly in the chair. Agnew was unfair in his vitriol directed against Fulbright, the senator charged. "The Vice-President demonstrated his complete mastery of the art of character assassination," he fumed.

Agnew at a luncheon praised a congressman for "working to get Fulbright out of Washington." Thereupon Fulbright stormed:

"The role of the Vice-President is more reminiscent of Dr. Joseph Goebbels in the thirties than that of Joseph McCarthy in the fifties because he speaks for a different brand of government than did McCarthy."

A single senator, cried Fulbright, is nothing to a Vice-President in terms of power to intimidate or control citizens. Fulbright's own tenure in the Senate was living contradiction. Further, senators of the immediate past like George Norris, the La-Follettes, Borah, Vandenberg, Robert Taft, Alben Barkley disproved his charge. They all challenged not just Vice-Presidents but Presidents without recourse to personal ire. Challenges to President Franklin D. Roosevelt rose and fell from senators countless times. Would Fulbright have suggested that Nixon was more powerful and cannier than FDR? To denounce Ted Agnew for Hitlerian tactics and imply that there was an analogy with the Nixon-Agnew Administration was ludicrous and vicious. Had Fulbright paid attention to even regular newspaper reading rather than his own clippings, he might have discerned some steady personalized diplomacy by the President in the field of foreign affairs.

It went off in letters to Soviet and Middle East leaders, through private conversations with Communist Chinese trouble-shooters, and in face-to-face discussions in the White House and Nixon's encounters abroad. The Chairman never took the time to reflect over these activities. Neither did his staff, eager to conform to, or butter up, their leader. Besides, the majority of the fifteen-member senatorial committee on Foreign Affairs was busier attacking this Administration, as they had the past one, than in understanding how the President was getting personally involved. It was at the White House level, with the President, that questions should have been asked. Fulbright, his committee and staff, simply relied on invective. It was fed partly by frustration from Secretary Rogers in golf rounds with Fulbright. They were old friends, as Rogers was an old friend, conversely, with President Nixon. Months before a public *cri de coeur* rocked the capital. Rogers grumbled about Kissinger's role as a senior Machiavelli foreign-affairs adviser to Nixon.

Henry Alfred Kissinger, German Jewish refugee at fifteen, was at forty-seven the President's adviser on national security. A distinguished professor at Harvard, a renowned member of the Eastern intellectual establishment, Kissinger in the course of a given day saw the President on business more than anyone else of his official family. The contact provoked Fulbright. Kissinger wouldn't come from his lair in the western wing of the White House to answer the Senator's questions. Executive privilege, something cherished by all Presidents, was always invoked. Kissinger looks the academician, brown hair rising from his forehead in small waves and blue-gray eyes behind horn-rimmed spectacles. His voice is deep, still tinged with a German accent.

Possessed of a razor-honed mind and capacity for judgment and decision, he had been bitterly assailed by Harvard colleagues for his role in advising the President on Vietnam. As a matter of fact, his former Harvard soulmates just about read him out of their ivy-bound intellectual ground rules. He should never have been with Nixon. A bachelor by divorce, Kissinger loves power and power plays. His bachelorhood gave him new steam. He squired pretty girls who also dote on powerful men. And he drove a fast Mercedes. His physique didn't square with most girls' dreams, not even today's liberated crowd. In physique he was not out of the ordinary: 5 feet 7 inches, about 170 pounds. Kissinger, to his critics, was "Dr. Strangelove," a hideous practitioner of evil power. He took this in a faintly amused, detached manner.

From the day Nixon announced his appointment, the State Department upper echelon hated his guts. They had known him well from his previous service as a consultant to Presidents. Those were transitory times. As the President's adviser, however, Kissinger was a separate power and a threat to department bureaucrats —and to senators like Fulbright. He had a "PL Pres" light on his telephone bank. Translated that meant "private line, the President." No senator has that. In their own ways, Rogers and Fulbright fretted about the mass of detail Kissinger proposed—and Nixon adopted—before actual negotiations with the Russians on

SALT. If they could be satisfactorily worked out, Nixon had a political gold mine coming up in 1972. On this subject, strategic arms limitation, Fulbright had only the sketchiest of notions. He was opposed to our ABM, period. Rogers usually talked in vague terms, signifying he knew a great deal, whereas the whole problem baffled him.

ABM foes and their lobbyists decried Kissinger—their Strange-love—as a vote to enlarge the Safeguard antiballistic-missile system came to a head. Steered mainly by Scoop Jackson, an amendment to block expansion was throttled, 53 to 45. Of the ten Republicans opposing, five were members of the Foreign Relations Committee. Fulbright was among five Democratic members of his committee in opposition. So busy were the anti-ABM Fulbright committee members criticizing "Henry's Plan"—giving no acknowledgement to Jackson, steeped for years in the problem—that they paid almost no heed to a dramatic turn of events in Europe. West Germany, under Chancellor Willy Brandt, and the Soviet Union agreed to renounce the use of force. Moreover, they affirmed the inviolability of the present borders in Europe. Overnight, it seemed, the long tussle over the Soviet-fixed Oder-Neisse frontiers of East Germany were thrust aside.

A new policy in the heart of Europe, affecting the Old World and the New, were on the drafting boards. Because Kissinger had throughout his career been actively interested in German affairs and, of course, spoke flawless German, Fulbright dismissed the Soviet-West German approaches lightly. Another Kissinger scheme, he snorted. The President and Kissinger had a large hand in supporting the project as seen by Brandt. But the committee chaired by Fulbright had not in three years taken the time to inquire into German policies towards the USSR, and vice versa. Military bases and the war in Vietnam apparently exhausted Fulbright and staff. When he could take time off he spoke to peace-in-Vietnam audiences. The one in Indianapolis, Indiana, a few months earlier was good. It also paid $5,000 for less than an hour's talk. Fulbright was in Al Capp's league. No matter how well fixed a senator may be, he likes a little extra. Take the vending machines in the Fayetteville, Arkansas airport. They belong to Fulbright. Ever try a sandwich or hamburger out of one? That's all you could get at the airport. Fulbright's revenge.

Hardly a Zionist, Fulbright was in the thick of the Middle East when headlines and TV shows tugged at the public consciousness. He had been a conspicuous but silent dissenter from the Senate's pro-Israel majority. After his staff prepared a thirty-seven-page speech, Fulbright read it to the Senate. He assailed Israel for lack of flexibility and foresight since the Six-Day War. Then the Chairman accused Israel and its friends in this country of exploiting American concern with Soviet involvement.

"It is the same old game of waving a red flag in front of the anti-Communist bull and many Americans are still falling for it," declared the Senator.

Came the Fulbright stinger: he praised Secretary Rogers but charged President Nixon and Kissinger with using cold war rationalizations. Their combined Nixon-Kissinger statements, declared Fulbright, amounted to "geopolitical hocus pocus." His aim was sharply clear: to bring Bill Rogers over on his side. Besides, Kissinger was a Jew and had to be very partial to Israel. To sweeten his blows, Fulbright proposed a pullback by Israel from all occupied Arab territories. For withdrawal, Fulbright recommended that the United States should work out a formal security treaty with Israel. As the loudest foe of new American commitments abroad, this proposal seemed a resounding about-face even with its high-handed demands. It turned out to be something in which Rogers was deeply interested. And it never got off the ground.

For a while it looked as if the Senate couldn't hear. At one point the chamber called it quits for a hot weekend. Only forty-nine members, two short of a quorum, could be mustered. It was final passage on a bill lots of voters thought urgent. The roll had been called for passage of a $5.2 billion public-works bill. As far as the books went, there was no other recorded instance of the Senate's being compelled to adjourn for want of a quorum while voting on the final passage of a bill. In its last stages the Senate session of the Ninety-first Congress was setting all kinds of no-achievement records. The imbalance was redressed a bit. Nixon was rebuffed when the Senate followed the lead of the House. It voted 77 to 16 to override the Presidential veto of a $4.4 billion education bill. Mansfield sniffed that priorities had to be reordered. He coined a clause: "It's so easy to vote millions for

ABMs and SSTs and then reject money for the ABCs." That's not the way education is launched these days. In any event, many who voted for the ABM also opted to override the veto. The Senate then tried to sustain momentum.

Members still grumbled that Nixon canned an old political plum with the postal reform bill. It was a bipartisan complaint. With a Republican President, GOP senators had hoped to pick up around five thousand postmasters and a couple of thousand rural letter carriers. Henceforth, the nation's thirty-two thousand postmasters would be selected on merit. To suit the occasion, Nixon declared: "There is no Democratic way or Republican way of delivering the mail." Still, senators in idle moments tried to figure partisan solutions to a new patronage problem. It was much more appropriate than some pesky legislation Senator Bayh introduced. He proposed that all top federal officials make full public disclosure of their private finances each year or face stiff fines and jail sentences.

To show his good faith, Bayh released a personal balance sheet. It revealed his family's net worth as of the summer to be just under $150,000. Total 1969 income amounted to $105,646. The Bayh bill, however, didn't call for listing free rides, hotels, and other largesse. His family and he got free hotels in Miami regularly. On the other side of the aisle, Senator Dole launched a drive to amend federal lobbying laws. He questioned activity in support of the Hatfield-McGovern amendment to shut off funds for the Vietnam war. Senatorial sponsors of the amendment received $480,000 to mount a publicity campaign for support of the end-the-war measure.

"At stake," observed Dole, "is whether the Senate is going to remain a deliberative body."

He must have had his terms mixed. The Senate for some time had become a deliberate body. Lobbies for and against legislation were in tremendous vogue. They also raised pots of money. The lists of names they acquired were coveted. John Gardner's Common Cause was eagerly wooed. It was supposed to span all parties. But the amount of money his outfit generated and lists of contributors were far more interesting to the senators. Common Cause was in the legislative lobbying arena as well as any utility.

The whole Senate looked up from those fact-and-figure sheets when the Tydings case broke with a roar. There had been no advance warning. A question of ethics was involved once more in the Senate. Senator Joseph D. Tydings, Democrat of Maryland, was charged with conflict of interest in an article in *Life* magazine.

A young, liberal Democrat, Joe Tydings was finishing his first six-year term as a senator. He had a reputation as a tough, former prosecutor of errant congressmen. Wealthy by inheritance, Tydings was a crusader for public disclosure of elected officials' financial data. He was only one of fourteen senators who made any public report on his personal finances. Tydings also was a close friend of the Kennedys and imitated many of their mannerisms. Within the exclusive confines of the Senate, his fellow club members were overwhelmingly overjoyed to hear that Joe Tydings seemed to be in trouble. *Life* magazine, through its top-flight investigative reporter Bill Lambert, had clobbered other personalities.

Most recent was the conflict-of-interest report that convicted Voloshen and Sweig, the high-and-mighty protégé and aide to Speaker McCormack. Many senators breathed relief that their names didn't come up in that case. Better than half knew Sweig pretty well. The magazine, among other previous revelations, had knocked Democratic Senator Ed Long of Missouri out of the box. He was shown to have accepted special fees from the Teamsters. Ed Long's retirement didn't benefit the Republicans in 1968. Young and capable Tom Eagleton got the Democratic nomination and won the election. Nevertheless, here in Tydings was another breed of new senator. And he was deep in the muck of conflict of interest. Already under fire by political opponents for his support of gun controls and by liberals for a tough crime bill, the *Life* story could not have been more inopportune for a senator facing a primary, let alone re-election.

Tydings was accused of failing to meet his own standards of ethical conduct in managing his personal fortune. Briefly the charges were: that just before he was sworn in as Senator, Tydings visited a government loan officer with a business associate. The amount the company—in which Tydings held nearly twenty-six thousand shares—sought was $7 million. It was for a foreign investment that turned out to be very profitable. Despite his demand that personal financial data be released by senators, Tydings didn't report 1967 income from the company where he held a large portfolio. Neither did his voluntary financial statement, supposed to be a model, show that nearly $2 million of his reported $2.5 million net worth was in the enterprise which secured the government loan.

He reacted, instead, like any other senator under such attack. Tydings claimed it was a Republican smear. He added that the Justice Department, headed by Nixon strategist Attorney General Mitchell, provided the "smears and innuendoes" to *Life*. All that was possible in this cannibalistic community under any administration. Nevertheless Tydings, only a few months before the *Life* magazine piece appeared, had lent his presence and services to his business partners. He flew with them to California on a merger deal that never panned out properly. Tydings did nothing illegal. The question of propriety was at issue. Repeatedly Tydings lent his personal and senatorial prestige to promote his own financial interests. It made a mockery of his self-promoted ethics standard of values.

The episode emphasized more clearly than ever a continuing failure of the Senate and the whole Congress. Firm and absolutely clear ethical standards have not been set up. Being a senator, a congressman, or a Cabinet member, for example, is a full-time job. It must be held with the deepest devotion to public responsibility. In short, that means: no law practices, no outside business interests, and all investments in trust until retirement to private life. Disclosure was hardly enough. The Senate—the whole Congress—had to be totally above suspicion of using public office for private enrichment. If that yardstick were applied without fear or favor in the presidential year of 1972, we would have a midget Senate and House of Representatives. The rancid Tydings case buzzed—still causes sweats and shivers—through election time.

His measures provoked much more debate and discussion than an amendment designed to bring about a volunteer army. Nothing was in the proposal to put an end to military conscription. That had to wait another year, when the Selective Service Law was due to expire unless renewed. The Senate amendment was sponsored by the strangest pair of Republicans imaginable. Architects were

Hatfield, superdove and anti-Nixon, and Barry Goldwater, screaming eagle and as conservative as sagebrush. They wanted dearly to
raise military pay to a level so that enough volunteers would
enlist to make the draft unnecessary within six to eight months.
In 1968, President Nixon had campaigned in favor of a volunteer
army. A presidential commission recommended big pay hikes to
create a manpower pool for military volunteers.

Senators, on this vote, ignored all their past attitudes, for or
against our role in Vietnam, pro and anti-military. Some supporters of the amendment advertised the proposition as an act to
end the draft. Ted Kennedy and a group of liberals opposed the
amendment. Usually they were on Hatfield's side. Kennedy was
against the basic concept of a volunteer army. He contended it
would discriminate against the poor, who were the only ones who
might be enticed by the higher pay. Liberal backers of Kennedy
tipped the balance. The amendment lost 52 to 35. Therefore,
the Kennedy team in this instance supported President Nixon,
who opposed Hatfield-Goldwater. It would be too expensive their
way, declared Nixon. Besides, the draft was essential in his view
as long as we had big forces in Southeast Asia. It was a curious
voting line-up: Kennedy and Stennis, Hart and Goldwater, as
indicators. Senator Goodell was for it but Javits opposed. Nobody
was willing to argue that servicemen were not underpaid. Hatfield
declared that twenty thousand soldiers were so underpaid that they
had to seek relief in welfare for their families.

At the Pentagon the brass never quite made up their minds
whether this rebuff from the Senate did them any good. There
seemed to be wheelbarrows full of proposals in the Senate to take
away from them more money and more contracts. McGovern, who
approved the Hatfield-Goldwater amendment, kept urging withdrawal of forces from Indo-China pronto. He also demanded strip-
ping from the Air Force money for a new bomber. Proxmire had
a fresh amendment that tore into a controversial Air Force transport. It was the C5A, built by Lockheed. And Lockheed, a massive
defense contractor, was showing signs of deepening financial dis-
tress. Wretched mismanagement, asserted Proxmire. He enlisted
a fairly independent Republican in the anti-Lockheed, anti-
Pentagon crusade. Freshman Richard S. Schweiker, Republican

from Pennsylvania, was a new ally. Another, an ex-career officer, tried to blow up the Pentagon's bureaucracy. Retired Marine Colonel James A. Donovan wrote that the overblown military bureaucracy was the single most powerful force in American life. Colonel Donovan, may have exaggerated. Admiral Rickover fought the same bureaucracy, winning more than he lost. The single most powerfully entrenched bureaucracy was in the Senate and the senators.

But the worst shock that ripped through the military with little sign of stopping was drug usage, addiction and its spread. In all branches of service the drug infection had risen to epidemic stages. It was pinpointed, like an addict's eyes, in Vietnam and the ceaseless clamor against our role out there. The Pentagon and its officials had long sought to pooh-pooh the idea of troops smoking marijuana and made light of the application of such hard stuff as heroin. Senators held endless hearings. The unfortunate aspect was their attempt to convert horrendous testimony and findings to further personal objectives. Not a single senator, proclaiming public service over self, ever tried to pursue the disease, solutions, and curatives without rushing into the public prints and media. It was as if they could scarcely wait to get testimony into the record and then lecture sternly.

Back in 1966, in Vietnam, I found marijuana usage among troops as common as looking for popular brand cigarettes in K-rations in World War II, It was dirt cheap. Using heroin— "scag," soldiers called it—was even then becoming a popular kick. Young doctors and psychiatrists in Vietnam, alarmed, were told they were getting hysterical over a few incidents. As the problem multiplied, the chains of command sought to suggest it was less than reported. By the time senators wheeled into solemn action, drug habits and addiction induced new international venality. The brass, which once suggested complainers were verging on the hysterical, became near hysterical in crash attempts to establish rehabilitation centers, controlled withdrawal units, and raids to cut off supplies. Even as therapy was introduced, starting surreptitiously, Pentagon specialists tried to whittle down the problem. Before a Dodd subcommittee, a witness blamed exaggeration in the media for the public's shock. Hearing the testimony of a host of former soldiers, who talked of combat units on marijuana and hard stuff, Dodd exploded: "It's people like you who aggravate the terrible problem by trying to hide it or pretend it's in hand. It's out of hand and it has to be stopped."

Heroin was being introduced into the United States through letters sent by servicemen. It was ingeniously sprayed on notes to be inhaled and smoked or distilled later. Throughout Southeast Asia, traffic was channeled by survivors of Chinese nationalist troops in Burma and Indo-China. Assistant Secretary of the Treasury Eugene T. Rossides, once an all-American back from Columbia, learned about the traffic. He had been actively engaged in cutting down the flow of drugs from Mexico into the States. There was cooperation in the venture. That was hardly so with many of our friends and allies. The dope traffic in Southeast Asia boomed. Our allies in Turkey and France paid little heed to choking off the trade. The Turks hardly bothered to keep farmers from planting the seeds like corn for later harvest. In France, especially around Marseilles, a port of entry, French authorities looked away from the up-to-date scientific laboratories that refined heroin and other drugs to be smuggled into the United States. Democratic Senator Walter Mondale, of Minnesota, cried out that friends were killing us with drugs. He urged that all aid be cut off from countries that do not cooperate to stop growth of opium and the like.

Then, the Army's own bastion for treatment of other ailments, Walter Reed Army Hospital, got to be something of a needle park. Users peddled drugs to fellow soldiers. Patients became runners for peddlers. On the broad lawns and in brilliant rose gardens LSD, heroin, marijuana, and "speed" all were available for a price. A Vietnam veteran confided that he sold drugs to a hundred or more fellow patients. He used the proceeds to buy his own fixes. First, the hospital authorities said huffily that the reports were all imagination. But they sent special policemen out to keep a vigil. The Pentagon's drug specialist, Frank Bartimo, said the problem had grown over a few years. Finally, all available controls were imposed as well as cures and amnesties. It would perhaps have been more immediately useful if the military followed the hard-headed example of George Meany. As soon as it came to his

notice that drug usage and peddling wormed their way into areas
of AFL-CIO membership, shop stewards alerted authorities. Union
clinics and specialists were available around the clock to handle
cases. Peddlers were routed out of plants. If arrests didn't scare off
the pushers, they were physically clobbered. The application of
power certainly benefited the community at large. Although he
didn't like emulating Meany in anything, Walter Reuther approved similar methods in United Automobile Workers areas of
infection. After Reuther was killed in a plane crash, successor
Leonard Woodcock continued the therapy against drug infiltration.

Curiously, no voices were raised to protest trade union handling
and disposal of drug pushing and addiction. There was an uproar
among many Democratic senators when Meany declared that the
"Democratic party has disintegrated." He warned that Leftist
extremists were taking over factions of the party in far-flung areas.
While the AFL-CIO generally backed Democrats, it also supported
a few Republicans. Meany was in a constant hassle with senators
who denounced American foreign policy, particularly in Vietnam
and where accommodation with the Soviet Union was urged. He
had deep suspicions of any overtures or openings toward the
USSR. In this regard, Meany had the counsel of Jay Lovestone, a
former American Communist who knew the demonology of Soviet
tactics. Reuther and then Woodcock were by no means as hard
nosed or astute as the Meany entourage.

To senators who complained that Meany's assessment of the
plight of the Democratic party boomeranged against them, the
AFL-CIO leader said that inflation would certainly harm the Republicans. He knew firsthand how President Nixon and his
strategists were trying to woo labor union members and their
votes. Meany had been to White House meetings and dinners
with Presidents ever since Roosevelt. The battle-scarred veteran
of nearly half a century of negotiations and picket lines was not
about to be seduced by charm at the White House. His 13.6 million members wanted continuing improvement. Unemployment
was on its way up. Part of it was due to phase-outs of defense
contracts and shutdown of military bases in America. Meany
didn't forget the senators who inveighed against the military and
came to him for help when their states were hit with plants closing
or transferring elsewhere.

In Washington, where grabbing for the jugular is an admired technique, the unwritten coexistence between Meany and Ralph Nader had special fascination. The young consumer crusader and the hard-bitten labor head disagreed over a great area of problems. Where the consumer was concerned, they complemented each other. To Meany this meant added protection for workers and union leaders. To Nader his work was aimed at benefiting essentially the little guy and his family. Where they disagreed there seemed to be a tacit decision to keep it out of a public wrangle. Actually, AFL-CIO people quietly hailed an out-of-court settlement by General Motors with Nader. It was for $425,000, tax free. Nader said the money arising from his invasion of privacy suit against GM would be used for "continuous legal monitoring of General Motors' activities in the safety, pollution and consumer relations area." Senators who were often challenged by Nader thought that Meany seemed pleased because GM also had to deal with the rival trade union organization, the UAW. With few exceptions, senators were jealous of Nader.

As a young lawyer, he shunned service with a prestigious firm. He was a loner and his appearances on TV were in great demand. Nader knew how to orchestrate charges and appearances. At least a dozen senators worried about whether he intended to go into politics and challenge any of them. Without any recruiting, Nader had vast numbers of young men and women with law and consumer backgrounds constantly demanding posts with him. Not a single senator on the Hill could command a fraction of those volunteers. Some, like McGovern, tried, to little avail. Usually senators tried to work both sides of the street in an effort to produce what they thought was harmony. Nader, for all his poor man's cultivation and calculated drama, was unsparing against government, management, and politicians. He went after the Department of the Interior and the coal industry for what he said was evasion of a new Coal Mine Health and Safety Act. He also waged a campaign against the Federal Aviation Administration. Nader wanted to ban smoking on all commercial flights. Smoking in the air, Nader felt, was a threat to health, comfort, and safety.

A United States District Court judge ruled against Nader. He didn't turn a hair. His Raiders took it higher. At the same time Nader charged that his old adversary, GM, hid proof that the

1960–63 Chevrolet Corvairs were unsafe. Angrily, GM retorted, no. Nader sent Transportation Secretary John Volpe a five-and-a-half page, single-spaced letter in which he charged that there were 600,000 of these models still on the road. He wanted owners notified. Fresh charges against the Corvair from Nader were first aired in public when Nader wrote "Unsafe at Any Speed." All the foregoing, from mine safety to GM, Nader and his troops undertook in a single week's activity. In the entire Senate, there was nothing that could come remotely close in a given year. Long after Nader proposed abolition of the Interstate Commerce Commission (ICC), Senator Mansfield advocated the same thing.

"The time has come when we should be concentrating on the consumer," declared Mansfield.

It was nice to realize that senators—Hart was a notable exception—feel compassion on occasion for the consumer. If there wasn't a Nader prodding, would there be as much interest? They manage, nevertheless, to form a defensive unit around one of their own in the exclusive club on unwritten ground rules of privilege. Senator Goldwater raised hell when Arthur J. Olsen was appointed spokesman for the State Department. He had been an experienced foreign correspondent. From Germany, Olsen wrote a story in 1964 that Goldwater had been in correspondence with a leading West German right-wing politician. It was denied by the politician. Goldwater bitterly contended this was used against him—raising neo-Nazi specters—in the 1964 campaign. His indignation was communicated forcefully to Secretary Rogers. A pillar of rectitude, Rogers backed off. The Olsen appointment was rescinded. The Senate did not have the slightest right of control in the matter. Senators Mansfield and Church, two more prominent senatorial friends of Olsen, shut up. Their standards were comparable in private shows of sympathy for gun control and knuckling under to the gun lobby by voting against control legislation.

Weightier matters in affairs of state concerned senators more than essential principles such as the Olsen case. There was a collective gasp when Chile chose the first freely elected Marxist president in the world. Fulbright had little to say. He was in the forefront of outlays the United States had made to South Korea, around a billion dollars for two divisions in Vietnam. What was his grasp of conditions in Latin America? The Chairman had some reports from a committee field man. He preferred looking into Vietnam. The White House played it cool. Its wrath centered on our Ambassador, Edward Korry. He didn't figure, annoyed White House higher-ups claimed, that Marxist Salvador Allende could make it. Allende barely did, over two other candidates who together amassed better than 61 percent of the vote.

More instant drama surfaced in the Middle East than a new turn for the worse in our own hemisphere. Arab guerillas hijacked three huge airliners and forced them down in the Jordan desert. Hijacking (or skyjacking) had been in grim vogue for some years. Many of our domestic planes were diverted to Fidel Castro's Cuba. Now costly airliners filled with many American citizens of Jewish origin were hijacked. Guerillas held passengers as "prisoners of war." They were to be exchanged for jailed guerillas in Britain, Switzerland, and Germany. The guerillas also blew up the three jets forced to land in the desert. Later, they exploded one that was set down near Cairo. All the sabotage was carried out in the name of the Popular Front for the Liberation of Palestine. It was guesswork who had control—if anyone—over the guerillas.

In his feverish desire to show accomplishment as a statesman, Secretary Rogers had come up with a strange peace plan for the Middle East. He had the project circulated to see its impact. The Rogers plan to keep Middle East peace in this case was to have a joint United States-Soviet force. It was the product of inexperience and feckless thought. Little sense of contemporary history and feelings of opposing forces were considered. The reach was for the stars, that fell with a thud on Rogers. President Nixon vetoed the idea. He would soon have a personal examination in the area with a trip into the Mediterranean and then to Tito's Communist-run Yugoslavia. The visit would be balanced by a journey to Franco's Spain.

With skyjacking dominating horror-stricken reactions from the Middle East, a visit from Israel's matriarchal Premier Golda Meir to the White House at hand, a method was devised for us to come to grips with hijackers. One evening Assistant Secretary of the Treasury Gene Rossides got a hasty White House call. He was consulted on feasibility of collecting Treasury agents to ride shotgun guard on our overseas flights. Be prepared, Rossides was informed, to come up with a program by Thursday. It was a Tuesday night. A nimble and unflappable man, Rossides worked out names and numbers. He made it with a program in hand by Thursday. Subsequently, his cool, to-the-point plan for sky marshals was adopted.

His backbreaking task was totally obscured by bloody fighting that broke out in Jordan between Palestine guerillas and Hussein's forces. Hostages from hijacked airliners were held in terror-stricken Palestine refugee camps in Jordan. Hussein fought for survival. Israeli forces were strengthened on the borders. Hysteria rang like firebells through the Middle East. Mrs. Meir saw President Nixon. Her government, she asserted, would not renew its part in peace talks until Soviet AA missiles were moved back to pre-cease-fire positions. They never were. Premier Meir met with most senators at a reception. They did not discuss substance. But they all glowed at seeing her again. The Arabs could never match Golda Meir. Nasser couldn't come close. Nor could Women's Liberation here. Fulbright sulked. President Nixon went off on his trip, first to Italy, where demonstrations against him were organized and kept in check. Then he went to an aircraft carrier of our Sixth Fleet in the Mediterranean.

All the plangent sounds of arms could be heard on Israeli frontiers with Jordan. Nixon's appearance on the carrier close to the Middle East carried a message. It was the unspoken suggestion of power communicated to the USSR. Nasser railed against us and Hussein bitterly assailed Nasser. It had all the ingredients for combustion. Senators and congressmen went for quick looks at Israel and possible fighting areas. They were running for office. As the old story goes, there are hardly any Arab votes in our elections. While Nixon, with principal Cabinet officers and Kissinger, studied Middle East reports on the carrier, an unexpected drama unfolded. The consequences were to be immense.

In a nonkosher restaurant in Tel Aviv, I dined with Israeli Intelligence chief, Lt. General Ahron Yariv. Short and powerfully built, with a ticking mind, Yariv had once been a military attaché in Washington. He made frequent trips there, one narrowly evading a hijack. Sitting with Yariv in a restaurant of Continental decor, I found him an engaging conversationalist host. The head-waiter, a former Romanian, came up to him, telephone in hand. Yariv plugged the line into a wall socket, remarking: "Just like a bad 21 Club." He spoke in Hebrew. I do not understand the language. But the drift of something urgent came across. Yariv's even voice was that much more rapid than usual. He cradled the phone, waited for me to finish coffee.

"Nasser is dead," said Yariv. "The Prime Minister wants an assessment."

We went to his office. Men in uniform, some looking like academicians and others in open-throated shirts were waiting. Yariv introduced me. A lean, tall colonel was introduced to me by Yariv as "our chief spy." He and I chatted for a few minutes. I said good-bye and Yariv escorted me to the door. In a double take, I asked him when Cairo Radio had reported the news.

"I should say within about an hour and a half," replied Yariv.

It was great one-upmanship. The news came within ten minutes of his estimate. That report on Nasser's death also flashed to the carrier aboard which Nixon was conferring with his top foreign-policy people. Obviously, the Russians would be in a dither. Egypt was a client state of theirs and they had invested billions from the Aswan High Dam to hardware and sophisticated missiles, complete with trained technicians. The fierce fighting in Jordan persisted. Syria invaded and then withdrew. Guerillas and Hussein patched up an accommodation. Nixon went off to visit Tito. A mammoth welcome greeted him in the Balkan capital of Belgrade. In the Austro-Hungarian architecture of Zagreb, in Croatia, Tito escorted Nixon. A pelting rain didn't diminish another mammoth turnout. Nasser was dead. Old friend and mentor on nonalign-ment, Tito, opted to stay with Nixon. Power dictates alternatives. No sentiment could be spared. Out of the welter of conspirators who had helped Nasser to take control nearly twenty years earlier, one of the less publicized personalities emerged. Named interim President was balding, swarthy, Anwar Sadat. He had his own plans—for later.

Nixon returned to Washington after his protocol visit to France. He had succeeded in making the power world feel that the presidential presence in neuralgic corners of the world was persuasive.

The Senate, which had, remember, by 55 to 39, rejected the Mc-Govern-Hatfield end-the-war amendment, had another idea. A cross section of doves and hawks, from Senators Javits to Jackson, urged Nixon to propose a cease-fire in the Paris negotiations. It had been aired before but not in so bipartisan a fashion. The project was passed on. Ambassador Bruce broached it skillfully. The North Vietnamese scorned it. Their forces had just been exposed to have been in a senseless slaughter of unarmed villagers. The grisly affair elicited little notice, as did the cease-fire plan.

Mid-term election fever was zooming. Impatience with anything else caused irritation in the Senate. Hatfield again hinted that he might not run for a second term, up in 1972. He mentioned financial reasons as well as lack of family life. As noted, the Administration didn't care for him and his ultradove attitudes. Critics blamed any financial difficulties on his lifestyle. His attractive wife and he dressed modishly and expensively. They entertained handsomely. Money? His $42,500 salary, plus $28,000 in lecture fees was more than he had ever earned in his life. The total of $70,500 was hardly the whole picture. For his staff, phones, six trips to and from Oregon, and other facilities, Hatfield drew $300,000 annually from the taxpayers. Add that to a free five-room office in Washington and another commodious office and staff in Oregon. Not bad for a struggling freshman senator. Some friends even thought they ought to raise a special $100,000 fund to help him meet extra expenses. It was hastily dropped when details seeped out in Oregon. Still, Mark Hatfield said he was deeply depressed by the state of Republican politics.

XII

END OF THE LINE
FOR THE NINETY-FIRST

Senator Percy was not so pessimistic. He had a personal fortune accumulated as a whiz kid for Bell & Howell. His standing in Illinois shaped up well, although his legislative record—as with most of his club members—gleamed with tinsel. Percy, striving to show that he represented "new Republicanism" (whatever that is), liked to be called a moderate. He didn't like the war in Vietnam but he was careful to avoid offending the President. Percy harbored ambitions. The Vice-Presidency? Still, he would run for re-election in 1972. Hatfield's indecision wouldn't keep Percy out of the race. Despite financial drawbacks, Percy observed that he had no intention of quitting the Senate. If necessary, he could fund his own campaign. "I complain bitterly," he said, "but I would fight anyone who would try to take the job."

That was a declaration of intention dear to Birch Bayh's heart. He was all for big reform. Lots of senators talked that way, especially with elections around the corner. Bayh, re-elected from Indiana in 1968, had sights centered on the Democratic nomination for President in 1972. His work on the Judiciary Committee, where he organized opposition to Haynsworth and Carswell, earned him some of labor's gratitude. He was most prudent to subscribe to Meany's dictum that labor won its gains through the "system." Don't destroy it, was Bayh's thesis, taken from the AFL-CIO, but make necessary reforms. In this quest at age forty-two, Bayh proposed a constitutional amendment that challenged the

Senate's imagination. He proposed to abandon the archaic electoral college system in favor of the direct election of the President
and Vice President.

His direct-election proposal made sense. Not to conservatives,
especially in the Southern states. One of Bayh's foremost opponents
in the in-fighting of debate was Senator Fulbright. He called himself a Senate traditionalist. Other colleagues on both sides called
Senator Fulbright other names, down to four-letter words. Most
were traditionalists in togetherness, likes, and hates. They also
were under constant attack from the outside. Institutions and
traditions, from the Presidency to the Senate, business and universities were under ceaseless assault. A direct election of the
President would remove lots of sting from critics.

Immovable Senate traditionalists showed early they weren't
to be moved. The Bayh amendment required two-thirds of the
Senate majority to abolish the system. Then it would be two-thirds
of the House of Representatives. And, finally, approval by three-
fourths of the states' legislatures. Some eternal compromisers
began to suggest a compromise. In their thinking, the electoral
college could be altered profoundly. How? The electoral vote of
each state would be apportioned among candidates to their share
of the popular vote or the number of congressional districts each
carried. Senator Bayh realized he was on to a striking new reform
issue. He heard compromise suggestions and filed them away.
Then he went to around thirty-five states with the direct-election
proposal in speeches and meetings. It was one-man, one-vote, and
at the end, the candidate with the greater number of votes became
President.

Most senators from small states with great electoral college
power were opposed. Interestingly, a sizable minority was not.
Take Republican Henry Bellmon, of Oklahoma, who made a
practice of doing little but proving party loyalty. In a stunning,
somewhat unique insight into topsy-turvy conditions, he said: "I
believe that greater danger exists in the present system than would
under a direct popular vote." The Senate debated, waffled, and
stalled directly. There were in the remarks evidences of unreason-
able fear of change. Sentiment showed, too, as well as nostalgia
and apologia. The Bayh amendment was actually talked into

another look later on. The Senate had to try to adjourn to campaign for those pesky mid-term elections. By 54 to 36 the Senate voted against cloture—electoral reform, the issue. Chances of it getting through and ratified for the 1972 presidential elections looked superthin.

Bayh, with his young, athletic good looks, was also busy running—he has since withdrawn—for 1972 as a Democratic presidential hopeful. He was not above, as reviewed earlier, accepting a few favors. For example, an Indianapolis industrialist helped pay the bills for around seven of the Senator's annual winter visits to Miami. The tycoon was Miklos Sperling. One of the hotels at which Bayh and family stayed was the Miami Hilton Plaza. "As far as I knew," Bayh said, "Sperling was to pay the bills." Sperling was godfather, political that is, to Bayh's public life. The Teamsters Union Fund held a $13 million mortgage on the Miami Hilton Plaza. Bayh claimed he knew nothing about it. One can be sure that the Teamsters knew Bayh would be there and who would pick up the tab.

Being a crusader-reformer needs more than a sound issue like direct presidential elections. Fellow senators generally knew about Sperling and his friendship with Bayh. The majority all had Sperlings of their own. It was of small consequence that Bayh once failed to pass the Indiana bar exam, one of a dozen who flopped. He at least took the exam himself and passed it later on. His once close friend, Senator Ted Kennedy, tried a stand-in for a test at Harvard. He also sought unsuccessfully in the realm of jurisprudence to have a family friend made a federal judge. It was questionable that the friend could submit to the rigors of a present-day bar exam. It had been "Birch and Ted" for a long time, including an unfortunate private plane crash that nearly cost both senators their lives. Even before the ghastly incident at Chappaquiddick, a gap between Birch and Ted developed. They remained friends, but the fervor went out of the relationship.

It was each man for himself. The division probably began at the conventions of 1968. Bayh tried hard to get the No. 2 spot for Humphrey. Kennedy people didn't care for the ambition nor for Humphrey. Later Bayh was after the brass ring but could probably be induced to take the second post, depending on the first aspirant. Right now, like other ambitious candidates for the presidential nomination, he needed money and national exposure. That sounds indecent, and all hopefuls behaved in varying indecent manners in order to win support. Although he played it coy, Muskie thought for public consumption that his move toward a presidential nomination looked just great. He had re-election problems coming up in Maine, but Muskie looked further ahead. Hoopla and money scrambles overshadowed events of normal, substantive concern to this country.

A government report circulated that radicals plotted to kidnap high United States officials. Because the report first emanated from the FBI, there was a reflex inclination by critics to disclaim the threat. Presidential top aide Henry Kissinger was a target. When he was watched by a bodyguard, loud guffaws came his way. It took only a little time before the priestly brothers, Dan and Philip Berrigan, were implicated with a group of their adherents. They had been involved in destruction of draft records and were in hiding. The subsequent arrest and case became almost as controversial as the one surrounding Angela Davis.

The Senate, so turned inward about its own status, gave the problem scarcely a second look. Neither did Senator Fulbright's committee take an especially hard look at on-again, off-again reports that the Soviet Union was constructing a base for missile-firing submarines in Cuba. Specially equipped Russian ships were calling at the port of Cienfuegos. U-2 flights kept taking photos. The Soviets denied they were building a base. In President Kennedy's time they also denied slipping in missiles. This hide-and-seek situation was too close to home. It didn't interest Chairman Fulbright. The issue has not been satisfactorily resolved yet. Another momentous event, hard by the continental United States, caused a shock temporarily. The government in Canada, under swinging Premier Pierre Elliott Trudeau, invoked emergency police powers. It began mass arrests of suspected members and sympathizers of a revolutionary organization that claimed to seek independence for French-speaking Canada. A British diplomat had been taken hostage, as had the Minister of Labor for Quebec Province. The diplomat was later released and his captors permitted to fly to Cuba. The Canadian official was murdered.

It was a terrible business, our government and Senators agreed. First things first: President Nixon would gamble by campaigning for Republicans in twenty states. Agnew was kneading the media with his knuckles and the purge was out for Senator Goodell. The Vice-President called him the "Christine Jorgensen" of the Republican party. The campaign was heading into its seamiest confrontations. The Democrats lamented loudly their lack of cash. That was the National Committee's moan. Individual candidates for the Senate managed nicely. Campaign 1970 was setting a spending record. For congressional races—Senate and House— about $100 million, more than half for TV time. The business of being a political consultant boomed. To veteran and trusted Senate staff members fell the election duty of helping to raise vast sums. The D.C. Committees, as always, were the best vehicles.

These legal and semiconcealed operations crossed party lines. Majority Leader Mansfield and Minority Leader Scott headed up committees to assist in bankrolling their people. A perusal of records available showed that groups representing shipping, savings associations, cable TV, coal, restaurants, Teamsters—names can be reeled off a yard long—all contributed to D.C. Committees. Senator Winston L. Prouty, Republican of Vermont, had four committees. His opponent, former Vermont Governor Hoff, had at least two. Other senators using D.C. Committees included: Montoya, Democrat of New Mexico, Moss, Democrat of Utah, Proxmire, Ralph Smith, Republican of Illinois; Ted Stevens, Republican of Alaska, and former Vice-President Humphrey, running for the vacated McCarthy seat in Minnesota. Just as old fellow club members did, Humphrey leased a cut-rate Lincoln Continental from the Ford Motor Company. He hadn't yet been elected anew but was figured to be a shoo-in against Congressman Clark MacGregor, a Nixon confidant and old OSS veteran.

Humphrey, in this instance, obtained a $750-a-year discount lease, as it is known. He used the chairmanship of a tax-supported scholarship center to get the lease. It was obtained in the name of the Woodrow Wilson International Center for Scholars in Washington. Humphrey paid for the lease himself. McCarthy? He was very much in politics, lending his name to "peace candidates." Just about all of them lost. He also held himself aloof, waiting to see how his separation from his wife would work out. In the interim, McCarthy had his fling at public poetry readings. His own poetry, of course. Little attention was paid to the activities of "Clean Gene" in the frenetic chase for campaign dollars.

Industry lobbies and labor organizations had to file donations to committees with Congress. Many D.C. committees raised upwards of $50,000 each. Few were willing to tell. A canvas showed only $386,761 donated in various Senate candidates' committees. It was the wee tip of the iceberg. As any Senate aide, charged with helping to raise money, knew, cash was an indispensable factor. Don't report it or report little of it. But cash was a must in renting cars, getting poll watchers, and adding office help. Some Senate staffers who scoffed at a briefcase as a Central European habit in which to hide salami sandwiches, bought them for campaign fundraising. Much easier that way, you know, to shovel in currency. Moreover, a staff man needing funds for trips to dollar donors, required cash to make the journeys. It could be as many as two dozen trips.

A rare step in the 1970 mid-terms was a public report filed by re-election D.C. Committee for Muskie. With a month to elections, the committee voluntarily filed a report with Congress. It showed at the time about $163,000 having been raised. Donors were from all over the United States, including a top official of IBM. The Muskie committee was taking no chances in view of controversy over fund-raising groups. The Tom Dodd case remained ever fresh. More recent was the indictment against former Senator Brewster. He had been charged with taking a bribe from a mail-order company lobbyist. It was through a "D.C. Committee for Maryland Education." The indictment was dismissed by a federal judge who held that senators while in office were covered by some magical immunity. Repercussions still rip through the Senate as an aftermath.

No matter the party affiliation, it was still most useful to have plenty of personal assets. Senator Kennedy held big fund raisers, while contributors turned away with covered smiles. At the Ethel Kennedy Hickory Hill estate, four thousand turned out. It was intended, naturally, for the little people. Cost: $15 apiece or $25 a couple. The big one was staged up in Massachusetts where Kennedy ran for re-election. The glitter attached to the name of Kennedy illuminated Boston Symphony Hall. The spectacle brought in 2,631 donors. They paid from $500, $100, $50 down to $10 into the Kennedy campaign funds. Total take: about $200,000. Guests got to see three generations of Kennedys, comedians, and composers, and sipped tepid champagne. Senator Hart didn't have to stage such blowouts in Michigan. His opponent was the wife of the former Governor and present Secretary of Housing and Urban Development (HUD), Mrs. Lenore Romney. It was as easy as running against a learner in ballroom dancing.

Money, though, meant something in New York. Governor Rockefeller had the scratch. His opponent, former Associate Supreme Court Justice Arthur Goldberg, had to scrape. A Kennedy brother-in-law, Stephen Smith, managed the New York Democrats. But no real Kennedy money came to the hapless Goldberg, a rhetorical room-clearer. Nor did Rocky take the band off the bankroll for floundering Senator Goodell. Some Rockefeller money somehow found its way into the campaign contributions of Conservative candidate James L. Buckley. He also got a large turnout of volunteer youngsters. Youth, on the whole, contributed little, in cash and carry, to the campaigns of most candidates. They seemed indifferent to the "purge" approach aimed at the Administration's elimination of Goodell. Democratic candidate Ottinger, spending his family's plywood wealth freely, begged Goodell to withdraw. He figured that he'd draw the lion's share of "liberals" from Goodell. That would make him, by those estimates, a sound winner over Buckley. Goodell had an intimation of a judgeship accommodation with Governor Rockefeller. Besides, what most people failed to realize: Goodell disliked Ottinger personally and intensely from their time in the House.

Although the Senate tried to build up a pre-election image as a law-and-order body, it recessed for the elections in factional disputes. From the floor senators turned their emotions heavenward. They worked into the night, after inveighing against crime in the streets and terrorist bombings. Liberal Democrats like Hart sought hard to channel more federal crime-fighting funds into the cities.

"The cities, that's where the crisis is," Hart told the Senate.

His effort to divert a greater share of the grants of the Federal Law Enforcement Assistance Administration was smashed to earth by a vote of 42 to 18. Senator Hart also lost another funding bill under the Crime Control and Safe Streets Act. Hart and Kennedy argued the cities were being short changed. Instead the Senate passed bills making it a federal crime to assassinate, kidnap, or assault a member of Congress or a member-elect. It's enough punishment, some members observed sourly, to read the daily remarks published in the *Congressional Record*. Anyway, the crimes that were specified had been dealt with by individual states previously. Other bills tightened security for the President and imposed the death penalty for conviction of fatal terrorist bombings. Hart tried to delete death penalties. Up stepped Senator McClellan. He paced the aisle and swung his arms.

"The arsonists, the revolutionaries, the sabotagers [sic] are running free in our country," he cried.

You can't coddle the criminals, contended the Senate's chief crime hunter. He tried, with a withering look at Hart, to arouse the Senate by saying: "One of our troubles in this country today is that they [presumably coddled criminals] get away with it." The Senate listened. It voted all the crime-fighting bills, turned its collective back on Hart and his associates, and rushed pell-mell to get the hell home to campaign.

The Democrats found their traditional top campaign issue— the economy. In a way this was a carry-over from the Depression days of Herbert Hoover and the New Deal panaceas of FDR. Because of the pent-up anger of customary lower middle-class Democrats at crime in the streets, campus upheavals, and sharp shooting at the "System" and "Establishment," the party worried about defections on a broad basis. But there was a long strike at General Motors. Unemployment had ascended to 5.5 percent. The bogey of the thirties was whipped into a 1970 specter by the Democrats. Although most of the nation's voters called themselves Democrats, the party's luminaries were scared.

They had nothing with which to rebut the Republicans. It narrowed down to something as simplistic as "Democrats could do the job better." Quite a few of the better-known Democrats in the Senate were girding for the presidential convolutions. It was amazing how they spent more time talking to voters about 1972 than about the mid-term elections of 1970. Those with longer range views began collecting contributions for 1971 and the phase leading to nominating conventions and primaries of 1972. To add to national Democratic confusion, the internecine and intramural bickering made it seem that they were fighting each other rather than Republicans.

In the more vocal and articulate foreground stood would-be makers and breakers of Democratic leaders. Professor John Kenneth Galbraith, for instance, was all for shucking many top Senate Democrats. In Texas he supported Republican George Bush over Democrat Lloyd M. Bentsen, who beat incumbent Senator Ralph W. Yarborough badly. The Galbraith believers felt they could destroy the Democrats and reshape the party in their own images. Their constituencies usually covered the salons at which they talked only to each other.

The Republicans, fortunate enough to have squeaked into the White House in 1968, exercised the boomerang strategy. President Nixon was the grand strategist. His 1968 campaign manager, Attorney General Mitchell, ran some interference. Vice-President Agnew carried the ground smack into the middle. Dent was the Southern strategist. Most of the nitty-gritty, north of the Mason-Dixon, was in Chotiner's hands. It included Maryland. For a year, however, Nixon tried to orchestrate the game plan to win control of the Senate. The size and scope of the effort was unprecedented in American history. Other Presidents, as Wilson and FDR, smarted and bridled against "a little band of wilful men" in the Senate who thwarted their policies. Interestingly, Nixon's drive was much less personal but more ambitious.

President Nixon needed seven Senate seats. By sheer numbers, that would have made it 50–50 with Agnew casting a tie-breaking vote. Had Nixon been successful, he would have stampeded the dozen or so Republican Senate votes often cast against him. They would have lined up dutifully like parade soldiers. This campaign, too, was the first in a new era: the sizzling seventies. After the first two years in office, the Nixon Administration could see how the Senate frustrated him. It rejected two of his nominees for the United States Supreme Court, cut back on his ABM plan, and nearly rejected the whole project. The upper house also compelled the President to slash defense spending, served as a national concentration point for opposition to his policies in Vietnam, and added more money than he wanted for Health, Education and Welfare.

Restructuring the Senate, Nixon style, would have muted a raucous, fractionalized club. Nixon's record as President was fairly substantial, once you removed partisan criticism or glowing zealotry. His unabated withdrawal of troops from Vietnam was toward peace. He had a fragile but working balance with the Soviets on arms. And he adroitly opposed Russian power probes in the Middle East. He was quite prudent in the exercise of presidential power. On the domestic front, Nixon compromised with adversaries on school integration, social security, trade, and welfare policies. As a political being, he was uncompromisingly militant, riding an untamed tiger around the nation.

All traces of civility in the campaign disappeared in the last ten days. It became a national dock-wallopers' brawl. The issues vanished. Nixon, usually in iron control of himself when he seethes, became emotional. Several of his veteran advisers and helpers, going back to 1946, tried unsuccessfully to get him back on the track of dispassion. It didn't work. The GOP had a five-to-one edge on funds. In reports made public, the Republicans showed seven leading national committees with gifts of $18.6 million. Five Democratic national committees reported $3.6 million. The reports of both parties were deceptive. Their books were crooked, but in legal style. The campaign took upwards of $100 million. Nobody will ever know the precise and true figures.

The slam-bang techniques of the Republicans had begun to backfire. They were running into a combination of pocketbook problems and their own fear-smear attacks. George Meany said he didn't trust the GOP. But he was careful to keep access clear. He did not assail Nixon by name. Meany, for example, never cared much for Agnew or John Mitchell. He considered them big-mouthed lightweights. Nor did Meany have any regard for Muskie. He referred to him as "Shmuskie," a sort of New Yorkese combination of part of the Senator's surname and *shmuck*, or dope. Election eve, though, the Democrats got together. After lots of telephoning to Muskie's colleagues and presidential hopefuls, Muskie was agreed upon as the party choice to do a paid TV broadcast on all three networks. Harriman, always careful with his multimillions and hatcheck tips, volunteered to guarantee the cost. That alone was sensational.

Back-to-back TV carried appeals by President Nixon and Senator Muskie. It was a bad show—for Nixon. His was a black-and-white film and emotional. Nixon had been at a stormy rally earlier at San Jose in California. The quality of his show was terrible. Muskie's was done in living color. It was a fireside chat from the roomy kitchen of a Maine friend. His speech was drafted by writer Richard Goodwin, whose talents can coruscate but whose collaborative instincts with those on high never guarantee loyalty. Once the Muskie film was hailed, Goodwin let it be known that he was the author. Muskie ever since tried to keep a no-man's land between them. Muskie had come across as a reasonable, reflective, and responsible personality. Thus did Muskie insure a front-running status for himself for the Democratic nomination.

How did Nixon screw up? Poor communications, euphoria, and the yes, Mr. President, toadying of immediate associates. When the Nixon team was warned well in advance of the poor quality of the taped show, the caution was laughed off. "We'll go, warts and all," exulted Mitchell. Even anti-Nixon voters were alarmed. Weren't the TV stations being guilty of unfairness, as Agnew always charged? Throughout the country, stations were swamped by complaining calls. The gist ran that TV deliberately set out to sabotage Nixon and make Muskie look good. It was ironic: the Republicans had all the money that could possibly buy a well-rehearsed tape of the President. It sure belied the pat concept among many Democrats about Nixon having been TV-packaged in 1968.

Election results were probably not a reflection of any last-minute swings because of the TV shows. If there ever was a Machiavellian Southern strategy, it was applied judiciously in the Northeast. It worked well there and in two border states. The Republicans managed to make a net gain of two seats in the Senate. It made the upper chamber stand at 55 to 45, not a very famous victory for President Nixon, who put so much on the line to get a better break in the numbers. The Democrats picked up some seats in the House of Representatives. The gains were modest and hardly as big as had been predicted in mid-term. More to the point, the Republicans lost their absolute majority of governors. They lost statehouses all over the country, going down to a distinct minority. Power bases—especially for 1972—require statehouse control for nominating presidential conventions.

Both parties licked their wounds and claimed to see glorious triumph at the mid-term election results. The net two gain in the Senate led President Nixon to proclaim an ideological victory. Survival tactics of most senators aimed at working accommodations—deals—not ideology. If anything, the outcome showed ticket splitting around the country. And an incredible ton of money spent and wasted.

Republicans lost: Smith, in Illinois, bewildered, zero appointee to fill in for Dirksen. Adlai Stevenson III won, but even Democrats wondered why. Memories of his father, probably. Out in California, George Murphy was swamped by Congressman John Tunney. Revelations about Murphy's profitable tie-up with Technicolor, plus a big drop in the vote for Governor Ronald Reagan, overwhelmed the ex-song-and-dance man. His replacement, however, had shown no sign of any brilliance besides being his father's son. Republican gains: in Tennessee, William E. Brock, 3rd, beat Albert Gore. That made two Republican senators for the state, noteworthy because it was the first time since Reconstruction. Robert Taft, Jr., squeezed through over parking-lot millionaire Metzenbaum. Taft kept Agnew from campaigning in Ohio and stayed away from the corruption-ridden remainder of the state ticket.

An unexpected Republican dividend: in Maryland, Congressman J. Glenn Beall, Jr., beat Joe Tydings soundly. Six years before, Tydings swept out Beall's father. The publicity suggested that conflict of interest cost Tydings dearly, as did his gun control support. Liberals also fell out with him because Tydings was so adamant about the "no-knock" anticrime law. Almost tongue in cheek, the State Department, ten days after the elections, said it could find no influence peddling by Tydings. The department is a professional career service all right, up there with the oldest professions in the world. In Connecticut, Lowell P. Weicker, Jr., scored over peace proponent Joseph Duffey and incumbent Senator Tom Dodd, the latter running as an Independent. Dodd took a quarter of the vote. He achieved a big goal, that of defeating the statehouse ambitions of former Democratic National Chairman John Bailey.

Yet the biggest satisfaction the Administration took in all the Senate contests was the victory of Buckley. Out went Republican Goodell, marked for the purge. It also was a singular victory for the backroom strategy of Murray Chotiner. Re-election of Harry Byrd pleased the White House. He ran as an Independent in Virginia. Neither the Democrats nor Republicans could lay a glove on him. Democratic reformists in the Senate didn't challenge Byrd's right to his seniority as long as he lined up with them for the party label. High-minded switch hitters, they didn't debate the Harry Byrd case long—around twelve minutes flat.

Really close ones for both parties that didn't change things were in Indiana and Nebraska. Senator Hartke had recounts facing him with a win of less than five thousand. The total seemed enough since the Republicans in the state exhausted their take-home vote in the rural areas. Hartke's most active allies, the Teamsters, did their job well. He was nervous for a while. Hartke threatened to hold up confirmation of the appointment of able and intelligent William D. Ruckelshaus to be head of the new Environmental Protection Agency. He so told Hugh Scott and other senators, unless the Republicans withdrew their legal action for a complete review. Hartke relented on Ruckelshaus. Making the deal was second nature to him.

Senator Hruska came perilously close to losing to a Democratic mediocrity. The piety and sanctimony of Hruska and his profitable, prurient movies in the state obviously caused mass revulsion. Occasional opposition remembrance of Nebraska's great Senator Norris almost did in Hruska. Norris, from the grave, could obtain almost as many votes as the walking dead represented by Hruska. Symington, keeping the seat warm for his son (he hoped), had a cliffhanger in Missouri. Voters out there were fed up with his hard-line-turned-soft-line tactics. Moreover, he paid little attention to the concerns of the state, and his opponent was a young and intelligent lawyer.

It was in the South and Southwest that the Administration saw its once rosy hopes go awry. A bright young Democratic candidate from Florida, Lawton Chiles, easily beat the Nixon choice, William C. Cramer. Over in Texas, LBJ took a hand. Bentsen, a wealthy former congressman, clobbered George Bush.

All the effort, planning, and energy didn't mean a thing without massive money to match. The principal cost was the outlay for TV. More reports to the Senate close to and after election time were ridiculous, and a mockery of the electorate. Because of the law, neither Bentsen nor Bush claimed to have received or spent a dollar. The Texas race cost close to $5 million. This was the sworn statement, too, of Tunney, of California. Both Hartke and his opponent, of Indiana, swore the same. Brock, elected in Tennessee, reported no gifts or outlays. He said he spent only $2,118.84 for travel and lodging. Loopholes in the law, of course, permit a candidate to report only what was received by him or with his knowledge. Try to get a candidate to admit anything like the sums expended. Yet they all know, down to the last thousand. How? By asking regularly.

With the vast sums spent, particularly for TV, the high-pressure makers of political images had little to say for themselves except that their services were needed more than ever. From the results, you would never know why. No matter the party, across the country, the analysts-consultants just about split even on winning and losing. Of the five top image-makers, they had twelve winners and eleven losers. For all the money and effort, someone could have stabbed a pencil in a list of names and done just as well. But the occultism of political consultants had been elevated into a kind of pseudoscience. It was the 1970s' answer to the medicine man.

An organization had even been founded. It was called the American Association of Political Consultants. Good thing it was "American." No other practicing parliamentary society could tolerate the mumbo-jumbo. Right after the mid-term elections, the association held a seminar in New York. Members exchanged trade secrets. Postmortems also were in order. As you could expect, consultants never jabbed at the opposition that were winners. The tables could easily be turned next time out. For example, F. Clifton White explained how Goodell's votes could never have gone to a

Democrat. The consultant who ran the show for Goodell agreed. White, by the way, had been big in Barry Goldwater's race in 1964. This time he was strategist for Senator-elect Buckley. While the association stroked members' backs, the most widespread but unseen apparatus of all filed facts and names.

Their activity was confined to learning all about political trends, possible helpers, and supporters—down to home phone numbers— for re-elected Senator Ted Kennedy. Massachusetts returned Kennedy handsomely, but not as heavily as six years before. In every major consultant's office for a Democratic candidate across the country was a Kennedy volunteer. Sometimes three or four. Certainly, they gave advice and stratagems for free to the candidates. But they did first things first: getting details in all states on who could help in a county, on the board of education. No office was too lowly or obscure to be tapped and asked for information.

It was the Kennedy political intelligence network getting up to date. There was not a single aspirant for the Democratic nomination in 1972 who could come close to the Kennedy files. Kennedy had more on tap with information than the whole collection of party candidates. It was uncannily what Chotiner suggested to the Republican strategists after the 1968 elections. He wanted to train cadres in the fifty states. They would make up a last third-of-the-century set of party centurions. Chotiner emphasized loyalty, not what money could buy in the way of analysts-consultants. The pay-for-play strategists in the White House won out, although Senator Scott was all in favor of Chotiner's idea.

The after-election quarterbacking persisted over a lame-duck return to Congress. It was the first post-election session in twenty years. A vast load of unfinished work remained. Little time was left to accomplish much. A bipartisan zest to work it out was indiscernible. Controversial money bills hung in Senate pipelines. They could, and did, trigger fights over foreign aid, defense, and the SST (supersonic transport plane). It was interesting to note the term "lame duck." In vogue first in eighteenth century England, it referred to a stockbroker who would not or could not pay his losses. So he had to "waddle out of the alley," the bargaining place. A better term could not have been invented for the Senate at this time and for some time past. Yet there were only seven of the thirty-one senators who ran who were unsuccessful. They waddled and squawked.

Senatorial attention got some diversion in the hard-to-get attitude of Mrs. Mary Mundt. The wife of the ailing senior Senator from South Dakota refused to permit husband, Karl, to resign. Republicans were getting vapors. The Republican governor, Frank Farrar, had been beaten. He had until January 5, 1971, to appoint someone else, should Mundt resign. Mrs. Mundt had no intention of allowing that. She liked being Mrs. Senator although her stricken husband hadn't been able to come to the Senate for a year. The chances were maybe never. He was up again in the presidential election year of 1972. A Democratic governor of South Dakota, when the time was feasible, could appoint a Democrat. McGovern was the other Senator.

The attention paid to Mrs. Mundt in the hectic post-election weeks was probably greater than at any time in Mundt's long career. She was invited to the White House. President Nixon went out of his way to be extra nice. He didn't directly suggest that Mundt resign. All his outriders did. Mary Mundt remained firm in her no. She suggested her husband might suffer another stroke if resignation was suggested. Later, in a melodramatic last-ditch act, defeated Governor Farrar sat in a Washington hotel. He waited in case Mrs. Mundt had a change of heart the last minute. Emissaries went back and forth as at a summit meeting. Farrar sat helplessly in his hotel room. He became the former Governor. Mrs. Mundt stayed triumphantly as Mrs. Senator.

Martha Mitchell sympathized with her. By this time the wife of the Attorney General generated her own decibel system every time she phoned or talked. Besides sympathy for Mary Mundt, Martha Mitchell observed that Republican losses in the elections were their own fault. She was eminently pleased, though, that Senators Gore and Goodell had been beaten. A bigger flap that involved her decision and her husband's building petered out in the Senate. She wanted a rush job done on five hundred feet of corridor hallways leading to her husband's offices in the Justice Department. It took 154 hours of overtime for painters. Cost was about $1,300 for a pale-blue face lift. It matched the Wedgewood blue in Mrs. Mitchell's Watergate apartment. A secretary in a Mitchell outer office looked at the newly painted walls and said: "It's enough to make you throw up." Her remark made the rounds quickly in Senate offices stung by Mrs. Mitchell's vitriol and by her derogatory references about some of their officeholders.

Lots of friendly and unfriendly senators would have shared her bemusement—real or fancied—when she was asked at a party about a new best seller. It was *The Greening of America* by Yale law professor Charles Reich. Mrs. Mitchell thought that it had to do with painting and the most recent controversy about her choice of colors in her husband's offices. Maybe a half dozen senators had taken the time to read and think about the Reich book. It was low-grade totalitarian thought. Its sustained popularity probably reposed in categories like Consciousness I, Consciousness II, and Consciousness III. A couple of elderly senators' wives bought the book thinking it was another sex manual.

Sudden death across the seas stopped the introspective Senate in its tracks briefly. A heart attack toppled in France the last of the giant-sized personalities of World War II. General de Gaulle was gone. Senators, in eulogies, tried to wrap themselves around some of his mystical grandeur. Many conveniently forgot how they knocked him for kicking NATO headquarters out of France, trying to put a gold drain on the dollar, and generally looking at the States as a semi-primitive creature. In death, he had become super. President Nixon and a high-powered entourage flew to Paris for special services. Most of the Senate wallowed in the courtesy of mourning. They returned to normal quackery—remember this was a lame-duck session—pretty quickly.

Senator Hart, next to Cooper the man who tried always to behave gentlemanly even with fiery critics, turned up with a grizzly Vandyke beard. He was unique, the only present-day bearded senator. Hart also had just been re-elected to his third term. Hughes thought that if eleven more senators would grow beards, he would, too. Then, there'd be no more fuss. Hart had promised his son he'd grow the beard if he won. He planned to keep it on for a couple of months. Being No. 1—with a beard, that is—pleased Hart so much that he stayed with it. Senator McGee regarded Hart and beard striding down a corridor and said wickedly: "I'm reserving judgment until he walks down the mountain with the tablet." Hart was always to be envied because his heart was as relatively pure as were his motives.

In serious business, the lame ducks quacked and singularly failed to override President Nixon's veto of the TV campaign spending bill. The vote was 58 to 34 in favor of overriding the veto. It was four votes short of the required two-thirds majority. Five Republicans who earlier supported the curb switched and acted to sustain the veto. This abject show in failing to provide a first step was deflected by Scott. He had voted against overriding, but he promised to draft a more comprehensive bill within the next year. Limitless spending was not only back in style but given a free hand, courtesy of the United States Senate. The analysts-consultants, who sanctimoniously backed the curb, were modestly enthusiastic. As a majority observed: we could have managed even with curbs and prohibitions.

The Senate's monumental failure was temporarily swept away by a series of simultaneous events. A commando force stormed into a North Vietnamese prison compound twenty miles west of Hanoi. It was a daring raid. But the POWs—a vital factor in negotiations —had long since been removed. Once revealed, the episode provoked a spate of senatorial declamations. Senator Fulbright said it represented escalation. Characteristically, Pell was moved to exclaim: "My God. . . ." The Foreign Relations Committee met to decide they wanted to hear Secretaries Laird and Rogers. On the Senate floor members accused and defended. Few, by the way, tried to exact anything but the first published details. Jackson called the effort sound and prudent. Hugh Scott attacked critics. From the floor Muskie called the mission another evidence of the follies of the Administration.

In an amazingly short time the Senate's alarums and excursions were kind of a dead letter. With news of the raid on one side of the world came the revelation of a dreadful episode in American waters. A Soviet sailor on a fishing boat off Martha's Vineyard— playground for many in the Camelot crowd—tried to defect. He gave himself over to the captain of a United States Coast Guard cutter, and was forcibly returned. It was a wretched example of craven stupidity in high places. Scapegoats were found fast. The

hapless defector from Lithuania was sent home and after a convenient spell, sent to prison. Quite a right of traditional asylum!
There was no outcry from Senators Fulbright, McGovern, Hatfield, and their supporters. It interfered with their concept of first
things first: Vietnam and the war. The Senate, you see, had become
totally incapable of dealing with more than one grave issue at a
time.

It followed much more naturally for most of the club members
to concentrate on inner politics—their own. Behind the scenes
dogged, all-work Bobby Byrd of West Virginia built himself up
steadily. He had no reputation beyond his own state, and Democratic liberals shunned or pretended to scorn him. He was, in
effect, assistant to Majority Whip Ted Kennedy. Yet as we have
noted, Byrd did all the drone's work. What he also did, just
before the mid-term elections, was to divide the $18,000 he re-
ceived for re-election purposes from the Democratic National
Committee. Himself a sure winner, Byrd apportioned the money
among Democrats facing tough contests. They were all to Byrd's
left.

This generosity was another tile in the Byrd mosaic to make
himself whip. He had begun the political IOUs approach twelve
years before. His colleagues had always looked on the whip's job
as an honorific joke until Teddy made his big show to defeat Russ
Long by 31 to 26 in 1969. After Chappaquiddick Kennedy had
become a dim figure in the Senate. Besides resentment that a
Kennedy could possibly get what he wanted for the asking, many
fellow liberals had nonideological grievances against him. One
was Alaska's Gravel. There were lots of condescending views about
Gravel. Some bordered on contempt.

Other weighty issues caused senators to pause lest their lips get
too tired. In a gesture of magnanimity, Vice-President Agnew
praised the American media as "the fairest, finest in the world."
His compliments added to the din of expertise. All the pre-
election punditry, added up, hardly squared with the results.
Nixon won, as the President claimed, or he lost, as his critics
contended. Casual perusal of most annual almanacs would show
that in 1966, 1968, and 1970, Democratic candidates for Congress
took 50 percent of the vote. Agnew's praise with suggestions of

how the media could do better qualified him for punditry with
the most prominent hydra-headed analysts. His benevolence didn't
last. How could it for so demanding a partisan?

The Vice-President was first to rush to the defense of FBI
Director J. Edgar Hoover. It's just as Martha Mitchell quipped
later: "If you've seen one FBI Director, you've seen them all."
Hoover was being criticized and sniped at more regularly than at
any time in his forty-five-year career. So he took off against one
of his more persistent critics, Ramsey Clark. Son of a former
Supreme Court Justice, Clark had been predecessor to Attorney
General Mitchell. That made him, of course, Hoover's boss.
Hoover, in a rare interview, called Clark a "jellyfish." Clark's
father, former Justice Clark, was "a good, strong man" in the view
of Hoover. The younger Clark shaped up worse than did the late
Bobby Kennedy by the FBI director's yardstick. Bobby also had
been a boss of Hoover in his tenure as Attorney General under
brother President John F. Kennedy.

"If there ever was a worse Attorney General [speaking of
Bobby] it was Ramsey Clark," declared Hoover. "You never knew
which way he was going to flop on an issue. He was worse than
Bobby. At least Kennedy stuck by his guns even when he was
wrong."

That was strong meat served up by Hoover. The critical lions—
privately Hoover called them hyenas and scavengers—chewed and
reared back. Hoover, they said, was senile and dictatorial. Maybe
he did some good once was a grudging concession, but it was high
time, in the name of God, for him to go. A living monument
doesn't trundle off. The pedestal would be empty. Hoover critics,
so irate, also failed to see his self-perpetuation methods. Counter-
charges after the comments on Clark entrenched Hoover with
the Administration. Martha Mitchell loved him, too. A pleasant
and publicized dinner with President Nixon extended the Hoover
timetable—his own. After all, even the Kennedys never dared
budge our only living monument in Washington, D.C. At least 90
percent of the Senate kept its collective mouth shut as well.

A few senators, among them Jackson and Scott, became aware
of quiet presidential diplomacy. Nixon had been most cautiously
working toward an approach to mainland China. All the steam

had gone out of a committee to make of Mao the ruler of a hermit people's republic. Mrs. Anna Chennault, the glamorous dragon lady, was unable even to check the Nixon trend one bit. Shrewdly she noted what was afoot. The United States said it was reexamining policy after Communist China won a simple majority for a seat in the United Nations. A two-thirds vote was required. That seemed assured next time out. Little reflex dismay emanated from the Administration. Nationalist China, via Mme. Chennault, worried aloud. They had to rephase, but the shift was irreversible.

Senator Fulbright and his committee hardly noted a comment about this revolutionary change in affairs of state. It may have been too difficult to read Peking tea leaves, since no staff members could even get a visa for a few days' study of conditions on the spot. Suffice it to say, Fulbright and members weren't filled in. They were enraged about something else that surfaced from the White House about the UN. Daniel Patrick Moynihan, leading Democratic intellectual on Nixon's staff, was picked as our next ambassador. The news circulated even before veteran career man, Ambassador Charles Yost—taken out of retirement by Nixon—was told about the appointment. It was classic crassness. The Kennedys, some years back, had a successor to our Ambassador to West Germany, Walter Dowling, before he knew it. First word "Red" Dowling got was when his wife told him as he went into surgery for a kidney ailment. First pleased, Moynihan then fiddled. He decided against the appointment. The leave of absence from Harvard was good for two years. It was about up. Moynihan, a capacious, unaffected martini drinker, returned to Harvard.

The Yost-Moynihan incident got buried beneath an avalanche of publicity and analysis of another personality, Nikita Sergeyevitch Khrushchev. He had been a big man, party secretary and all-powerful in the Soviet Union, for ten years. Toppled by a Kremlin cabal in 1964—led by burly, nose-picking Leonid Brezhnev and ally Alexei Kosygin—Khrushchev became an unperson. Now his memoirs were published. The *Time-Life* empire paid a fortune. The negotiations were in the James Bond mold. A few senators, their curiosity piqued, asked how the memoirs were obtained. They didn't get an answer. Neither did the CIA. The

Soviet middleman was Victor Louis. He's a shadowy one. Louis was the only Russian to drive a Mercedes convertible in Moscow. He lived it up. Of Louis it could be said that if he promised to sell his grandma, he'd deliver her.

The memoirs of Khrushchev, in book form, entitled *Khrushchev Remembers,* first appeared in installments in *Life* magazine. All inside and outside men of the Senate tried their demonological infrared on the stories. Speculation outstripped the text. Were there voice tapes smuggled out? Did Soviet security, the KGB, deliberately handle the transaction? By coincidence, the revelations thrust aside the disgraceful and forcible return of Soviet sailor Simas Kudirka from one of our Coast Guard cutters. The KGB also had a hand in that act. But the Khrushchev memoirs, while not necessarily a cultural gem, got far more attention than the sailor. His was supposed to be unvarnished, living history.

Our foreign relations defenders in the Senate did not see fit to utter a phrase in behalf of the imprisonment of brilliant dissident Soviet writers like Andrei Amalric. Nor did the committee complain about the indignity in the harassment of Nobel Prize-winning writer Alexander Solzhenitsyn. When internationally known cellist Matislav Rostropovich protested, the KGB wouldn't let him travel. Senator Jackson deemed it worthwhile to remind colleagues of the Soviet techniques as he had, in another vein, about the enforced second-class status for Jews in the USSR. Senator Fulbright had too much of Southeast Asia on his plate. He couldn't be bothered to take time out to study Soviet affairs. Those issues had been ghost-written for him earlier in a tome that dealt with new realities and old myths as he saw them. Responsibility for affairs of state lay heavy on the United States Senate.

Even in the last gasp of the ninety-first session, the Senate found it irresistible to belt the military around. Senate critics like Proxmire, McGovern, and Hatfield ignored a Pentagon disclosure of significance: the forces would be cut by 600,000 by mid-1972. Shrinking budgets and rising personnel costs were the reasons. In themselves the explanations were inadequate. Senatorial critiques centered not just on waste but on whether the total manpower in the military establishment was useful or necessary. The Defense Department hardly responded to the challenge. By mid-1972 it would have 2.7 million in all branches, about the same as the total had been before the buildup in Vietnam in 1965.

A branch of the services came off suddenly better than all the others. It may have been due to the fervor of modish-looking new Chief of Naval Operations, Admiral Elmo R. Zumwalt, Jr. The name "Elmo" caught on delightedly with senators. And Zumwalt's flood of directives to change institutions in the Navy were charmingly different. Most senators critical of the Pentagon in regard to the Army and Air Force somehow shied away from any attacks on the Navy. It had become sort of our own latter-day senior service. Zumwalt's instructions for change were called by his supporters and his haters, "Z-grams." He ordered special things in keeping with the times: no professional discrimination against officers and men who grow neat sideburns, beards, or mustaches. Motorcycles were allowed on bases. A Navy man owning one could wear any color helmet he liked. Liberty wouldn't end at night but last until morning.

In addition to improving morale and presumably effectiveness, the mod Admiral approved more rational dress regulations. Men in clean and neat work clothes could go off base, or into snack bars, without the endless uniform changes traditional in barracks life. Zumwalt even ordered commanding officers to stop painting their ships unnecessarily simply to please scheduled visiting admirals. He really tried the traditionalism of old-line salts. More, he aggravated them by urging black officers to stand up for their rights and for those of fellow blacks. Zumwalt also launched a program that would result soon thereafter in promotion for the first time of blacks to the rank of rear admiral. Anyone could see revolution, therefore, in the Navy; or maybe it was going to hell.

Marine Corps General Lewis Walt thought that maybe Americans had been naïve on the nature of the war in Vietnam. The Marines, as we are taught early, are the shock troops of the Navy. Chalk up another aberration for Zumwalt's operations.

Senators were opening their barrages on the Army. Senator Sam Ervin told his colleagues on the floor that a former Army Intelligence agent charged that the Army spied on new Senator Adlai Stevenson, former Illinois Governor Otto Kerner, and Democratic Congressman Abner Mikva. Another eight hundred civilians also were spied on, declared Judge Sam. Political surveillance was applied during the officeholders' campaigns. Ervin was good and sore about information he acquired. He said that we were rapidly becoming a "dossier society." Details on lives—the census just showed upward of 204 million Americans—were contained in everything from credit card ratings to Social Security. The use of Army spies, in Ervin's view, was unpardonable. Once more the most vocal, instant support rallying to Ervin was from left-of-center forces. While colleagues in the club were annoyed that a member could have been watched; most didn't care what happened to or about young Stevenson. They were by now wholly outraged that the Army was getting around to conceding widespread use of drugs in Vietnam.

It was marijuana at this time—only later would the brass acknowledge large-scale addiction to hard drugs like heroin, bought so cheaply in Southeast Asia. The chief of an Army psychology section informed a Senate subcommittee chaired by Senator Hughes that a poll he made of outgoing enlisted men showed more than half had tried marijuana at least once in their lives. One out of every six, he reported, was a habitual user in Vietnam. Overall, half reported using pot in Vietnam on occasion. Hughes and fellow senators were staggered shortly thereafter to hear testimony that four men in every plane load of 154 paratroopers were likely to be on heroin or other hard drugs. Then the Defense Department, which used to say that drug addiction in the military was not widespread, began to admit that they had a major problem on their hands. They were groping for answers. In a somber understatement, compatible with the pace and mood of the ninety-first session in the Senate, Armed Services Committee chairman Stennis said of infectious drug usage: "I think it is one of the gravest national problems that we have."

As chairman of his committee, Stennis might have also pondered the wrenching problems of racial unrest. A Pentagon group had gone to overseas bases and found disturbing, disquieting conditions. A report noted: "The problems found overseas are not unlike the media have made them appear." The semantics used would make a reader wonder where the blame rested. Instead of having them aired fully and impartially before his committee,

Stennis sought steadily to defend segregationist policies. They had to be in a constitutional form, you understand. Thus, he embraced bills a strange new ally advocated. Stennis, from Mississippi, found himself in tender togetherness with Senator Abe Ribicoff from the state of Connecticut. Ribicoff demanded a national policy of school desegregation. The North was too hypocritical, only carping at the South.

There was something pointed in Ribicoff's terminology. Much was made of *de jure* and *de facto* situations. Most Northern liberals were livid with Ribicoff. He was trying hard, went the sneers, to be second best. That meant he wanted the support of Stennis and Southerners he could attract to back a Ribicoff pursuit of the Democratic nomination for Vice-President. Senators can sure take the scalp off a fellow member. Dodd, who had helped Ribicoff to the first Senate seat, and later felt the sting of cold correctness, dripped with acid when the Stennis acclamation for Ribicoff's plan became a general talking point. Long before he had to appear before Stennis, as chairman of the Ethics Committee, Dodd savagely called him the biggest bigot around. Of Ribicoff, the off-the-cuff remark from Dodd was, "Abe is at your throat or your feet."

The Ribicoff school desegregation project got plenty of discussion and heat. So busy was the end-of-term Senate with backed-up legislation that the bills were put away for early reconsideration in the ninety-second session. Senator Stennis and his colleagues studied a case that was dramatically in the public eye. The trial of 1st Lieutenant William L. Calley, Jr., had begun just before 9:00 A.M. at Fort Benning, Georgia. He was on trial as a mass murderer at My Lai in Vietnam. It was a court-martial before a six-man jury. There was a lot at stake: the integrity of United States military justice—and Calley's life. Calley had three lawyers. Royal blue drapes covered the windows and a wall of the large room in the one-story brick-and-frame building. Calley was accused of the premeditated killing of 102 men, women, and children, a muggy day in March 1968.

Unmindful of public dismay and disfavor, Pentagon bureaucrats kept up a little money-making operation on the side. It was for the Defense Department, not personal. Nearly a million dollars a year was being collected from private businesses operating in the Pentagon. Nothing wrong with that, but only a part got back to the Treasury. How? Half went to the Defense Concession Committee. In turn, the committee used $250,000 a year to finance social clubs, dinner dances, and tennis tournaments for Pentagon employees. The arrangement was—still it—unique in the federal government. That little caprice caused senators to scoff when the Pentagon's auditing officials claimed that inflation really ate up any peace dividend accruing from war's end in Vietnam. At peak, the Vietnam War in 1968 cost about $20 billion a year. By the end of June 1971, it was sliced to $10 billion. Nothing could be channeled back into health and education programs. Department of Defense pay raises consumed $4.6 billion of the $10 billion drop. Piled on top was a $300 million boost in military retirement pay. Then inflation drove up costs. The image was as dark as many returning servicemen found when they got back from Vietnam to hear themselves reviled as criminals. What a lovely war!

Fighting their counteroffensive from the Senate with the well-financed lobbies that mushroomed to assist, Senate doves paused with their adversaries. A political event occurred which had been long expected. Secretary of the Interior Hickel was called into the President's office. Nixon fired him. Once regarded as a docile dope, Hickel had become a short-term hero to anti-Nixon senators. He had come to symbolize disloyal public dissent as did former Senator Goodell. Out he went, together with six aides the White House dismissed with him. Oh, how the anti-Nixon senators loved him. Hickel was Rudolph the Red-nosed Reindeer in reverse. Into his post came Maryland Congressman and Republican National Chairman Rogers C. B. Morton. A bear of a man who could dance to a presidential tune, Morton became hipped on conservation. Isn't that what every Secretary of the Interior is supposed to be?

"The party is tired of quarreling with each other," said Tennessee's Senator Howard H. Baker, Jr. "Instinctively, we feel the time has come for us to pull together."

The instinct may have been there, as Dirksen's son-in-law Baker wanted to believe. But a recasting of the staffs in the White House had Republican senators wondering who would really be in charge, excluding the President. Byzantium practice is a White House rule of political survival. Senators Mansfield, Scott, and all the veterans of the Senate knew the rules, firsthand. So did many of the self-thrusters in the domain of reform. Essentially they resented the intrigues and the techniques because these were power plays and those looking in from the outside were neither consulted nor tapped. Their inherent beef was that they were cold-shouldered from our own kind of permanent purge. They all blinked hard when Secretary of Labor George Shultz was appointed by Nixon to head the newly created Office of Management and Budget.

Crew-cut Erlichman, Seattle lawyer and amateur photo snapper, was chosen to direct the Domestic Council. It was like being chief watchdog of the domestic scene, especially in the ebbs and tides of political fortunes. Erlichman, with Haldeman, had been keeper of the keys to the President's office. He still worked in tandem with Haldeman. Shultz, in seventeen months as Secretary of Labor, had won complete confidence from Nixon. He also was liked by senators who pursued interest in civil rights coequality. He had a gift for compromise and a touch for reconciling politics and principle. Hard-to-please George Meany got along with him. Shultz was about equal in the pecking order with Haldeman. As an economist and former dean of the University of Chicago Graduate School of Business, he was experienced in many fields. But he had none in foreign affairs. And his hand-to-hand battle in politics was largely limited to reading. Therefore, he could be no "Assistant President." That relieved guardians of their own power in the Senate and White House.

In their subjective manners they studied closely the effect the resignation of one of the Administration's top black officials—some senators insisted he was No. 1—would have. He was James Farmer, founder of CORE (Congress for Racial Equality) and a pillar in civil rights. Farmer resigned as Assistant Secretary of HEW. He didn't knock Nixon, who sent him a "Dear Jim" letter of thanks and regrets. Farmer, then fifty and a big man physically, said he chafed under a ponderous bureaucracy. He thought he could get more done from the outside. When he entered government under

Nixon, Farmer had been verbally pistol-whipped by more radically motivated blacks and whites. Obviously he was a great find for the Nixon Administration. His calling was really oratory, not bureaucracy. But Farmer wanted, as he said, to have a taste of government power for his cause. It was not altogether satisfactory, but the experience was neither bitter nor sour. There were around 150 blacks in top federal positions. Nixon haters pointed skeptically to the fact that like Washington's own Mayor, Walter Washington, they were mainly holdovers from the Democrats. True, but they also could have been pigeonholed or fired. The only black man on the President's personal staff was Robert J. Brown, a personable public relations counselor from North Carolina. He worked with Bobby Kennedy in 1968. After Kennedy's death he was recruited for Nixon. Brown took his lumps from the same assortment of critics as did Farmer. He managed quietly to do all right.

The Senate—civil rights proponents or otherwise—didn't dwell long on speculation of Farmer's future and his actions. They were in the main highly upset when one of their own, a veteran member of the club, carried out a long-standing threat and promise. Humorless, hard-working Senator John J. Williams not only withdrew from office but sought a retirement age limit. He had turned sixty-five. Time to get out, he said long before. A member of the Senate for twenty-four years, he refused to seek re-election. His constitutional amendment would make it mandatory for federal judges and members of Congress to step down at age seventy. Federal judges can be on the bench for life if they keep their noses clean. It happens to be true of a great many in the Senate, too.

Williams's amendment, also introduced by his successor, Republican Congressman William Roth in the House, would have affected Scott, who won re-election at sixty-nine. Mansfield, also re-elected at sixty-six, would have been in his last term. That disposed of the majority and minority leaders. Of thirty-three Senators whose terms end in 1972, sixteen would be barred from running because they would be sixty-five or older. Only Cooper, at sixty-nine, announced he intended to retire. Two more, Mundt and Anderson, could not have run but were in failing health, anyway. Half of the sixteen also were Republicans. There were

Allott, Case, Cooper, Curtis, Len B. Jordan, Mundt, and Margaret Chase Smith. Jordan was seventy-one; Mundt, seventy; Mrs. Smith, seventy-three. At least she didn't look it. The Democrats affected would have been Anderson, seventy-five; Eastland, sixty-five; Ellender, eighty; Everett Jordan, seventy-four; McClelland, seventy-four; Jennings Randolph, sixty-eight, and Sparkman, seventy. It's a gloomy geriatrics review. Without fuss and farewell, Williams left the Senate. "I'm just going to walk out the door," he said. And he did.

Senators have a way of wishfully thinking that an act like Williams' is nothing personal but intended really for another colleague. An age cut-off caused some to shudder, others planned tactics to block the proposal. They concentrated on the SST for a while. Conservationist senators like Muskie and Jackson found themselves on opposing sides: Muskie against and Jackson in favor. The supersonic transport headquarters was Boeing in Jackson's state of Washington. Continuing the project meant jobs in a state where unemployment kept rising. Transportation Secretary, patent-leather-headed John Volpe, didn't have the persuasion and lobbying techniques of anti-SST.

In the Senate, critics of the program had active assistance from lobbyists on conservation and welfare as well. Plenty of money was spent by the lobbyists in an eight-month fight. George Meany was in favor of the SST. So was President Nixon. But they bided their time until just before the last phase of the floor fight in the Senate. Senator Proxmire, who led the anti-SST campaign, got national attention. It made him think, too, in presidential terms. Amazing what a little prominence can do to a politician. Lobbyists kept clamoring about conservation and reordering national priorities. The SST wasn't in their rearrangements. By a vote of 52 to 41, the Senate halted federal funding of the SST. The White House had wanted another $290 million to continue development of the controversial 1,800-mile-an-hour jetliner. On the other side of the world the vote was hailed by the Soviet Union. It had its own SST and began taking advertisements in the best capitalist manner so as to sell their superjumbo jet.

Out of the melee involving the Senate and the SST emerged a fresh feud—that between Muskie and Jackson. In the conservation field years ahead of Muskie, a bill by Jackson over national land-fill use was blocked by Muskie. Chairman of the Senate Interior Committee, Jackson wanted to bring his bill to the Senate floor. Muskie, chairman of a subcommittee and seeking status as "Mr. Clean" in ecology, put a personal "hold" on the Jackson bill. Senators normally do that when they try to block an appointment, not necessarily a bill. And Jackson was much senior—but not in age—to Muskie. Although annoyed by many more recent Muskie turnabouts in policy, Jackson blew on this calculated affront. Muskie already was making appointments to a staff for his presidential nomination ambitions. In the wings, Jackson prepared to line up labor support. Jackson said he would see how far he could get himself. His challenge could only hurt Muskie badly. Off the Senate floor, Proxmire and Jackson composed SST differences—for a spell. They agreed to have it held over until the following March, around ninety days, to see what would happen by then. This was in the tradition of Senate compromise. You win, show magnanimity, and prepare to belt your opponent out of the ballpark for good the next time.

Out of the backbiting, backfiring Senate chamber, nearly all the members were dumbfounded by a presidential appointment. Handsome, former Texas Governor John B. Connally was picked by President Nixon to be Secretary of the Treasury. Except for the inner family of the White House and Senators Scott and Griffin, virtually everyone else was in the dark. Connally, everyone remembers, was badly wounded in the same car he rode sitting next to President Kennedy, on that leaden November day in 1963 in Dallas. Connally was a protégé of former President Johnson. An open bid for winning Texas was on the way from the White House. Except for Senator Jackson, LBJ had only contempt for all the other Democratic aspirants. In the Senate, after catching a second breath, members wondered what the Connally appointment could mean to John Tower, a Republican up for re-election in 1972. The 1972 races were of much more importance than legislation in this lame-duck session. In their state of shock over the Connally appointment, the Senate managed to raise federal civilian pay by $2.2 billion. It covered 4.3 million civil service and military people. The Senate is never loath to take care of its

own and what is regarded as its own. The vote was close: 40 to
35, and the Senate limped toward statutory cut-off time of the
Ninety-first session, January 3, 1971.

Between fits and starts of the lame-duck legislators, a few internal political affairs were shaken down. These are usually dearest
to most senators' psyches. In the Republican party, twenty-eight
senators backed Bob Dole to replace Morton as National Chairman. Tobacco-chewing William B. Saxbe, Republican from Ohio,
didn't like the idea. Dole, he complained, didn't represent the
mainstream of the party. He was too conservative, said Saxbe.
Scott thought that a full-time chairman, not a senator, might be
better. It was difficult to do both jobs well, observed Scott, who
had done both as a congressman twenty-odd years before. Dole had
the majority of Republican senators. Nixon wanted him. Besides,
for 1972 the President and John Mitchell would be calling the
shots. Saxbe and other anti-Dole men relented. Because he was
a Democrat, Senator Ernest (Fritz) Hollings didn't care about
the Dole matter. He was much more concerned about another
kind of dole, with a small "d"—that of the Hungry American.
From South Carolina, where Strom Thurmond seemed impregnable, Hollings jabbed the Nixon Administration in the bread-
basket. Hollings accused the Republican leadership of getting food
to less than one-half of America's 15 million hard-core hungry.
The Administration, said Hollings mournfully, was sabotaging
federal programs.

Hollings put his accusations in a book on the hungry. That
kind of complaint had never been lofted by anyone in South
Carolina before. He lambasted the food-stamp and commodity
programs. Total mishandling, declared Hollings. Administration
specialists heatedly replied, not at all. They countered with some
shrewd and cunning rebuttal, taking the programs for the hungry
espoused by McGovern as poorly planned and executed. Why
didn't Hollings talk about that? But the Democratic Senator from
Thurmond's state got congratulatory messages and an avalanche
of visits from Southern blacks for his efforts. These prompted
him to say that if he had fifteen minutes with President Nixon, he
would be able to convince him to triple money for feeding programs. Why hadn't he?

"I'd have to go through Harry Dent," was Hollings's reply. "Do you think I could get through?"

The Senate tried to make amends for Hollings's complaints—largely ignored by his fellow club members—with a boost in Social Security benefits. It was a unanimous vote, 81 to 0 in a roll call. Passage meant a 10 percent increase, around an extra $10 billion. An iron-sided powerful congressman, Representative Wilbur Mills, prevented enactment quickly. Mills, from Arkansas and a personal friend of Senator Fulbright, staked out finances as his major field. He had also gone to Harvard graduate school. A House-Senate conference was essential for the Social Security hike. The House had a narrower version, to fit the frame of Mills's thinking. It wanted a 5 percent increase. Thus, both houses had to work an accommodation. Later the same go-around occurred with revenue sharing from federal funds to state and city governments. President Nixon had worked out a $5 billion program. Mayors and governors, regardless of party line, wanted the sharing project at once. Urban centers were disintegrating; welfare rolls had gone up with no end in sight. Mills and anti-Nixon senators like Muskie sneered at the White House offer. Mills came up with a package of verbiage wrapped with a ribbon of thought—anti-Nixon. Alarmed by Democratic mayors' criticism of his own stand, Muskie had a plan. He wanted to wed it with the Nixon program but give it a Muskie label. He was, after all, trying to win the Democratic presidential nomination and unseat Nixon. Federal revenue-sharing was booted around as the plight of the cities approached a national blight.

Pleased with poll results showing he had large personal "identification," Senator Fulbright was restless with all these domestic considerations. In the lame-duck session he didn't mind mini-filibusters. Fulbright was long winded in trying to talk to death civil rights proposals. He found a talking ally on a measure concerning his vigil in foreign affairs. Alaska's Gravel, on the make for prominence and always suspect to Democratic and Republican liberals because of a penchant to work a deal with all factions, teamed up with Fulbright. They wasted a couple of days of a congested calendar. The Fulbright-Gravel alliance filibustered against a foreign aid bill that contained $255 million for assistance to Cambodia. The legislation contained clear language prohibiting the President from sending in ground troops or advisers to Cambodia, anyway. A vote finally taken by the dawdling exclusive club beat back the Fulbright-Gravel filibuster.

As a one-issue chairman, Fulbright paid no attention to an explosion in Poland. Workers in Baltic ports struck against the Communist-run regime of Wladyslaw Gomulka. He had been returned to power in the short-lived Polish riots of October 1956. Reform was then in the air. The triumph and tragedy of the Hungarian uprising stopped Polish reform. Gomulka behaved nearly as devoted to the Soviet line as did goat-bearded Walther Ulbricht, the Russian's East German proconsul. The worker riots in Poland blew Gomulka out of office. It was another evidence that the system of the Gomulkas and their power-driven comrades in the USSR does not work. Senator Fulbright paid the episode no heed. He stuck with his priority and single issue: Vietnam and the war. Both Senators Fulbright and Kennedy sent their own representative to Paris. What for? To talk to and interview North Vietnamese and Communist delegates, in negotiations for a couple of years with the United States and South Vietnamese. It was hardly an act of statesmanship. All that emerged was publicity and assertions from the other side that could be found on any of their records.

In the Middle East, Fulbright apparently has thought it unnecessary for years to visit combustible Arab and Israeli areas or even to send his instant experts to solidify prejudgment. Senator Jackson went out to Israel. His committee on Government Operations and Security has long provided Jackson with a chance to study international issues as they affect the United States. Fulbright couldn't snipe at Jackson for having a "pro-Israeli constituency," either. When asked why he did not coordinate more of his committee's efforts with those of Jackson's, Fulbright replied sharply: "Senator Jackson is trying to undercut me."

In his report, later called "The Middle East and American Security Policy," Jackson noted: "I have often thought that, in its foreign policy, the Soviet Union is like a burglar who walks down a hotel corridor trying the handle of all doors. When he finds one unlocked, in he goes. Looking back on the history of the last decades, it is unfortunately all too clear that Egypt and the other radical Arab states were such unlocked doors. It is too late now to try to keep the Soviets out. But we *can* limit the amount of mischief they will be able to do from these bases of operation. . . ."

Quite a contrary assessment from Fulbright, creator of what he contended were old myths and Communist bogeymen. The affection in unilateral citadels of "liberalism" held for Fulbright because of his constant criticism of our part in Southeast Asia was getting frayed a bit because of his views on the Middle East. Yet his civil rights positions, or lack of them, rarely entered the pro-Fulbright support from these enlightened quarters. It took some notes by a Columbia University professor to attempt to establish a perspective. Henry Graff, the historian, met privately with former President Johnson over a four-year period in the LBJ Presidency. At a session with Johnson and his advisers in 1965, Graff made notes saying:

"I asked the President how he explained Fulbright's opposition to the Administration's position on the war in Vietnam. [Fulbright only the year before managed the Tonkin Gulf Resolution right through the Senate.]

" 'It's some little racial problem.' Fulbright, who had studied at Oxford, simply 'cannot understand that people with brown skins value freedom, too.' 'I say,' added the President as if it were not for the first time, 'if you want a social revolution in the Dominican Republic, why don't you start it in Little Rock?'

"The allusion was to Fulbright's denunciation of the United States' armed intervention in 1965 and his stand on integration in his home state in 1957.

" 'Fulbright,' the President went on, 'had opposed wage and hour legislation, had favored the Dixon-Yates contract, was against the poverty program, and had voted against every civil rights bill.'

" 'Some people say he votes against civil rights bills because that's the only way he can get elected in Arkansas. I'll tell you why he votes against civil rights: he's against civil rights.' "

That was LBJ, of course, a partisan himself. But his comments on the civil rights attitudes of Senator Fulbright are shared by just about every Northern Democratic senator. Some have told him so right to his face, though they share his anti-Vietnam policies. Most say so to each other, a kind of private clublike inquest. There are a half dozen senators, on either side of the chamber, who can mimic Fulbright and his drawling reflections with devastating accuracy. They do this regularly and convulse colleagues in laughter. But say right out what LBJ said? Almost none of them. He would be right in there, senior senator of the glamor committee, as a blundering Senate staggered through shamefully dilatory final days of the Ninety-first Session. Members were pleased to remind critics that the Supreme Court upheld the Senate vote on rights of eighteen-year-olds to vote. It was up to three-fourths of the fifty states to ratify the amendment in time for the 1972 elections. There would be full speed ahead in the Senate—to prepare for national elections.

Never in American history had so many United States senators —all Democrats—set such store on a presidential nomination. The fact that a full year of work and legislation in the Ninety-second session had to be tackled bothered few. In the last days of the Ninety-first, the Senate ran through nine roll call votes one day. It included decisions to kill welfare reforms and trade bills for the year. Compatible with Senate responsibility, Senator Muskie was absent. He was deeply involved in briefings for a trip to Europe and the Middle East. Why he could not have kept pace with external affairs in the past year was inexplicable. Muskie had set his sights on a presidential nomination and prepared the ground as long as two years earlier. Muskie's office—like other Democratic offices—received a call from the cloakroom each time the bell rang for a vote. But he was too busy learning about statecraft to be bothered. He wasn't alone. About one-third of the Senate was absent in a series of crucial votes.

The absentee events augured the condition and future of the Senate for the next two years. They will go down as the Ninety-second session in antiseptic record books. But the Senate was prepared as the stage on which the poor players would fret, strut, and play tricks on the voters. Elections 1972 was the name of the game. Nearly all the players were unworthy of their self-appointed roles.

XIII

THE SENATE—NEARLY
TWO HUNDRED FEET
OF CLAY

The United States Senate, despite tradition and built-in seniority privileges, has become a springboard for presidential ambitions. Little time is expended except by a handful to draft and research legislation. Most senators, in a bipartisan way, try to claim at least a piece of the national stage to promote themselves and acquire something of a household name. As a result, there is an incredible senatorial scramble to pick off the Democratic nomination for President in 1972.

There was a brief respite when Senators Harris, Hughes, and Bayh dropped out in rapid order. Lack of money, little interest among the electorate, and in Bayh's case, his wife's serious illness were the principal reasons for the dropouts. But into this breach sprang two other senators. There was battle-tested Hubert Humphrey, a freshman again after being his party's candidate in 1968. Humphrey took to dyeing his thinning hair. It came out brown with red tints here and there. His clothes became what he took to be the latest styles—bell-bottomed pants and Edwardian jackets. But he could still talk a blue streak like the old Humphrey and become emotional.

Humphrey, who is seldom inclined to keep a grudge, was sore at Ed Muskie. After all, it was Hubert who made Muskie by selecting him to be his vice-presidential candidate in 1968. But Muskie scarcely even bothered to say hello after Humphrey returned to the Senate. Hubert was in the way as a nuisance. Besides, Humphrey had die-hard supporters with money locked up.

The other senator was the most unlikely of all the senatorial candidates. He was Vance Hartke, a pudgy man of self-proclaimed liberalism and under-the-counter attachments to special interests. He announced his intentions when his squeak-through re-election triumph was still contested in the courts. Hartke's backers were an interesting and gamy bag. They ranged the special-interest front from the huge mail-order house of Spiegel, Inc., in Chicago to the Teamsters. Hartke is on subcommittees that review legislation dealing with each of these groups' special concerns. Other senators in the race, as primaries drew close, scoffed at Hartke. There were some who thought that he was running so that the Justice Department wouldn't look into complaints from the Republicans. A couple thought that he was running just because Bayh had gotten a fair amount of limelight. But nearly all agreed that Hartke was out to show his main moneyed backers that he could command some national attention that would be good for them and vice versa in the immediate future.

The records and performance charts of the aspiring Democratic senators, with the notable exception of Jackson and Humphrey, are a study in mediocrity. This has been an unfortunate tendency of most senators seeking the Presidency since World War II. The late Republican Senator, Robert A. Taft—known as "Mr. Conservative"—took his work and role most seriously. The Taft record was one of thorough preparation and dedication to sound legislation as he saw it. The late President, John F. Kennedy, was at the bottom of the heap as a senator. He didn't like the drudgery, thought of himself in a bigger mold. JFK reflected on this before the 1960 campaign got rolling in earnest. If he was beaten, Kennedy observed, then he'd return to the Senate and buckle down to being a devoted, hard-working senator. His late brother, Bob, never indulged in that type of reflective philosophy. Bobby Kennedy also was impatient with what he regarded as the humdrum requirements of a junior senator from New York. For years he had been with the making of great national and global policy. His Senate record was do-little to do-nothing. But so was Nixon's as a senator.

As a senator, Goldwater—the last Republican nominee for President before Nixon—compiled a record that might have been consonant with colleagues of an earlier day, say, 1880. It is absolutely pure and honest. There is nothing in the Goldwater record that can be mistaken as being compassionate toward labor or the underprivileged. Yet Goldwater will vote to support Nixon as often as does Jack Javits. And Javits, who has seen his hopes of becoming the first Jewish vice-presidential nominee disappear in the wheeling and dealing of the presidential sweepstakes, likes to be called a liberal.

Lyndon B. Johnson, of course, was the most notable senator of contemporary times to become President. It is almost forgotten, however, that LBJ was a senator only about eleven years, less than Muskie. In that short time he rapidly rose to Democratic leader and then majority leader. He was probably the wiliest political persuader of the twentieth-century Senate. He steered legislation as a conservative-centrist. Becoming President, Johnson used that lode of experience and due bills owed him for past favors to ram through a strong civil rights bill, major income-tax reductions, and a war on poverty. All these accomplishments have been largely ignored. LBJ got involved in a war in Southeast Asia, and all his expertise became generally suspect.

With Humphrey, a former and present senator, narrowly beaten in 1968, it would seem high time for another line of political trade to push for the candidacy. A few have, but the best they can seem to manage is to try for a little veto impact. Not a single state governor has been considered even briefly for the presidential nomination. That goes for the Vice-Presidency, too. Florida's young and tough-minded Governor, Reuben Askew, was suggested as an afterthought by Mike Mansfield. In his first term as governor, Askew said thanks but that he didn't see getting anywhere that high this time.

The dilemma of governors within the national political picture was pinpointed around the swimming pools and posh hotels the autumn of 1971 in San Juan, Puerto Rico. There was a governors' conference. The Democrats were holding a heavy edge: 32 to 18 Republicans. That kind of margin, even a generation ago, could automatically have raised several names as potential presidential candidates. Not a single governor was mentioned this

time out. In 1968, the out party—Republican—talked of Governors
Nelson Rockefeller (New York), Ronald Reagan (California), and
George Romney (Michigan). Even in 1964, at such a conference,
the names of Nelson Rockefeller and William Scranton (Pennsylvania) were mentioned with some excitement.

Of course, active and former senators were selected to head their
tickets in 1964. The same thing happened in 1968; 1972 will also
have past and present senators running as the nominees of both
major parties, as the polls keep claiming, and gambler Jimmy the
Greek, in Las Vegas, contrives his betting odds. What are the
chances for a non-senator making the grade? A conversation with
Jimmy the Greek put them, as he told me, "conservatively" at
200 to 1.

The only exception to the domination of candidates from the
Senate has been George C. Wallace, past and present Governor
of Alabama. Yet even his candidacy in 1968 had to be taken outside
the Democratic Party structure. Whatever success Wallace enjoyed
have been as a loner, a maverick. He has not had any tangible help
from fellow governors. Still, Wallace persists in calling himself a
Democrat. In lambasting the idea of busing school children to
achieve white-black racial balance, the Alabama governor has
achieved another success, compelling aspiring Democrats to
soften their views on busing. This, in turn, has angered blacks
seeking a piece of the 1972 political action. Wallace also early
showed how much of a spoiler he can be by making believe that
he is the truest of Democrats and running as one in primaries.

"He's unworthy of the party label and he isn't a Democrat any
more than I'm a Republican," grumbled Scoop Jackson.—"He's
unconscionable and a demagogue of the worst kind"—Muskie.—
"Let him stick with his so-called American Independent Party"—
McGovern.—"A divider; a hater, thrives on prejudice"—Humphrey.

"Oh, let 'em call me all the names they want," Wallace said
affably when I chatted with him in Washington. "They know
that I'm right and they're wrong. I can get people on my side.
Can they? I'll bet I can draw bigger crowds than any of them."

Wallace may well be right for the wrong reasons, but he can
attract crowds. His disposition to the press and the rest of the
media is even benign today. Wallace, whose wife Lurleen died,

has remarried. The new Mrs. Wallace is a comely Southern belle.
Cornelia Wallace sees to it that food stains don't stay on his tie
and jacket any more. When I reminded Wallace about a fiasco
for the press traveling with him in 1968, his wife said firmly that
it would never happen again. It was a cold night in Flint, Michigan. Blue-collar workers showed a big interest in the third-party
candidate from Alabama. His campaign strategists, indignant at
media coverage, took this convenient opportunity to ignore overnight hotel accommodations for the press. So, bags were tossed
into a parking lot and were located in darkness with the aid of
flashlights. And the press was on its own for the night.

Then, as four years later, Wallace never asked nor received help
from fellow governors. He took to guffawing aloud at what this
last governors' conference did for the first time in history. It set
up a liaison with the Democratic National Committee. The reason? To try to guarantee a voice in party affairs. For at least a
hundred and fifty years it had been just the other way around.
Governors shaped the ticket. If the National Committee wanted
something, it came to governors on its hands and knees. Today
governors are so enmeshed with their in-state problems they have
their hands full. As noted earlier, their money problems are so
acute that they must depend on Washington to bail them out.

Senators, therefore, find that influence to keep states out of
bankruptcy is in their grasp through appropriations. They command immediate national media attention for this specific advice
and consent. Similar influences come their way in proposing or
rejecting legislation putting more bite in civil rights programs,
education, welfare, and the entire spectrum of minority problems.
Senators have been quick to sense the transfer of great power to
them from their own states and over regions.

Certainly in the last dozen years—particularly since the elections
of 1968—many senators believe they can run the White House far
better than the incumbent. The crisis of confidence in our govern-
mental-political system rubs off more on local and state-elected
officials than on senators. Since a senator is doing business away
from home, he takes comfort in the belief that he has left almost
all his problems behind in his home state. His senatorial pedestal
is almost invulnerable.

But to voters at large and party workers of all parties, public officials appear unresponsive to their requirements. That goes maybe double for senators shielded in the camouflage that they are removed from the local scene and have become instant states-men—all one hundred of them. A disappointed group in from Montana visited both its senators, Mansfield and Metcalf. They also called on some Eastern and Far Western senators. Their pithy, bitter summation: "Up there [the Senate] we have nearly two hundred feet of clay." It was a grim conclusion to which senators should pay heed. Across the country today, in polls and interviews, the majority of our citizenry believe that most politicians cannot be counted on to tell the truth.

Somehow, most of the Senate feels that this deep gap in credi-bility applies to everyone else but its membership and special sanctum. The self-deception adds massively to the problem of restoring some kind of balance in credibility. Senate belief in its omniscience and its own compassion has contributed enormously to conviction that a senator can make a splendid President to lead us Hansels and Gretels out of the terrifying woods. Senators speak loftily of charisma that they enjoy. The rise of the percentage of self-styled independents to better than a quarter of the electorate ought to dispel the illusion.

This special coequality on which senators draw as a political birthright was affronted by Mrs. Margaret Chase Smith. She roasted, in her proposed constitutional amendment, absentee fel-low senators, moonlighters on the lecture circuit, and junketeers. Free-loading travel has come some sophisticated distance since the days when senators like Elbert Thomas, of Utah, asked a con-ducting officer on an Air Force plane as it jockeyed for a landing approach: "Son," demanded the Senator, devoutly occupied with postwar foreign affairs, "why do they sometimes call this Budapest, sometimes Bucharest, and sometimes Belgrade?" Senators, on tax-payer-sponsored trips, usually know where their arrival sites are located these days. Yet they won't forget and will hardly forgive Mrs. Smith for her scolding and advocacy of expulsion for absenteeism.

Her proposal sparked the salacious gossip of Mrs. Smith's as-sociation with her administrative aide. The Senate can use its collective forked tongue when someone bruises the membership's ego. Among other points Mrs. Smith noted was the absences of supposedly public-spirited senators, like McGovern. Through early October of 1971, she declared, McGovern missed 41 percent of the votes. Her amendment demands expulsion for any member of Congress—House or Senate—who misses 40 percent of the votes in any session. In a national election year, she pointed out forcefully that absenteeism was bound to become worse. Among the most flagrant truants she uncovered, besides McGovern, were Bayh and Harris. The last two, having dropped out, appear more often now.

The lucrative lecture circuit also bothers Mrs. Smith. She made a point of revealing that McGovern earned $24,035 on the platform in 1970. He was right up there among the big lecture earners. Muskie made more but he was in demand where the fees were usually bigger. The Muskie take from the circuit was $35,626. But he appeared for votes in the Senate 69 percent of the time. It usually meant a quick visit to vote and then off again to another political engagement. The most pathetic absentee has been Mundt, stricken in early 1970 and unable to appear in the Senate ever since.

Offended senators are always a substantial majority. They temporarily put away their feelings, and the proposal of Margaret Chase Smith, in cold storage. Images and issues in a presidential year must be regilded. Defense of the public interest, for or against President Nixon, had to be staked out quickly. One was easy enough to support, although neither the Senate nor the White House can predict where it will lead: the strategy of youth with millions of new voters over the age of eighteen. Tacked on was something more predictable, that of currying favor with the voters over sixty-five. While they represent 10 percent of the population, the over-65s cast 17 percent of the votes in 1970.

To enhance the earnest image of the Senate, a new campaign curb on contributions and spending was passed. It went through all the stages and the conference with the House after Nixon successfully challenged the dollar checkoff concept. Senators, led by stubby, rhetorical John Pastore, hailed the victory. An election year miracle, declared Pastore, who wrote much of the language. To the electorate spending a dime per registered voter, a limit on radio-TV of six cents might look useful. The gaps were frustratingly enormous. Committees unauthorized specifically by a candidate could still spend as if money went out of style. Stopping them could be considered abridgment of freedom of speech.

The real opportunity was discarded: a tough-minded Federal Elections Commission. It would have scrutinized all contributions received and reported. Instead, reports go to toothless tabbies: the U.S. Comptroller General, the timid secretary of the Senate, and the clerk of the House. After the useless Corrupt Practices Act of 1925, the new limitation was held up as a famous victory, for an electorate so much in the dark. A realistic, albeit unpopular, view was seen by Senator Hart. "It took us nearly fifty years to get even that," he noted. "Another fifty years of this and we may not even be in business."

Hart was one of the few leading senators persevering at his job and not trying to wrest the nomination for President. His depressing realism recalled statements by Clifford Case, the lean Republican liberal from New Jersey. On its own, Case maintains, the Senate won't reform itself. Reform is urgent, but too many of his colleagues want the status quo, the self-perpetuation of the interests and enhancement in this glorified body of one hundred.

Nearly a century ago when he was a young political scientist fired up with a zest for reform, Woodrow Wilson hoped to make the Senate over into something in the mold of the British parliamentary system. More realistic so late in the twentieth century would be reform that could adapt features from Britain and eliminate objectionable features totally incompatible with today's realities. One key issue is the issue of debate. The Senate prides itself on the rule for endless debate. That is an old and tricky device. But only if members employed far fewer prepared speeches and were required to speak for or against proposals on the floor would we know something about them and their attitudes. This has long been an issue of interest to Senator Cooper, who will not run for re-election.

Cooper would like to see a substantive curb on written speeches. Many of them are read to empty chambers. They are calculated room clearers. Speaking up, in Cooper's view, could have an additionally desired effect, that of making the Senate more interesting and attractive to the young. He observed: "We also could find out who the good speakers and the bad speakers are and we may even learn who really studied bills, amendments, and proposals." It would be most useful to the electorate to see—as in the House of Commons, or even in the House of Lords—senators fast enough on the feet to dissect a proposition at a given moment. Their traditional colloquies are studded with poor grammar, bathos, and mutual appreciation.

As a committee system, senators rely inordinately on the abilities and talents of committee staffs. Within their own offices, other staffers research, help prepare legislation, and usually provide the internal Senate advice and consent. The senators could improve the depth and insight into their assignments by first taking a profound look at the work of the committees or subcommittees that they serve. Many standbys are hacks who acquired bureaucratic cunning over the years, and little else. They are professional survivors at best. Changes at intervals and the infusion of fresh blood and talent would help greatly in acquiring up-to-date information and opinions.

The question of seniority must be solved sensibly. The longevity of a senator and his ability to get re-elected move him up the ladder on committees. There have been proposals, from former Presidents like Lyndon Johnson to political analysts, that the job of being President should be confined to one term of six years. He would therefore concern himself with all outstanding national business and not use up at least a year thinking of re-election. The same length of time—six years—also should be a most adequate term for a senator to serve as head of any committee. It is a senator's normal term after a regular election. If he has established, before coming to the Senate, for example, special talents and interest in welfare, defense, foreign affairs, or economics, then even a freshman senator should not be compelled to work his passage through seniority. Reform could place a freshman at the head of a committee, elected by his colleagues for what he knows and not for how long he has been re-elected.

Certainly there are senators who proved their talents despite the system of seniority. Through the years these members have managed re-election, too. But they could rotate their position within the committee. Their experience and dedication would encourage newer elected members to replace them. By being re-elected, these same veterans could then one day return to top place, provided it was by vote of their fellow committeemen.

The need for more deliberation over all-important issues has hardly been more urgent than in this period as we close out the century. We have senators, like Javits, who drift in and out of committees to show their interest. The normal time period is about forty-five minutes, often as little as five. Attendance without a good grasp of what the problems mean never makes for anything better than snap judgment.

Some accepted standard of ethics must be the highest priority in any attempt at change and reform. A committee already exists, but it is most charitable unless it is forced to act by a rare burst of publicity. George Murphy's outside income and allowances from an industry were allowed. So has been the standing joke in the Senate about the "bought" label applied to Senators Hartke and Hruska's money-makers in seedy movies. Before he was beaten for re-election, liberal millionaire Joseph Clark, Democrat of Pennsylvania, got up on the floor and detailed his outside income and holdings.

Senator McGovern, in a burst of candor, revealed his assets—a couple of houses and some stock that was held in a blind trust. It was an obvious campaign gimmick because McGovern had plenty of time even a year earlier to show a tidy $250,000 or so net worth. One might wonder how McGovern acquired so solid a nestegg. There have been five McGovern children to educate, and taxes take a big bite. But the lecture platform provided McGovern, like many other senators, with fees that double the annual salary of $42,500. If a speaker were not a senator, especially one of some consequence, he'd hardly be invited to speak for thousand-dollar fees.

Lectures that are all that valuable should be the property of the public a senator is elected to serve. His staffers usually prepare and research the material. They, too, are paid by the taxpayer. Therefore, the product does belong to the electorate. Articles and books should fall into the same category. Irascible former Senator Wayne Morse often stated that the Senate was supposed to be a goldfish bowl. Let everyone see how the members feed and swim. A requirement to list all assets—really going public if the Senate means to serve the public—would go a long way toward re-establishing some public confidence. It should be done at the beginning of each session. In a listing included or attached, a senator should provide details, if any, of outside industries that contribute toward his maintenance in the job. It could be a free trip or no hotel bill for the family. And all gifts must be returned if they have any real value. Former Senator Paul Douglas used to return any present worth more than $2.50. It is a good yardstick.

But reformers in the Senate scarcely ever raise their voices except in private. They grumble—and fall back, hardly inclined to come to grips with the formidable bloc that insists on the status quo. They complain bitterly about seniority. Yet when one of their own happens to possess seniority, they complain loudly if he fails to obtain rights owed him under seniority. Often, change-minded Senators oppose use of the filibuster. This is particularly true when Southerners and conservatives try to block legislation in the vast arena of civil rights. But these same reformers never hesitate, however, to filibuster when it seems useful to their own tactics. They cannot have it both ways and even pretend reform. In pursuit of change, there is little cohesion. Strategy for reform usually collapses when a senator sails off by himself. Everyone is ready to become Sir Galahad for TV.

In working habits the Senate is hung up on its own parliamentary ground rules of procedure. It requires unanimous consent to suspend the rules to cope with the workload before the floor. Any senator, whether out of caprice or malice, can cut off business by refusing to agree. Both the refusals and the unanimous consents occur far too frequently for the benefit of active and relatively smooth Senate work. A dissenting senator is free to invoke his objection. He then jabbers about issues totally unrelated to the one before the membership. Should the majority leader take advantage of the dissenter's absence to ram through a unanimous-consent deal, a grudge springs up that can be more harmful in the long run. Similarly, unanimous-consent agreements are being contrived with very few senators present. Too often, a handful of senators acknowledge a unanimous consent. Then they proceed to business that most of their other colleagues have little opportunity to examine. A tiny percentage, in short, exercises its will day to day in the name of the United States Senate.

The Senate, which so proudly extols its constitutional role in advice and consent over foreign affairs, mainly grumbles but does not take on the White House. Complaints about the President usurping the Senate's function in such a sensitive area have been growing louder since early 1968 when a political Tet offensive stormed against LBJ. Nevertheless, the Senate has been steadily yielding ground to the Presidency in the conduct of foreign affairs over the last fifty years. The self-indulgent reasoning for this now regular transfer of responsibility has been ultrasimplistic. Presidents supposedly have access to far more information daily on the crosscurrents of global events than any senator or group of senators. But if the Senate wants to insist upon the return of its lost prerogatives, it's not impossible. They have only to threaten, as does Fulbright, with their financial power.

It means quite simply cutting down—or cutting out—appropriations in areas certain to spark a demand for accommodation and perhaps coequality with the White House in foreign affairs. To show the displeasure of the Senate, appropriations are slashed, usually in the feeblest of areas such as foreign aid. In high dudgeon, the Senate also has threatened eliminating foreign assistance altogether. It cooled off and reversed itself. But with all the threats and complaints the Senate has not taken any real action by majority legislation to restore what it claims is an inherent right. Virtually the same attitude characterizes the Senate's attitude in complaining about military expenditures and the growing power of the Pentagon. At hearings malcontent senators mangle discomfited brass. A military budget is cut one year only to be refreshed and even increased the next with Senate concurrence.

About ten years ago, the same Joe Clark who upset fellow senators by revealing holdings and outside income also lambasted his colleagues. "The Senate establishment as I see it is almost the antithesis of democracy. It is not selected by any democratic process. It appears to be quite unresponsive to the caucuses of the two parties, be they Republican or Democratic. It is what might be called a self-perpetuating oligarchy with mild, but only mild, overtones of plutocracy." Clark took the skin off his colleagues, mind you, at the height of the New Frontier of John F. Kennedy. A new and exciting era was supposed to have illuminated the way for the nation.

More in sorrow as is his senatorial attitude, Majority Leader Mansfield replied: "What I believe those who complain of an 'establishment' are, in the final analysis, complaining against is the ever-present fact of frustration, the frustration of working in this body, the frustration of half a loaf, the frustration of compromise that of necessity is always with us. Who among us does not feel this heavy cloak of dissatisfaction? Less than an absolute power to achieve one's will is the essence of frustration. Yet less than absolute power to achieve one's will is also an essential of democracy. The process of democracy is therefore frustrating, and let us be sure that when it ceases to be so for any group or faction, at the same time there will have ceased to be a democracy."

Clark's go-getting supporters pretended to find crumbs of comfort in Mansfield's views. They shifted gears to more watchful waiting than demanding reform after Clark was beaten in 1968. Mansfield, quietly living up to his formula of half a loaf, remains in the Senate. It is a kindly supervision that Mansfield exercises, aware of the fire in the ashes of reform that get stoked up. Let them glow, is Mansfield's view, but not burn. Status-quo, half-a-loaf senators see merit in the Mansfield approach. Nobody gets hurt, true. By prevailing they steer the Senate into a snooze right through the seventies. The inherent dangers of an awakening, irate giant can be catastrophic even if do-it-yourself reform in the Senate takes the do-nothing, easy way out.

Ralph Nader has recognized what is at stake. His stern, near-evangelistic criteria synthesizes much of the prevalent mood in the United States. It is a yearning to do more with life, with an American dream as he sees it. Committed to make America a reconditioned, livable world, Nader is putting together his most ambitious project ever: A thousand-member team of his raiders will investigate Congress itself. He is out to restore what the politicians sitting in Washington evaded: the restoration of confidence and a full measure of public service. In his opinion, "Nothing remotely compares with the Congress as the hope of reclaiming America."

Just looking into the Senate, with its proliferation of powerful
standing committees and subcommittees, will probably tax Nader's
investigators to the limits of their resources and talents. Although
all are technically answerable to the public, there exists a built-in
ability in the Senate and its apparatuses to stall, to evade unpleasant problems. A demand to subpoena a committee's records,
for instance, will consume a huge slice of the Nader team's time
and ingenuity. Most senators and their foremost advisors on committees would show at least an inclination to cooperate if they
only emulated part-time Nader's own lifestyle.

Few would be willing to go all the way as Nader has done. He
works sixteen hour days; lectures fees of around $2,500 go into
his Center for Study of Responsive Law and subsidiaries. Book
royalties and the settlement from General Motors also have been
used in that way. Across the country and abroad in Europe and
Asia, Nader has managed to transcend cynicism and credibility
gaps. Even to the most bitter critics he epitomizes the man on
the level. He shrugs off personal attacks, and they have started as
well from the Senate and the House. The most common criticism
is that Nader's own organization is becoming big business, including fund raising. But he doesn't take a penny for himself.

More preoccupied with the Presidency, 1972, the Senate doesn't
see Nader's challenge as a primary concern. But Nader has proved
that he can be an exorcist in just about every field he has entered,
from the environment to hot dogs. He has never minced language,
either, calling sham, deception, and incompetence when he finds
them. He also just compiled a manual for student action and
awareness. If college students contribute to Nader's fund only
3 percent of what they spend on personal pleasures, they could
create the biggest lobbying force in America. This is the kind of
language the Senate understands. It is the potential of force.

Without sarcasm, Nader has declared repeatedly that Congress
is a constant underachiever. Hence the need for his mammoth
inquiry. He doesn't want to green America but to reform ingrown
institutions. His commitment to reclamation is also predicated
on a premise that asks: "Who is to say that our congressmen and
our senators would not welcome the participation of the people?"
For openers to his investigation, Nader gave some answers in a
lawsuit. He linked the White House to a smelly deal on increasing

milk prices. At the same time Nader disclosed fat contributions made by milk producers to senators and congressmen.

As a grateful gesture for the government hiking milk prices—which Nader charged would cost the public about $125 million annually—producers forthwith contributed $322,500 to the Nixon campaign. Another $2.5 million was on hand, his suit asserted, to be contributed. But Democrats also benefited from the milk producers' kindly charity. Humphrey and Muskie were among them. In 1970 and 1971, Humphrey received $15,625 in milk help. A contribution of $5,200, in December 1971 alone, went to Humphrey. Muskie received $3,936 in 1970. A big surprise disclosed that Senator Proxmire received $9,000 in milk contributions. A professed consumer advocate from the dairy state of Wisconsin, Proxmire publicly frowns on handouts.

While Nader tries to create—or restore—the American dream, the Senate plays out an intramural game of strategy. It is far less glamorous than competing for the Democratic presidential nomination. Yet its importance can mean the shape and character of the Senate for the foreseeable future. The prize is that of majority leader. Soft-spoken, soft-thinking Mike Mansfield is a weary sixty-eight. His Senate term isn't up until 1976. But there exists the strong possibility that he may step down in 1973 and concentrate on his main interest, which is foreign policy. Busy in the background is assistant leader and whip, Bobby Byrd.

The same Bobby Byrd upset the re-election of Ted Kennedy to whip. Just as Byrd collected due bills from moderate and liberal senators to beat Kennedy, his omnipresent black memo book keeps meticulous tabs on later favors to colleagues. The times, occasions, and dates are precisely noted. Anti-Bob Byrd senators, with growing consternation, discern the whip's momentum for aspiring to the leadership post. Byrd will dismiss all such suggestions—for now. Mike Mansfield can always stay on the job, if he wants it. After more than ten years in this often thankless but all-important role—with its direct links to the White House—Mansfield may really be ready to become plain Senator Mansfield and thereby shun all the problems of patriarchy.

He has sought, in a noncontroversial way, to infuse fresh blood into the political system in and out of the Senate. Mansfield is proud of his responsibility as a principal sponsor of legislation